Warp and Weft of Wonderment
volume 1

Warp and Weft of Wonderment

volume 1

Ngakma Mé-tsal

2025

Aro Books WORLDWIDE,
PO Box 111, 5 Court Close
Cardiff, Wales, CF14 1JR

© 2025 Ngakma Mé-tsal Wangmo

All rights reserved. No part of this book may be reproduced in any form or by any means electronic or mechanical, including photocopying, recording, or by any information storage and retrieval system, without permission in writing from the publisher.

First Edition 2025

ISBN: 978-1- 898185-68-0 (paperback)
ISBN: 978-1- 898185-69-7 (ePub)

For further information about Aro Books WORLDWIDE please see http://aro-books-worldwide.org/

To obtain copies of all our publications please visit https://www.lulu.com/spotlight/arobooksworldwide

contents

Foreword by Kyabjé Lhatsé Trülku Rinpoche		9
Map 1 – Lands of the Mahasiddhas		10
Map 2 – Provenance of the Mahasiddhas		11
Map 3 – Silk Road and Ögyen		6
Prolegomenon		13
One:	Jalandhara – *the net-possessor*	45
Two:	Minapa – *the whale siddha*	63
Three:	Goraksha – *the nondual cowboy*	79
Four:	Kankaripa – *the bereaved lover*	95
Five:	Subhadra – *the dakini choreographer*	111
Six:	Dombhi Héruka – *the tiger rider*	131
Seven:	Saraha – *consort of the fletcher's daughter*	151
Eight:	Sarvaripa – *the deer hunter*	171
Nine:	Shatakshi – *the mother of tigers*	187
Ten:	Baruni – *the surbdahar playing whore*	205
Eleven:	Bhagarvi – *the terrifying wanton*	225
Twelve:	Vinapa – *the vajra vainika*	249
Thirteen:	Lu'ipa – *the piscatorial viscera epicurean*	277
Fourteen:	Chamaripa – *the nondual cordwainer*	297
Fifteen:	Lila Vajra – *the regal hedonist*	319
Sixteen:	Tantipa – *the vacuous carpet-weaver*	335
Seventeen:	Khadgapa – *the lord of larceny*	353
Eighteen:	Shyama – *the cloud-weaver*	375
Nineteen:	Kanhapa – *the miraculous exhibitionist*	393
Twenty:	Sarvagjna – *the eccentric monocular seamstress*	419
Twenty-one:	Manibhadra – *the perfect housewife*	439

SER LHATSE SANG-NGAG RAPTEN LING MONASTERY
Lhatse Temple, Gyashod Town, Serda County, Karze Prefecture, Sichuan Province, China P.O. 626600

༄༅། །བྱེར་གཞི། །

སྤྱིར་སངས་རྒྱས་ཤཱཀྱ་ཐུབ་པའི་བསྟན་པ་འདི་ལ་རྒྱ་གར་འཕགས་པའི་ཡུལ་དུ་མདོ་སྔགས་ཟུང་འབྲེལ་གྱི་སྟོན་པ་མཆོག་པའི་ཁྱུ་མཆོག་དང་གྲུབ་པའི་དབང་པོ་སོ་སོ་གྲགས་པས་འདས་པ་ཞིག་བྱོན་པ་ལས། ཀུན་གྱི་ཐྱེར་སྟོན་པ་གྲུབ་ཆེན་བཀའ་བརྒྱུད་ཙུ་ཙུ་བཞི་ཞེས་རྒྱ་བོད་གཉིས་ན་ཕྱི་ཉི་ཟླ་ལྟར་ཡོངས་སུ་གྲགས་པ་དེ་དག་རྣམས་ནི། སྤྱི་ལུགས་ཨ་སིདྡྷའི་བྲིད་དང་། སྟོད་ཕྱོགས་མ་ལ་ཡ། སར་ཕྱོགས་བྲཾལ། ཡུལ་དབུས་མ་ག་དྷ། ཡུལ་མཐའ་འཁོབ་རྒྱ་དཀར་མིན་རྫོ་ན་གར། སོ་མ་པུ་རི། ཤྲིང་ཁྲིགས་ནར་གྱི། ཁ་ཆེའི་ཡུལ་དང་ཉེ་བར་རྫོང་པུ་རིའི་ཡུལ། སུ་ལི་པུ་ཊ་ན་གར། མརྐ་ཡོང་། གོ་ཀྱི་དྲི། ཨོ་རྒྱན་ཡུལ། ཀུ་རུ་པ། སྲིན་ནུ་མེ་ཏྲ་ཨོ་དྷུ་པུ་རི། དེ་སྟྲྲི་ཀོ་ཏ། ཨོ་ཏེ་བི་ཤ་ན་ག་ཨིནྡྲའི་ཡུལ་སོགས་སུ་སྐུ་བལྟམས་པ་དང་། བཙུན་ལུགས་འདས་ཀྱི་འདི་བསྟན་པ་འདི་ལ་རིགས་མི་གཏོགས་མི་གཏོགས་བཀབ་པ་རིན་པོ་ཆེ་གཉིས་གསུང་པ་བཞིན། གྲུབ་ཆེན་དེ་དག་རྣམས་ནི་བྲམ་ཟེའི་རིགས་དང་། རྒྱལ་རིགས། རྗེ་རིགས། དམངས་རིགས་སོགས་རིགས་བཞི་པོ་དག་ལས་བྱུང་བའི་གྲུབ་ཐོབ་སྐུ་མཆོང་སྟོབ་ལྡན་པའི་ཚུལ་འཛིན་པ་ཤིན་ཏུ་ཆེ་སྟབས་ལ་དད་པའི་ཚུལ་འཆར་བཀུར་གར་འཕགས་པའི་ཡུལ་གྱི་ཡུལ་དབུས་མ་ག་དྷ་སོགས་སུ་བྱོན་ནས། དགེ་བའི་བཤེས་གཉེན་མཚན་ཉིད་དང་ལྡན་པ་ལས་དགེ་བསྙེན་དང་རབ་བྱུང་གནང་ནས་གྱི་སོམ་པ་ཞེས། མདོ་ཕྱོགས་གཙོ་བོར་གྱུར་པའི་འདུལ་ལུང་སྟྲེ་བཞི་དང་འཁོར་ལོ་དང་པོའི་དགོངས་དོན་བདེན་པ་བཞི་དང་རྟེན་འབྲེལ་ཡན་ལག་བཅུ་གཉིས། བར་བའི་དགོངས་དོན་ཐབ་མོའི་བུ་དང་རྒྱ་ཆེན་སྤྱོད་པ་སོགས་ལ་ཕེས་གསས་བསྟོམ་གསུམ་མཐར། སྐུ་ཚེ་སྨྱུག་པ་ཐབས་མང་དགའ་བ་མེ་པའི་ཆེ་ལ་བར་མོ་གསར་སྤྱོད་དོ་ཛེག་པའི་བསྟན་པ་ལ་བསྟེན་ནས་ཐུན་མོང་གི་དངོས་གྲུབ་བརྒྱུད་དང། ཐུན་མོང་མིན་པ་སྤྱག་རྒྱ་ཆེན་པོ་མཚོག་གི་དངོས་གྲུབ་བསྐྱེད་པ་ནི་སྐུ་ལས་ཡིན་ལ། འདིར་དེ་དག་གི་ལོ་རྒྱས་རྣམ་ཐར(རོ་མཚར་བའི་རྒྱ་མཚོ)ཞེས་པ་འདིའི་ཉིད་པཚིགས་སྒྱལ་སྒྲགས་འཆར་རིན་པོ་ཆེའི་གསུང་སྟོབ་སྲོགས་མ་ཎེ་རྒྱལ་གྱིས་ད་བྱིད་ཡིག་ལས་བསྒྱུར་བའི་ཉིན་དུ། གྲུབ་ཐོབ་དེ་དག་གི་འབྱུང་ཡུལ་དང་། རབ་ཏུ་བྱུང་ནས་དགེ་བའི་བཤེས་གཉེན་བསྟེན་ཚུལ། མདོ་ཕྱོགས་གཞུང་ལུགས་རབ་འབྱམས་ལ་ཐོས་བསམ། མཛད་ཆོས། མཛར་རྡོ་རྗེ་ཐེག་པའི་ཅི་ལས་ཐབ་མོ་བཀྲུལ་བ་ཤུགས་ཀྱི་སྟོབ་པ་ལ་བསྟེན་ནས་སྤྱུར་ཏུ་མཆོང་གི་དངོས་གྲུབ་བརྙེས་པ་སོགས་ཤིན་ཏུ་མཚར་ཞིང་ཕྱིན་རྒྱལ་ཅན་འནུ་ཀྱི་རྣམ་པར་རྣམས་གསལ་པོར་བཀོད་ཡོད་པ་དང། རྣམ་ཐར་འདིས་ནི་རྗེས་འཇུག་གི་སྐྱོབ་པའི་རྒྱལ་དང་པ་བསྐྱེད་ཅིང་བྲཾར་བའི་སྲོན་བསྐུལ་བ་དང། གནས་སྐབས་དང་མཐར་ཐུག་གི་ཐན་བདེ་ལུས་པ་འབྱུང་བའི་རྒྱུ་འབྱུང་བ་དང། རྒྱ་ཆེའི་ཀྲེགས་པ་པོ་རྣམས་ལ་ཡང་དལ་རབ་པའི་ནང་དུ་རྒྱུས་སུ་བྱུང་བའི་ཉིད་བསྟན་གྱི་ལོ་རྒྱལ་འབྱུང་ཆོས་དང། སྐབས་དེ་དག་རྣམས་སུ་ཡུལ་མིའི་གོམས་སྲོལ་དང། འཚོ་བྱེད་སྨན་རྩིས་སོགས་ཀྱི་ལོ་རྒྱས་ཐྱེལ་བར་མ་ཟད། གྲུབ་ཆེན་དེ་དག་རྣམས་ཀྱི་རྣམ་པར་བཟང་པོ་ལ་མཚར་བའི་སྟབས་རྗེས་སུ་འཇུག་འདོད་ཀྱི་སྐྱེ་བ་སོགས་ཀྱི་དགོས་པ་མང་པོ་ཡོད་པ་ཡིན་ནོ། །

ཞེས་གསར་ལྷ་རྩེ་དགོན་པའི་བསྟན་པའི་བདག་པོ་དགོན་སྒྲུབ་པ་པདྨ་རིག་འཛིན་ཕྱོགས་ལས་རྣམ་རྒྱལ་བས་ཕྱི་ལོ་ ༢༠༡༨ ཟླ་ ༡༠ པའི་ཚེས་ ༢༩ ཉིན་བཏང་པོར་ཕྱིར་འབྱོར་༎

SER LHATSE SANG-NGAG RAPTEN LING MONASTERY
Lhatse Temple, Gyashod Town, Serda County, Karze Prefecture, Sichuan Province, China P.O. 626600

In general, regarding the teachings of Buddha Shakyamuni, countless learned masters and accomplished lords appeared in Noble India who combined the Sutrayana and Vajrayana approaches. Among them, the most prominent were the Eighty-Four Mahasiddhas, who became as famous as the sun and moon in both India and Tibet. They were born in various places including:

Sri Lanka (Singala), Southern Malayalam, Eastern Bengal, Central Magadha, the frontier regions of Gahur and Saindhonagar, Somapuri, the city of Skyaner, near Kashmir in Rajapuri, Saliputra Nagar, Shravasti, Kaushambi, Oddiyana, Kamarupa, Shrinendra, Odantapuri, Devikota, Odivisa (or Kalinga), and other regions.

As Buddha Shakyamuni said *'In my teachings, there is no caste or royal family lineage – it is the training which is primary.'* Initially, these great accomplished masters came from the Brahmin caste. They primarily studied and meditated on the *four sections of the Vinaya* from the Sutra tradition, the meaning of the *Four Noble Truths from the First Turning of the Wheel, the Twelve Links of Dependent Origination,* and from the *Middle Turning, the profound view and vast conduct.* In the latter part of their lives, through following the profound rapid path of the many secret mantra methods of Vajrayana, they achieved the eight common siddhis (accomplishments) and the supreme uncommon siddhi of nondual realisation.

This text called *'Warp and Weft of Wonderment'* is a *marvellous thread of tales* containing their life stories and biographies, written in English by the tantric master, Ngakma Mé-tsal Wangmo under the guidance of Chog-trül Ngak'chang Rinpoche *(supreme incarnate vajra-holder)*. It clearly presents their astounding and blessed biographies, including: *the Mahasiddhas' birthplaces; how they followed their religious teachers; how they studied the vast tradition of Vajrayana; and how they swiftly achieved supreme accomplishments through the profound rapid path of Vajrayana conduct*

These biographies generate faith in the minds of followers and plant seeds of liberation, becoming causes for both temporary and ultimate benefit and happiness. For the broader readership, they also: *inspire readers to understanding of Buddhist historical characteristics across many centuries; offer insights into the customs and ways of life of people during those periods; and, follow the excellent example of these great accomplished masters with wonder and admiration*

Written by 'öntrül Pema Rig'dzin Chokle Namgyal, the doctrine holder of Sér Lhatsé Gompa, on the auspicious day of October 24, 2024.

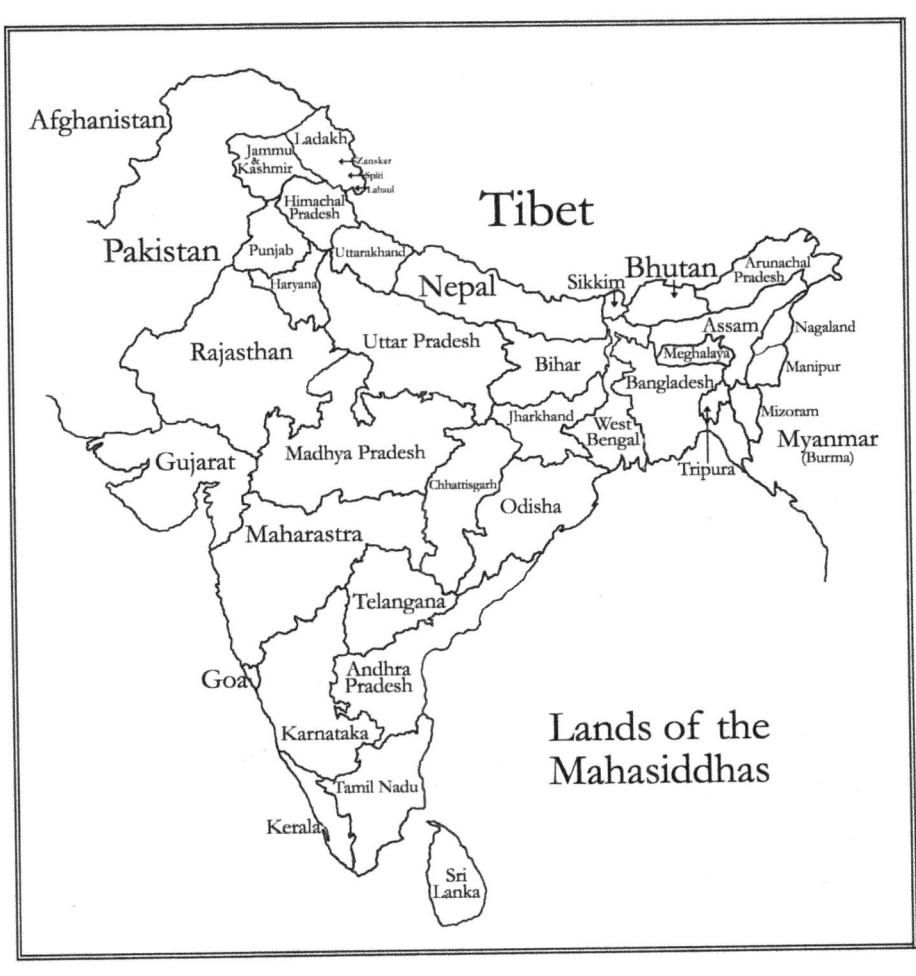

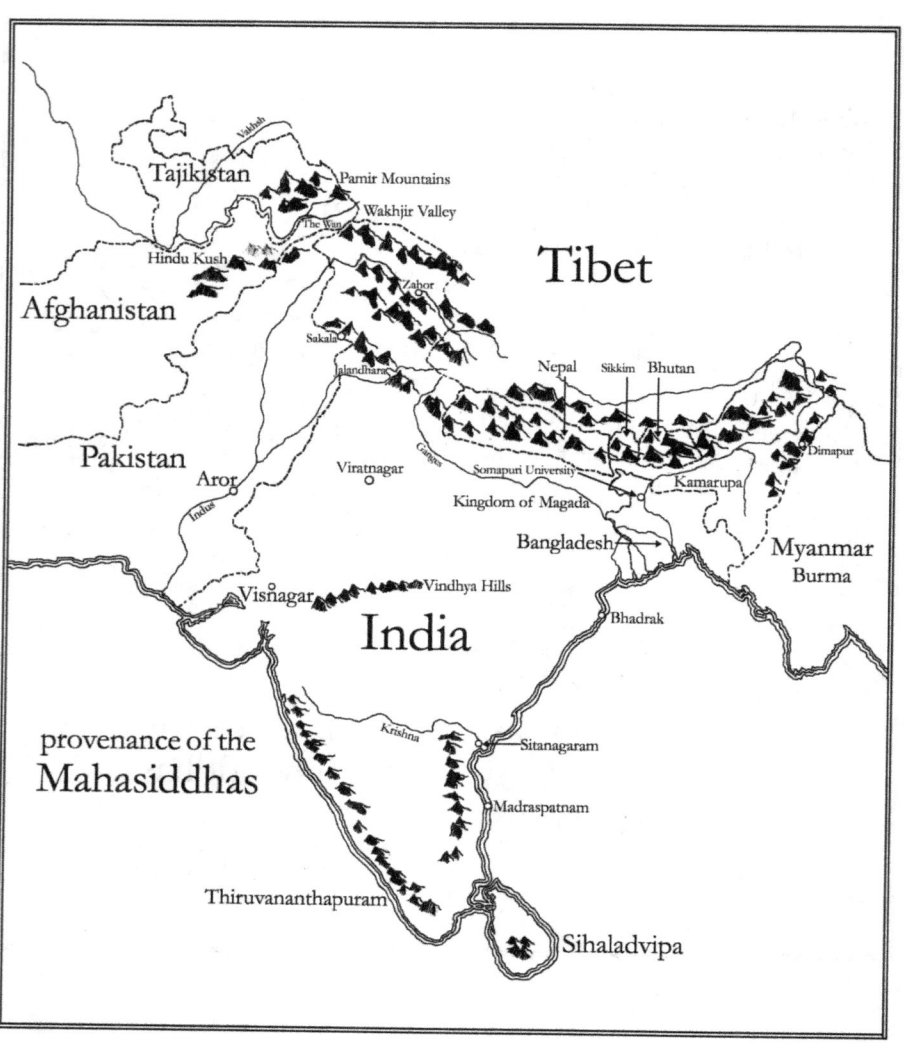

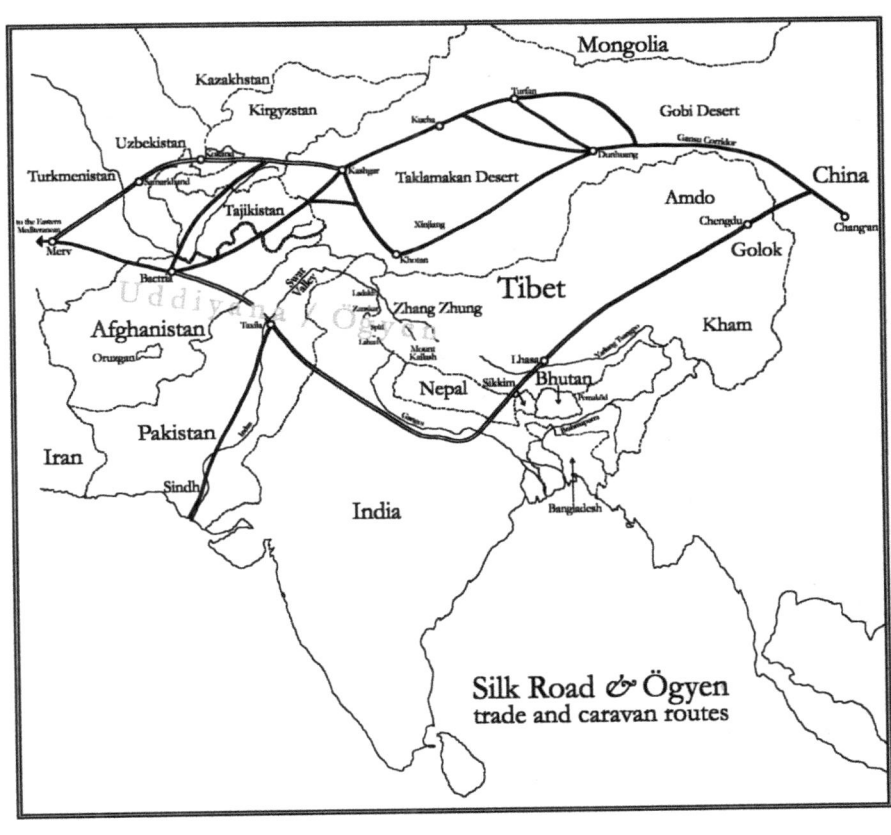

Prolegomenon

Ngakma Mé-tsal Wangmo[1]

The early 1990s – my first years studying with Ngak'chang Rinpoche[2] and Khandro Déchen[3].

The sangha was engaged in group retreat in West Wales. Days filled with teaching, silent sitting meditation, yogic song, physical yogas, craft work, and laughter. There was always laughter. In the evenings, after dinner—if no empowerment was scheduled—we were treated to readings from the Aro gTér Lineage History. I loved to hear these inspirational accounts of great practitioners – living on the eastern margins[4] of the Tibetan plateau at the turn of the 20th century. On the evening I remember particularly, we were listening to the account of the life of Jomo Pema 'ö-Zér[5]. Jomo Pema 'ö-Zér was the mother of Khyungchen Aro Lingma[6] – the discoverer of the Aro gTér and founder of the Aro gTér Tradition[7].

I was unaccountably moved by the hagiography[8] of Jomo Pema 'ö-Zér. She was immediately inspirationally present – and stayed with me as I headed for bed. She remained with me through my dreams. I was still thinking of her the next morning as we gathered for breakfast.

---

[1] *sNgags ma me rTsal dBang mo* / སྔགས་མ་མེ་རྩལ་དབང་མོ་. A ngakma *(sNgags ma /* སྔགས་མ་ or *sNgags mo /* སྔགས་མོ་ */ mantrini)* is a female holder of Vajrayana ordination. The male equivalent is a ngakpa *(sNgags pa /* སྔགས་པ་ */ mantrin).*

[2] *sNgags 'Chang rin po che /* སྔགས་འཆང་རིན་པོ་ཆེ — Ngakpa Chögyam Ögyen Togden *(sNgags pa chos rGya mTso o rGyan rTogs lDan /* སྔགས་པ་ཆོས་རྒྱ་མཚོ་ཨོ་རྒྱན་རྟོགས་ལྡན་ */* b.1952)

[3] *mKha' 'gro bDe chen /* མཁའ་འགྲོ་བདེ་ཆེན — Khandro Déchen Tsédrüp Rolpa'i Yeshé *(mKha' 'gro bDe chen tshe grub rol pa'i ye shes /* མཁའ་འགྲོ་བདེ་ཆེན་ཚེ་གྲུབ་རོལ་པའི་ཡེ་ཤེས་ */* b.1960)

[4] Kham *(khams /* ཁམས་ *)* and Golok *(mGo log /* མགོ་ལོག་ *).*

[5] *jo mo pa dMa 'od zer /* ཇོ་མོ་པ་དམ་འོད་ཟེར

[6] *khyung chen A ro gLing ma /* ཁྱུང་ཆེན་ཨ་རོ་གླིང་མ་ */* 1886–1923 – Great Garuda who tastes the Primordial A.

[7] The Aro gTér Tradition includes the gTérmas of Jomo Chhi'méd Pema *(jo mo chhi' 'med padma /* ཇོ་མོ་ཆི་འམེད་པདྨ་ *);* gTértön Rang-rig Togden *(rang rig rTogs lDan /* རང་རིག་རྟོགས་ལྡན་ *);* and Jomo Pema 'ö-Zér.

[8] Ancient Greek *hagios* 'holy' and *graphia* 'writing' – biography of a saint. Early Christian hagiographies consisted of biographic descriptions of a saint's deeds and miracles. As the term is used here, it also applies to visionary history.

After morning practice, I asked Ngak'chang Rinpoche and Khandro Déchen if it would be possible to receive empowerment to practise her as a yidam[9]. My question received a *"Who knows, many things are possible…"* answer – and a substantial grin from Rinpoche. It was only later that day, still obsessively thinking about Jomo Pema 'ö-Zér, that it occurred to me that—of course—I couldn't practise her in that way. She was a figure from lineage history, not a yidam. I felt a little stupid for not having realised this before – and for having asked the question. Now I feel unendingly grateful for that stupidity, because a few weeks later Rinpoche and Khandro Déchen gathered a small group of disciples together at their house in Penarth for the evening – and something remarkable took place. Once we were sitting together in the shrine room, Ngak'chang Rinpoche and Khandro Déchen gave the empowerment of Jomo Pema 'ö-Zér – as a yidam.

It was a transmission given in the *extremely non-elaborate*[10] mode of Dzogchen[11]. It transpired that the most important Aro gTér lineage Lamas[12] existed in yidam form. They came from a gTérma which had not yet been openly revealed. Although it was never discussed—or even mentioned—it had always been obvious to me that Rinpoche, as lineage holder of the Aro gTér, must be a gTértön[13].

---

[9] *yid dam gyi lha* / ཡིད་དམ་གྱི་ལྷ་ / *ishta devata* – awareness being; wisdom being; personal 'deity'; meditational 'deity'.

[10] Rab-tu trö'mèd wang-kur *(rab tu sPros 'med dBang bsKur* / རབ་ཏུ་སྤྲོས་མེད་ཀྱི་དབང་བསྐུར་)

[11] *rDzogs chen* / རྫོགས་པ་ཆེན་པོ་ / *Mahasandhi or Atiyoga* – Great Completeness.

[12] Lama *(bLa ma* / བླ་མ་ / *guru)*

[13] *gTer sTon* / གཏེར་སྟོན་ – revealer of religious teachings and practices which have been concealed by Guru Rinpoche and Yeshé Tsogyel *(ye shes mTsho rGyal* / ཡེ་ཤེས་མཚོ་རྒྱལ་)for future revelation, or which have emanated from the spatial dimension of reality.

He had not received the teachings and practices of the Aro gTérma cycle —*in person from any living Lama*—in his lifetime. It must therefore have been received from Aro Lingma in vision[14]. That evening however, we learnt that not only was he the third revealer of the Aro gTér[15], but that he also held another gTérma – the Zér-tsal Thugthig[16] which had been predicted by Kyabjé Düd'jom Rinpoche Jig'drèl Yeshé Dorje in 1975. This gTérma contained a series of Lineage Lamas as yidams.

We were asked not to speak about what we had received that evening, or the existence of the Zér-tsal Thugthig. This remained secret from all but a few close disciples for over two decades. Rinpoche said that he was concerned not to appear to be making claims of this nature. He was concerned that people should be interested in Nyingma[17] Vajrayana, rather than him.

Lama Tharchin Rinpoche knew that Ngak'chang Rinpoche was a gTértön however – as did Lama Tharchin Rinpoche's son, Dung-sré A'gyür Rinpoche[18], who I was to meet years later in Bodhanath[19], Nepal. Dung-sré A'gyür Rinpoche seemed to feel it was fairly well known that Ngak'chang Rinpoche was a gTértön – and was surprised that we didn't know.

---

[14] See: Ngakpa Chögyam—*Goodbye Forever – the Miscellaneous Memoirs of an English Lama*— Volume I—Chapter 1—Aro Books WORLDWIDE—2020. *Goodbye Forever* is the title of the series of volumes that deal with Ngak'chang Rinpoche's life as a Vajrayana Buddhist. It is a parallel series to the four volumes of *an odd boy* which deal with Ngak'chang Rinpoche's life as an artist, poet, and Blues musician.

[15] Khyungchen Aro Lingma passed the Aro gTér to her son, gTértön Aro Yeshé, both as a transmission whilst she was alive, and again in visionary form after she attained rainbow body. She also gave transmission of the entire Aro gTér to the two sangyums of Aro Yeshé: Jomo A-yé Khandro and Jomo A-shé Khandro. Khandro Déchen is the incarnation of A-yé Khandro, as confirmed by Kyabjé Künzang Dorje Rinpoche and Jomo Sam'phel Déchen Rinpoche.

[16] *zer rTsal thugs thig* / ཟེར་རྩལ་ཐུགས་ཐིག — the Zértsal Thugthig was also predicted by Khyungchen Aro Lingma.

[17] *rNying ma* / རྙིང་མ — the most ancient form of Buddhism in Tibet, dating back to the time of King Trisong Détsen *(khri srong lDe bTsan /* ཁྲི་སྲོང་ལྡེ་བཙན་ */ 755–797)*

[18] *gDung sras A 'gyur*/ གདུང་སྲས་ཨ་འགྱུར

[19] Jarung Kha-shor *(bya rung kha shor /* བྱ་རུང་ཁ་ཤོར་ */ Khasti Chaitya)* is seven miles from the centre of Kathmandu. It is predominantly a Tibetan cultural area, and home to many Lamas – particularly Nyingma.

It came as news to the wider sangha when it eventually became apparent. This happened in 2016 when I spoke at the *First International Conference of Vajrayana*[20] in Bhutan. On that occasion the conference speech and published paper both alluded to Ngak'chang Rinpoche as gTértön Zér-tsal Lingpa[21].

It was also in Bhutan that we witnessed the meeting of Ngak'chang Rinpoche with Kyabjé Düd'jom Rinpoche Ten'dzin Yeshé Dorje[22] – the current incarnation of Kyabjé Düd'jom Rinpoche Jig'drèl Yeshé Dorje[23]. He had predicted the Zér-tsal Thugthig gTérma more than 40 years before. Due to circumstantial time constraints this remarkable and joyous meeting was held at the roadside in Paro. There was much smiling and laughter as Kyabjé Düd'jom Rinpoche Ten'dzin Yeshé Dorje recalled knowing Ngak'chang Rinpoche – and remembered being introduced to Blues[24] by him.

There was another remarkable and equally joyous meeting in Nepal during that same pilgrimage when we witnessed the private audience between Ngak'chang Rinpoche and Kyabjé Düd'jom Rinpoche Sang-gyé Pema Shépa[25].

---

[20] *A Mandala of 21ˢᵗ Century Perspectives – the First International Conference on Tradition and Innovation in Vajrayana Buddhism*, held in July 2016 in Thimphu, Bhutan.

[21] *zer rTsal gLing pa* / ཟེར་རྩལ་གླིང་པ – Rinpoche only agreed to being mentioned as a gTértön in this paper because the audience was highly educated in terms of Vajrayana and it could therefore not be avoided. In Bhutan, gTérma is far less unusual than it seems to be in the Tibetan diaspora or in Tibet.

[22] *sKyabs rJe bDud 'Joms rin po che bsTan 'Dzin ye shes rDo rJe* / སྐྱབས་རྗེ་བདུད་འཇོམས་རིན་པོ་ཆེ་བསྟན་འཛིན་ཡེ་ཤེས་རྡོ་རྗེ

[23] *sKyabs rJe bDud 'Joms rin po che 'Jigs bral ye shes rDo rJe* / སྐྱབས་རྗེ་བདུད་འཇོམས་རིན་པོ་ཆེ་འཇིགས་བྲལ་ཡེ་ཤེས་རྡོ་རྗེ

[24] See: Ngakpa Chögyam—*Goodbye Forever – the Miscellaneous Memoirs of an English Lama*—Volume I—Chapter 1—Aro Books WORLDWIDE—2020. Ngak'chang Rinpoche sang *Hoochie Coochie Man* at his request. The current incarnation of Kyabjé Düd'jom Rinpoche Jig'drèl Yeshé Dorje is an aficionado of Blues, and plays guitar.

[25] *bDud 'joms sangs rGyas pa dMa bZhad pa* / བདུད་འཇོམས་སངས་རྒྱས་པདྨ་བཞད་པ / 1990–2022 who resided mainly in Tibet and Nepal.

On that occasion Kyabjé Düd'jom Rinpoche Sang-gyé Pema Shépa told Ngak'chang Rinpoche that he remembered him being there when he gave the *wang*[26] of the entire Düd'jom gTér in his previous lifetime, both in Tso Pema[27] and Bodhanath. He said *"Ngak'chang Rinpoche, you need no further teaching from me – but you should always feel free to communicate with me, whenever you choose."* He pointed out that there was the Aro gTér and Zértsal Thugthig to teach – so there was no need for Ngak'chang Rinpoche to be concerned about teaching the Düd'jom gTér. He looked forward however, to coming to Drala Jong[28] and was happy that Ngak'chang Rinpoche wanted to make his retreat centre available to Düd'jom gTér Lamas. He looked at the photographs of Drala Jong and said that he was extremely pleased with its appearance. There were many signs in what he saw which made him confident that Nyingma practice would flourish there.

Back at the beginning of the 21st century however, the existence of Zér-tsal Lingpa and the Zér-tsal Thugthig were still secret to all but a few. After that first evening's transmission, without mentioning it to anyone—other than Rinpoche and Khandro Déchen—Jomo Pema 'ö-Zér became my main yidam practice. With that developing practice, came a desire to know as much as I could about this astonishing woman. I started to ask Rinpoche and Khandro Déchen questions about her life and practice. It became clear that Jomo Pema 'ö-Zér was herself a gTértön– a treasure revealer. Over the course of time, Rinpoche started to talk about her gTérma of the Eighty-four Mahasiddhas[29]. This became my new obsession. I learnt of the unusual nature of this particular cycle of Mahasiddhas[30].

---

[26] *dBang* or *dBang sKur* / དབང་ or དབང་སྐུར་ / *abhisheka* – empowerment.

[27] *mTsho padma* / མཚོ་པདྨ་ – Rewalsar in Himachal Pradesh, northern India.

[28] *sGra bLa lJongs* / སྒྲ་བླ་ལྗོངས་ – Drala Jong Nyingma Retreat Centre, Wales.

[29] Drüptob gyèd çu tsa-zhi *(grub thob brGyad cu rTsa bZhi* / གྲུབ་ཐོབ་བརྒྱད་ཅུ་རྩ་བཞི་ / *caturasitisiddha)*

[30] Drüpchen *(grub chen* / གྲུབ་ཆེན་) – one who has achieved great accomplishment.

They were all available to be practised as yidams with mantras – and contained methods of Dzogchen men-ngag-dé[31].

Over the ensuing decades, each visit to Rinpoche and Khandro Déchen would elicit further discussion of Jomo Pema 'ö-Zér's gTérma – and I started to practise the Mahasiddhas as yidams as I received transmission of them in turn. My fascination was such that I kept notes on all that Rinpoche told me of these Eighty-four Mahasiddhas from the outset. When my *sangyab* Ja'gyür Dorje[32] moved over from Sweden however, he instigated the recording of all such conversations. Over the years Rinpoche gave increasingly detailed hagiographies of the Mahasiddhas I was practising – and it became clear that something extraordinary was happening. We were hearing accounts of the adepts of Ancient India – but we were hearing them now, from a person who was in all probability, a modern-day Mahasiddha. Chögyam Trungpa Rinpoche[33] was regarded as a Mahasiddha – so there was no reason why the same should not be true of Ngak'chang Rinpoche. He was, after all, gTértön Zér-tsal Lingpa. That was the name indicated by Kyabjé Düd'jom Rinpoche – and here he was in the living room of a Georgian terraced house in Penarth, in the Vale of Glamorgan, Wales.

The accounts Rinpoche was giving were entirely relevant and applicable to the present moment. They were also inspirational for Vajrayana practitioners – and, potentially, for the general public.

---

[31] *rDzogs chen man ngag sDe* / ཛོགས་ཆེན་མན་ངག་སྡེ་ – series of implicit instruction.
[32] Naljorpa Ja'gyür Dorje *(rNal 'byor pa 'ja' 'gyur rDo rJe* / རྣལ་འབྱོར་པ་འཇའ་འགྱུར་རྡོ་རྗེ་)
[33] Surmang Trungpa Chökyi Gyamtso *(zur mang drung pa chos kyi rGya mTsho* / ཟུར་མང་དྲུང་པ་ཆོས་ཀྱི་རྒྱ་མཚོ་ / 1940–1987) – a Mahasiddha and gTértön born in Kham; and the 11th incarnation of Surmang Trungpa, of the Surmang Gompa. His main Lamas were Shéchen Kongtrül Pema Dri'mèd Lekpa'i Lodrö *(zhe chen kong sPrul padma dri 'med legs pa'i bLo gros* / ཞེ་ཆེན་ཀོང་སྤྲུལ་པདྨ་དྲི་མེད་ ལེགས་པའི་བློ་གྲོས་ / 1901–c.1960); Kyabjé Dilgo Khyentsé Rinpoche *(sKyabs rJe dil mGo mKhyen brTse rin po che* / དིལ་མགོ་མཁྱེན་བརྩེ་ / 1910–1991); the 16th Gyalwa Karmapa *(rGyal dBang karma pa* / རྒྱལ་དབང་ཀརྨ་པ་ / 1924–1981); and Khenpo Gangshar *(mKhan po gang shar dBang po* / མཁན་པོ་གང་ཤར་དབང་ པོ་ / b. 1925).

As time passed, we not only recorded, and took notes, but also wrote accounts of when and where Rinpoche revealed each hagiography – with the questions and answers which followed each rendition. It is these stories and conversations which make up this book: the first twenty-one hagiographies of the Eighty-four Mahasiddhas which constitute the gTérma of Jomo Pema 'ö-Zér.

The following introduction provides some context and explanatory information for those who are unfamiliar with the history of the Mahasiddhas, Vajrayana, the Nyingma Tradition, or the Aro gTér. Ultimately Rinpoche's recounting of these hagiographies requires no introduction – the stories can stand alone and represent themselves, of themselves. I hope that they are found to be as astonishingly inspirational for the reader as they are for me.

———————•———————

The title *Warp and Weft*[34] *of Wonderment*[35] refers to the nature of reality as nondual luminosity sparkling through the fabric of dualistically fixated conditioning. It also refers to the nature of realisation as rolpa[36] – the effortless uncontrived play of emptiness and realised form. *Warp and Weft of Wonderment* also refers to the body of teachings and praxis of Vajrayana. The practices of Tantra and Dzogchen are exemplified in the lives of the Mahasiddhas – the great adepts of early Vajrayana practice in India. Finally *Warp and Weft of Wonderment* refers to the transformational accounts of the Eighty-four Mahasiddhas from the gTérma of the female gTértön Jomo Pema 'ö-Zér as recounted by Zér-tsal Lingpa in Wales, the west of England, Cornwall, and the Himalayas.

---

[34] gyüd *(rGyud /* རྒྱུད */ Tantra)* means 'thread' or 'continuity' and is a term which relates to weaving. Tantra (तन्त्र) literally means loom, weave – warp and weft. The verb-root *tan* means 'to extend, spread, to spin out, weave, display, compose'.

[35] gyü-ma *(sGyu ma /* སྒྱུ་མ */ maya)* – means wonderment, enchantment, magical display, mirage, or wizardry.

[36] *rol pa /* རོལ་པ – nondual play.

Vajrayana is a Sanskrit word. In Tibetan it is *Dorje Thegpa*[37]. *Do* means 'stone', and *je* means 'lord'. Together they refer to the *lord of stones* – the diamond. It is the *lord of stones* because it is indestructible and cuts through all other substances. This is the *vajra nature* – the indestructible lucid lucent empty ground of being. *Thegpa* means vehicle. A *thegpa* is a method of approaching the body of teachings we know as Buddhism or *chö*[38]. The word *chö* means *as it is*. All the teachings and methods within *chö* are ways of coming to understand—and integrate with—reality, 'as it is'. Each *thegpa* presents a different possible approach to the teachings. They each provide an alternative modality, not just a different level of teaching. Each vehicle is its own paradigm. Although there are principles which are consistent throughout the range of the nine *thegpas* of the Nyingma, they do not necessarily concur with each other.

Any class of teaching which is described as a vehicle, is recognised as having a base, a path, and a fruit: a place to start, methods to practise, and a result of following those methods. A *thegpa* is a means of gaining realisation which is entire unto itself. Each *thegpa* however, has its own *principle and function* – and the methods employed are multifarious. They can vary dramatically – and can even contradict each other, depending on the base. When it is understood that each *thegpa* is predicated upon a specific level of experience – all inconsistencies between *thegpas* are seen in terms of pragmatics. A knife and fork function far better than a spoon when eating rare steak – but a spoon comes into its own when faced with soup.

Vajrayana is the *thegpa* of Tantra and Dzogchen. In the Nyingma tradition of Himalayan Buddhism, we speak of the six classes of Vajrayana, which comprise the three outer Tantras: *Kriya Tantra, Upa or Carya Tantra*, and *Yoga Tantra*; and the three Inner Tantras: *Maha Yoga, Anu Yoga*, and *Ati Yoga* – better known as Dzogchen.

---

[37] *rDo rje thegs pa* / རྡོ་རྗེ་ཐེགས་པ་
[38] *chos* / ཆོས་

The Mahasiddhas were the first practitioners and masters of Vajrayana in the Indian Subcontinent[39] and in the Himalayan countries, including Tibet. They attained nondual realisation through following the Inner Tantras. The Sanskrit word *Tantra* means *thread* or *continuity* – and is related to Sanskrit terms which deal with weaving. In this context, Tantra refers to a practice and a view in which emptiness and form are the *warp and weft* of reality. Emptiness is seen as being the medium of continuity. To recognise that indestructible emptiness is the thread of continuity which exists throughout the fabric of experience, is to be free to let the texture of reality be *what it is*. Dualism is the failure to recognise this – and the consequent compulsion to continually divide the form qualities of existence from their emptiness aspects. This division creates the web of duality within which entrapment is woven. The core principle and defining characteristic of the Inner Tantras is *transformation* – in contradistinction to the principle of *purification* in the Outer Tantras and the principle of *renunciation* found in Sutrayana. In Sutrayana the teachings and practices renounce attachment to form in order to experience the emptiness quality of being. In Outer Tantra the teachings and practices explore a new dimension of form – in which form needs to be seen as pure and empty of referentiality. In the Inner Tantras, the base is the experience of emptiness as *the ground from which form arises in natural purity*. The path of Inner Tantra is therefore the experience of *the natural arising of form from emptiness* – of which the fruit is nonduality. One approaches nonduality through riding the energy of duality – and form is embraced as nondual appearance.

The core principle and defining characteristic of the *innermost Tantra*, Dzogchen – is *self-liberation*. *Self-liberation* means *of itself – it liberates itself*. That is to say, without the intervention or assistance of anything else – *being* simply relaxes into its natural condition. The base is the nondual state.

---

[39] India, Pakistan, Afghanistan, Nepal, Sikkim, Bhutan, Myanmar, Bangladesh, Sri Lanka, and the Maldives. The Buddhist area also included Thailand.

The path consists of methods by which one returns to the nondual state whenever it has been lost. Dzogchen is known as a 'fruit path' because the base, path, and fruit are the same – nondual awareness or rigpa[40]. Rigpa is the path, the support for the path, and the result of the path.

The greatest exemplars—the forebears of these practices of transformation and self-liberation—were the Mahasiddhas. It was they for whom the attainment of nondual awareness was the ultimate siddhi[41] – or greatest accomplishment. The Sanskrit word Mahasiddha describes a realised tantric adept. In Tibetan the word is Drüpchen – master of accomplishment. *Maha* is Sanskrit for 'great' and a *siddha* is 'one who has siddhis'. Siddhi means accomplishment – and refers to both relative siddhis[42] – miraculous powers; and the absolute siddhi[43] – nonduality.

Warp and weft of wonderment refers to the lives and praxis of these Mahasiddhas which are woven through the very fabric of Tantra into the lived experience of Vajrayana practitioners today.

Magical Mastery of Method

The epoch of the Mahasiddhas occurred between the 3rd and 13th centuries across a large area of northern India and the Himalayas. The methodology of the Mahasiddhas arose from visionary revelations designated as Tantra. The Tantras were received from Shakyamuni Buddha manifesting in the form of various *long-ku yidams*[44]. Mahasiddhas were those who, through practising *drüpthab*[45], attained both nondual realisation and supranormal capacities.

---

[40] *rig pa* / རིག་པ་ – instant presence, nondual awareness, presence of awareness, nondual presence.
[41] ngödrüp *(dNgos grub /* དངོས་གྲུབ་ *)*
[42] thun-mong gi ngödrüp *(thun mong gi dNgos grub /* ཐུན་མོང་གི་དངོས་གྲུབ་ *)*
[43] chog-gi ngödrüp *(mChog gi dNgos grub /* མཆོག་གི་དངོས་གྲུབ་ *)*
[44] *longs sKu yi dam* / ལོངས་སྐུ་ཡི་དམ་ / *sambhogakaya, ishtadevata* – beings within the visionary dimension.
[45] *sGrub thabs* / སྒྲུབ་ཐབས་ / *sadhana* – method of accomplishment.

We have accounts of Mahasiddhas who performed feats of clairvoyance, psychokinesis, and alchemy, but these extraordinary abilities were held to be of little interest compared to the absolute accomplishment – liberation from duality.

Although one meaning of drüpthab is *liturgical text*[46], drüpthab has a far wider meaning. It also refers to the personal methods of practice given to aspirants by their teachers. The genius of these methods lies in the fact that they conjure with essential Vajrayana principles in relation to individuals and their individual predilections. Unlike the renunciate discipline of Sutrayana, the inner discipline of Vajrayana provides a methodology of transformation and self-liberation through which the dualistic neuroses are not renounced – but specifically cultivated as the context for energetic transformation. Vajrayana holds that the neuroses are simply dualistically distorted aspects of nonduality. They provide therefore, the supreme opportunity in terms of discovering nonduality. The greater the neurosis, the greater the potential for nondual liberation. No style of personality or confusion is beyond potential transformation. No human being is too distorted to achieve realisation.

The distorted qualities of practitioners are—in fact—the dynamic linkages which enable access to their intrinsic nondual nature. A thief who became the disciple of a Mahasiddha was instructed to steal the entire phenomenal universe in his mind. An indolent was given recumbent practices.

Whatever orientation—*be the person a camel-riding caravaneer, housewife, gourmet, glutton, wastrel, prostitute, king, moron, launderer, child manual-labourer, libidinous satyr, nymphomaniac, blacksmith, impoverished ex-patriot, depressed son of fallen gentry, bird-catcher, warrior, puritan, poet, mythomaniac, swindler, sensualist, farmer, market gardener, cowboy, fisherman, hedonist, musician, arrow maker*—all a person required was devotion to the teacher and utter willingness to apply the exact nature of their individual drüpthab.

---

[46] A chant manual which accompanies the practice of visualisation and mantra.

The Mahasiddhas had little interest in the Buddhist bureaucracy, monastic establishments, or codified cerebral conventions of their time. They abandoned institutional settings in favour of mountain caves, uninhabited islands, forests, and charnel grounds. Many adopted itinerant lifestyles roaming between remote villages in the Himalayan and Karakorum ranges – living outside the boundaries of common orthodoxies.

The Mahasiddha path however, was not one of renunciation of anything within the outer physical material world *or* within the inner emotional world. Their 'renunciation' was *the renunciation of referentiality* – the renunciation of dualistic orientation. Mahasiddhas were therefore, also to be found breaking with convention in towns and cities, in palaces and courts – and, in every walk of life. Moving beyond conditioning was radical. It was shocking, given the rigid confines of the prevalent social stratification of the varnas.

The varna system divided society into four castes[47] – and one *classless* category of outcastes[48]. There were the Brahmins[49], Kshatriyas[50], Vaishyas[51], and Shudras[52]. The Brahmins held the most power in the Hindu/Buddhist world. They were primarily priests, but also scholars and teachers – the spiritual and intellectual leaders of society.

---

[47] Mi-rig zhi *(mi rigs bZhi* / མི་རིགས་བཞི་) – the four varnas, castes, or social classes.

[48] Harijans – kuntum *(kun gTum* / ཀུན་གཏུམ་). Ngak'chang Rinpoche chose to use 'Harijan', which was Mahatma Gandhi's word for untouchable or outcaste. Harijan—a term which is no longer in favour—is not a varna, therefore they are outcastes i.e. outside the caste system – often sweepers and latrine cleaners. They are also referred to as kyi-zan *(khyi zan* / ཁྱི་ཟན་ – of low caste; dol-rig *(gDol rigs* / གདོལ་རིགས་) – outcaste, class of untouchable; dol-pa *(gDol pa* / གདོལ་པ་) – outcaste, untouchable, vile, lowly, base; and rig-nan *(rigs ngan* / རིགས་ངན་) – barbarous.

[49] Brahmins: dram-ze-rig *('bram ze'i rigs* / འབྲམ་ཟེའི་རིགས་) – priests and the priestly class.

[50] Kshatriyas: gyal-rig or dro-wa'i wang *(rGyal rigs* or *'gro ba'i dBang* / རྒྱལ་རིགས་ or འགྲོ་བའི་དབང་) – lords of beings; rulers and warriors; members of the military or governing class; warriors of princely descent. Shakyamuni Buddha was a Kshatriya.

[51] Vaishyas: je-rig *(rJe'u rigs* / རྗེའུ་རིགས་) – the bourgeoisie; officials; doctors; landowners; merchants, traders; skilled manufacturers.

[52] Shudras: mang-rig or kang-kyé *(dMangs rigs* / དམངས་རིགས་ or *rKang sKyes* / རྐང་སྐྱེས་) – the plebians; unskilled workers, servants to Brahmins, Kshatriyas, and Vaishyas.

The second varna in the social hierarchy were the Kshatriyas – the rulers, warriors, and high-level administrators of society. Shakyamuni Buddha was born a Kshatriya. The third in the social hierarchy were the Vaishyas – bureaucrats, accountants, merchants, academics, teachers, doctors, and traders who materially contributed to the economy. The fourth were the Shudras: the farmers, artisans, labourers, peasants, and servants who worked in service to the higher varnas. There were also those who had no status. They belonged to no varna – and were *a-varna*.

The justification of this social stratification was linked to the concept of karma from previous lives as understood in Hinduism. The Chandogya Upanishad[53] proclaims *"Those whose conduct here has been good will quickly attain some good birth – birth as a Brahmin, birth as a Kshatriya, or birth as a Vaishya."*. People's position in society remained fixed for life – and members of a varna were expected to consort only with others of their own varna. The priestly Brahmins were religiously concerned with maintaining perceived purity: the eating of meat and drinking of alcohol were deemed unclean and to be avoided, as was consorting with those of the lower varnas.

The Mahasiddhas were not constrained by such religious or societal conventions. Their methods therefore, embraced the fields of the senses in order to realise their authentic nature. No activity, occupation or circumstance was precluded from practice. Indeed, many drüpthabs of the Mahasiddhas employed sensual enjoyment as the object of meditation. Alcohol, meat, secular music, dance, and sexuality were renounced by both Hindu Brahmins and Buddhist Sutrayana monastics. They were not however, renounced in the Inner Tantras – and could therefore be employed by yogis and yoginis as the means to realise nonduality.

---

[53] छान्दोग्योपनिषद् – one of the oldest in the *Chandogya Brahmana* of the Hindu Sama Veda. 9th in the *Muktika* canon of 108 Upanishads.

The Mahasiddhas thus broke free of the restrictivism of Brahminic societal control. They frequently broke all the conventions of *varna stratification* and lived on the margins of mainstream society. They were highly ethical – but ethical according to nonduality, rather than according to artificial morality and systematised ethics. They contravened puritan mores – and any form of societally manipulated morality. It is not possible to manipulate someone who has moved beyond all reference points and whose only controls and commitments are to kindness and awareness. The essence of Vajrayana is anarchism. Anarchism, in this sense, means 'adhering to no externally imposed governance, government or administration'. Anarchism—as the naturally manifesting *inner governance of awareness*—is unconditioned, present, direct, and utterly responsible. The Mahasiddhas were therefore highly threatening to the establishment, and posed a direct challenge to Brahminic supremacy.

Within the lives of the Mahasiddhas there is no uniformity in terms of gender, background, capacity, lifestyle, personality, or predilection. Without exception however, they all meet with a teacher who gave them transmission of realisation in the form of individual drüpthabs. Without exception their liberation relied on devotion to the vajra master[54].

The Dangerous Friend

The practice of Vajrayana is not possible without the teacher, the Lama. The Lama is the source of empowerment in Tantra. Without empowerment the practice of Tantra is meaningless – or at best futile. Without real experience of empowerment, it is impossible to maintain the fundamental *damtsig*[55] or commitment of Tantra. This fundamental *damtsig* is to sustain the experience of transmission through practice – and ultimately in every moment.

---

[54] Dorje Lopön *(rDo rJe bLo dPon /* རྡོ་རྗེ་བློ་དཔོན་ */ vajracarya)* – as distinct from the ge-wa'i shényèn or 'spiritual friend' of Sutrayana *(dGe ba'i bShes gNyen /* དགེ་བའི་བཤེས་གཉེན་ */ kalyanamitra)*
[55] *gDam tshig /* དམ་ཚིག་ */ samaya* – vow, commitment.

The Lama is the source of transmission in Dzogchen – and without transmission, the practice of Dzogchen is impossible. In Dzogchen, transmission means 'non-ritual introduction'. It is divided into three[56]: *direct transmission, symbolic transmission,* and *oral transmission*.

Direct transmission[57] is Mind-to-Mind communication between Lama and disciple which can happen at any moment and according to any circumstances. *Symbolic transmission*[58] is when some essentially potent object is displayed along with cryptic oral indications, which incite understanding. *Oral transmission*[59] is when a verbal clarification is given either of nonduality, or of the practices which facilitate its realisation. These are often referred to as the *pointing-out instructions*[60] or as *mere indication*[61].

The primacy of emptiness within Sutrayana influences the rôle of the teacher. In Sutrayana, teachers are simply conduits for the teachings – and there is nothing personal or particular about their presentation. The personality of the teacher is irrelevant and potentially an obstacle to the teaching. Personality is a symbol of form, and Sutrayana teachers should reflect emptiness. Teachers in Sutrayana renounce the form of their individual manifestation in order to accurately reflect the nature of the teachings. The teacher is kind, supportive, and offers advice and instruction. Although the teacher might challenge students' conceptual structures and assumptions, this is done in a gentle manner and at the level of the intellect. The teacher is reliable and safe.

---

[56] ka'i gyüdpa sum *(bKa'i brGyud pa gSum /* བཀའི་བརྒྱུད་པ་གསུམ *)* – the three transmissions.
[57] Gong gyüd *(dGongs brGyud /* དགོངས་བརྒྱུད *)*
[58] Rig'dzin da-gyüd *(rig 'dzin brDa brGyud /* རིག་འཛིན་བརྡ་བརྒྱུད *)*
[59] nyèn gyüd *(sNyan brGyud /* སྙན་བརྒྱུད *)*
[60] ngo-trö kyi dam-pa *(ngo sProd kyi gDams pa /* ངོ་སྤྲོད་ཀྱི་གདམས་པ *)* – also referred to as *pointing out the nature of Mind*: sem kyi ngo-trö *(sems kyi ngo sProd /* སེམས་ཀྱི་ངོ་སྤྲོད *)*. In Dzogchen, the pointing-out instructions are often called the 'introduction to rigpa': rig-pa'i ngo-trö *(rig pa'i ngo sProd /* རིག་པའི་ངོ་སྤྲོད *)*
[61] jod-du 'mèd *(brJod du 'med /* བརྗོད་དུ་འམེད *)*

Students move at their own speed, and there is no sense in which their rationale is in danger or under threat. This is one of the reasons why Sutrayana is known as the gradual or graduated path.

The teacher in Vajrayana is known as the vajra master. The personality of the teacher is a *symbol of transformation* – and the vehicle by which the teachings are expressed. The personality of the vajra master expresses the very quality of the path which is most important – the fact that the elemental neuroses do not have to be removed or avulsed. The elemental neuroses can become the apparitional array of *nondual greed, nondual rage, nondual lust, nondual suspicion,* and *nondual phlegmatism.* The vajra master is able to paint *continually arising pictures* of the manner in which neuroses can be transformed into transparent manifestations of nonduality.

In terms of Vajrayana, the personality of the Lama is indispensable as a means of showing disciples that their own personalities are open to transformation. Because of this, the Lama may appear 'unreliable' and 'unsafe'. The vajra master will threaten students' insistent grip on maintaining the particular illusions of duality to which they are so fiercely attached.

Chögyam Trungpa Rinpoche coined the term 'dangerous friend' for the vajra master. The danger of such a friend is *that which is the inherent threat* to fixed and limited perceptions. The pace of change for disciples can be swift and dramatic, or even immediate. This is why Tantra is known as the short path and Dzogchen as the instantaneous path.

In *Wearing the Body of Visions*[62] Ngak'chang Rinpoche and Khandro Déchen write:

'The Lama is the ecstatic, wild and gentle figure who short-circuits one's systems of self-referencing. The Lama is the only person in life who cannot be manipulated. The Lama is the invasion of unpredictability one allows into life, to facilitate cutting through the convolutions of interminable psychological and emotional processes.

[62] Ngakpa Chögyam and Khandro Déchen—*Wearing the Body of Visions*—Aro Books Inc—1995

'The Lama is the terrifyingly compassionate gamester who re-shuffles the deck of one's carefully arranged rationale.'

It is just such Lamas—and just such devoted disciples—who appear in the hagiographies of the Mahasiddhas. *Dad'dun*[63]—devotion—such as that shown by the Mahasiddhas for their remarkable teachers, is vitally and viscerally important in terms of both Tantra and Dzogchen. The meaning of dad'dun is 'rapturous insight' or 'perfect appreciation' – the open-ended appreciation which sees the value of: the teachings, the teachers as the transmitters of the teachings, and the lineage of transmission itself. Dad'dun is knowledge and skill coupled with direct experiential understanding, so devotion is based on the development of spiritual experience through practice. The more *practice insight* disciples have, the more they value their Lamas – because they know that they have travelled beyond the horizons that they are trying to reach. That is the basis of their Dad'dun. Dad'dun in Vajrayana is that which recognises either nonduality – or the *possibility* of nonduality.

Text and gTérma

The stories of these remarkable teachers and their disciples are recounted in texts which give collections of eighty-four Mahasiddhas. There are a number of such *lists of eighty-four* – the two most famous being known as the Abhayadatta Sri list and the Vajrasana list.

Abhayadatta Sri was a northern Indian scholar dating from the 11th or 12th century, who compiled a text called the *Caturasiti-siddha-pravrtti*. This text was translated into Tibetan by Mondrüp Shérab[64] and is known as the Drüpthob Gyèd chu Tsa-zhi lo-gyü[65] or 'Histories of the Eighty-four Siddhas'. Only the Tibetan translations of this Sanskrit text seem to have survived.

---

[63] khyer-shé dad'dun (*khyer shes kyi dad 'dun* / ཁྱེར་ཤེས་ཀྱི་དད་འདུན་)
[64] *sMon grub shes rab* / སྨོན་གྲུབ་ཤེས་རབ་
[65] *grub thob brGyad bCu tsa bZhi'i lo rGyus* / གྲུབ་ཐོབ་བརྒྱད་བཅུ་ཚ་བཞིའི་ལོ་རྒྱུས་

The Vajrasana list is contained in the *Caturasiti-siddha-bhyarthana* by Ratnakaragupta of Vajrasana, Bodhgaya in Bihar, northern India. This text was translated into Tibetan by Dorje Denpa[66] and is known as drüptob gyèd chu tsa zhi sol deb[67].

Despite difficulties of analysis due to variations in spellings and regional names, it is possible to ascertain that there are only 34 Mahasiddhas who occur on both lists. This means that there are some 135 Mahasiddhas referred to on the two lists combined. There were in fact known to be more than a thousand Mahasiddhas – and their hagiographies were gathered together in groups of eighty-four. This is because the number eighty-four was seen as symbolically 'complete' – and therefore represented a larger, possibly infinite, number. The lists of eighty-four thus represent *all* Vajrayana practitioners who achieved nondual realisation in one lifetime through the practice of the Inner Tantras. Many Vajrayana lineages extant today descend directly from these Mahasiddhas providing a living link between both Indian and Himalayan Buddhism, and between the first spread of Buddhism in Tibet and the present day. In 2014 the 17th Gyalwa Karmapa said *"Actually, there are many more than eighty-four Mahasiddhas. These highly accomplished masters, both men and women, can be found in India, Tibet, and even in Europe where they may remain unknown."*[68]

Although we know that there were many female Mahasiddhas in India and the Himalayan countries, there are none listed on the Vajrasana list – and only four on the Abhayadatta Sri list: *Manibhadra*[69] – the Perfect Wife; *Lakshmincara* – the Princess of Crazy Wisdom; and, *Mekhala* and *Kanakhala* – the Two Headless Sisters.

[66] rDo rJe gDan pa / རྡོ་རྗེ་གདན་པ

[67] grub thob brGyad bCu tsa bZhi'i gSol 'debs / གྲུབ་ཐོབ་བརྒྱད་བཅུ་ཙ་བཞིའི་གསོལ་འདེབས

[68] According to Ngak'chang Rinpoche, both Kyabjé Düd'jom Rinpoche Jig'drèl Yeshé Dorje and 'Khordong gTérchen Tulku Chhi'mèd Rig'dzin Rinpoche (*'khor gDong gTér chen sPrul sKu chhi' 'med rig 'dzin* / འཁོར་གདོང་གཏེར་ཆེན་སྤྲུལ་སྐུ་ཆི་མེད་རིག་འཛིན) said the same in the 1970s. Kyabjé Künzang Dorje Rinpoche confirmed this was the case to me independently in 2005.

[69] Manibhadra / མ་ཎི་བྷ་དྲ – was one of the previous incarnations of Ngak'chang Rinpoche.

The absence or paucity of women on these lists is not indicative of the number of female Mahasiddhas – nor of the attitude towards women in *essential Vajrayana*. It is the result of the lists having been compiled by monastic scholars in a patriarchal society[70]. Here, in the gTérma of Jomo Pema 'ö-Zér, we have another collection of Eighty-four Mahasiddhas. Some sixty of these Mahasiddhas can be found on the Abhayadatta Sri list – but there are also twenty-six female Mahasiddhas. We find Manibhadra and Lakshmincara from the Abhayadatta Sri list and a further twenty-four:

Subhadra – *the dakini choreographer*; Shatakshi – *the mother of tigers*; Baruni – *the surbdahar-playing whore*; Bhagarvi – *the terrifying wanton*; Shyama – *the cloud-weaver*; Sarvagjna – *the eccentric monocular seamstress*; Srirudra – *the lesbian crocodile tamer*; Maha'abala – *the virago*; Niguma – *the queen of the charnel grounds*; Sukhasiddhi – *the impoverished housewife*; Sanatini – *the giggling dakini mathematician*; Nandana – *the horsewoman*; Surasa – *the skull-juggling woman*; Niranjana – *the lion rider*; Ishani – *the nondual wandering woman*; Chandika – *the unpredictable jesting dakini*; Sharvani – *the laughing dakini*; Sharanya – *the corpulent dancing girl*; Sadabhuja – *the sister of wolves*; Kirati – *the fastidious fruit-picker dakini*; Kalaparani – *the skull-bearing queen*; Shambhavi – *the snake-clad dakini*; Vidhyadurga – *the beautiful butcher dakini*; and Amritambhu – *the naked moon-gazer*.

For the teachings and practices of Vajrayana to maintain their accuracy and relevance as they are passed from one generation to another, the Nyingma tradition has two major styles of transmission: ka'ma[71] and gTérma[72].

---

[70] This was more the case in the 2nd spread of Vajrayana. In the 1st spread—from the time of Guru Rinpoche and Yeshé Tsogyel to the assassination of Langdarma—women played a far greater rôle. Yeshé Tsogyel had over 3,000 female disciples.
[71] *bKa' ma* / བཀའ་མ
[72] *gTer ma* / གཏེར་མ

Ka'ma—words of the Buddha—is known as *long transmission* and refers to oral transmission of the early translations of Buddhist teachings passed on in unbroken succession from Lama to disciple up until the present day. gTérma, meaning 'treasure', is known as *short transmission* and refers to teachings hidden by Guru Rinpoche and Yeshé Tsogyel in the 9th century to be discovered at a later date.

Tulku Thöndup writes in *Hidden Teachings of Tibet*[73]:
'In order to prevent the deep teachings and sacred objects of Tantra from becoming mixed, diluted, or lost in the distant future, and in order to maintain their blessing powers afresh for future followers, Guru Rinpoche and Yeshé Tsogyel concealed them. They are discovered at the appropriate time by realised masters through their enlightened power.'

gTérma is therefore a phenomenon in which 'new' cycles of teaching and practice emerge at the appropriate time. They therefore resonate with the current gestalt – and address the mind-set of the moment. This periodic arising of gTérma means that spiritual conventions never become literalistically fixed or culturally ossified. In contradistinction, these teachings retain vitality and relevance. There are different ways of classifying gTérma. The most prevalent taxonomy within the Nyingma Tradition gives Sa gTér – *Earth gTérma*, and Gong gTér – *Mind gTérma*. These are the two categories of gTérma which were concealed by Guru Rinpoche and Yeshé Tsogyel. Sa gTér are physical texts or objects. Gong gTér are teachings secreted at the level of Mind. The gTértön—treasure revealer—is the discoverer of the gTérma. In the Nyingma tradition gTértöns will be the incarnation of realised disciples of Guru Rinpoche and Yeshé Tsogyel[74].

---

[73] Tulku Thöndup—*Hidden Teachings of Tibet – an explanation of the Terma Tradition of the Nyingma School of Buddhism*—Wisdom Publications—1986.

[74] Ngak'chang Rinpoche is an incarnation of Aro gZa' Druk-tsal Shèldrakma *(A ro gZa' 'brug rTsal shel brag ma /* ཨ་རོ་གཟའ་འབྲུག་རྩལ་ཤེལ་བྲག་མ་ *)* – a female disciple of Guru Rinpoche, although not one of the 25 direct disciples. She was rather, one of the 25 direct disciples of Yeshé Tsogyel.

Kyabjé Dilgo Khyentsé Rinpoche said:

"In many instances, after bestowing an empowerment or giving a teaching, Guru Rinpoche made the prayer: 'In the future, may this treasure arise in the mind of such and such gTértön.' While doing so, he would focus his prayers and blessings on the gTértön, usually an incarnation of one of his disciples. When, due to Guru Rinpoche's blessings, the time comes, both the words and the meaning of the treasure arise clearly in the gTértön's mind. The gTértön can then write these down without having to think."

There is also a category of gTérma called dag-nang gTér[75] – *Pure Vision gTérma*. These are visionary teachings received from realised beings other than Guru Rinpoche. These will be Lamas such as Mönmo Tashi Khyi'dren[76]. Alternatively, they can be revealed by manifestations of Guru Rinpoche and Yeshé Tsogyel in the sphere of vision as experienced by the gTértön. If teachings are revealed for a second time from a past gTérma, they are known as yang gTér[77].

Discussion of gTérma is complex and sometimes contentious. Further exploration therefore lies beyond the scope of this prolegomenon. More detail however, can be found in Tulku Thondup's *'Hidden Teachings of Tibet'*.

Hidden Yoginis

Jomo Pema 'ö-Zér was recognised as an incarnation of Mönmo Tashi Khyi'dren by her adoptive aunt, Jomo Chhi'mèd Pema[78]. Jomo Pema 'ö-Zér was about four years old when her mother, father, and older brother died of smallpox. Other relatives proved unwilling or unable to take her in, and she was left to be brought up by her 'aunt' Jomo Chhi'mèd Pema, who happened to arrive in the area at that time.

---

[75] *dag sNang gTer* / དག་སྣང་གཏེར་
[76] *mon mo bKra shis kye'u 'Dren* / མོན་མོ་བཀྲ་ཤིས་ཀྱིའུ་འདྲེན་
[77] *yang gTer* / ཡང་གཏེར་ — the Aro gTér at this time is a yang gTér.
[78] Jomo Chhi'mèd Pema was a Dzogchen long-dé practitioner, Lama, and incarnation of Niguma, the sister of Naropa.

It is unknown whether Jomo Chhi'mèd Pema was Jomo Pema 'ö-Zér's actual aunt, or some other relative or friend of the family – but she became her adoptive mother.

As far as most people were aware, Jomo Chhi'mèd Pema lived alone and herded a few goats who provided her with milk. She was regarded as an eccentric, who was erratic but not entirely unapproachable. She was actually a powerful ngakma who could converse with the local mountain protectors. She had a weighty teng-ar[79] made of pebbles. She wore rings on her ring fingers made of the same kind of stone – known as kLu-dor[80], or serpent stone. There were heaps of stone all around her dwelling – but not in the style of the usual Mani walls[81]. The stones were not carved or painted, but rather she would *inscribe* mantras on them with her fingers, using rain-water. These mounds of pebbles from the river were arranged in circles and other shapes around her home in the form of a kyil'khor[82] – but no one was aware of that, because the shapes did not conform to anything commonly understandable.

She was observed by locals to have the habit of carrying stones, sometimes of prodigious size, for many miles. When questioned as to the nature of her task, she would reply *"The stones are in the wrong place. I am merely correcting the situation because the stones are helpless in effecting the necessary change themselves."* She had a vast depth of knowledge, connected with the protectors, which concerned where certain stones should be – and therefore she treated them as living beings. She could read meaning in the positions in which she found them, and gave agricultural advice on the basis of what she saw. Jomo Chhi'mèd Pema knew the positions of all the large rocks in the river.

---

[79] *phreng ba* / ཕྲེང་བ / *mala* – Vajrayana rosary or mantra beads.
[80] *kLu rDor* / ཀླུ་རྡོར
[81] Walls built of mani stones which have been inscribed with mantras or sacred syllables.
[82] *dKyil 'khor* / དཀྱིལ་འཁོར / *mandala* – totality, centre and periphery; cosmogram; efflorescence, manifesting as centre and periphery.

When they happened to shift in position, she made predictions concerning the weather – in terms of the best times to sow and harvest barley. If large river rocks moved, she would always know immediately. It would usually portend change in weather or in other outer circumstances. The local people would often ask her advice on weather conditions as she was known to have considerable power as a controller of weather. In spite of her flamboyant peculiarities and outré idiosyncrasies, people would seek her help in terms of many basic life issues.

The inside of her hut was full of pebbles which had some connection with the local Mountain Protectors. She was known as a healer, and would tap, slap, or hit people with different kinds of pebbles when they were afflicted by diseases. She would click pebbles together, and listen to the sound they made, as a method of mo[83] divination. She also used to entertain the young Pema 'ö-Zér by the many sounds she could make with stones.

At one time, when she was very young, Pema 'ö-Zér fell and hit her knee on a large rock whilst she was playing outside their stone dwelling. When Jomo Chhi'mèd Pema heard her crying, she came out immediately with a large stick and gave the rock a severe thrashing. *"She is the mother of a Buddha!"* she shouted – warning it to take good care of young Pema 'ö-Zér in future. Pema 'ö-Zér was moved by the sight of the beating the rock had received. She felt sad and ashamed for having implicated the rock in an injury sustained merely through her clumsiness. Thereafter, she treated the rock with kindness and respect. Every day she made small food offerings to the rock and apologised for the beating it had received as a result of her carelessness. Jomo Chhi'mèd Pema often gave young Pema 'ö-Zér teachings in this way, and Pema 'ö-Zér was advantaged by this teaching style to profound effect. She learnt a great deal from her aunt about stone—from the smallest pebbles to huge boulders—in terms of the nature of the Mountain Protectors.

---

[83] *mo* / མོ

This strange and eccentric yogini—Jomo Chhi'mèd Pema—taught Jomo Pema 'ö-Zér Dzogchen long-dé[84] and Dzogchen men-ngag-dé. Jomo Chhi'mèd Pema never chanted texts or used any kind of ritual implements. She had no shrine or thangkas in her home. People therefore assumed that she was poor, and ignorant of religious conventions – but always asked for her help when personal misfortunes overtook them. She did have disciples who visited her, but they always came secretly at night and gave no outer sign of coming to visit a Lama. This was demanded of them by Jomo Chhi'mèd Pema as she did not wish the local people to know anything about her other than that which she chose to reveal to them.

Jomo Chhi'mèd Pema would attend teachings when important Lamas came to the area, but she would sit in a state of non-conceptual equipoise rather than take note of the actual language used. She would rarely perform mudras or participate in the recitations when wangs were given. The monks therefore assumed that she was merely a pious simpleton. This suited her purpose, and so she made no effort to give any other impression. When the teachings or empowerments were concluded she would sometimes leave the gompa giggling quietly. She would smile at people whilst nodding her head vigorously, which others found rather disconcerting. When asked any question she would often only reply *"Yes!"* and nod her head a great deal.

As a child living with Jomo Chhi'mèd Pema, Pema 'ö-Zér received a gong gTér of Yeshé Tsogyel manifesting as Mamo Ékajati[85]—protector of the Dzogchen teachings—and this gTérma remained a major practice throughout her life.

---

[84] *rDzogs chen kLong sDe* / རྫོགས་ཀློང་སྡེ། – series of space.
[85] *Matrika* or *Matari É ka dza ti'* / ཨེ་ཀ་ཛ་ཏི། / *ma mo ral gCig ma* / མ་མོ་རལ་གཅིག་མ།

Love and Liberation

In her early adolescence, Jomo Pema 'ö-Zér received a prediction from Jomo Chhi'mèd Pema: *"One day you will find that I have gone. You will know when this time has come, because I will not return from one of the regular journeys I make. If more than three months pass in which I have not returned, you must take that as the sign to leave the area and begin the life of a wandering yogini. There will be nothing you should take with you apart from your clothes."*

Jomo Pema 'ö-Zér passed through her early adolescent years with this idea firmly implanted, so she avoided making a life for herself in the area where she and Jomo Chhi'mèd Pema lived. The local people found Jomo Pema 'ö-Zér as eccentric as her aunt, and therefore human contact was minimal. Local people avoided both of them unless they wanted to approach Jomo Chhi'mèd Pema for mo divinations or other such services. Jomo Chhi'mèd Pema rarely accepted any form of offering for the help she gave, only food and occasional sundry materials which fulfilled the everyday needs of herself and her niece.

When Jomo Pema 'ö-Zér reached the age of nineteen, Jomo Chhi'mèd Pema left without warning as soon as the year's weather had become sufficiently clement to allow travel. She had adopted the habit since Jomo Pema 'ö-Zér's early teens of leaving home without warning and without bidding her niece farewell. Jomo Pema 'ö-Zér had no idea at these times whether her aunt would return, or whether it was the appointed time of Jomo Chhi'mèd Pema's predicted vanishment. Sometimes Jomo Chhi'mèd Pema would be gone for several days, sometimes weeks, and occasionally for longer than a month. Because of this unusual behaviour, Jomo Pema 'ö-Zér became accustomed to isolation and to the sense in which her aunt was no longer a functioning parent. During the phase before this final departure, Jomo Chhi'mèd Pema had given her niece a great number of transmissions and had provided her with the most detailed explanations of Dzogchen long-dé.

After three months of her aunt's absence had passed, Jomo Pema 'ö-Zér realised that her aunt and Tsawa'i Lama[86] was gone and would not return. She remained at her aunt's house for some weeks longer simply to practise. One morning she awoke and went to sit on the mountainside overlooking her aunt's dwelling. She had not long entered a state of absorption when she realised that the loud crashing sound she was hearing was Jomo Chhi'mèd Pema's house collapsing. The house had been nothing more than an assortment of boulders with strategically placed timbers and holes packed with hardened mud. When Jomo Pema 'ö-Zér went back to look at the ruins, there was no sign that the pile of rock which remained had ever been a dwelling.

Her only remaining possession was her bedding which she had taken as a sitting mat, and so she rolled up her blankets and started walking northward as her aunt had instructed.

She wandered for a number of years. Sometimes she met and practised with other wandering *gö kar chang lo'i dé*[87] practitioners. Mainly her time was spent alone. After five years, she met with a Lama called Rang-rig Togden. He recognised her immediately as a highly accomplished practitioner, and requested transmission from her. At first, she claimed to know nothing, but Rang-rig Togden was not easily dissuaded. He had observed her sitting in the crags of a mountain slope with a great many ravens circling over her head. She was sitting in a place to which there was no possible access by climbing which he could establish. She had been sitting there for some days – so Rang-rig Togden remained where he was, practising in her presence. His practice had been of such a profound nature during that time that he became certain that the presence of the ngakma was the cause of his greater clarity. One morning as he sat in meditation, Rang-rig Togden realised that she was sitting right in front of him.

[86] *rTsa ba'i bLa ma* / རྩ་བའི་བླ་མ་ – root teacher.
[87] *gos dKar lCang lo'i sDe* / གོས་དཀར་ལྕང་ལོའི་སྡེ་ – White-skirted Long-haired Series; the Tradition of Vajrayana ordination; ngakpas and ngakmas, naljorpas and naljormas.

He was unable to account for how she had appeared there, only moments before she had been sitting a fair distance away. Jomo Pema 'ö-Zér also had no idea how she came to have been in either place – but recognised that this was a time and situation of which Jomo Chhi'mèd Pema had spoken.

Rang-rig Togden, was a powerful Lama and an extremely strong and muscular man. He had been born into the A-kyong clan from Golok. Until meeting with Jomo Pema 'ö-Zér, he had been a wandering gÇodpa[88], but Pema 'ö-Zér instructed him in the practices of Dzogchen long-dé which she had received from her aunt, Jomo Chhi'mèd Pema. After that he had visions of Yeshé Tsogyel, Tashi Khyi'dren and Mandarava[89]. Jomo Pema 'ö-Zér and Rang-rig Togden practised all their lives together in caves as a yogic couple[90]. They spent their elder years in semi-open retreat. When they were in their early sixties Jomo Pema 'ö-Zér had a vision of Yeshé Tsogyel which lasted seven days. When the vision dissolved back into *chö-nyid*[91] she was left with the knowledge that she was going to give birth to a daughter.

Their daughter was an incarnation of Jomo Menmo, the great female Nyingma gTértön. She was herself a gTértön who came to be known as Khyungchen Aro Lingma, the revealer of the Aro gTér cycle.

When Khyungchen Aro Lingma was sixteen or seventeen years old, Jomo Pema 'ö-Zér and Rang-rig Togden took *rainbow-body*[92] together.

---

[88] gÇod pa / གཅོད་པ་ – a male practitioner of gÇod (gÇod / གཅོད་) – the practice of cutting attachment to corporeal form.

[89] Yeshé Tsogyel, Tashi Khyi'dren, and Mandarava – the three principal consorts and disciples of Guru Rinpoche.

[90] See: Khandro Déchen and Ngakpa Chögyam—*Entering the Heart of the Sun and Moon*—Aro Books Inc.—2021 – a commentary on the Khandro dPa'wo Nyi-da Mélong Gyüd (*mKha' 'gro dPa bo nyi zLa me long rGyud* / མཁའ་འགྲོ་དཔའ་བོ་ཉི་ཟླ་མེ་ལོང་རྒྱུད་)

[91] *chos nyid* / ཆོས་ཉིད་ / *dharmata*) – reality: the space of being and existence in which there is no distinction or differentiation.

[92] ja-lü (*'ja' lus* / འཇའ་ལུས་) – rainbow body; dissolution of the physical body at death into a body of light.

Khyungchen Aro Lingma sewed them into a white tent after they had given her final advice, instructions, and predictions. She then retired to a distance of twenty-one paces to begin her practice. Seven days later she opened the tent and all that was left of Jomo Pema 'ö-Zér and Rang-rig Togden were their respective clothes, hair, fingernails, toenails, and nasal septa. It is a highly unusual event for two people to achieve rainbow-body together at the same time – but it was something that Jomo Pema 'ö-Zér had predicted many years before, and it left a profound and lasting impact on Khyungchen Aro Lingma.

gTértöns and Tales of Transformation

Jomo Pema 'ö-Zér had passed her gTérma to her daughter Khyungchen Aro Lingma who in turn passed the gTérma to her son and heir, Aro Yeshé. Aro Yeshé took incarnation as Ngak'chang Rinpoche. He then received the Aro gTér and ancillary gTérmas—as yang gTér—from Khyungchen Aro Lingma, as predicted by Kyabjé Düd'jom Rinpoche Jig'drèl Yeshé Dorje. These gTérmas included Jomo Pema 'ö-Zér's gTérma of the Eighty-four Mahasiddhas and the Thangtong Thugthig[93] of her *sangyab*[94] Rang-rig Togden.

As the third discoverer of the Aro gTér, Ngak'chang Rinpoche is known by his gTértön name – Zértsal Lingpa[95]. He and his wife—and *sangyum*[96]—Khandro Déchen, are the current lineage holders of the Aro gTérma cycle and all the nested gTérmas.

---

[93] Rang-rig Togden *(rang rig rTogs lDan /* རང་རིག་རྟོགས་ལྡན *)* received the Thangtong Thugthig *(thang sTong thugs thig /* ཐང་སྟོང་ཐུགས་ཐིག *)* from Thangtong Gyalpo *(thang sTong rGyal po /* ཐང་སྟོང་རྒྱལ་པོ */* King of the Empty Plain /1351–1485) who was a cag-zampa *(lCags zam pa /* ལྕགས་ཟམ་པ *)*—Iron Bridge Maker—and mind emanation of Guru Rinpoche.

[94] *gSang yab /* གསང་ཡབ means 'secret father' or male consort of a female Lama.

[95] *gTer sTon zer rTsal gLing pa /* གཏེར་སྟོན་ཟེར་རྩལ་གླིང་པ

[96] *gSang yum /* གསང་ཡུམ means 'secret mother' or female consort of a male Lama.

The yang gTér of Jomo Pema 'ö-Zér's gTérma, revealed by Ngak'chang Rinpoche, contains: the cryptic hagiography for each Mahasiddha; their iconographic description; and the mantras necessary for their practice as *yidams*. Yidam is the major transformative practice of Tantra. The yidam —awareness-being—is a symbol of the realised state. The practice of yidam is one in which one's *self-definition* is dissolved into emptiness – from which one arises in the form of the yidam. This is the practice of *wearing the body of visions* [97].

The hagiographies as presented here benefit immeasurably from having been told by Ngak'chang Rinpoche – as he is a gifted and accomplished narrator and raconteur. He has fleshed out the hagiographies from the gTérma, bringing the stories vividly to life with wit and wisdom.

Ngak'chang Rinpoche said: *"I owe my ability to write narrative and dialogue, entirely to Kyabjé Künzang Dorje Rinpoche. It was he, who encouraged me to write the accounts of Tibetan Lamas he'd narrated, in a form which would make 'enjoyable reading in your own country'. He was keen that the accounts should be lively – and not constricted by Tibetan cultural stylistics. He told me that he knew that the West had a great heritage of literature. He'd even heard of Shakespeare as a master storyteller whose plays had been performed for over 500 years. He hoped that someone would one day translate Shakespeare's plays into Tibetan. Fortunately he was not relying on me for that. He told me that I knew what Western stories were like from having studied a great deal of Western literature – and that I should be able to tell the tales of these Tibetan Lamas in an appropriate way. At the time, I was not a writer. I had written poetry from an early age – but I'd never written a textbook, let alone a novel. I therefore seriously doubted my ability in this respect. However, although I doubted my ability, I did not doubt Künzang Dorje Rinpoche – so, I threw myself into the endeavour. I was surprised when the task proved less arduous than I'd imagined. Again, Künzang Dorje Rinpoche was right – and I was wrong.*

---

[97] See: Ngakpa Chögyam—*Wearing the Body of Visions*—Aro Books Inc.—1995

"The results can be seen in Wisdom Eccentrics[98] *which recounts the collection of Lama stories with which he regaled me – along with the manner in which I was interrogated as to their meaning."*

Each hagiography in *Warp and Weft of Wonderment* contains pointing-out instructions from Dzogchen men-ngag-dé given as drüpthab by each of the Mahasiddhas to their disciples. The disciples, having followed the drüpthab, become Mahasiddhas themselves – and in most cases go on to be the teachers of their own disciples. The lineage of the transmission of nonduality thus continues.

So, this list of the Eighty-four Mahasiddhas is a living tradition. It provides not only inspirationally didactic tales, but also the possibility of transformation through yidam practice, and liberation through Dzogchen men-ngag-dé instruction. For those familiar with presentations of translated Mahasiddha stories from other sources, there will be an obvious difference in these hagiographies. Most obvious perhaps is the far greater number of female Mahasiddhas and teachers of Mahasiddhas. This is a more accurate reflection of the number of realised female practitioners at that period of time. They appear here as rôle models for women practitioners today and as a source of inspiration for male practitioners.

There is a Dzogchen perspective *throughout* the telling of the hagiographies – not simply in the overt Dzogchen men-ngag-dé instructions. This is not found in other collections of Mahasiddha hagiographies. There are many references to *ro-chig* [99] for example – the *one-taste* of two aspects of experience which mirror *emptiness* and *form*.

---

[98] Ngakpa Chögyam—*Wisdom Eccentrics*—Aro Books Inc.—2011
[99] *ro gCig* / རོ་གཅིག་ – one-taste.

These may be: stasis and movement; desire and aversion; lust and disgust; complacency and dread; hope and fear; sound and silence; indolence and industry; lassitude and dynamism; fascination and ennui; excitement and tedium; gravity and gaiety; horror and euphoria; possessions and possessionlessness.

The stories are also more concerned with real life in as much as the situations are frequently not as idealistic as they are often presented – and, nor are the motivations of the aspirants. There is an absence of beatific vision too, and of Mahasiddhas becoming Buddhas in the visionary sense. Despite nondual realisation these Mahasiddhas remain *in-and-of-the-world*. They continue the lineage of teaching and transmission. Perhaps the most enjoyable difference is the interactive and frequently humorous nature of the communication between the Mahasiddhas and their disciples. The Mahasiddhas are not bland holy-men and holy-women. They are powerful characters who display a grounded earthiness to which it is easy to relate. They can be tricksters too – often manifesting mercurial and playful temperaments as part of their method of transmission.

What we see is a gestalt which does not feel as distant as ancient India. It is one which could in fact, be translated into contemporary Western terms with few changes. This is the remarkable *warp and weft of wonderment* we have received from the Mahasiddhas Tashi Khyi'dren and Jomo Pema 'ö-Zér – through gTértön Zér-tsal Lingpa.

One: Jalandhara – the net-possessor

Jalandhara *(dza' la nDha ra / ཛཱ་ལ་ནྡྷ་ར)* / Drawa 'Dzinpa *(dra ba 'dzin pa / དྲ་བ་འཛིན་པ)*
Disciple of: dakinis *(five khandromas – mKha' 'gro ma lNga / མཁའ་འགྲོ་མ་ལྔ)*
Teacher of: Tantipa, Kanhapa, Kankaripa, Chatrapa, and Maha'abala
Varna by birth: Shudra

Early autumn. in Frogs' Leap – the Penarth home of Ngak'chang Rinpoche and Khandro Déchen, in the Vale of Glamorgan, South Wales.

Frogs' Leap is a Georgian mid-terrace house, built in 1849. It is one of the two original houses in the street. It retains many original features: doors with iron locks; fitted wooden cabinets; Welsh dressers; and sash window-casements. The floorboards show the delicate tracery of treated woodworm under the varnish. The staircase is carpeted with the Axminister *Red Turkey* [1], acquired at a house clearance auction. The white walls are largely bare of pictures—apart from a few ancient relatives on the upper staircase—and a framed print of Albrecht Dürer's *Das große Rasenstück* [2].

We had retired after dinner to the sitting room, and Ja'gyür and I were sitting in front of the window in our usual place on the Italian replica Louis XVth chairs—obtained from a used-furniture emporium—upholstered in red and blue Turkestani-pattern fabric. Ngak'chang Rinpoche and Khandro Déchen have a facility for finding surprisingly economical household furniture and furnishings. Much of their furniture has been inherited from their deceased parents, and from German grandparents and great-grandparents. The window in the living room opens directly onto the pavement.

---

[1] Axminister *Red Turkey* is a large pattern carpet *(predominantly red – but containing blue, green, and yellow in descending order)* that can often be seen in hotel reception rooms.
[2] *The Great Turf* – a watercolour painting by Albrecht Dürer—Nürnberg—1503. This is a study of a group of weeds including a dandelion. The work is considered one of his masterpieces.

It is lower than other front windows in the street – the house having been a sweet shop a hundred years previously. Confectionery and ice creams were sold through the window to passing customers. Penarth—known as *The Garden by the Sea*—was an elegant seaside destination for Victorians and Edwardians.

Rinpoche was sitting opposite us, in his accustomed seat—another of the Louis XVth chairs— with his legs resting on a similarly upholstered footstool. Khandro Déchen sat in yet another of these chairs, also near the window, against the backdrop of ancient leaf-green linen curtains. The curtains were unusual in being lined with green cotton rather than lining fabric. I commented on it and Khandro Déchen said *"People outside also have to look at the curtains."* She chuckled. *"We liked them because people can have something pleasant to see from the outside – rather than a bland absence of detectable hue."*

Although it was still early autumn, the evenings had become chilly, and Rinpoche wore an unusually huge grey-brown Irish Fisherman's cardigan. It was huge when he bought it, but due to his having shed over seventy pounds in weight since it was purchased – it was now massive. *"I see no reason to discard it"* he smiled *"when it has served me so well since 1989 – and Ngakma Nor'dzin and Ngakma Lé-kyi have both spent a great deal of time repairing it."*

There was a multi-coloured crocheted blanket laid over Rinpoche's legs. It had been made by his great grandmother, Clara Schubert. It had been repaired many times – but, so perfectly, that it looked new. We each had a glass of Barolo, as a case had arrived from Italy as a gift. We settled in for the evening, and conversation turned to the hagiographies of the Mahasiddhas from the gTérma of Jomo Pema 'ö-Zér. I asked Rinpoche *"Where would you start Rinpoche, if the stories were to be published? Which would be the first hagiography to be told?"* Rinpoche looked quizzical, so I continued *"Is it possible to put them in historical order?"*

"*I'm not a vastly competent taxonomist – so organisation, classification, compartmentalisation, cataloguing, and categorisation, are not exactly my forté.*" PAUSE "*I feel we would need to commence with Mahasiddha Jalandhara [3]. It's not possible to create a coherent chronology – or not one which would function in terms of placing every teacher of a Mahasiddha before the Mahasiddha disciple. There are various patterns which could be created, but those patterns wouldn't function as structures for the entire group.*"

"*Many of the Mahasiddhas*" added Khandro Déchen "*were disciples of one Mahasiddha, and teachers of others. The time frames aren't necessarily neat and tidy, so if you tried to force them into a linear sequence, it wouldn't work.*"

"*Life doesn't tend to be a linear sequence*" Rinpoche chuckled. "*My life certainly isn't. 'This' cannot always be said to lead on to 'that'. Sometimes there is no clear route from 'here' to 'there'. As Ogden Nash wrote 'You can't get there from here'. Be that as it may, Jalandhara taught more of the Eighty-four Mahasiddhas than any other – and those students, in turn, became teachers of others. We should therefore start with Jalandhara. There are other reasons too, which might become clear as the hagiographies unfurl.*"

"*Would you give the transmission now, Rinpoche and Khandro Déchen?*" I asked hopefully.

"*That's certainly possible.*" Rinpoche smiled and Khandro Déchen nodded.

---

[3] Jalandhar is the name of a place which included the Upper Doabas from the Ravi to the Satluj. The country takes its name from the Daitya King, Danava Jalandhara. The earliest historical mention of Jalandhar occurs in the region of Kanishka. A council was held near Jalandhar in around 100 AD, in the time of the Kushan King of northern India, for Buddhist scholars to collect and arrange the sacred writings of Buddhism. In the 7th century, when Chinese pilgrim Hiuen Tsang visited India during the reign of Harsha Vardhana, the Kingdom of Jalandhar extended 167 miles from east to west and 133 miles from north to south. It included the hill states of Chamba, Mandi, and Suket *(Himachal Pradesh)* and Satadru or Sirhind in the plains. There were 50 Buddhist monasteries in Jalandhar alone.

"*O yah*⁴..." Rinpoche began – in the way that his Lama, Kyabjé Künzang Dorje Rinpoche often began when he related stories of historic Lamas⁵. "*Jalandhara was a working-class hero – not necessarily John Lennon's 'Working Class Hero'*⁶, *but a lad born of the Shudra varna...*"

His family was a poor—yet healthy and sturdy—family in Togar⁷. His parents, despite robust physique and hardiness, died of cholera when Jalandhara was six years old. He was abandoned by indifferent relatives, who felt they owed him no responsibility. He thus wandered off on his own – having the surprising confidence that he could, somehow, find his own way in the world. He had been brought up in the higher reaches of the river Vaksu⁸ which flows from an ice cave at the end of the Wakhjir valley, in the Wan⁹ of the Pamir Mountains¹⁰. He was, due to his mountain upbringing, a hardy and resourceful lad: brave, unafraid, and resilient. He knew the topography well—knew how to survive without undue fuss or trepidation—and therefore became an adult by force of sheer necessity.

---

⁴ *'ong yag* / ཨོང་ཡག — a phrase that means a variety of different things according to tone, inflection, facial expression, and hand gestures. It encompasses *delight, astonishment, surprise, pleasure, gratification, satisfaction, agreement, ambiguity, disbelief, suspicion, ennui, languor, fatigue, impatience, irritation, irascibility, frustration, negative judgement, and censure.*
⁵ See: Ngakpa Chögyam—*Wisdom Eccentrics*—Aro Books Inc.—2011
⁶ John Lennon—*Working Class Hero*—Plastic Ono Band—1970.
⁷ Turkestan.
⁸ The river Oxus.
⁹ Wan is an area of north-eastern Afghanistan which forms a land link between Afghanistan and China: a long narrow salient, 140 miles long and 10 to 40 miles wide. Part of Badakhshan, Wan separates Badakhshan of Tajikistan in the north, from Khyber Pakhtunkhwa and Gilgit Baltistan of Pakistan in the south. The name Wan also applies to the route along the Panj River and the Wan River to China, and the northern part of the Wan is then referred to as the Afghan Pamir.
¹⁰ The Pamir Mountains are formed by the junction of the Himalayas with the Tian Shan, Karakoram, Kunlun, and Hindu Kush ranges. They lie mostly in Badakhshan, Tajikistan, and Afghanistan. To the north, they join the Tian Shan mountains along the Alay Valley of Kyrgyzstan. To the south, they join the Hindu Kush mountains along the Wan of Afghanistan, Gilgit, Baltistan in Pakistan. To the east, they end on the Chinese border in a range including the Kongur Tagh and Kunlun Mountains.

Jalandhara had many names throughout his life – many of them *place names* such as: Wakhjir, Wan, Aror[11], Viratnagar[12], Oddiyana[13], and Jalandhara. This was due to the fact that he became well known and respected in all these places, and, because no one knew him well enough personally to know him by name. In this he was similar to Guru Rinpoche, who also had many names; one name being Ögyen or Oddiyana because—like Jalandhara—he manifested in that land.

Jalandhara was a highly independent, spirited boy – and therefore did not fret unduly about his abandonment. He was naturally kindly, open-minded, and curious, and the area in which he lived provided him with many avenues for his curiosity. The wandering life suited him and he earned his keep with the many caravans which plied their ways across the rugged yet startlingly beautiful terrain.

He became so skilled with camels and other pack animals that by the time he was ten years old he was able to offer his services easily to those who valued his experience. He was soon able to buy two Bactrian[14] camels—one to ride and one as a pack-animal—and equip himself with his own tent.

---

[11] Aror was the ancient capital of Sindh, originally ruled by the Ror Dynasty, which was followed by the Rai Dynasty and then the Brahman Dynasty. Present day Rohri is now situated close to Sukkur.

[12] Viratnagar – present day Bairat. Viratnagar was the capital of Mahajanapada. The ruins of the Bijak-ki-pahadi, a Buddhist chörten from the 3rd century BC—in Viratnagar—is the oldest Buddhist structure in India.

[13] Oddiyana / Uddhiyana – or Ögyen *(o rGyan /* ཨོ་རྒྱན *)* in Tibetan, is the birth place of Guru Rinpoche and the origin of Vajrayana. The physical location of Ögyen is disputed and open to conjecture by scholars who posit **a.** the Swat Valley region of present-day Khyber Pakhtunkhwa, Pakistan, close to the Afghanistan-Pakistan border; and **b.** Odisha in eastern India. Ngak'chang Rinpoche and Khandro Déchen hold that Ögyen extended as far west as Oruzgan, the central area of Afghanistan.

[14] The Bactrian camel *(camelus bactrianus)* is a large, even-toed ungulate native to the steppes of Central Asia, which has two humps on its back. The name 'Bactrian' comes from the ancient region of Bactria. The domesticated Bactrian has served as a pack animal in Inner Asia since caravans existed. With their forbearance of cold, drought, and high altitude they were much valued on the Silk Road.

He named the older camel Al Ghaab—because he only drank once every two days—and the younger camel, Al Ra-be'a, because he only needed to drink every three days. These—he had learned—were the traditional names which signified each camel's habit of drinking.

As he grew older, he became increasingly hardy and increasingly skilled in every aspect of living in the wilds and tending to pack animals. He had become the youngest professional caravaneer and was known at many caravanserais on the eastern end of the Silk Road[15]. He became an extremely proficient rider, who was known to be fearless yet judicious; daring yet prudent. Rather than building a business for himself however, Jalandhara was content simply to travel and to learn anything from anyone who had some specialised knowledge. He loved to learn about history and of the many cultures and religions of the people who travelled through the Wan. There were many travelling yogis and yoginis —spiritual practitioners of many different lineages—and he asked them questions whenever he met them. Yogis and yoginis were his most prized informants, and he soon began to seek them out.

When he was twelve years old he happened to meet a local aristocrat returning from a hunting expedition in the mountains. The aristocrat was wracked with grief by the demise of his son, who had fallen to his death in a crevasse. The body was irretrievable and the man was tormented not only by the loss of his son, but by the emotional impossibility of telling his wife. His wife had lost two children to sickness and regarded their remaining son as her sole comfort in life. On seeing Jalandhara, he was struck by the astounding similarity between Jalandhara and his lost son. The lads were close in age and build and even the tone of their voices was alike.

---

[15] The Silk Road was a huge network of trails that stretched over 4,600 miles of desert and mountains – largely travelled by camel caravans. Camel caravans travelled in convoy with people walking alongside the camels which carried their goods to market. Camels were well-suited to this work, as temperatures ranged between 122° and -50° Fahrenheit – and camels carry both water and fat in their humps. Because the towns were often far apart, caravans were supported by caravanserais: roadside inns where food and water for travellers and their animals was available.

On observing this remarkable similarity, the aristocrat spoke with Jalandhara and eventually made a suggestion. He would adopt him as his son. Could he play the part to his wife's satisfaction? That was the only problem. The father *could* claim the lad had fallen—hit his head on a rock—and thus lost his memory. The question of his lack of court graces *could* possibly be put down to the accident as well. He could explain to his wife that the blow to the boy's head had left him bereft of social skills – including the facility for refined speech. This was perhaps a little far-fetched, but he knew that his wife would be only too happy that her son had not died, and would therefore not be naturally given to suspicion. They were some months away from home, so there would be time at least to train Jalandhara a little in the arts of refined speech.

Jalandhara considered the idea – but wished to decline. He had no desire to leave his life on the open road. When it was explained to him however, that the aristocrat's wife would be inconsolable, Jalandhara accepted on the condition that he was allowed to keep his camels. He had no wish to cause the lady pain if it could be helped, but he would not desert his camels, for fear of their being abused by caravaneers who were less caring of their animals.

Jalandhara was therefore dressed in appropriate clothing and taken home. On the way he learnt as many modes of formal address as the aristocrat could teach him and his adoptive father was amazed by the lad's learning abilities. In a matter of days, he had begun to sound quite like his own son – and he started feeling hopeful as to the success of his ploy. Jalandhara seemed naturally gracious and extremely bright. Jalandhara asked many questions about his new home and about the customs and views of the Kshatriya varna to which he would belong. He remembered everything he was taught, which was immensely pleasing to his new father. The aristocrat grieved his lost son, but after three days he found that the highly pleasant distraction that Jalandhara offered made his grief easier to bear.

He would after all have to act normally with his wife or she would suspect something. He would have to act as the cheerful husband he had always been, and, as the days went by on the road with Jalandhara, this seemed increasingly plausible.

When they arrived at Jalandhara's new home, the story was explained. Although his new mother was upset, she was delighted that her son was unhurt. Jalandhara—being a kindly lad—made a perfect son; far better in fact, than the one he had replaced. He was good-natured, unspoilt, and hardworking. He honoured his new parents quite naturally. His new mother, for her part, considered the *bang-on-the-head* her 'son' had received, to have been the best thing that ever happened to him. His loss of memory wasn't wonderful—and his new and rather surprising fondness for camels was peculiar—but life lay in the future rather than the past.

"There are always camels in the accounts of Jalandhara." Khandro Déchen smiled *"I enjoy them – and how they always function as part of the teaching given by Jalandhara."*

Rinpoche rearranged the blanket over his legs and lifted his wine from the three-level wooden Victorian cake stand next to his chair *"And they are —very much—personalities."*

I took the chance to comment *"I think I see another reason why the hagiography of Jalandhara needs to be first, Rinpoche. It's the similarities between him and Guru Rinpoche. The account mentions that they both were called Oddiyana – but I'm also thinking about the parallels between their lives in terms of King Indrabhuti finding Guru Rinpoche as an eight-year-old and taking him home to the palace and adopting him as his own son."*

"Yes" Khandro Déchen nodded. *"Jalandhara is regarded by some as a manifestation of Guru Rinpoche.*

"Kyabjé Künzang Dorje Rinpoche said that Jalandhara was not separate from Guru Rinpoche — that Jalandhara was an emanation of Guru Rinpoche. He also said that Ögyen was further west than people thought. He located it as extending into Afghanistan."

"He said that many images of Guru Rinpoche have a slight Arab appearance" Rinpoche continued *"and this is something I noticed when I was in Afghanistan."* PAUSE *"Jalandhara could be seen as an emanation of Guru Rinpoche whose quality was concerned with integration — integration with society. This is why he allows himself to be adopted. He continually arrives in ordinary places. He simply appears —wherever it is—and becomes known as having come from another place. He was often known as having come from Jalandhar. Like Guru Rinpoche, he had lived his life, up to a certain age, mysteriously. Jalandhara lived as a caravaneer on the Silk Road, where he collected teachings whenever he could. That area of the east was a confluence of everything interesting that was available at the time. Both Guru Rinpoche and Jalandhara sought it out. By the time Jalandhara meets the five khandros in the charnel ground he's completely prepared for what is going to be imparted to him."* PAUSE *"I imagine you might wish me to tell you more about that?"* Rinpoche raised his eyebrows — and I nodded eagerly.

Jalandhara was happy in his new home, and the uneasiness of living with a deception gradually dwindled. His new mother was exceptionally kind. His new father was an honourable man, who remembered well that Jalandhara was reticent about participating in his scheme. He therefore allowed Jalandhara considerable freedom in terms of seeking out itinerant teachers who could avail him of the secrets of existence. Mystics of all kinds were therefore always invited to the household and given alms.

As the years went by Jalandhara's new father increasingly experienced Jalandhara as his own son and theirs was a happy family — apart from the fact that Jalandhara kept having dreams in which a beautiful woman appeared and told him *"You cannot remain here forever with these Kshatriyas. Your future is in the wilderness. That is where you belong."*

Thus, Jalandhara's wanderlust began to return. He was not a lad to be cosseted too much, and so he became increasingly restless with his life of comfort and ease. His mother was always nervous about him making expeditions into the mountains lest he have another accident like the one that caused him to lose his memory, but his father said that it would not be good to deprive their son of his freedom. He secretly worried that Jalandhara would leave home if he were not allowed sufficient liberty to roam. After all, he'd found the boy enjoying a life on the open road, and it obviously suited him so well that he was not tempted by the life of luxury he'd been offered. Conversations ensued between the son and his adoptive father and it was agreed that Jalandhara would be allowed more freedom to roam on his own without servants. This pleased Jalandhara for a year, but by the time he was fourteen his spiritual practices began to suggest that his life was not what it should be. The beautiful woman appeared increasingly in his dreams telling him *"You cannot remain here forever with these Kshatriyas. Your future is in the wilderness. That is where you belong."*

Apart from the growing desire to return to his life in the wilderness, it became increasingly painful to Jalandhara to be wealthy when others were poor. It also became difficult for him not to have the time to pursue religious practice as deeply as he felt necessary, due to the social life with which he had to engage as the son of a Kshatriya family. He found the conversation of the affluent to be rather tepid and domestic, and their attitudes decidedly docile. Their opinions all seemed to be based on hearsay and hand-me-down platitudes rather than on any real experience of the world. He had great experience of the world and of the wonderful variety of peoples it contained. He knew when statements were based on prejudice and ignorance – but not being able to contradict such statements became increasingly irksome.

When Jalandhara was sixteen the beautiful woman in his dreams started to become insistent.

"You must leave these Kshatriyas soon! Your future is in the wilderness practising as a yogi! If you stay here, you will never realise the nondual state!"

Something had to change. Jalandhara realised that the woman in his dreams had to be taken seriously. She knew who he was and what his life had been. She knew of his deep-rooted interest in religion and the knowledge that could be gained from experience. Her words accorded completely with his own view of life—and he wished to heed her advice—but he was deeply saddened to have to disappoint his adoptive parents. He considered slipping out of a window after dark and disappearing. He always put it off to a later occasion however – for a time when his mother might be less upset by his sudden vanishment. The problem was that this day never seemed to arrive. There was always another important social gathering at which he would be missed, and his mother so obviously enjoyed his presence that he felt deeply troubled at the thought of having to leave her.

In his seventeenth year however, the decision was made for him. The beautiful woman appeared and told him *"You may now remain with the Kshatriyas as long as you are needed – but your tenure will be brief. Your adoptive mother and father will soon pass beyond missing you. You may then depart for the wilderness – which is where you belong."*

Soon after this dream, his mother and father fell ill with cholera. He remained with them, caring for them until they died. Once left alone, he set about giving away his entire inheritance to the care of the poor and sick. Once the house and all its contents had been distributed, the beautiful woman appeared and told him *"Now you are free to leave. You may depart for the wilderness, which is where you belong. When you have travelled for some time however, you must find a charnel ground in which to practise. When you have found this place, I shall return—with my sisters—and give you instructions which will serve you as a yogi throughout your life."*

The next day, he took to the road. He took only his hardiest clothing. He took his one remaining camel—Al Rab-e'a—and provisions for travel. He then set out into the wilderness. After some months of journeying, he found himself approaching a charnel ground. This seemed opportune and so he entered the area and settled to practise. Remembering what Shakyamuni Buddha had done, he decided to remain in practice until he gained realisation. There was forage aplenty for his camel, so he left Al Rab-e'a free to wander.

On the first night the beautiful woman in his dreams became a reality—a waking vision—a blue dakini, who told him *"You must now remain here in the wilderness where you belong – until you attain nondual realisation."* She, and her four sisters, each gave him transmissions, which he put into practice immediately and continued on the following day. Having practised as instructed for three months the dakinis appeared again.

The yellow dakini sang:

> *"Contemplate all phenomena, whether inner or outer, as inseparable from mind, speech, and body."*

The white dakini sang:

> *"Allow mind, speech, and body to be subsumed by the solar and lunar channels of the subtle body and let those dissolve into the central channel."*

The red dakini sang:

> *"Once the entire phenomenal world is found to be within the central channel, condense the experience into a single essential-point and eject it through the crown of your head."*

The green dakini sang:

> *"On accomplishing this you will know the indivisibility of emptiness and ecstasy."*

Finally, the blue dakini sang:

> *"Finding the presence of awareness in that sensation – you will achieve the nondual state and hold the miraculous net of the phenomenal universe in your hands."*

With that the yellow dakini dissolved into the white dakini – and she in turn into the red, green, and blue dakini. Finally, the blue dakini merged with Jalandhara and his own experience of identity dissolved into space.

Jalandhara followed this instruction of the dakini transmission and realised the nondual state in three days. He spent the rest of his life teaching methods of nondual realisation to over three hundred disciples including a group of those named as Mahasiddhas.

As Rinpoche concluded the hagiography, I had to ask about the dakinis *"How is it most useful to think of them? As simply the wisdom aspects of reality, or should we think of them as actual beings?"*

"That" Rinpoche raised his eyebrows *"is a contemporary Western question."* PAUSE *"There's nothing wrong with that however. That is where we are – but it is valuable to remember that there are other frames of reference."*

"With respect to khandros, or dakinis" added Khandro Déchen *"there is no need to regard them as either. There is no need to compartmentalise them."*

"The khandros in these hagiographies" continued Rinpoche *"are 'as they are'. They are as the sky – is as it is. Or as the sea – is as it is. It's not worth trying to make linear sense of dakinis – or relate them to something unnecessarily specific. So, whether they are simply 'aspects of visionary reality' or 'five actual women', is not worth examining. They can simply be as they are. We do not have to define them any further."*

"Those five practices, those given by the dakinis…" I asked *"…it feels as if you don't really need any more instructions than that, do you?"*

"*Indeed*" replied Rinpoche. "*They are five cha-tra*[16]—*aspects—of the same practice. It's a kyil'khor. So, within that kyil'khor there is everything that is required. Jalandhara simply receives everything there is to receive. Beyond that… the other Mahasiddha stories are simply different aspects of how one would approach the nondual state.*"

We sat quietly for a while. Another question bubbled up. "*… about Jalandhara being known as 'the net-possessor'… could you say more about the nature of the 'nondual net' as it's understood in Buddhism?*"

"*It's the spatial interconnection of everything – but not an eternalistic structure. It's not limited by eternal meanings.*" Rinpoche paused. "*Connectedness arises as a 'sparkling' in which connectedness momentarily appears.*" PAUSE "*That's why I sent out that story of Popeye the other day. I discovered that Popeye—the cartoon character —was based on the real-life Polish gentleman, Frank 'Rocky' Fiegel who had emigrated to America in the late 1800s. He was a merchant seaman for twenty years. He later became a bouncer and a renowned storyteller. The photograph of Frank Fiegel looks remarkably similar to the cartoon character. Somehow from an obscure Polish gentleman – we now have the Popeye phenomenon. Everyone knows Popeye. Popeye connects with everyone – of a certain age group at least. This is one aspect of the fundamental richness of existence. There's this. There's that. 'This' leads to 'that' – and 'that' leads to something other. It is not like the Hindu Net of Indra* [17].

---

[16] *cha phra* / ཆ་ཕྲ

[17] This is the net of the Advaita Vedanta tradition, which is monist. It holds that 'All is One' and that self is both eternal and subsumed in Brahma – the 'Godhead'. The Advaita Vedanta *Net of Indra* has, at each intersection, a jewel. Each jewel is perfectly clear and reflects all the other jewels in the net in the way that two mirrors placed opposite each other will reflect an image ad infinitum. The jewel symbolises an individual consciousness that is an aspect of the 'Godhead'. Every jewel is intimately connected with all other jewels – and a change in one jewel creates a change in every other jewel. In Buddhism the term 'Net of Indra', refers to the Yeshé gyü-trül drawa *(ye shes sGyu 'phrul drwa ba* / ཡེ་ཤེས་སྒྱུ་འཕྲུལ་དྲྭ་བ) – magical net of primordial wisdom. The Gya-chin gyü'trul le'u lèg *(brGya byin sGyu 'phrul le'u lag* / བརྒྱ་བྱིན་སྒྱུ་འཕྲུལ་ལེའུ་ལག) teaches: **a.** the holographic nature of phenomenal reality in which every individual nondual point of the hologram is sympathetic to all other points; **b.** this does not posit a substantive eternal identity in terms of continuity; **c.** this does not posit a particular single source point from whence all phenomenal reality arises; **d.** primordial wisdom; **e.** the illusory nature of conditioned appearances; **f.** primal creativity; **g.** the mirror-like *nature of Mind*. The Hindu and Buddhist descriptions of the Net of Indra can seem little different – but the Buddhist *Net of Indra* is nondual and the Advaita Vedanta *Net of Indra* is monist.

'It doesn't all have a meaning that goes back to 'God' – as a putative 'self-created creator'. It does however, have a 'meaning-ness' in and of itself – in the moment. It's the efflorescence of human vibrancy, which people can suddenly experience. Then, this can be communicated."

Rinpoche paused and carefully sipped his Barolo *"Students must sometimes wonder why I post such items on our social media groups. Why suddenly this account of Popeye?"*

"Yes. I did wonder" I laughed.

"Why? Because if you're actually alive – you can be aware of such phenomena. You can hear of such connections. You can read about the origin of Popeye – and that is —genuinely—delightfully interesting. Khandro Déchen and I, like to encourage people to be interested *in life. Boundless non-referential fascination is possible. You can't know everything about everything – but sometimes you come across something which is inexplicably moving, poignant, inspiring, magnetic, or beguiling. I never knew this Polish gentleman existed. Now I do. And now I know something about his life. It's fascinating how someone—in Penarth, Wales—knows about a Polish gentleman who existed last century. I didn't know about him the day before. That is magical. When people start tuning-in to the magical quality of life, they find themselves more authentically alive."* A faint smile began to play on Rinpoche's face. *"So, you see… Popeye could have been a Mahasiddha. He's the kind of character who could have bumped into Jalandhara – and then, everything would have changed for him. It simply requires that accident"* Rinpoche laughed *"but you don't have to make anything of that."*

"Maybe" Khandro Déchen grinned *"I should paint a thangka of Popeye."*

That was too funny and I guffawed *"Can we…"* I laughed again *"… approach identifying these threads of connection as a practice? Or is tèn'drèl*[18] *simply a recognition of that interconnectedness?"*

---

[18] *rTen 'brel* / རྟེན་འབྲེལ

"It's simply recognition. It's important not to make anything of it – but simply, to be delighted. That is what's important. Just as it was when I was in Bodhanath in 1971. That was when Kyabjé Düd'jom Rinpoche asked me to tell him about my life – and I mentioned being the vocalist for Savage Cabbage. The Savage Cabbage Blues Band had not long ceased to be. It was still at the forefront of my mind, so I told him about it. He was then curious to hear Blues, and asked me to sing for him. That was a slightly terrifying idea. Letting rip with 'Hoochie Coochie Man' in front of Düd'jom Rinpoche was not comfortable. You can't sing Blues quietly – or at least I can't. I have to belt it out or not bother. The translator looked aghast – as if I might be a dangerous lunatic. Fortunately, Düd'jom Rinpoche enjoyed it – and his enjoyment was obvious. The translator monk perceived Düd'jom Rinpoche's smile and breathed a soundless sigh of relief at my presently being within the bounds of normality. Then of course he wanted Savage Cabbage translated into Tibetan. It came out as Bèd-tsé Ya'mèd[19]."

"Then, in October 2021" exclaimed Khandro Déchen "his incarnation, Kyabjé Düd'jom Rinpoche Ten'dzin Yeshé Dorje—who plays guitar—happens to have a love of Blues. He tells gTértön Drukdra Rinpoche about it – and he passes this information back to us. We send videos of the contemporary Savage Cabbage Blues Band – and they are enjoyed. That is tèn'drèl. It's utterly delightful—the connection between lives—Ngak'chang Rinpoche with Düd'jom Rinpoche Ten'dzin Yeshé Dorje's past incarnation – reunited through Muddy Waters and Chicago Blues. This is where truth is stranger than fiction."

"Not that we should build a thesis on that basis" Rinpoche explained. "It's simply the efflorescence of being."

"It seems" I commented "that we find it hard not to make anything of it though. As if we're desperate for everything to mean something?"

"Yes." Rinpoche shrugged "there is that tendency – especially in New Age circles. Unfortunately, that seems to have entered mainstream thinking to a certain extent.

---

[19] bad tshe ya 'med / བད་ཚེ་ཡ་མེད

"The problem is that by trying to 'expand' an experience—by manufacturing meaning—you actually contract it. It forces experience into a box – in which 'this' relates to 'that' and 'that' relates to 'this'. Then 'this' and 'that' mean something else – and therefore… ad nauseam. Whereas… nothing has to relate to anything – and yet it is delightful. So simply because Kyabjé Düd'jom Rinpoche Ten'dzin Yeshé Dorje remembers my singing Blues in 1971, doesn't mean anything about 'me' – or nothing extraordinary, at least."

"Of course" smiled Khandro Déchen "if one wishes everything to have meaning – it is possible, from one point of view. Everything does mean something. It means each one of us is going to die. That's what everything means. That's the only meaning – other than being born. We will sleep tonight. Maybe we'll wake up tomorrow. Maybe we won't. Who knows?"

With that, Rinpoche and Khandro Déchen stood up. *"Sleep well – perchance to dream!"* Khandro Déchen smiled.

"Ay, there's the rub!" laughed Rinpoche. *"For in that sleep of death what dreams may come – when we have shuffled off this mortal coil, must give us pause. There's the respect that makes calamity of so long life* [20]*."* Time for bed. Maybe I would wake on the morrow. Maybe I wouldn't.

---

[20] Shakespeare—the *'To be or not to be'* soliloquy—*Hamlet*—1600.

Two: Minapa – the whale siddha

Minapa *(mi' na pa /* མི་ན་པ *) /* Khyim nya Gyalpo *(khyim nya rGyal po /* ཁྱིམ་ ཉ་རྒྱལ་པོ *)*

Disciple of: kLu-chen *(kLu chen /* ཀླུ་ཆེན *)*
Teacher of: Goraksha
Varna by birth: Shudra

Cadgwith on the Lizard Peninsula in Cornwall.

Ja'gyür and I were with Ngak'chang Rinpoche and Khandro Déchen in Cornwall. They go to Cadgwith once a year, every year, for various reasons – one being *The Devil's Frying Pan*. It is a place connected with the protectors, particularly Damçan Nod-jin 'barwar Mé-zér[1] – a minion of Dorje Legpa[2].

We were delighting in late morning on the Lizard, the most southerly peninsula of the British mainland. Rinpoche put on the 'Enid Blyton'[3] sandals he'd had made by E Vogel's Boots[4] in New York. He knows Jack Lynch, the proprietor, as a friend. Jack has made various items of footwear for Rinpoche – some from photographs. Rinpoche called them 'Enid Blyton' sandals because the style dates to that era, and he liked their distinct 1930s character. Rinpoche has specific clothes for Cornwall, amongst which are his Peterman[5] 'Irish Pub Shirts'. These are faded blue, coarsely woven cotton collarless shirts. He had replaced the collar bands with white linen in order to allow the insertion of collar studs.

---

[1] *dam can gNod sByin 'bar bar me zer /* དམ་ཅན་གནོད་སྦྱིན་འབར་བར་མེ་ཟེར – Stormbringer; he who works the bellows for the Vajra Blacksmith, Damçan Garwa Nagpo *(dam can mGar ba nag po /* དམ་ཅན་ མགར་བ་ནག་པོ *)*. Damçan Nod-jin 'barwar Mé-zér is the protector of Drala Jong

[2] *rDo rJe legs pa /* རྡོ་རྗེ་ལེགས་པ *) / Vajra Sadhu* – one of the three protectors of the Nyingma Tradition.

[3] Enid Blyton 1897–1968 – English children's writer, whose books have been worldwide bestsellers since the 1930s. She is best remembered today for *Noddy*, *The Famous Five*, and *The Secret Seven*.

[4] E Vogel was established in 1879 by Egidius Vogel in Lower Manhattan. The tradition continued through the years with: 2nd generation Harold Vogel; 3rd Jack and Hank Vogel, 4th Dean Vogel; and now, Dean Vogel's cousin – Jack Lynch.

[5] An American retail company founded by John Peterman in 1987 after buying a *duster*—a horse-riding coat—in Wyoming and receiving many compliments. He manufactured 2,000 coats and in 1988 published the first catalogue, offering distinctive reproductions of antique clothing and clothing worn in films, illustrated and described in literary style.

Since buying these shirts in the late 1980s, they have developed mysterious holes, which he has hidden with floral embroidery. They are now covered with flowers in the five colours. I have noticed that there is always a reference to Vajrayana in whatever Rinpoche wears – if you can detect it.

We took a short stroll from *Pink Cottage*[6] out on to *The Todden* in the limpid air of bright August sunshine, to watch the fishermen return from the ocean with their crustacean catch. *The Todden* is a rocky spit of land which rises thirty feet above the sea. It separates the two coves. Cadgwith is a fishing village of lofts, capstan houses, and cellars, with local stone walls and thatched or slated roofs. The village has its origins in the mediæval era, and the felt-history of the place seeps from every cobble of its steep streets – so I had moments of feeling entirely out of time. From *The Todden* promontory, we could look down on both inlets: *Fishing Beach* or *Working Cove* to the north-east, and *Little Beach* – the swimming cove to the south. Pointing seaward from *The Todden* are two rocks called *The Island* and *The Mare* which draw the eyes out through all shades of blue to the sea and sky horizon shimmering in the distance. At low tide, the two beaches are connected by a strip of rocky sand between *The Todden* and *The Island* – but at that hour, of this particular morning, the tide was heading towards its high mark. The crystal clear, deep turquoise water was rising through the gap. We were lucky – the bench which perched on *The Todden* was free of walkers and beach-goers. We could thus settle to feast our senses and gaze at the incoming fishing boats being dragged up the shingle by the communal tractor. My nose filled with the subtle scent of fresh sea spray rising from the waves below. I caught the pungent undertow odour of less fresh fish from old lobster pots stacked not far from our feet.

---

[6] Standing at the top of Little Beach, *Pink Cottage* is one of the original thatched cottages in Cadgwith.

Two: Minapa – the whale siddha

The air was filled with the piercing cries of the wheeling gulls high overhead, and the grunts and chugs of men and motors below. Minutes passed in wordless ocean gazing. I was absorbed by the lucent sparkles on the rolling swell of the waves, and the manifold blue, green and purple hues from patches of shadow and seaweed. My eyes however, kept returning to the activity on *Working Cove* below to our left. The recently beached fishing boats started unloading their morning spoils: brown crab, spider crab, lobster, and maybe monkfish or conger eel. The fishermen had been out at sea before dawn. They were still working steadily and continuously – barking requests for help from their fellow piscators amidst occasional roars of mirth related to long-standing banter. There were others down on the shingle too, both emmets[7] and locals – but it was easy to spot the fishermen.

"You can tell they're fishermen, can't you…" I commented. *"Even if they weren't dressed in sou'westers and hauling boxes of crab in the cove, as they are now. Even when you see them quaffing beer and singing sea shanties in the Cadgwith Cove Inn you can easily spot which of them spend their lives on the ocean. It's something about their demeanour… something in their eyes…"*

"Quite so – the nam'gyür[8] of the fisherman" smiled Rinpoche. *"Each one could be Minapa – the whale siddha. I imagine… you might like to hear the hagiography?"*

"I most certainly would" I replied. *"I can't think of a better place, or time."* I turned my gaze up and out towards the horizon. I settled my mind to listen.

Minapa was a Shudra, born of a Bengali fishing family in the sea port Samudrabandara in Madraspatnam[9] on the Coromandel Coast.

---

[7] British archaic or dialect word for 'ant', used in Cornish dialect to denote a tourist or holiday-maker.
[8] Nam'gyür – demeanour, *physically sensed and sensing characteristics*, a way of being in the world which communicates both outwardly to the environment, and inwardly, or reflexively, to oneself.
[9] Madraspatnam, or Madras, is now known as Chennai. It is situated in the Bay of Bengal, in the Tondaimandalam province between the Pennar river of Nellore and the Pennar river of Cuddalore.

Rinpoche began to recite:

> "*On the Coast of Coromandel where the early pumpkins blow,*
> *In the middle of the woods*
> *Lived the Yonghy-Bonghy-Bo.*
> *Two old chairs, and half a candle,*
> *One old jug without a handle –*
> *These were all his worldly goods,*
> *In the middle of the woods,*
> *These were all the worldly goods,*
> *Of the Yonghy-Bonghy-Bo,*
> *Of the Yonghy-Bonghy-Bo.*[10]

There was no particular need for me to quote Edward Lear… but the reference was somehow pleasing.[11]"

Minapa learned the skills of the fisherman's life from an early age, and his father was proud of him for his courage, skill, and intelligence. His mother loved him for his kindness and for the keen duty he showed to his father. He was eager to learn—eager to pull his weight in the family economy—and eager to become a fully functioning adult.

When his father was too old to work, Minapa took over completely. He cared for his parents until they died, then continued, completely alone. He realised that he should have sought a wife, but he had always been too busy with his training, his work, and eventually his responsibility to his parents. By the time he realised that there would be no one to care for him in his old age, it was too late – and he decided to let the future look after itself. He was not saddened by the shape his life had taken because he loved his work and loved the sea.

---

[10] Edward Lear (1812–1888)—*On the Coast of Coromandel – The Courtship of the Yonghy-Bonghy-Bo*
[11] Ngak'chang Rinpoche often quotes poetry – as disparate as Shakespeare, Yeats, Edward Lear, Ted Hughes, and the Beat Poets.

Minapa was accustomed to isolation, having spent most of his waking life in a boat on the ocean. He was well attuned to the weather—to the moods of the sea—and had an intuitive grasp of the nature of his environment. He was not a man of any intellect. He had no education. He was illiterate in terms of societal considerations – but extremely well-versed in the grammar of sailing and fishing. He was an accomplished navigator, knowing the patterns of the stars, sun, and moon. He was possessed of great strength and endurance. The art of fishing had taught him patience. It had taught him the need of alertness to the dangers of a life at sea. It gave him a mind which was both quiet and vigilant. In order to survive, he needed to know every sign of bad weather, and every indication which arose from the movement of waves.

Minapa was a man who would be categorised as a *natural sage*[12] – a person who has developed realised qualities simply through living and through past-life experience. He was a kind and generous man – but a man with a steady mind, accustomed to silence and lacking the need to be entertained. He loved the changeable nature of the sea, and asked nothing of it other than being what it was, however it was. He was never bored. He had no ambition to be other than he was. Being a fisherman, he had come to terms with the possibility of death – and, because of this, he was relatively fearless. He had often helped others in peril on the sea, and had taken great chances to rescue others from drowning.

As chance would have it, he cast his line one day and hooked what seemed to be an enormous catch. It proved however, more than that for which he had bargained: it was a whale. He tried to let go of the line but became ensnared and dragged down into the ocean. As the whale ingested Minapa's line, it drew him further down and eventually he was swallowed by the whale. Curiously this saved him from drowning – but imprisoned him in the whale's belly.

---

[12] Trang-srong *(drang srong* / དྲང་སྲོང་ / *rishi)*

Minapa was accustomed to isolation and so he had no fear of his imprisonment. He had no fear of darkness, as he sometimes fished at night when the sky was overcast and therefore entirely dark. He had food enough to eat as the whale constantly swallowed small fish – and although they had to be eaten raw, they kept him alive. His main problem was thirst, but fortunately the whale had swallowed some flotsam and jetsam amongst which were jugs of water and wine.

After some days in the belly of the whale, Minapa heard voices. He was aware that they were not human voices, but nonetheless he understood them. The voices were those of two nagas[13]. One was a student, and the other a teacher. The student asked questions about the nature of reality. The teacher answered. The student however, suffered a wandering attention and would occasionally lose the thread whilst the teacher was answering. After giving one answer the teacher asked *"Have you understood what I have told you or has your mind drifted?"* Minapa had heard the discourse of the naga, and, even though he had never received Dharma teaching, he understood perfectly. He replied *"Yes, I understand your teaching – and I am grateful for hearing it."* The naga was surprised on hearing these words from a human, and replied *"These were not words for a human being to hear. Having heard what you have heard – you cannot now return to the human realm."*

"But how will I live in the belly of this whale?" replied Minapa.

"That is not necessarily my concern. I did not place you inside this whale."

"Yes... I do not hold you or anyone else responsible."

"Those are words of strength and wisdom" replied the naga. *"Is there more you would say – before I take my leave?"*

"Only that I shall die here."

"That is true" replied the naga. *"You cannot breathe in the realm of the nagas, even if I were to release you from this whale."*

---

[13] Lu *(kLu /* 𑀎 *)* – nagas are beings who inhabit the dimension of the water element.

Two: Minapa – the whale siddha

"Then there is no more to be said" replied Minapa matter-of-factly.

"You are brave…" the naga mused considering the problem *"… and you are undaunted by death. How did you come to be within this whale?"*

"I was out on my boat and the whale took my fishing line. Then I was swallowed when the line was caught round my arm and I could not release myself from it."

"Ah – a killer of fish…" the naga replied with disapproval *"…this does not endear you to me. I am not inclined to be merciful to one who shows no mercy."*

"Yes… you are right…" replied Minapa *"…as you see the world – I have killed your kindred."*

"And as—you—see the world?"

"As I see the world… Well, I see it as human beings see it – and, as I was taught to see it by my father. We see fish as food. We are poor. We live by the sea, so we see the sea as our source of nourishment. I do not say it is right. I only say that this is all I know."

"That is… reasonable" replied the naga. *"It is true that the karmic perception of all beings is what it is – and you do not seem evil by predisposition. It could be that I can overlook this fault, grievous though it is in my eyes. Now tell me further – did you deliberately choose to overhear my teaching?"*

"No. It was entirely accidental. I only realised I was overhearing something when it was too late to decide whether to listen or not – and by then I found it too interesting not to listen. That is why I answered when you asked the question as to whether your student's attention had wandered."

"Well… I would know if you were lying – and I perceive that you do not lie" the naga replied, and proceeded to think deeply about the problem. After some hours, he decided that Minapa was a worthy vessel for the teaching he had overheard.

"Ordinarily I could not let you return to the human realm—but I see your mind—and I believe you will benefit beings with the knowledge you have gained. I shall cause this whale to cough you onto the shore, and there you must begin your life as a yogi. The only condition I make is this: you may no longer be a fisherman. The lives of fish are sacred to us – so instead of fishing, you must become a fish who lives above the sea."

"How is this possible?" asked Minapa.

"You must follow the teaching you have overheard, and you must develop the qualities of a fish. You must develop these qualities for a month before you are coughed up onto the beach. The whale's belly shall be your retreat cave."

"What are the qualities of the fish that I must develop?" enquired Minapa.

"They are the qualities of the perfect tantrika. The fish—like the perfect tantrika—swims effortlessly in the stream of whatever arises. The fish dwells in the pervasive ocean – just as tantrikas dwell in the experience of the pervasive rTsa rLung[14]. Fish live in water but are never wetted by it – just as tantrikas dwell in the appearance of duality without being distorted by it. They dwell within samsara but they are not of samsara. The fish never sleeps just as the tantrika never loses awareness in the waking state or the sleeping state. The fish has large unblinking eyes – just as the tantrika has large unblinking eyes, which see everything without involvement in convoluted discourse. Integrate with the essence of this teaching and you will become Minapa—the whale siddha—the fish for whom you have always sought."

Rinpoche paused in his telling. He looked at me with raised eyebrows, and the slight upward hand gesture I knew so well. I wondered if he had realised, I had a question forming in my mind.

"I can see the qualities of a fish being the qualities of a perfect tantrika" I began "but it seems like maybe the qualities of a fisherman, of Minapa himself, could be useful qualities for a practitioner too?"

---

[14] rTsa rLung / ཙ་རླུང་ – the spatial channels and winds of the psychophysical energy system of the body.

"Indeed" Rinpoche replied. *"Anybody whose life involves learning skills, developing the ability to learn from circumstances extremely quickly, the ability to be solitary, and the ability to face death on a daily basis, has the makings of a practitioner. With fishermen—in boats on their own—out on the sea fishing… it's a dangerous occupation."*

"We know that from talking to Nigel Legge[15]*"* commented Khandro Déchen.

"And these fine fellows on the beach below" I added. *"Ja'gyür and I spent an evening with them—well, a late night actually—and they told some hair-raising stories. So, as you were saying Rinpoche, it's a dangerous occupation."*

"And… in that situation" continued Rinpoche *"the more you know, the better. Being able to read the sea and the sky. To know a storm is coming. To know what something—anything—means. To be utterly attuned to the environment. These things make people ideal candidates for practice. They have skill. They have awareness – and application. There's independence, autonomy, and self-reliance. All the qualities are there."*

There was a pause. We all gazed first at the fishermen on the beach, and then, out to sea.

"Minapa then practised as he had been instructed" Rinpoche continued *"and, in a month, he had attained the nondual state…"*

At that moment the naga became aware of Minapa's realisation – and, as he had promised, came to speak with him.

"You have fulfilled your promise—practised with diligence—and now I perceive that you have achieved the result. The whale shall now take you to the shore, where you will be delivered onto dry land. We shall never meet again in this life but I believe that you will remain true to your word and never return to the life of a fisherman."

---

[15] *The Fisherman's Apprentice*—BBC—2015. Nigel Legge appears—with Monty Halls—in this BBC documentary.

The whale swam to the nearest coast where the naga caused the whale to cough Minapa onto the beach. Once standing on the sand, Minapa saw a large congregation of people. They had never seen a whale come so close to the shore before. They had gathered on the beach curious to see what it would do. Suddenly the whale had opened its mouth and let out a loud rushing of air and water – and there stood Minapa before them. They were astounded. They asked him—after they had recovered from being shocked into silence—how he came to emerge from the mouth of a whale. Minapa recounted his experience. He kept the naga's teaching secret but sang a song of realisation for the people.

> *"The fish yogi swims effortlessly in the stream of whatever arises.*
> *The fish yogi dwells in the pervasive ocean of the experience of the pervasive rTsa rLung.*
> *The fish yogi lives in the water of dualism – but is never wetted by it.*
> *The fish yogi dwells within samsara – but is not of samsara.*
> *Never sleeping the sleep of delusion – the fish yogi never loses awareness in the waking state nor the sleeping state.*
> *The fish yogi's unblinking eyes see everything without involvement in convoluted discourse."*

The Raja of the land soon came to hear of Minapa and presented him with gifts in order that he should remain for some time and be of benefit to his people. Minapa did as he was asked, but eventually, he was moved to travel and offer teachings in many other places. *"A fish must swim"* he told the Raja. *"A fish never remains in one place – but must move with the flow of the ocean. Likewise, I must move with the flow of circumstances and find myself where I am needed."*

Minapa took his leave the next day and returned to his home. There he found his fishing nets and line which he took down to the shore and burnt, calling out *"I shall never fish again – but shall walk towards the mountains and serve people wherever I may."*

Those who had known him before asked him *"Why are you behaving like this? Are you a madman – that you burn the tools of your livelihood?"*

"Is it madness to keep one's word?" Minapa replied.

"No" the fishermen responded *"but it is madness to destroy good nets."* At this Minapa sang them a song of realisation:

> *"I am the madman who no longer draws beings to their deaths
> And who has thus abandoned the boat of misery in token of promises made.
> I am the madman who meditated beneath the sea – yet breathed no water.
> I am the madman who dwelt in the belly of a whale – yet was not eaten.
> I am the madman delivered safely to the shore, by the whale who dined upon him.
> I am the madman who cut the lines of duality which hook the senses.
> I am the madman who revealed the links of interdependent origination as both form and emptiness.
> I am the madman who liberates the Net of Indra[16] into nondual space."*

On hearing this, some of the fishermen sneered. Others were inspired—even though their understanding of his words was lacking—and were able to perceive him as a Mahasiddha. The inspired fishermen left with Minapa. They became his disciples and each of them realised the nondual state after some years of practice. Those who sneered eventually came to hear of Mahasiddha Minapa's miraculous appearance from the mouth of a whale, and heard it confirmed by many who had gone to the beach to see it. The sneering fishermen were ashamed of their reactions to Minapa. They went in search of him – but never found him.

Mahasiddha Minapa lived to a great age and wandered continually, giving teachings all over India and Nepal.

---

[16] The Net of Indra referred to here is the monist net of the Advaita Vedanta tradition, and not the net referred to in Buddhism.

Rinpoche finished the telling. I remained silent allowing the tale to percolate, trying not to rush to conclusions or questions. I was acutely aware of the perfect poignancy of hearing such a story in such a place and in such company, sitting on a rocky coastal outcrop with the sea stretching in front of me. The potential Minapas continued to work on the shingle below. Eventually a question coalesced.

"Is there a reason" I asked *"that Minapa meets a naga as his teacher—a non-human water element being—as opposed to a human teacher? Could he also have met another teacher like Jalandhara and learned from him, or is there a reason that he needs a being from another dimension?"*

"It's not that he needed such a teacher" Rinpoche replied *"but Mahasiddhas who were entirely independent operators—people who didn't have problems—were the ones who tended to have non-human teachers. They had non-human teachers perhaps because they had no problems, other than those which life-circumstances occasionally threw at them. Minapa could have continued being a fisherman for the rest of his life. He could have been perfectly content out on the sea—on his own—just doing what he did and being what he was."*

"Human intervention" added Khandro Déchen *"manifests when the potential Mahasiddha has a personal problem which the teacher can help them explore or explode."*

Silence ensued in which I wondered what the average citizen would make of the story. *"What would you say to people who said that whales were incapable of ingesting anything as large as a human being?"*

"I'd say" Rinpoche sang *"Oh Minapa, he lived in a whale; Lawd Minapa, he lived in a whale; That saint made his home in a mammal's abdomen; Yeah, Minapa, he lived in a whale.*

*"Oh it's—**so**—necessarily so; Oh it's—so— necessarily so; The things that yer gonna…"* [17] He burst out laughing.

---

[17] George Gershwin—lyrics by Ira Gershwin—*It Ain't Necessarily So*—from the opera *Porgy and Bess*—1935

A moment of silence. *"You see…"* said Khandro Déchen *"the fact about whales is entirely irrelevant."*

"So we may as well see it as fact?" I asked.

"Yes—but also 'no'—and maybe neither" replied Rinpoche. *"You could simply cease to divide 'real' and 'unreal' as if it had to be one or the other."* PAUSE *"As a tantrika… one doesn't have to be an eternalist literalist—or—a sceptical nihilist. The hagiography belongs to a culture. If you belong to that culture – then you enjoy that culture. This is an extremely bad example – but why do rationalists, scientists, and marine biologists leave mince pies and glasses of whisky for Santa Claus?"*

"Or why" added Khandro Déchen *"if they don't go so far – do they leave presents for their children to find under the Christmas tree as if Father Christmas has left them there, when an adult cannot descend a chimney? People put on this charade even when they're not Christian – not that it's even an entirely Christian tradition."*

"A Swiss lady once pointed out to me that William Tell was apocryphal" Rinpoche smiled *"and I paraphrased Chhi'mèd Rig'dzin Rinpoche—on the subject of dragons —replying 'Until I die, I believe in William Tell!'* [18] *– and anyhow did Rossini compose the William Tell Overture*[19] *in vain?"* PAUSE *"What is there to believe or not believe? It's the same with Robin Hood. These are marvellous stories and human societies are enriched by them."* PAUSE *"So… the salient point in this hagiography of Minapa"* concluded Rinpoche *"is the Dzogchen men-ngag-dé instruction. Swim effortlessly in the stream of whatever arises; dwell in the pervasive ocean of the experience of the pervasive rTsa rLung. Live in the water of dualism – but never be wetted by it. Be in samsara – but not of samsara. Kyabjé Künzang Dorje Rinpoche once said something similar: 'Air of 'khorwa breathing – but changchub be outbreathing.' So, inhale the air of dualism – but exhale compassion."*

---

[18] Wilhelm Tell, the folk hero of Switzerland, was an expert mountaineer and crossbow-marksman who assassinated Albrecht Gessler, the tyrannical reeve of the Austrian dukes of the House of Habsburg positioned in Altdorf. Wilhelm Tell's defiance and tyrannicide encouraged the population to open rebellion. He is considered the father of the Swiss Confederacy.
[19] The William Tell Overture is the overture to the opera *William Tell* composed by Gioachino Rossini. William Tell premiered in 1829 and was the last of Rossini's 39 operas.

Silence ensued again. This time the pause was disturbed by the noisy arrival of a large family of tourists surrounding us with high volume inanities—ice creams—and the clear intent to park themselves on *The Todden* for the afternoon.

"*O yah… I think this might be time to find Ja'gyür*" Rinpoche said "*then we can mercilessly wreak revenge on a plethora of Ann's pasties[20].*"

I nodded. We rose from the bench and turned for *Pink Cottage*.

As Rinpoche walked ahead of me, I noticed the family of invaders all pause in their chatting and licking to stare after him. I saw Rinpoche through their eyes and thought I would probably stare too – he was dressed in his 'Cornwall attire' which included a scarlet white-polka-dotted neckerchief and a sizable brown Tricorne[21]. I was used to passers-by gazing somewhat nonplussed after Rinpoche. He himself seemed oblivious to the reaction to his appearance.

At that moment Rinpoche glanced back at me. "*You know…*" he grinned "*an interesting part of the hagiography is the part in which he keeps his vow, by burning his nets. Those around him—who'd known him before—think he's an idiot.*"

"*That's reflective of the way anyone is viewed*" added Khandro Déchen "*if one does, says, or wears, anything out of the ordinary—if one gives up security—if one ceases to buy into whatever seems 'normal' to the herd… then 'the herd' looks at you as if you were an idiot.*"

---

[20] *Ann's Famous Pasties*. Ann Muller's shop in Lizard makes traditional hand-made Cornish pasties using beef from the Lizard peninsula, Cornish potatoes from Manaccan, swede and onion from Leedstown, Dove's organic flour and—in cheese and onion pasties—Davidstow Cornish cheddar.

[21] The tricorne is a hat, popular during the 18th century. At the peak of popularity, it varied greatly in style and size, and was worn by aristocracy and citizenry alike, as common civilian dress and naval uniform. The distinguishing characteristic was that 3 sides of the brim were turned up—*cocked*—to form a triangle around the crown – which made it impervious to wind.

Of course, Khandro Déchen had noticed the gawping emmets. Rinpoche had not. At least, I thought, not in particular – but then he commented *"It's a privilege to be endowed with the facility to dispense entertainment with such utter paucity of exertion."*

Three: Goraksha – the nondual cowboy

Goraksha *(go ra kSha /* གོ་རཀྵ *)* / Balang Srung *(ba gLang srung /* བ་གླང་སྲུང *)*
Disciple of: Minapa
Varna by birth: Vaishya

Onset of spring at Drala Jong. Early morning in the gently warming day – taking a short stroll before breakfast.

Rinpoche was attired in an ankle-length buffalo-hide horseriding coat from Montana. He wore his characteristic 'Montana Crease' hat, with the broadest brim and highest crown. He has hats in various colours: black, grey, brown, acorn, blue, green, and white. An impeccably incongruous vaquero, yet somehow looking entirely at home amidst the teeming green of a Welsh valley.

"*Do you miss Montana, Rinpoche?*" I asked.

"*Yes…*" he responded equivocally. "*It was an ideal pool of time – but a pool of time which ended, as do all such interludes. Düd'jom Rinpoche told Tharchin Rinpoche* [1] *there was a Bé-yul* [2] *in the north-west of Montana—a Hidden Land— which is why we made pilgrimages there for a while. This place—here—is also ideal, apart from the absence of horses to ride.*"

"*What did you like about Montana – apart from the horseriding?*"

"*The people. The way the people appreciated their culture. People on the street often stopped me to say 'Thank you for keeping up the old traditions.' I'd then tell them 'I'm English,' and they'd reply 'Thank you anyway – it's important to us.' Then there was the lady in a pizzeria who asked if she could have her photograph taken with me. 'I said 'Certainly, I'd be happy.' After the photograph was taken she said 'I've always wanted a picture of myself with a real Montana cowboy.'* " *I replied 'But I'm English…' and she replied 'No one will know.'*" Rinpoche laughed. "*I found that delightful.*"

---

[1] Lama Tsédrüp Tharchin Rinpoche *(bLa ma tshe sGrub thar phyin /* བླ་མ་ཚེ་སྒྲུབ་བར་ཕྱིན *) /* 1936–2013) – an important Nyingma Lama of the gö kar chang lo'i dé. 10th Family Lineage Holder of the Repkong Ngakpas. Ngak'chang Rinpoche and Khandro Déchen are good friends with his elder son Dung-sré A-gyür Rinpoche, who lives in Yang-lé-shöd, Nepal.

[2] *sBas yul /* སྦས་ཡུལ – a hidden land of Guru Rinpoche and Yeshé Tsogyel.

"She was a tourist from Florida" said Khandro Déchen. *"There were so many wonderful human confluences in Montana."*

We headed up the track from the Drala Jong farmhouse, listening to the raucous greeting of the cockerels as we passed, and watching out for the circling of the red kites overhead. We stayed on the grassy centre of the track where bursts of bright sunshine-yellow from the dandelions leapt out of the luscious verdancy of the new-growth grass. As we rounded the first corner, we paused at the wooden five-bar gate which led into one of the fields belonging to Huw, the dairy farmer. We paused and rested—our forearms on the top bar of the gate—breathing in the view. The fields fell away from where we stood, in gentle rolls and pleats down the valley. The grass was drenched in dew, radiant with early morning sun. It provided the perfect backdrop for the herd of Friesian cattle which ranged across the slopes.

As we watched the cows meandering their masticatory thoroughfare across the fields, Rinpoche launched into the hagiography of Goraksha, the nondual cowboy. *"So, Goraksha was born in Dimapur* [3], *on the banks of the Dong-siri river* [4] *in the east of India. That would have been during the reign of Raja Devapala…"*

Goraksha's family were incense merchants of the Vaishya varna, who—having fallen on hard times—had to take drastic measures to survive. When financial crisis overwhelmed the family, Goraksha's father had to hire him out to a local cattle baron in order to supplement their income. Goraksha was not averse to this work as it took him out into the countryside – a place he loved. It enabled him to gain a broader sense of fragrance than that provided by incense.

Goraksha had been trained from an early age in the art of incense-making – and thus was possessed of an acute sense of smell.

---

[3] Dimapur is the largest city in Nagaland. In the Middle Ages, it was the capital of the Dimasa Kachari rulers. Dimapur was derived from Dimasa Kachari: *Di* means 'water', *Ma* means 'large' and *Pur* means 'township'.

[4] Dong-siri—now known as Satluj—means 'Ravine of Peaceful Habitation'.

Goraksha loved the fragrances of wild herbs and flowers and soon became able to detect the presence of leopards or tigers, simply by smelling them on the breeze. Tigers were a great danger but they did not appear often. Leopards, on the other hand, were numerous – so, Goraksha armed himself with a long and heavy staff in order to keep them away from the calves. They would not attack full-grown cattle but the young were always in grave risk of being taken. The other cowboys would not risk their lives to protect their bovine charges from leopards – but Goraksha was always alert to their presence and would always go to defend the calves. The other cowboys were incredulous as to why Goraksha would risk his life in such a way. *"Are we paid to risk our lives? No. Why should we risk being mauled by leopards just so that our employers can make a better profit?"*

Goraksha was equally incredulous *"Isn't it supposed to be our duty as cowboys?"*

"It's not our duty to die…" they replied *"…or be horribly mauled."*

"Well…" Goraksha mused *"… why would you not wish to help these poor calves? Do you not feel sorry for their plight?"*

"Yes… we do feel sorry for the creatures – but not sorry enough to take the kind of risks you take."

Goraksha was a kindly generous lad and bore his comrades no ill will for their cowardice and lack of responsibility, in spite of his being the lone protector of the calves. The only aspect of his life about which Goraksha was dissatisfied was the curtailment of his education – for he knew that without education he would be unable to study Dharma. To be an incense manufacturer had naturally led him to think about the purpose of incense, and from that standpoint a growing fascination with Dharma had evolved. There was no time in the life of a Bengali cowboy to devote to education or to gain access to Dharma, and he therefore had no knowledge of how to practise.

All he knew concerning practice, was that it required sitting motionless, and so he spent evenings, late into the night, simply sitting still. He had no preoccupation to disturb him—unless he caught the scent of a leopard on the wind—and so his silent sitting naturally began to bear fruit without instruction and without his being cognisant of any change that was occurring through his informal engagement with meditation.

Rinpoche stood back from the gate, pausing for a moment. I voiced what had occurred to me as I listened. *"He's like Jalandhara and Minapa, in that he seems to be very much at home in the natural world. Do all the Mahasiddhas show such sense field integration with their physical environment?"*

"Mostly… In ancient India living as part of the natural world was what everyone did unless they were royalty. You wouldn't find as much today, of course."

"People are even removed from cooking now" commented Khandro Déchen. *"Removed from making meals with real ingredients. People have become enslaved to convenience food and fast food."*

"Perhaps, we should make it even faster" laughed Rinpoche. *"Cut out 'the middle man' by flushing it directly down the defæcatorium."*

"It's sad" continued Khandro Déchen. *"Cooking has become a chore, rather than a creative art."*

"About once a month" added Rinpoche *"I make caramelised onions. It's the same process every time – but every time I'm delighted when the onions begin to brown. It was an accident, originally. I was busy and left the onions cooking for too long. Three hours later they were a little burnt on the sides but the middle was delicious, so I worked out how to achieve that without the burning. I've perfected the art now. I boil them first, then place them in the oven for an hour at 240°F. Then I leave them all day at 160°F, adding water and stirring, every hour or so. This reduces the onions until they look like chutney.*

"It's always enjoyable even though I know what's going to happen. There's always a sense of success even though I never doubt that the process will be successful. It's always joyful to see it happening again." Rinpoche leant back on the top bar of the gate and continued the hagiography.

One evening, several leopards appeared and badly mauled a calf before Goraksha could fend them off. No one came to his aid and he was mauled himself in his effort to protect the helpless creature. Finally, the leopards left—unable to take the calf—and Goraksha was left wounded, yet tending the wounds of the calf.

In this sad condition he was found by the Mahasiddha Minapa. *"I saw the vultures circling…"*

"I saw them too" answered Goraksha.

"What did you think when you saw them?" asked Minapa.

"I thought…" mused Goraksha *"… they are probably waiting for the calf to die – or for me to die."*

"Yes… you are right, young fellow. That is usually why vultures circle – and that is why, when I saw them, I came here thinking some poor creature might be dying. I came here to see if I could give some assistance."

Goraksha was surprised to see a rather strange man—whose skin appeared to be tinged with green—speaking to him.

"Thank you, kind sir" replied Goraksha. *"I would be grateful if you would help me bind my wounds. I have tended to this poor calf but I cannot bind my own wounds well enough on my own."*

"How did you come to receive these wounds?"

"From the three leopards who were trying to take this calf."

"Were there no other cowboys to help you?"

"No, good sir – or, rather, yes, but they are afraid of the leopards. I do not blame them for not coming. I did not call out to them for help, and so they had no knowledge of my situation."

Minapa considered the young lad carefully as he tended his wounds, and said *"You will not know this – but before I became a yogi, I was a fisherman. That job was a similar job to yours. Both livelihoods contain an element of risk. They also offer the chance of death. These are excellent qualifications for the life of a yogi. Have you ever considered that you might practise Dharma?"*

"I have considered it, good sir..." sighed Goraksha *"... but, since the difficulties of my family, I have not been able to pursue my education. To study Dharma, one must be educated and there is no possibility of that now. But I do try to meditate, even though I have no instruction other than remaining motionless."*

"Where did you learn about remaining motionless?" Minapa asked as he tended to Goraksha's wounds.

"I have observed the monks" Goraksha replied *"and that is what they do when they are not studying. So... from that I understood that being motionless and studying must be the two most important things for a monk. This is sad for me because although I can sit motionless, I cannot study and therefore the gate of religion is closed to me."*

"Ah..." laughed Minapa. *"I see – you have learned society's conditioned ideas of what is expected in terms of religion. Study has its value – but it is not absolutely necessary. To remain motionless is a great skill – and this is absolutely necessary. This skill will serve you well in terms of practising Dharma."*

"This is the most marvellous news! Are you a holy man to speak as you do?"

"I am not sure if I am a holy man or not – but, as I said, I am a Buddhist yogi and therefore I can tell you what a Buddhist yogi would tell you."

"So, you think there is some possibility for me to practise religion?"

"*Certainly — besides being able to sit motionlessly, you have other advantages which may be lacking in most monks.*"

"*You astonish me, reverend sir. What possible advantage could a cowboy have?*"

"*Showing such kindness to the calves in your charge. Kindness is a rare and indispensable necessity of Dharma.*"

"*Is kindness so uncommon?*"

"*Yes. Most people are like your cowboy colleagues: kind only when it is of no inconvenience to themselves.*"

"*That is a sad way to live*" commented Goraksha.

"*Yes… and it is also cowardly… which leads me to another great quality you possess — bravery. Bravery is a rare and indispensable necessity of Dharma. No one can practise Dharma if they are cowardly, or if they live in the avoidance of risk. All you need, young lad, is transmission and essential teaching on the nature of Mind.*"

"*Where can I find such transmission and teaching, reverend sir?*" asked Goraksha. "*And even if I found it, how would I be able to make an offering to receive it?*"

"*You have not only found this transmission and teaching*" laughed Minapa "*but you have also paid handsomely for it.*"

"*How is this possible?*" Goraksha gasped.

"*You have made the offering I require. The offering you have made has been your kindness to the calves in your charge, and your courage in the face of grave danger.*"

Goraksha thanked Minapa effusively for his offer of teaching and transmission. "*But how will I be able to practise, living the life of a cowboy?*"

"*That is simple*" replied Minapa. "*There are many who imagine that the practice of Dharma requires time that is free of other activities, but living the life of a monk, in itself, is no guarantee of accomplishment. Some monasteries are merely sanctuaries for the idle and self-obsessed. Chanting all day long is no guarantee of gaining wisdom.*

"*Reciting mantra with a congested mind will avail nothing but more congestion. Silent sitting may well occur in these places – but sitting and doing nothing is no guarantee of realising emptiness. Everything I shall teach you, can be incorporated—exactly—into the life you have. Then, through being a cowboy yogi, you will show others that they can do the same. You will therefore be of great benefit to others.*"

"*But what of the need for study? How will that be possible living the life of a cowboy?*"

"*That is simple*" replied Minapa. "*There are many who imagine that the practice of Dharma requires great intellectual knowledge. That however, is only required of intellectuals – and even then, there is no guarantee that they will achieve liberation through that means. I gained all I needed in the belly of a whale – so you may gain all you need in the compassionate solitude of your profession. All you need is to live exactly as you have always lived, but having received transmission, and having gained a precise knowledge of how to practise in your situation.*"

Goraksha felt inspired by a deep and abiding devotion for his vajra master, the Mahasiddha Minapa, and absorbed everything he imparted concerning view, meditation, and action.

"*The qualities of the perfect cowboy are those of the perfect tantrika.
Cowboys live naturally in the unfabricated world, where they devote themselves to the protection of others.
Cowboys dwell in the sense of pervasive responsibility which connects them with all beings.
Cowboys must transcend hope and fear in order to live ascetically as they do;
They therefore dwell in the appearance of duality without being distorted by it.
They dwell within samsara but they are not of samsara.
Cowboys are always alert—whether awake or asleep—to the dangers that exist for others;*

Just as tantrikas never lose awareness in the waking state or the sleeping state.
Cowboys have ears which hear what is carried by the wind, and noses which sense whatever is carried by the wind;
Just as the tantrika has senses which are open to the entire phenomenal world.
Cowboys see, hear, taste, and smell everything without involvement in convoluted discourse.
Integrate with the essence of this teaching
And you will become Goraksha—protector of herd-like humanity—and attain liberation."

Goraksha practised as he had been instructed, and after three years he attained the mundane siddhis. Having realised the fruit of practice this far – he had little work to do. The leopards became tame amongst the herd he tended and visited him from simple affection. When leopards were nearing death, they came to lie at Goraksha's feet with the intention that he should take their pelts once they were dead, and in this way Goraksha eventually came to wear leopard-pelts as clothing.

The cattle baron became aware of his remarkable cowboy and reestablished Goraksha's father in his incense business. He told Goraksha that if he could teach the other cowboys something of his art, he would be free to come and go as he pleased. He told Goraksha that he would always support his father's business in times of hardship.

Goraksha's peers—on observing the tame leopards—naturally asked Goraksha for his secret. He gave it to them freely—as he had been given it—and they all became accomplished yogis. Goraksha however, was not satisfied with the mundane siddhis. He knew this was not the end of accomplishment and set out to find Minapa.

When he found Minapa, his vajra master said *"I have awaited your arrival and can only tell you this.*

"Now that you have protected your charges and passed your knowledge to those who have taken your place, you must now devote yourself to imparting this knowledge as widely as you can. There is no need for you to seek the ultimate siddhi – as the ultimate siddhi will now seek you. Simply live in the service of others, and the ultimate siddhi will be born naturally in the stream of your awareness."

Goraksha followed this instruction and attained nondual realisation after twelve years had elapsed.

As the hagiography ended, we watched as one of the cows seemed to notice us properly for the first time. She ambled slowly over to the gate as if we might have something interesting to offer. *"Humanity being herd-like reminds me of your frequent warnings to us about the propensity for mindlessly following fashion"* I mused *"… about all conditioned thinking, in fact."*

"Ah yes, herd behaviour – one has to root it out!" Rinpoche gave a thespian yell of glee. The cow lifted her head and looked right at us. *"Practitioners need to show they have integrity. They need to show that they're not herd animals. This cow is less of a herd animal than some people we've met. See – she's come to visit us, unlike the other unexceptional bovines."*

"Unfortunately, most people border on the bovine" added Khandro Déchen. *"Fashion is herd behaviour and herd behaviour is a major problem in the world."*

"When I was young" sighed Rinpoche *"there was a fashion for racist 'humour'. I didn't like it because I'd come across Black American music at age eight – and Black Americans were my heroes."* PAUSE *"I never liked racist 'humour' for that reason – and also because my German grandmother had told me that racists were not as evolved as animals. Those people around me were not necessarily 'bad people' – but racist 'humour' was the 'humour' of the time. They just didn't think about it. The same people no longer subscribe to racist 'humour', they've come to recognise that it's not funny. They thought it was funny because everyone else thought it was funny. Like sexist 'humour', eventually people realise that it's not funny either. It's not funny because ethnicity and anatomy are not intrinsically comical."*

"Schadenfreude too" said Khandro Déchen *"… laughing at the misfortune of others. It's all herd behaviour. In-groups and out-groups. It's primitive. Herd behaviour is primitivism. People feel safe having a certain view and they join in with the view of everyone else."*

Some moments of silence passed.

"I saw a lot of it at school too" Rinpoche continued. *"In those days everyone was a Marxist."*

"Were you a Marxist?" I asked.

"I was probably more of a Groucho Marxist" Rinpoche laughed. *"Or that's what I used to tell people. Actually, I was an anarchist and remain an anarchist today – freedom with responsibility. Back then however…"* Rinpoche smiled *"… to be accepted, one learnt the Marxist language—employed the Marxist words and phrases —and that's how you let people know what you were. You had a political view – and you shared that with everyone else around you. Sometimes it had nothing to do with whether you believed it or not. And ten years later many of those Marxists were voting Tory. That is not necessarily an invalid choice – but it has to be a real choice borne out of research and personal conviction."* PAUSE *"People don't think."*

"By 'not thinking' Rinpoche, do you mean people don't think for themselves?"

"Yes. They don't tend to question the idea they hold to be true. Flanders and Swann [5] make fun of that in their 'Song of Patriotic Prejudice': The English, the English, the English are best, I wouldn't give tuppence for all of the rest! The rottenest bits of these islands of ours, We've left in the hands of three unfriendly powers, Examine the Irishman, Welshman, or Scot – You'll find he's a stinker, as likely as not.'"

"It happened with Rinpoche and the Queen Mother" Khandro Déchen grinned.

---

[5] English comedy duo. Michael Flanders (1922–1975) – lyricist, actor, and singer. Donald Swann (1923–1994) – composer and pianist. They first worked together in a school revue in 1939 and eventually wrote more than 100 comic songs together.

"*Some years ago*" laughed Rinpoche "*I was walking down the High Street in Penarth. There was an exhibition about the Queen Mother in a charity shop window – and I caught myself sneering as I walked past. That sneer hit me almost immediately! Why was I reacting in this way? I thought: 'you miserable, loathsome, little excrescence…' We have to catch ourselves reacting like this. So, anyhow, I had to analyse the situation. I had to assess – had I come to this 'sneering position' through independent thought? And no, I had not. It was a hangover from the early 1970s, when I was at Art School. That's where that 'sneer' came from. It was the general attitude of that time to the Queen Mother and the Royal Family. I realised that it was something that I had never questioned. I could however, question it now.*"

"*So, Rinpoche bought a set of Queen Mother Centennial mugs*" smiled Khandro Déchen. "*We use them every day and it's ever-so-slightly amusing to observe the politically correct parents of Ræchel's friends eyeing them with 'certain expressions' on their faces.*"

"*An old friend of mine—a student of Namkhai Norbu Rinpoche—had come to dinner with her husband*" Rinpoche announced. "*They sat at the dining table whilst we busied ourselves with final touches to the fondue. They had noticed the dinner plates celebrating the Queen's Diamond Jubilee and the dear lady commented to her husband in vague horror 'D'you think they're royalists?' Khandro Déchen heard, and peeping round the corner said 'Of course.' It was a funny moment. Nothing more was said about it. I think it must have thrown them into a state of nonconceptual shock.*"

"*Of course*" added Khandro Déchen "*Chögyam Trungpa Rinpoche regarded himself as a loyal subject of the Queen.*"

"*Himalayans tend to be a marvellous blend of feudalism and anarchism.*" PAUSE "*We're not archetypical royalists—we just see the value of heritage—and would far rather have the Queen, than a fair few of elected heads of other countries.*"

"*So, people need to be willing to question themselves*" I concurred as we watched four more cows move steadily up the field to join the first at our gate.

"Yes… but not in a neurotic manner" replied Khandro Déchen. *"One simply needs to be open for it to occur."*

There was a pause after which Rinpoche added *"It has to be there in the moment. 'Ah! I have a decided attitude here!' Then one asks: 'Did I come to this through independent research? Or have I just picked up on what's around me? Have I merely adjusted myself to my peer group? Have I just taken up someone else's point of view – and adopted it without consideration?' These questions need to occur – if one is a practitioner."*

Five cows coming to check us out seemed to be the tipping point for the whole herd. They now all started heading our way. Our field of vision was soon filled with heaving black and white flanks, and our noses with the sweet smell of warm cow breath as they all jostled for prime gate position. There were now thirty or more cows finding us fascinating, but our eyes were drawn to the one who had remained at the far hedge, either not interested in us or with other things on its mind.

"Not that one should reject the herd, either" Rinpoche turned and smiled *"because that is just another fashion. If there's something the herd is doing which one authentically likes then there's no problem with it. I could sing 'Land of Hope and Glory' at the Last Night of the Proms, simply because it was enjoyable. It would not have to be an act of jingoistic patriotism, nationalistic fervour, or xenophobia. It's not that one has to reject everything. Having to be a 'hard-wired rebel' is herd mentality."*

"Feeling superior to others because 'I'm a rebel', is vapid" Khandro Déchen commented. *"We have no interest in rebelling against anything for the sake of rebellion. With 'rebel mentality' or obsession with being unorthodox or counter-culture, one is basically just part of another herd. Why refuse to wish people 'Happy Christmas' because you're not a Christian? It's always a problem when one has to establish one's identity according to mandatory socially imposed rules – either by accepting them or rejecting them. Both can be equally clichéd."*

Then Rinpoche quoted *"Cowboys dwell in the sense of pervasive responsibility. It connects them with everyone and everything everywhere. Cowboys transcend hope and fear to live ascetically as they do. They dwell in the appearance of duality without being distorted by it. They dwell within samsara but are not of samsara."*

We stood a while longer, listening to the sounds of bovine butting, bumping, and chewing the cud – all accompanied by the thud of hard hooves on beaten earth.

"Seeing the fixed patterns of herd mentality is absolutely primary, in terms of Vajrayana" Rinpoche concluded. *"Undermining it, in oneself, is probably one of the major practices. Many 'Western Buddhists' are herd animals. Chanting 'for the benefit of all sentient beings' can be merely cataleptic – a catatonic catechism."*

"Why couldn't it be 'for everyone'? Why is it 'all sentient beings'? Are there beings who are not sentient?" asked Khandro Déchen. It was a pertinent rhetorical question.

"We have to think about what we're saying and how it distances us from people who are not Buddhist" added Rinpoche. *"You can't have conversations with non-Buddhists if you pepper your speech with jargon and stock phrases. Kyabjé Künzang Dorje Rinpoche shouted 'thom-yor!'*[6] *at me every time I used a Buddhist stock phrase. Stock phrases need to be avoided in everyday speech, and Buddhist technical language needs to be reserved for teaching situations. This is particularly important if you are coming to Buddhism as a 'new religion'. What many people do, is learn how to look and sound 'like' a Buddhist. This often means walking around with a teng-ar round your neck and decorating your house with a plethora of Buddhist pictures. There were some people in Cornwall who created a wall to ceiling collage of an admixture of Buddhist and Hindu images culled from National Geographic magazines."* PAUSE *"It was creative… in some ways."*

There were a few moments of silence. Then we turned away from the gate and walked back down the track towards the farmhouse for breakfast.

[6] *'thom yor* / འཐོམ་ཡོར་ – idiot.

I was enjoying the gentle babbling accompaniment of the stream trickling in the drainage ditch alongside the track, and the patches of palest-of-yellow primroses on the bank below the hedge. I was also wincing slightly inside thinking of all the 'Buddhist pictures' that had graced my walls down the years. It occurred to me that there were almost no Buddhist images in Ngak'chang Rinpoche and Khandro Déchen's home, outside the shrine room. There was only a framed photograph of Kyabjé Künzang Dorje Rinpoche.

I asked Rinpoche about this and he replied *"Our 'empty white walls' are Vajrayana images, although… they may derive more from Zen than Vajrayana – or perhaps Sweden. Scandinavians seem to like white and wood – although, that may be apocryphal."* PAUSE *"Be that as it may Kyabjé Künzang Dorje Rinpoche and Kyabjé Düd'jom Rinpoche Jig'drèl Yeshé Dorje are—always—there, in everything."* PAUSE *"There is an old photograph of Kyabjé Düd'jom Rinpoche—with Sangyum Rig'dzin Wangmo⁷—which was taken in Tibet. It hangs at my bedside."* PAUSE *"The photograph was given to me by Kyabjé Düd'jom Rinpoche."*

---

⁷ *gSang yum rig 'dzin dBang mo* / བདུད་འཛོམས་གསང་ཡུམ་རིག་འཛིན་དབང་མོ་ – also known as Düd'jom Sangyum Kushog Rig'dzin Wangmo *(bDud 'joms gSang yum sKu shog rig 'dzin dBang mo* / བདུད་འཛོམས་གསང་ཡུམ་སྐུ་ཤོག་རིག་འཛིན་དབང་མོ་). Mother of Dé-kyong Yeshé Wangmo *(bde skyong ye shes dBang mo* / བདེ་སྐྱོང་ཡེ་ཤེས་དབང་མོ་), Chhi'mèd Wangmo *('chi 'med dBang mo* / འཆི་མེད་དབང་མོ་ – second eldest daughter), Shen'phen Dawa Rinpoche *(gZhan phan zla ba* / གཞན་ཕན་ཟླ་བ / 1950–2018), and Tsé-ring Pen'dzom *(tshe ring phan 'dzom* / ཕན་འཛོམ་ – their younger daughter), who was a hidden dakini often in retreat. She attained parinirvana on 27ᵗʰ of August 2014 at Yeshé Nyingpo in New York. Ngak'chang Rinpoche met her in Bodhanath and in London.

Four: Kankaripa – the bereaved lover

Kankaripa *(kang 'ri pa /* གང་3ི་པ *)* / Ken-ru Zhab *(keng rus zhabs /* གང་རུས་
ཞབས *)*
Disciple of: Jalandhara and Subhadra
Teacher of: Subhadra
Varna by birth: Shudra

On pilgrimage in Bhutan with Ngak'chang Rinpoche, Khandro Déchen, and sangha.

It was our first day and we were travelling from the airport in Paro valley to the capital, Thimphu. This is one of the best roads in the country and it's possible to make the forty odd miles in just over an hour. The road is cut through the rock of the high hills which line the route following the rivers: first the Paro Chu and then the Wang Chu – the river which flows through the valley of Thimphu. Just before we reached the confluence of the rivers at Chuzom, we broke our journey to practise at Tamchog Chakzam. This is the iron chain-link suspension bridge built in 1433 by the gTértön and realised polymath, Thangtong Gyalpo – who is sometimes described as the Leonardo Da Vinci of Tibet.

We pulled off the road and took in the view of Tamchog Lhakhang across the river, perched on the otherwise deserted hillock directly above the bridge. The Lhakhang is still in the hands of Thangtong Gyalpo's descendants and maintained by the Chagzampa lineage he founded. Within the walls of the Lhakhang are several paintings and shrines depicting Thangtong Gyalpo and his emanations – but on this occasion our interest lay more with the ironwork than with the temple. We followed the steep path down towards the bridge in the fierce heat of the sun, our vision filled with clear blue mountain skies and the red iron-rich earth of the steep barren hillsides.

The bridge is constructed of multiple lengths of iron chain secured by square whitewashed gatehouses on opposite banks. The remarkable non-rusting wootz iron[1] of which the hand-forged links were made had been there from the 1400s until it was washed away in extreme flooding in 1969. Sections of the chain were salvaged and kept at the Lhakhang until 2005 when the King of Bhutan ordered the rebuilding of the bridge.

The bridge was recreated in its original form using the salvaged chains and unused links from other bridges built by Thangtong Gyalpo throughout the country. The iron links of the recreated bridge we now stood on were almost 600 years old, with much of that iron likely to have been mined locally. The mouths of ore tunnels are still visible in the mountainsides around the Lhakhang. The water below us was not deep, but rushed fast and furiously under the bridge. Numerous windblown strings of prayer flags added to the sound and movement which filled the senses. As students headed to the river banks, hillsides, or Lhakhang for solitary practice I followed Rinpoche and Khandro Déchen as they headed down river and then settled to sit on one of the many boulders that lay partially in and partially out of the swiftly flowing water.

After sitting quietly for some time Rinpoche said *"Whenever we were in Montana, I was unaccountably attracted to the splendid, shallow, fast-moving rivers – they were marvellously rock-strewn. They contained occasional great boulders, just as they have here. I sat and gazed at them for hours."* Rinpoche laughed *"Now I know why! They were exactly like this river! I have never been here before in this life – but I remember this place. There seems to be a memory, some sort of connection sparkling through. It's intermittent, but… there's a sense in which Aro Yeshé is seeing through me or I'm seeing through him."* PAUSE *"It's rather peculiar…"* PAUSE *"… probably just fancy or fantasy."*

I was understandably moved by this statement – as I was entirely unaccustomed to Rinpoche saying things of this nature.

---

[1] Wootz iron is a 'crucible steel' characterised by band-patterns and high carbon content. The bands are formed by sheets of microscopic carbides within a tempered martensite or pearlite matrix. It was a pioneer steel alloy made in India in the 1st century BC.

Four: Kankaripa – the bereaved lover

I knew him to be rather reticent about such matters. I was silent for a while and then asked *"Is it possible for anyone to experience such a connection to a place from lifetime to lifetime? If you have a strong connection to the land in a particular location, might you be drawn there in the next lifetime?"*

"It's certainly possible. Yes" Rinpoche responded.

Following my thought through, I asked *"Does that mean that we're more likely to take rebirth in the same kind of land as the one we're connected to?"*

"Yes. If one is Bhutanese, one is more likely to be reborn in the Himalayas than the Netherlands, Amazon Basin, Antarctic, or the fens of East Anglia." Rinpoche gazed at the river as he continued *"This is because we follow what's similar or familiar, unless there is a substantial accident which throws circumstances."*

"Such as an avalanche?" I asked, knowing that Aro Yeshé—Ngak'chang Rinpoche's previous incarnation—had died in an avalanche.

"Yes. That was substantial – as it were." He laughed. *"Accidents happen."* PAUSE *"The Nyingma are sometimes known as 'The Accident Lineage'[2] and Kyabjé Düd'jom Rinpoche Jig'drèl Yeshé Dorje spoke of 'the bad luck of the Nyingmas'. When he told me about this however, it was a matter of no great consequence. He laughed about it and said 'Good luck—bad luck—this only alternation coming. Always—good luck—when practising, possible coming."* PAUSE *"Most people are reborn more-or-less where they were before, simply because that is what happens naturally."* He gestured to the river before him *"Like water gravitating to the lowest point. It's not going to flow up the hill. That is not the nature of water. Just as air moving from high pressure areas to low pressure areas."* PAUSE *"We call it wind."*

We sat quietly again. This time I was acutely aware of the water itself. I placed my feet in the river below the boulder, feeling the chill and the power of the downward surge.

---

[2] It was Chögyam Trungpa Rinpoche who spoke of the Nyingma as *The Accident Lineage*.

"I've heard you talk before about the possibility of reconnecting with practice across lifetimes." I pondered "I guess that might be the same, if there's sufficient familiarity?"

"Ah, yes. That is far more likely in fact" Khandro Déchen replied. "If you're authentically immersed in practice, then you'll reconnect with it. As in life, if you really like something, or if you really want something and you never let go of the idea of wanting it, eventually, you'll get round to getting it."

"I remember…" Rinpoche mused "seeing a National ResoPhonic guitar for the first time when I was 14. It was at Farnham Folk and Blues Festival in the grounds of The Bush Hotel [3]. It was a Tricone model played by Mike Cooper [4]. I was astonished by it. As soon as I saw it, I wanted one. Then Jo Ann Kelly [5] came on with a 12-string guitar, and I thought: 'Now I want a National 12-string!' Then forty years later, I have three. This is because I became friends with Don Young, the owner of the company which produces them. We go to dinner with Don and his wife, Hillary. So, connection happens. I don't believe it's accidental. I was simply obsessed for forty years. So, if you keep something strongly in mind – eventually circumstances connect."

Rinpoche paused, and I wondered "And is it because practice is more important than anything else that we're likely to reconnect with it? Or is it that there's a chance of reconnecting with anything that you're passionate about?"

Rinpoche smiled "It could be anything about which you're passionate – within reason. Obviously if I'm passionate about becoming the King of Britain – that is not going to happen." PAUSE "It's a matter of being open to taking advantage of opportunities. There was a lady—a guitarist who attended teachings in California— who had recently bought a wooden National ResoPhonic. I'd already ordered a 12-string from them and received it.

---

[3] *The Bush Hotel* was a 'coaching inn' built in 1618 and mentioned in William Makepeace Thackeray's novel *The Virginians*.
[4] English Country Blues guitarist / vocalist / b. 1942 – famous for his lap-slide style. He is personally known to Ngak'chang Rinpoche.
[5] English Blues guitarist / vocalist / 1944–1990 – respected for strong vocals and Delta-style guitar. She was personally known to Ngak'chang Rinpoche.

"It was the first one they'd ever made, but I'd never been to the National factory or met Don Young. On hearing this, the lady telephoned and asked if it was possible to have a tour of the factory. I would never have thought of that." Rinpoche laughed. "Don tried to put her off by saying 'You'd have to wear hard hats because there are always things falling off the ceiling. It's a dangerous place.' This was comedy—of course—as he was just trying to deter her. She wouldn't be deterred however. The tour was arranged and as Don showed us around the factory he said 'We have orders coming from all over the world. Some English dude just ordered a 12-string Tricone'. I smiled and said 'That was me – and you made the previous 12-string Resolectric.' Don broke out into a huge grin 'Oh, so—you're—the dude!' Those were the first two 12-string guitars National made – but now they're part of their catalogue. Don and I became friends from that point onward. It was curious how that happened so naturally."

Rinpoche dexterously removed some earwax with a hair grip—as was often his custom—and continued *"Be that as it may, if you have any degree of persistence in anything, it goes somewhere. It's a vector. It doesn't have to be particularly spiritual – although Don always said that I had a religious devotion to Nationals. It happens with everything. Anywhere where you have such a vector, there's the possibility for connection and reconnection. Obviously, this also occurs with practice – but with far more power."* Rinpoche smiled and turned back to gaze at the river.

"What about relationships and reconnecting with people you're close to in other lifetimes?"

Rinpoche grinned *"I wouldn't bother thinking too much about that."* PAUSE *"Although… perhaps, I could relate the hagiography of Mahasiddha Kankaripa, the bereaved lover?"* I nodded – so Rinpoche commenced.

"Kankaripa was born in Magadha[6] "he smiled *"more-or-less where Bihar is now. He was a Shudra. He married a lively, pleasant, and affectionate girl, also a Shudra, called Padmini. They settled down to an extremely happy married life together and enjoyed each other's company to the fullest…"*

Being a Shudra he had no religious pretensions and therefore felt free to enjoy connubial delight with a wife who was similarly inclined to make the most of the physical passion which united them. Kankaripa was a kind generous man who appreciated what he had and was devoted to his wife's happiness in every aspect of her life. Kankaripa and Padmini continued to behave toward each other as they had behaved during their courtship, and therefore, they remained as happy with each other as they were on their wedding day.

Existence being what it is however, Padmini unexpectedly took ill and died. Kankaripa was inconsolable in his grief. Padmini was taken to the charnel ground – but Kankaripa was unable to leave her there. He sat with her, keeping a constant vigil lest beasts of prey should eat her. The poor man wept sporadically – but no matter how much he cried, he never came to the end of his tears. It was then that Mahasiddha Jalandhara hove into view, riding his camel – as ever. Jalandhara observed the wretched state of Kankaripa from a distance and made his way towards him. He rode his camel up to within a yard of Kankaripa, but Kankaripa remained entirely unaware of him. Jalandhara dismounted and stood next to Kankaripa waiting to be noticed, but Kankaripa continued to cry, as if nothing else in the world existed other than himself and the intensity of his misery. Once Jalandhara had observed him for a while, he asked *"Dear young man – why are you sitting here weeping next to the corpse of this woman?"*

---

[6] Magadha was one of the sixteen Mahajanapadas—great countries—of ancient India. The nucleus of the kingdom was the area of Bihar, south of the Ganges; its first capital was Rajagriha *(Rajgir)* then Pataliputra *(Patna)*. The ancient kingdom of Magadha is heavily mentioned in Buddhist texts with respect to advances in science, mathematics, astronomy, religion, and philosophy in the Indian Golden Age.

Kankaripa was so absorbed in grief that he didn't hear Jalandhara. *"Hey, young man!"* Jalandhara repeated at greater volume *"Why are you sitting here weeping next to the corpse of this woman?"*

Still Kankaripa heard nothing – so Jalandhara had to shout *"Hey! You! Young man! I said 'Why are you sitting here weeping next to the corpse of this woman?' You look as if you've been here for days – yet you are no yogi."*

Kankaripa finally noticed – but could make nothing of the words he'd heard, so Jalandhara had to repeat himself a fourth time *"Hey! You! Young man! I said 'Why—are—you—sitting here—weeping—next—to—the—corpse—of—this—woman!?' You look as if you've been here for days – yet you are no yogi. I'd be mightily obliged if you would answer me!"*

Kankaripa stared at him and was only able to say *"This… is Padmini—my wife—she has died and there is no use in my living on any further."*

"Yes…" sighed Jalandhara *"…it is a great sadness – but everyone dies sooner or later. Didn't you realise that? My parents died when I was six years old. That was sad too – but I continued to live."*

"Yes…" wept Kankaripa *"…but we loved each other so much."*

Jalandhara shook his head sadly *"Yes… I can well imagine – but if a bride and groom give each other flowers at their wedding, one will take flowers to the other's grave. You must know this. Birth is a terminal illness – is it not?"*

"If this is samsara – then it is better if I died too."

"The fact that we are born and die is not samsara, young man. Samsara is the fact that we want it to be otherwise and try to convince ourselves that it is otherwise or that it can be otherwise. And as to your dying alongside your wife – that would be of no help to you or your wife. That would merely cause you to be reborn in an ever-repeating mess – in which finding Padmini would become ever more hopeless. Maybe… it is time you practised Dharma – you know… this—would—be a good opportunity."

"But what is the purpose? If Dharma will not bring Padmini back — what use is it to me?"

"Certainly Dharma will bring Padmini back! Why do you think I am here talking with you if not to help you with your difficulties? What d'you think I came here for — my wretched health, or something?" Jalandhara smiled.

"Then I will practise Dharma."

"Not so sudden, my friend. I will not deceive you" Jalandhara confided in a kindly manner. "Dharma will bring Padmini back — because we all take rebirth. It is just a matter of where and when she will return to the physical world."

"But the world is vast and there are countless people in countless places — how would I ever find her again?"

"That is not a question I can answer — and even if I could, it would do you no good."

"So, what can you tell me — that would do me good?"

"I can tell you that finding does not always come from searching."

"But what other means is there for finding other than searching?"

"There is no 'way' in terms of 'how' you would imagine a way to be. You see... even if you could search the entire world, you might only find her at the point of your own death."

"What is this 'way that I cannot imagine'?"

"Embodying Dharma."

"Yes... It is true... I cannot imagine that at the moment — but I will try. Can you say just a little more so that I will be able to begin and feel inspired with the sense that Padmini will be somewhere?"

"Alright then... If you are to find your wife again it will occur through the auspices of your tèn'drèl — your real connection.

"If there was a great connection between you, whose main nature was kindness – then it is possible that circumstances will bring you together again. The problem is that you cannot live for this possibility. You must live life in the best way you can – and that means: practising Dharma. You are more likely to meet Padmini again through practising Dharma than through searching the world for her rebirth. Even if you were to become a Maharaja and send envoys across the world, there would be no guarantee – so Dharma is your major option."

At this, Kankaripa's eyes took on a look of hope, and his face a look of openness to possibility. *"How should I practise Dharma? Where should I go and what should I do? Will you help me?"*

"Certainly, I will help you – why else do you think I'm here?" Jalandhara replied, and then set about instructing Kankaripa in the manner of making a funeral pyre for his wife. Jalandhara performed all the necessary rites for the cremation and for the stages of her experience through the bardos – and in each activity he taught Kankaripa details of what was necessary. Instructing Kankaripa in this way, as he was performing the rites, took an inordinate length of time – but Kankaripa was keen to learn. He was keen to learn because every aspect was Dharma – and it was Dharma which was the most likely to reunite him with Padmini.

Once all the preparation was concluded, they cremated Padmini with further rites. Jalandhara was not accustomed to performing such lengthy ceremonies, but they formed the basis of the teaching of Dharma – and because the rites were centred on Padmini, Jalandhara had Kankaripa's full and undivided attention. He was, in fact, the perfect disciple. The force of his devotion and yearning combined to sharpen his intellect and the power of his concentration.

They remained in the charnel ground for forty-nine days after the cremation. There was always, mysteriously, food for them to eat and water to drink from the stream that flowed between the trees.

Once the forty-nine days of the bardos were over Jalandhara gave Kankaripa instructions on how to practise.

> *"Visualise your wife as the dakini who resides in the vast space of reality.*
> *She is both the form that you see in your mind and the space from which she arises.*
> *See her as indistinguishable from space – and you will never be separated from her.*
> *Try to obtain her – and you will be parted from her.*
> *Allow her to be empty and she will naturally manifest her form.*
> *Attach to her form and she will manifest her emptiness."*

Kankaripa understood this teaching immediately *"I am amazed, venerable sir – that I understand what you have imparted!"*

"You have understood, dear fellow, because you have listened so carefully for so many days through the many complex preparations for your wife's cremation. I should tell you though—because I must be honest with you—that all those rites were not entirely necessary. I shall no longer teach you through outer forms, because you now understand the essence of Dharma and outer forms are not necessary. I had to employ them at the beginning because you had no experience with Dharma or with understanding teachings that related to the nature of Mind."

"I am deeply grateful for your teaching, venerable sir..." Kankaripa stated with tears of devotion in his eyes *"... and for the way in which you gave it. I am a practical man and, it is true, I could not have understood such an abstract teaching without first being introduced to it through ceremonial rituals."*

"This is the way that Dharma is taught to many. Usually, many years are needed before Dharma is sufficiently understood to form the basis for the essential teaching. Your devotion to Padmini—and to me through your love for Padmini—has allowed you to understand the essential teaching within mere weeks. This is a good sign that you will not only achieve realisation of the nondual state, but that you could also discover the rebirth of Padmini."

At this, an even stronger devotion for Jalandhara arose in Kankaripa.

Rinpoche paused, and I said *"Jalandhara makes it very clear that enacting the funeral rituals and death rites was not actually necessary, that he just goes through the process as a method to instruct Kankaripa in practice. It makes me wonder if there's a degree to which everything other than men-ngag-dé instruction is like that – not actually necessary?"*

"Well, this has to be a 'yes and no' answer" Rinpoche smiled. *"You see, it's certainly the case that Dzogchen is all that is necessary. However, there is a broad spectrum in terms of 'what we are', and 'how we are'. We need to eat and drink in order to survive – and that is not Dzogchen. A grey nutritious paste could be developed – and, yes, you could live on that. It would not however, satisfy the tongue, nose, or eyes. We need variegated sustenance. Obviously, if you invite friends to dinner, you don't merely offer something you took from the freezer and microwaved. You cook something fresh and delicious. You take time and effort to set the table attractively. All those additional aspects—the candles and freshly laundered napkins—make a pleasant situation in which one's guests feel welcomed. And so, with practice, we have our shrine rooms. They don't have to be painted with the traditional stripes – but when they are, those stripes have history. They provide a context in a number of ways. Also, although the Aro gTér is mainly based in Dzogchen, we also have Mahayoga aspects."*

"It's not that Mahayoga has less function" added Khandro Déchen. *"Mahayoga has many functions which support silent sitting. A problem only arises when people mistake the supportive practices for the main practice."*

After a moment Rinpoche continued *"In this particular hagiography, Jalandhara is using Mahayoga methods to distract Kankaripa – as well as instruct him. When Kankaripa is involved in the rites, he's doing something for Padmini, something related to her. He's not merely wallowing in his grief. Doing something for her extends the situation. He feels involved with her – but he's engaged with practicalities. This dissipates his anguish, which is necessary in order that he is able to see beyond it."*

"Is that in part why employing supporting practices rather than silent sitting can be useful if someone's in some kind of distressed emotional state?" I asked. "Is it distracting them from it in order to move them beyond being stuck in it?"

"*Certainly*" Rinpoche nodded. "*That is the efficacy of 'supporting practices' in such situations.*" PAUSE "*You know, Jalandhara notices Kankaripa in the first place, because he's in a state of such intensity. Intensity is always potentially workable – if someone can open themselves up to being worked with. Which—in the end—Kankaripa can.*" Rinpoche chuckled and continued with the hagiography.

Kankaripa remained in the charnel ground practising as he had been instructed for six months – and throughout that time he was supported in his practice by offerings of food that were left for him by people he never saw. The intensity of love he felt for his wife—and the intensity of devotion he felt for Jalandhara—facilitated a one-pointedness which fuelled his practice. After six months he realised the fruit of Jalandhara's teaching and understood that his wife was inseparable from his own inner khandro – and that his inner khandro was inseparable from space.

Kankaripa—consequent to his attainment—remained in the charnel ground for 16 years, at the end of which, a young woman appeared in the dimension of physical reality. She had all the appearance of the khandro he had visualised – and also that of his deceased wife Padmini. She was the Mahasiddha Subhadra – the dakini choreographer. Kankaripa joyfully took her as his teacher and consort and they began a life of wandering. They travelled to all the charnel grounds visiting small villages between each – and in each village Subhadra danced and Kankaripa wept. People —on seeing the joy of Subhadra's dance—sometimes asked Kankaripa why he wept – and he always answered "*I cry with grief that my wife has gone and I cry with joy that she has returned. My tears are the one-taste of misery and ecstasy.*"

Some would then ask him why his wife never spoke and he would always answer "*What would she say that has not already been said in her dance?*"

Those who understood the meaning of Kankaripa's statement requested teachings, and gained realisation.

As the hagiography concluded and I heard of Kankaripa meeting Padmini again in the form of the dakini Subhadra, my thoughts returned to the idea of continuity of connection between loved ones after physical death. *"There's certainly an idea in Christian culture"* I commenced *"that you might meet again in heaven those whose loss you grieve, isn't there? I'm wondering what's the most useful way to think about the possibility of meeting again in terms of Vajrayana?"*

"That possibility is a trap" replied Khandro Déchen *"that's best avoided."* PAUSE *"Of course, Kankaripa does meet Padmini again, but he meets her after sixteen years – and she's deaf and dumb. It's therefore not the total 'Mills and Boon'[7] happy ending . He's together with her again. They are happy – but it's not the same. The problem would be wishing everything to be exactly the same as it was – whenever it was."*

"Staying the same is not even the case with someone with whom you've been married for many years" added Ngak'chang Rinpoche. *"Khandro Déchen is not the same lady I met thirty odd years ago. She has become a different person. There's an illusion that until one dies, nothing changes – but of course, it does. We all change all the time. Husbands and wives become progressively wrinkly. Khandro Dechen might have married a man whose hairline was receding – but the situation has deteriorated somewhat seriously."*

"So" continued Khandro Déchen *"the idea of rebirth meaning that one will be in contact again, is not really something we would advocate. You will either meet people again, or you won't. Even if you do reconnect, it will not be the same."*

"I know two people." added Ngak'chang Rinpoche, a little wistfully. *"I knew them when I was at school – but our relationship has changed. They've become different people.*

---

[7] A publisher founded in 1908 by Gerald Mills and Charles Boon. In the 1930s they began specialising in escapist fiction for women.

"We still know each other, but sometimes I feel as if we only know each other… because we once knew each other. We could now easily not know each other. We have little in common other than our past – and that is not remembered with any great concurrence as to facts. What we remember is contradictory. There are often such impasses with old friends. People tend to freeze each other in former modes." PAUSE "It can be awkward."

"If one has changed, it can be vexing to be related to as if one was forty years younger, with whatever foibles one had at that time" laughed Khandro Déchen. "It does not worry me – but, to be treated as if one hadn't matured since one was 16 years old could irritate some people. So, the time to appreciate anyone is now. It's not tomorrow. It's not next week – or with some idea that you'll meet them again in another life. The time is now and the next life is tomorrow."

A horn blast echoed across the valley. "And now—it seems—the time has come to depart for a new life" Rinpoche added. "We are called to the coach, by the horn of death – or the horn of Gabriel[8]."

It was time to drive on to Thimphu to meet Kyabjé Dung-sré Garab Dorje Rinpoche[9] and his wife Khandro Rinchen Paldrön[10]. We were expected for an audience.

---

[8] Archangel Gabriel blows the horn to announce Judgment Day.
[9] sKyabs rJe gDung sre dGa' rab rDo rJe / སྐྱབས་རྗེ་གདུང་སྲེ་དགའ་རབ་རྡོ་རྗེ is the son of Kyabjé Dung-sré Thrin-lé Norbu Rinpoche (sKyabs rJe gDung sre phrin las nor bu rin po che / སྐྱབས་རྗེ་གདུང་སྲེ་ཕྲིན་ལས་ནོར་བུ་རིན་པོ་ཆེ) – and grandson of Kyabjé Düd'jom Rinpoche Jig'drèl Yeshé Dorje.
[10] mKha' 'gro rin chen dPal gron / མཁའ་འགྲོ་རིན་ཆེན་དཔལ་གྲོན

Five: Subhadra – the dakini choreographer

Subhadra *(su' bha' sGra /* སུའ་བྷའ་སྒྲ *) /* Zhu Zangmo *(bZhu' bZang mo /* བཞུའ་བཟང་མོ *)*

Disciple of: Sharanya and Kankaripa
Teacher of: Kankaripa
Varna by birth: Vaishya

A cool overcast August afternoon in Cadgwith. The perfect time and weather for a picnic at the Minack Theatre, near Porthcurno.

'Minack'[1] means 'a rocky place'. It is an open-air theatre perched on rugged granite cliffs which slope precipitously to the sea ninety feet below. Set in the wild beauty of the Cornish coast, Minack welcomes many thousands of visitors each year for both daylight, and starlight evening performances. They enjoy the ocean views and experience the magic of live performance in this remarkable place. There were no tickets available for shows on any days of our Cadgwith stay this year. A visit to see the theatre itself—and the fabulous subtropical gardens which have been planted around the open-air arena however—was still a delight.

We were met by a profusion of colour. The subtropical grandeur of rare plants from across the world, coaxed into riotous glory on the steep slopes and rocky outcrops, was magnificent. The agaves, aeoniums, and agapanthus carpet the cliffside, woven through the winding paths. Low rock walls and rope edges lead down to the theatre below. Beyond the theatre we looked out over Porthcurno Bay towards craggy headlands and the Lizard peninsula where Cadgwith lay on the grey horizon.

Having enjoyed the sight and fragrances of planted Art at this *garden on the edge*, we descended to the stone seating terraces of the theatre to enjoy our picnic luncheon.

---

[1] *Meynek* in Cornish.

There are also grassed terraces to seat the audience but no chairs for performances in this theatre. The stage area is poised on the cliff edge with hexagonal stone slabs on the ground. Although there is no roof, there are stone pillars, balustrades, arches, and a balcony. The theatre appears as if it were part of the ancient world – yet it is less than a hundred years old. It holds the story of the Minack's master builder – the remarkable Rowena Cade.

Rowena Cade was born in 1893. The First World War and the death of her father brought an abrupt end to her genteel Edwardian life in Cheltenham. In the early 1920s she moved to Cornwall and bought the Minack headland for one hundred pounds. Here she built her home, Minack House, which we passed as we arrived. It sits on the clifftop above the theatre. In 1929 she became involved with a local open-air production of Shakespeare's *A Midsummer Night's Dream*. Later—when the theatre company wanted to stage *The Tempest*—Rowena Cade offered them the use of her cliff garden for the performance. This meant she had to create an *acting arena* and somewhere for the audience to sit. So, Rowena Cade and a few helpers set to. They worked without diggers and heavy machinery. They used hand tools to shape the stage and terraces with Rowena Cade carrying sand up the cliff in sacks from the beach below. She continued working on the theatre well into her eighties, dying in 1983, a few days before her ninetieth birthday. She was an artist as well as a builder and throughout the theatre she etched complex designs into the wet concrete with an old screwdriver.

As we descended the terraces towards the stage, we paused to read a memorial to Rowena Cade—a granite plaque marking her achievements set into one of the walls—and we talked of what a remarkable woman she was. Rinpoche commented as he continued down to the stage area *"A plaque is perhaps unnecessary for me – she is present in every stone and every vista of this place."*

Five: Subhadra – the dakini choreographer

As I watched Rinpoche, standing centre stage, he made such an unusual and arresting sight that it occurred to me that the other visitors might be wondering if he were part of an impromptu performance, and that he was about to burst forth into speech or song. He wore his tall-crowned, wide-brimmed, green 'Montana Crease' hat which had seen some years of mountain horseriding in the forests north of Kalispell. He was dressed in green Austrian 1930s *carpenter's lederhosen* and matching leather waistcoat, decked out with his grandfather's gold 'Double Albert' watch chain. Beneath the waistcoat he wore an emerald green suede Bavarian farmer's shirt. His double-length pale green moss crepe cravat was tied with a *four-in-hand* knot. He sported a pair of 1940s snap-fastening green ankle boots.

Perhaps disappointing some visitors, Rinpoche returned to where we sat without uttering a sound. *"I was almost moved to sing 'Come into the Garden Maud' – but didn't wish to frighten the children"* he grinned.

"They may have enjoyed it, Rinpoche" I replied *"especially as there is no performance at the moment."*

Rinpoche span round from looking at the sea and his green leather ankle-length Luftwaffe greatcoat swirled dramatically in the wind.

I commented *"…shame we couldn't get tickets for the play."*

Rinpoche made a gesture with his hands that betokened 'c'est la vie'. *"Yes indeed"* he replied. *"I relish the performances here in particular."* Then, after a pause *"I have always had great respect for thespians. It strikes me that acting is an Art which could enhance one's ability to visualise – to arise as the yidam. It's an Art form I have never approached – ars longa vita brevis* [2]*"* Rinpoche mused. *"Perhaps instead… I might venture an account which concerns performance?"* I agreed with delight and Rinpoche explained *"It concerns two other remarkable women – which seems appropriate under the circumstances."*

---

[2] Latin: Art is lengthy – life is brief.

He gazed across the sea into the blue distance for a moment and announced, almost theatrically *"The hagiography of Mahasiddha Subhadra, the dakini choreographer."*

We settled on the terraced seat to listen as Rinpoche began *"Subhadra was born in Singhala. That, of course, is now Sri Lanka. She was a deaf-mute from birth. The times being as they were, despite her being rather beautiful, Subhadra was considered societally unbecoming – and therefore unsuitable for marriage…"*

When this was explained to her, she made signs to her parents to the effect that she wished to become a nun – but the monastic rule forbade applicants with such disabilities. Being deaf and dumb she was unable to access any form of education other than the reading and writing skills her parents had imparted to her. When she enquired through sign language what she could do with her life – her parents assured her that they would look after her. She could however, not tolerate the idea of being a burden to them. She wanted to learn any manner of skill in order to make her own way in the world. Her parents however—being Kshatriyas—were averse to her learning an artisan's trade. They asked her which of the Arts she enjoyed. She informed them that she loved to dance.

Subhadra was sent to various dance masters but none would take her on the basis that—with her disability—she would be too hard to teach. Having discovered that there was nothing she could do in life, Subhadra sat alone in her room weeping. Her parents too, were deeply distressed. They attempted to assure Subhadra that she could still have a pleasant life – but Subhadra could see no hope in a life where she could have no rôle and where she was unable to practise Dharma.

After some days, a rotund voluptuary arrived at their front door and introduced herself. Her name was Sharanya and she was a dancing girl. She said *"I have come to teach your daughter to dance."*

Five: Subhadra – the dakini choreographer

Subhadra's parents sent her away because—to them—she was obviously a Shudra and they had no wish to allow her into their home. *"Why does a Shudra girl come to our front door – have you no sense of propriety?"*

"If I am to teach your daughter dancing – I shall have to enter your house. So the front door seemed appropriate."

"We have no need of a Shudra dancing teacher, thank you very much indeed. You may find interest on the other side of town."

Sharanya departed with a smile saying *"I do not blame you for disparaging me because I am a Shudra[3] – but I may be the only dancing teacher in this town who will instruct your daughter."*

"Please, just go away" they replied and closed the door.

Sharanya however, was entirely unperturbed. She returned every day – and although she approached by the tradespersons' entrance, she made the same statement *"I have come to teach Subhadra to dance."*

After three days Subhadra's parents told their servants to leave her standing there. After a week they told their servants to drive her away with stones – but in spite of this, Sharanya came every day and danced for an hour in different places slightly more than a stone's throw from the house.

After three weeks Subhadra noticed Sharanya and went out to see her. She made signs to indicate that she wanted to learn to dance and Sharanya replied in signs that she was extremely well qualified to give her exactly the instructions she needed to be the greatest dancer of the land.

Subhadra went immediately to her parents and told them about Sharanya's offer of tuition.

---

[3] Sharanya was actually a Dombhi. The Dombhis were a theatrical, musical, entertainer varna – from whom the gypsies originated. They were a low varna – but one whose members were admitted to the homes of the higher varnas.

Her parents were deeply unhappy about the prospect, but eventually—giving in to their daughter's pleas—they spoke with Sharanya. *"Explain to us what you are able to teach our daughter and we shall consider this proposal – but first, how will you communicate? Can you both perform and understand the language of signs?"*

Sharanya answered them in sign language which she performed so gracefully that the parents lost the meaning in their fascination at watching her. She therefore had to answer a second time, more slowly, in order to give them time to read her signs.

"That is well and good but we shall not tolerate mere folk dances. What you teach must only be the highest form of dance.[4]"

"I teach the Bharatanatyam [5] from Tamil Nadu; the Chha'u and Odissi [6] from Odisha, West Bengal, and Jharnd; the Gaudiya Nritya from West Bengal, Kathak, Uttar Pradesh, and Bihar; the Mohiniyattam from Kerala; the Kuchipudi [7] from Andhra Pradesh; the Thang-ta and Manipuri from Manipur; and other dances from the dimension of realisation."

"How can you claim to know all these forms?" the parents asked rather sharply.

---

[4] Dance is considered to have been received as gTérma by Bharadamuni *(bar dwa dza thub pa / བར་དུ་ཛ་ཐུབ་པ་*)—an ancient sage—and written down as the treatise on performing Arts, the Natya Shastra. He is dated to between 200 BCE and 200 CE, but estimates vary between 500 BCE and 500 CE.

[5] Bharatanatyam is a classical dance from Tamil Nadu, practised predominantly by women. Accompanied by Carnatic music, its inspiration derives from the sculptures of Chidambaram.

[6] Odissi—also known as Orissi—is one of the eight classical dance forms of India. It originates from the state of Odisha, in eastern India. It is the oldest dance form of India. There are three books of Odissi, the classic treatise of dance. Bas-reliefs from the 1st century BC in the hills of Udaygiri *(near Bhubaneshwar)* confirm its antiquity. It is particularly distinguished from other classical Indian dance forms by the importance of Tribhangi (threefold independent movement of head, chest, and pelvis) and upon the basic stance known as Chauka. This dance is characterised by various Bhangas *(stances)*, which involve stamping of the foot and striking various postures as seen in Indian sculptures. The common Bhangas are: Bhanga, Abhanga, Atibhanga and Tribhanga.

[7] Kuchipudi—dating from the 2nd century BC—is a dance from Andhra Pradesh. Kuchipudi is the name of a village in the Divi Taluka of Krishna district, near the Bay of Bengal. The performance begins with stage rites, after which the characters introduce themselves with a Dharavu *(a small song and dance composition)*. This introduces the mood and character in the drama. The drama then begins, accompanied by Carnatic song and music. Ornaments worn by dancers are made of lightweight Boorugu wood.

"I have no need of claims beyond saying that I have mastered all forms of dance."

"How did you learn them, then?"

"I have no need of explanations – but if you wish I shall demonstrate them all."

The parents nodded with morose acceptance and Sharanya began to dance. The parents were shocked to discover that Sharanya was the most wonderful dancer they had ever seen in spite of her being rather plump. They discovered that she did indeed know every dance to which she had referred – but long before she had shown every dance, the parents agreed that she could teach their daughter. Sharanya was not only highly experienced with each form of dance, but was superior to any of the teachers they had approached as prospective tutors for their daughter. None of those teachers had Sharanya's universal knowledge of dance and none performed them so well. An agreement was therefore made – as long as Sharanya always entered the house in secret by the rear entrance. The servants were bound to secrecy and the tuition commenced.

"First I shall teach you the Bharatanatyam. This is the subtle and sophisticated dancing Art of Tamil Nadu. It is—visually—a dynamic, earthy, yet precise style. It contains a variety of movements with an emphasis on striking the floor with the feet combined with leaping and rotating. The fundamental postures are balanced positions, with elongations that provide a linear quality. The style has equal measures of beauty and strength; deliberate and rapid. To dance, one must first understand the body and the hand positions, and the musical context – and for that you will have to use all your other senses to 'hear' the music. Rhythm is the vital essence of dance which entwines body and melody. Understanding the nature of dance, is understanding the heartbeat of dance. It is a practice of communicative awareness. The hand positions in Bharatanatyam frame the body in symmetrical lines. There are positions where the hands are stretched above the head; positions around the body; and, positions that are stretched downwards.

"The symmetrical patterns formed around the body describe the relationship between the inner space of the dancer and the outer space of the phenomenal universe around her. Watch as I demonstrate. Imitate the movements of each phase after me."

Sharanya taught Subhadra in this way for a month. She was proficient within a week – but by the end of the month she excelled all expectations; so Sharanya went on to teach Manipuri.

"Manipuri requires great restraint – but without arresting fluidity in movement. No matter how intricate or vigorous the dance, the regulation is perpetual – and through this, you display ceaseless ease of movement. This however, must always be understated: there's no sharp angularity in any movement. Each movement merges into the next, creating the sense of timelessness. The smooth flow of the movements results in the fluidity and continuity of body line and mood. The style is never aggressive – it is affectionate yet reserved. Overstatements of mood through facial expression would ruin the dance. All movements—whether horizontal or vertical—are spherical and pour from one rounded movement to another, forming spirals. The hands and wrists must move with marvellous suppleness. There is no conclusiveness to any movement. Every movement is based on strength – yet the greater the strength, the greater the need for command and discipline. Your power as a dancer is not a force which is expended, but a force which is encompassed: pulsing and replenishing its source. The observer who lacks awareness will often fail to perceive the cogency and splendour of Manipuri."

Sharanya taught Subhadra in this way for a month. She was proficient within a week – but by the end of the month she excelled all expectations; so Sharanya went on to teach her Odissi.

"Odissi is a lyrical style of dance which adheres to physical norms that are significantly different from those of other dance forms. Its subtlety is essential and the body postures are not merely factors in the lexicon of the style. A posture by itself can communicate a meaning and each movement can be a teaching in itself. Torso movements are a specialty of Odissi – and correspond directly to the positions and movements of the lower half of the body.

"The lower limbs remain steady in relation to torso movement. The hips do not move – but rather, the upper torso gently undulates on a vertical axis. The head moves in contradistinctive directions with respect to the torso. The movements in Odissi are lyrical due to the spiral nature of the style. The neck movements follow the natural tilt of the head in relation to the angle of the torso and maintain a central line with that of the upper half of the body – with the neck moving laterally, rather than being tilted. The hands move around the frame of the body in various ways. Circular movements and semi-circular extensions of the arms moving upwards or downwards from the breasts to the sides. So—like this—one hand is placed above the head, encircling, whilst the other hand traverses the line of the leg."

"Like this?" indicated Subhadra.

"Yes – that is perfect. You see, dance is an expression of your joy in movement. Odissi is based on a wealth of techniques and abounds in cryptograms handed down over many centuries. Through the positions of the feet—the toe-and-heel exchanges—and the physical positions—contradistinctive movements—the dancer constantly takes on attitudes which are visually delightful – speaking, as they do, of the intrinsic purity of the phenomenal world."

Sharanya taught Subhadra in this way for a month. She was proficient within a week – but by the end of the month she excelled all expectations; so Sharanya went on to teach her Mohiniyattam.

"The Mohiniyattam follows the Bharatanatyam system closely – but the knees spread out and the steps are firm. The arms open wide – but the movements remain rounded and graceful. The musical accompaniment for Mohiniyattam is supplied mainly by the conductor, who sings and also plays hand-held cymbals. The drummer plays the madhalam [8]*.*

---

[8] The madhalam is a drum made of jackfruit wood. It has two skins for playing, made out of leather, which have different sounds. The madhalam is a heavy instrument which is hung around the waist of the person playing. The player stands whilst performing. The madhalam is a vital instrument in traditional Kerala percussion ensembles such as Panchavadyam, Keli, and Kathakali orchestras.

"Also, there is often a wind instrument player who might play the nadhaswaram [9]. Now you will have to watch these instruments in order to see how the music develops — and this will take great awareness."

Sharanya indicated that she would ask her parents to hire musicians — and they agreed. The three musicians on arriving and meeting Sharanya, informed the parents that Sharanya was not a Shudra, but a Dombhi. The parents were embarrassed by their error and apologised to Sharanya. They asked her however, why she had not corrected them in their assumption that she was Shudra — but she replied, with an undetectable grin, that it was not her place to correct those of higher varnas. Three musicians were always there when Sharanya taught Subhadra — and she began to concentrate on hearing the music with her eyes.

"You will also learn to hear the drum with your feet because the sound will be felt in the floor even when the floor is made of marble."

Sharanya taught Subhadra in this way for a month. She was proficient within a week — but by the end of the month she excelled all expectations; so Sharanya went on to teach her Kuchipudi.

"Kuchipudi is the impeccable balance between three: nritta, nritya, and natya. Nritta is a rhythmic sequence that concludes a song or a verse. Nrityas are rhythmical passages followed by alternate interpretations. Natyas are complete dance-drama stories. Unlike Bharatanatyam, Kuchipudi employs undulating hand movements and rapid tempo. The deployment of laya — rhythm, tandava — rhythmic footsteps, and abhinaya — expression, is important and must include three steps.

---

[9] The nadhaswaram, (nadaswaram, nagaswaram, or nathaswaram) is a classical musical instrument played in Tamil Nadu, Andhra Pradesh, Karnataka, and Kerala. It is the loudest non-brass wind instrument. It is similar to the north Indian shehnai — but longer, with a hardwood body and a large flared bell made of wood or metal. It is a key musical instrument and part of the family of instruments known as mangala vadya *(auspicious instrument)*. It is usually played in pairs, and accompanied by a pair of drums. It is often accompanied by a drone-oboe called an ottu. The body of the nadhaswaram is made out of acha wood. The nadhaswaram has seven finger holes, and five additional holes drilled at the bottom which can be filled with wax to modify the tone. The nadhaswaram has a range of two and a half octaves.

"It begins with facial expressions and eye movements, followed by hand gestures and ultimately movements of the entire body. Kuchipudi concerns gestural language—which is often difficult for the uneducated to understand—but you will learn to speak with gestures that communicate to everyone whether they have learnt the gestures or not."

"Is there then some advantage in my not being able to hear or speak?"

"Certainly Subhadra. That is why I sought you out. You have both the desire to dance and the desire to practise Dharma. Because you cannot hear or speak, your mind is less congested with concept. You understand how to speak and hear in signs – so eventually the whole phenomenal world will be a communication to you and from you outward to all phenomena."

Rinpoche ceased speaking. I listened to the intermittent high-pitched cries of the gulls piercing the deep rumble of the tide battering the rocks below. After some moments, I asked *"Can you explain how the phenomenal world communicates, Rinpoche?"*

"There is nothing to explain. It simply communicates. There is no method. It's simply here – being what it is."

"That is the nature of its communication" added Khandro Déchen. *"You either experience it, or you don't."*

"And…" I enquired *"in terms of it being a communication through signs?"*

Rinpoche turned *"Well, let me put it this way"* he smiled. *"If you're a being who communicates through language—and communication occurs which is not linguistic—then there will be signs and symbols. When a cat wishes to frighten a predator, for example, it causes its hair to stand out. This makes the cat seem larger than it is. That's a sign or symbol which conveys the message 'Be gone miscreant malefactor! I'm a bulky belligerent bellicose barbaric beast!'"* Rinpoche chuckled. *"That is not language. This is a sign – a sign which communicates. That's very much the way with animals. They have that way of expressing their messages."*

"*And… what about phenomena that are usually deemed non-sentient?*" I asked. "*I was thinking about Jomo Chhi'med Pema reading the position of the rocks in the river for example. Could you describe that as communication from the phenomenal world through signs?*" Rinpoche nodded agreement. I continued "*But if there's 'some form of consciousness' directing the communication… I suppose there's nothing much to say about that, is there — other than that it's there?*"

"*If there was an intellectually expressible answer to this*" Rinpoche smiled "*then it wouldn't be a sign. You can give an intellectually expressible answer to something that is intellectual. With whatever is not intellectual—and that which is not expressed in language, or movement—there's nothing which can be said. It's something you either experience or not. That is all that can be said by way of explanation.*"

"*So…*" I ventured "*in the transmission of the phases of drala[10] practice that you give, the instructions encourage the possibility of experiencing the communication, of being able to read the signs?*"

"*Indeed — but the 'reading' is not interpretive. 'This' is not converted into 'that' in order to be understood.*" Rinpoche smiled and continued "*Subhadra derived great joy from her dancing lessons, but she felt an enduring disappointment at being denied both marriage and a religious life…*"

When Subhadra expressed this to Sharanya — Sharanya revealed that she was a tantrika. She was the Mahasiddha Sharanya—the corpulent dancing girl—and therefore there need be no obstacle to the practice of Dharma. There was also no obstacle to her finding a husband — but that would have to wait until a future point when it would prove entirely appropriate.

Subhadra learnt the intricacies of classical dance with great ease and within a year she became highly accomplished. Being deaf and dumb there was little in life for her, other than practising her Art in most of her waking life.

---

[10] sGra bLa / སྒྲ་བླ — the sentience of the phenomenal world.

It was not long, with the teaching of Sharanya, before she found herself dancing in her dreams and mastering the practices of mi-lam[11] and gyü-lü[12].

Rinpoche looked across at me with enquiringly raised eyebrows, so I ventured *'Would mastering gyü-lü simply be the recognition of the empty nature of phenomena?'* Rinpoche nodded *"Yes. When there's no difference between awareness in the sleeping state and waking state."*

He took up the hagiography again.

When Subhadra accomplished the entire range of Sharanya's teaching, Sharanya told her she was ready to be presented at court – where she would, without question, be accepted as a royal dancer. Subhadra's parents were doubtful, especially when they were informed that they should mention Sharanya as having been Subhadra's dance teacher – but having witnessed Subhadra's dancing, they felt they had no choice but to make the approach to the royal court of Indrabhuti [13].

---

[11] *rMi lam rNal 'byor* / རྨི་ལམ་རྣལ་འབྱོར་ – dream yoga; one of the six yogas of Niguma and Naropa.

[12] *sGyu lus* / སྒྱུ་ལུས་ – yoga of the illusory body; one of the six yogas of Niguma and Naropa.

[13] Indrabhuti *(rGyal po i nDra bhu ti /* རྒྱལ་པོ་ཨི་ནདྲ་བྷུ་ཏི་ or Dza Gyalpo / *rDza rGyal po* / ཛ་རྒྱལ་པོ་ / King Gyalpo Dza of Zahor *(za hor rGyal po dza* / ཟ་ཧོར་རྒྱལ་པོ་ཛ་) – was the first recipient of Mahayoga. He taught himself intuitively from a Mantrayana text that fell from the sky onto the King's roof along with other sacred objects and relics. Dza Gyalpo was also the teacher of Kukuraja. 'Indrabhuti' can refer to several Maharajas from Oddiyana or Zahor who were key figures in the early transmission of Vajrayana: **a.** Indrabhuti the Great *(i nDra bhu ti chen po /* ཨི་ནདྲ་བྷུ་ཏི་ཆེན་པོ་); **b.** Indrabhuti the Intermediate *(i nDra bhu ti bar pa /* ཨི་ནདྲ་བྷུ་ཏི་བར་པ་); **c.** Indrabhuti the Younger *(i nDra bhu ti chen po'i sras /* ཨི་ནདྲ་བྷུ་ཏི་ཆེན་པོའི་སྲས་), also known as Lawapa, Kambalapada, or Shakraputra – was the son of Indrabhuti the Great; **d.** King Indrabhuti of Oddiyana, King Dza or King Ja (Dza Gyalpo / *dza rGyal po /* ཛ་རྒྱལ་པོ་) – the adoptive father of Padmasambhava. Kyabjé Düd'jom Rinpoche Jig'drèl Yeshé Dorje wrote *'Some say that King Ja was none other than Indrabhuti the Great, who had been empowered by Buddha Shakyamuni himself, but others maintain that he was Indrabhuti's son. Some even believe him to have been Indrabhuti the Intermediate. Thus, there are various dissimilar opinions – but, because ordinary persons cannot imagine the emanations of great sublime beings, perhaps they are all correct. And yet, upon examination of the chronology, we find he is described as a contemporary of master Kukuraja. For this reason, he may well be an intermediate Indrabhuti. Moreover, the great accomplished master Kambalapada and this king are contemporary, whether or not they are in fact one and the same person. He is also the approximate contemporary of Vidyavajra* (Rig'dzin Dorje / *rig 'dzin rDo rJe /* རིག་འཛིན་རྡོ་རྗེ་), *Saraha, and Jalandhara.'*

Indrabhuti—the Mahasiddha Monarch at whose court Subhadra was to dance—knew the name Sharanya immediately. He also immediately recognised Subhadra's capacity for nondual realisation in witnessing her dance. He thus summoned her to his private chambers and gave her transmission of the drüpthab of uniting stasis and movement. She engaged with this practice immediately and recognised nonduality through dance.

She lived at the royal court as a dancer for a year – but then Indrabhuti summoned her parents to the palace and explained that their daughter had attained nondual realisation and should take the life of a wandering yogini. *"She will never want for food or shelter and she will be of great benefit to those who cannot easily understand Dharma."* Subhadra's parents were distressed but—knowing that Indrabhuti was their Raja and also a Mahasiddha—accepted his decision with grace. They bade their daughter farewell and she left the palace so entirely joyfully that her parents were happy with their daughter's fate.

Subhadra roamed throughout India teaching through dance – but only to those who were not fixated on the intellect. Many uneducated, illiterate, unsophisticated people were thus able to comprehend the highest levels of Vajrayana, directly through experience. After a year of solitary wandering and giving transmission-performances, she wandered into a charnel ground to dance for the animals there. No sooner had she begun to dance than she saw a yogi—the Mahasiddha Kankaripa – the bereaved lover—and took him as her consort. Kankaripa recognised her immediately as the mirror image of his dead wife Padmini whose dakini image he had visualised before he came to be known as Kankaripa – the bereaved lover.

As Rinpoche concluded the hagiography, we noticed that the theatre had emptied. We were now the only visitors seated amongst the grass and stone. We would no doubt soon be asked to leave as the Minack staff made preparations for that evening's performance.

Before we gathered our belongings however, I felt compelled to ask about Subhadra 'hearing with her eyes and her feet'. *"This sounds like the 21 sem'dzins, Rinpoche – in terms of awareness moving across the senses?"*

"Yes, but it's not from the Aro gTér. There are many different sets of 21 sem'dzins. Chögyal Namkha'i Norbu Rinpoche[14] *taught a set, for example. And there are some sem'dzin which are not part of any set of 21. They're simply individual. Any practice which 'holds' the nature of Mind falls into the category of sem'dzin – as with the Aro Mélong sem'dzin and the vajra melodies."*

After a moment I added *"The sem'dzins, where you hear through the eyes—or where you experience the other senses through the namtog*[15] *of taste for example—they seem like they are really useful for everyone to practise in terms of unravelling our compulsion to compartmentalise experience?"*

"Certainly. Synæsthesia was of great interest in the late 60s, of course. Every other Rock song concerned synæsthesia." Rinpoche sang *"Put your head down to the ground, And listen to your mind, If you can't spell what you found, I know that you're not my kind, I can hear the grass grow, I can hear the grass grow, I see rainbows in the evening*[16]*."*

Rinpoche chuckled, almost imperceptibly *"It was part of the psychedelic era – which was an inadvertent revisiting of the Surrealist Art movement. So, it's not something so unusual. It's probably unusual now – but Surrealism tends to resurface throughout history. I have traced it as far back as Giuseppe Arcimboldo*[17]*."*

---

[14] chos rGyal nam mKha'i nor bu / ཆོས་རྒྱལ་ནམ་མཁའི་ནོར་བུ / 1938–2018 – one of the foremost Dzogchen Lamas of the 20ᵗʰ and early 21ˢᵗ centuries. Born in Der-gé, Kham, he was recognised as the incarnation of A'dzom Drukpa *(a dzom 'brug pa /* ཨ་འཛོམ་འབྲུག་པ *)* by Palyül Karma Yangsrid *(dPal yul kar ma yang srid /* དཔལ་ཡུལ་ཀར་མ་ཡང་སྲིད *)* and Shéchen Rabjam Rinpoche *(zhe chen rab 'byams /* ཞེ་ཆེན་རབ་འབྱམས *)*. When he was three, the 16ᵗʰ Gyalwa Karmapa recognised him as the mind incarnation of Pema Karpo *(pad ma dKar po /* པད་མ་དཀར་པོ *)* and Druk Shabdrung Ngawang Namgyal *('brug zhabs drung ngag dBang rNam rGyal /* འབྲུག་ཞབས་དྲུང་ངག་དབང་རྣམ་རྒྱལ *)* – the first Chögyal of Bhutan.

[15] rNam rTog / རྣམ་རྟོག – that which arises in the mind.

[16] Roy Wood.—*I Can Hear the Grass Grow*—The Move—1967

[17] An Italian painter (1526–1593) famous for creating portraits comprised of fruits, vegetables, flowers, and fish.

"I know you and Khandro Déchen don't advocate the use of hallucinogens, Rinpoche."

"Well, it's a little more than not advocating, we specifically contraindicate narcotics – unless they are medically prescribed by qualified doctors. Kyabjé Düd'jom Rinpoche was adamant that narcotics were extremely harmful. He said the same of tobacco – which is why we do not accept smokers as students, unless they are prepared to stop smoking."

"So… what about the expansion of experience across the senses… would you encourage that *as valuable?*"

"Certainly – but you don't need hallucinogens for that. I've never had any interest in hallucinogens, because I've always been able to access synæsthesia naturally. I would imagine this is true of all artists. One couldn't really be an artist were this not the case." PAUSE "I remember once… being in Morgan's department store in Cardiff – before it closed. This was back in the 80s. I was with a doctor I knew at the time, and he was buying something in the haberdashery department. I was standing waiting for him, staring at the cotton reels – when, suddenly, he whispered 'Stop looking at those cotton reels, people will think you're on something.' Most people seem to need to ingest substances in order to look at cotton reels and enjoy them. Everyone can experience this however. It's not difficult." Rinpoche smiled. "Salvador Dalí [18] when asked whether he took drugs, replied 'I do not take drugs – I am the drugs.' Anyone who is used to silent sitting will gradually gain this kind of experience – or anyone who had an audience with Kyabjé Düd'jom Rinpoche. He was also 'the drugs' – but in another league altogether. Dualised normality was overawed by his presence."

I sat with that for some moments before returning to the subject of synæsthesia. "Is the reason that we don't seemingly do it more naturally, just part of our addiction to keeping hold of form?" I asked. "I mean, that we don't want that kind of blurring across the senses?"

---

[18] Salvador Domingo Felipe Jacinto Dalí i Domènech, Marquess of Dalí of Púbol (1904–1989) – a Spanish Surrealist artist renowned for technical skill, precise draftsmanship, and strikingly bizarre images.

"Well, it's partly social indoctrination – and partly autonomic reflex" replied Khandro Déchen. *"It's concerned with conditioned expectations and with self-preservation."*

"It's a way of 'reading' the world" continued Rinpoche. *"So, for example, when you look out of the train window—or car window—the eyes track backwards and forwards in order that the countryside doesn't blur. That of course is useful, because you don't want the landscape to be blurred. There might be dangers out there which need to be registered; such as bears, wolves, wild boars – or even wild bores."*

"This was how it was in the past, of course" added Khandro Déchen. *"Now, it might be a city street at night – with its possible human dangers."*

Rinpoche stretched his legs. *"With respect to 'freeze-framing' what we see, this is why some sem'dzin involve deliberately fixing the eyes so that the background does blur, in order to override this autonomic reflex. We have all kinds of autonomic responses which keep us safe. They have a function – but we need to be able to override them. The problem is that they tend to spread into areas where they're not necessary. There's nothing dangerous about looking at cotton reels."*

"And smelling and hearing and tasting…?" I queried.

"Yes. We ignore the senses, where there's no referential profit in them" replied Khandro Déchen. *"So, 'gazing' doesn't pick raspberries or self-aggrandise. Human beings become accustomed to certain modes – and to sensing in certain ways and certain settings. If you spend time amongst allegedly primitive people, you find that they have senses which we lack. This is because they need those senses to stay alive. They can hear approaching animals of which we would be completely unaware. We can retrieve those sense capacities. It's not that only preindustrial people have those perceptions – it's merely that we've lost them. The more one examines this, the more one discovers that, wherever and however people live, they develop senses which accord with the environment."*

"The Inuit have many different words for snow" added Ngak'chang Rinpoche. *"Even in our culture, skiers have a variety of words for snow.*

They talk about mashed-potato snow, champagne powder, and polystyrene[19] snow. This is because snow is important to them. They're going to be moving at speed across it – so they need to define it. Khandro Déchen is fond of birds and when she hears their song, she can identify them. To me there's just this delightful chirping, chirruping, twittering, and tweeting. 'Khordong gTérchen Tulku Chhi'mèd Rig'dzin Rinpoche—being the incarnation of Khye'u-chung Lotsa[20]—was also very fond of birds. I can't tell the difference between most of them. This is because I've not devoted time to ornithology. Wherever you dedicate time to anything, the capacity to perceive in that area, evolves. It's the same with all the sense perceptions. They can all open up if we allow them free attention."

With that, Rinpoche picked up his leather satchel and two US Army rocket bags[21]. Khandro Déchen hefted the wickerwork picnic basket. We commenced the steep climb back up the stone theatre steps and headed for the car park. I paused to put on my jacket and Rinpoche was then slightly too far away for me to catch his final comment. *"I'm sorry I didn't hear that, could you say it again?"* I called, and Rinpoche repeated *"Of course—being **deaf**—Subhadra's mind was less congested with concept."* He grinned and continued up the track.

"Being deaf" explained Khandro Déchen *"meant that she was perfectly poised for receiving transmission."*

---

[19] *Styrofoam* in US English.
[20] *khye'u chung lo tsa' ba* / ཁྱེའུ་ཆུང་ལོ་ཙཱ་བ་ – 'boy translator', one of the 25 disciples of Guru Rinpoche. He became a translator as a boy. His incarnations included Traktung Lingpa *(khrag Thung gLing pa* / ཁྲག་འཐུང་གླིང་པ་) and Kyabjé Düd'jom Rinpoche Jig'drèl Yeshé Dorje.
[21] WWII US 'M1 paratrooper bazooka bags' which were popular with hippies in the late 1960s and early 1970s.

Six: Dombhi Héruka – the tiger rider

Dombhi Héruka *(do mBi he ru ka /* དོམ་བི་ཧེ་རུ་ཀ*)* / Dol-ma'i Traktung *(gDol ma'i khrag 'Thung /* གདོལ་མའི་ཁྲག་འཐུང*)*
Disciple of: Virupa and Varuni
Varna by birth: Kshatriya

October 2019, pilgrimage to Bhutan.

Rinpoche had been camping with disciples at Bumdrak[1] above Taktsang—*The Tiger's Nest*—in Paro valley. Bumdrak refers to the footprints of a hundred thousand dakinis, left in the rock of the cave walls. These are now enshrined in Bumdrak Lhakhang. It was a long, steep, and hot day's trek to the campsite below the Lhakhang. At almost thirteen thousand feet, the nights were well below freezing – and that, combined with the altitude, can cause headaches at first.

After two nights camping, Rinpoche and disciples breakfasted early round the fire in the icy morning mountain air. They then walked the three-hour descent through pine and rhododendron forest to arrive at Taktsang from above, before the crowds started to ascend from the valley below. The Taktsang complex of white golden-roofed Lhakhangs appears to have sprung like a tiger from the sheer rock face. A splendorous awe-inspiring sight.

---

[1] *'bum brag /* འབུམ་བྲག — an important pilgrimage site, considered to be a second Tsa-ri *(tsa' ri gNyis pa /* ཙ་རི་གཉིས་པ — a sacred mountain in Tibet.). In the cliffs to the right of the lhakhang is the wrathful yidam Düdtsi 'khyilwa *(bDud rTsi 'khyil ba /* བདུད་རྩི་འཁྱིལ་བ / *Vajramrta* or *Amrita Kundali*). To the left are a hundred classes of wrathful and peaceful yidams. In the centre are the yidams of the kyil 'khor of Dorje Nam'jom *(rDo rJe rNam 'joms /* རྡོ་རྗེ་རྣམ་འཇོམས / *Vajra Vidarana*), the Thunderbolt Subjugator. Bumdrak is reached by walking from Ögyen Tsé-mo *(o rGyan tse mo /* ཨོ་རྒྱན་རྩེ་མོ*)* or 'ö-Sel gang *('od gSal gangs /* འོད་གསལ་གངས *)* for two and a half hours through a pleasant forest. From Bumdrak there is a panoramic view of the entire Paro Valley and the mountains beyond. One can descend to Paro via Chöchong tsé Rinpung Gompa, the ruins of Nen-ying Dzong, Sangchen Chö'khor and Kunga Chöling. The stream which flows down from Bumdrak is the source of the Shèlkar-chu which falls through the ravine next to Paro Taktsang.

There are four main Lhakhangs built around the eight caves where Guru Rinpoche practised in the 8th century, all of them interconnected by staircases of steps carved into the rock. Having spent time practising in the small Dorje Tröllö cave, Rinpoche visited the Hall of a Thousand Buddhas cut out of the cliff face, where a large statue of a tigress is located. The statue represents Tashi Khyi'dren, Guru Rinpoche's Bhutanese consort, who manifested as a tigress and flew to Taktsang carrying Guru Rinpoche on her back. As the midday heat and visitor numbers increased, Rinpoche began the descent from Taktsang intending to pause for a cold drink at the cafeteria perched on the mountainside almost half-way down.

Unbeknownst to Rinpoche, Khandro Déchen was hiding at the cafeteria to surprise him. She had been exploring a secret valley of Dorje Phagmo whilst Rinpoche was away at Bumdrak. Their reunion was delightful to witness, full of smiles and laughter. Rinpoche showed no signs of having spent two almost sleepless nights in the cold high altitude. Like Khandro Déchen, he wore his white to-nga[2] and tamchu[3] with the five-coloured garuda brocade gomthag[4], and five-element coloured shawl. He also wore his white, wide-brimmed, high-crowned 'Montana Crease' hat – which helped to keep off the intense sun.

As we sat on the cafeteria terrace with a view across to Taktsang, the vivid colours of Rinpoche's robes in the fierce sunlight—against the violet-blue sky backdrop—seemed almost luminous. A vividly clear reflection of Taktsang appeared in each lens of his round, frameless, mirrored sunglasses. Conversation turned to the vista before us with the colossal and remarkable self-arising face of Dorje Tröllö which fills the cliff face above Taktsang.

---

[2] *thod sNgags* / ཐོད་སྔགས་ – gö kar chang lo robe waistcoat.
[3] *grwa phyu* / གྲྭ་ཕྱུ་ – gö kar chang lo skirt.
[4] *sGom thag* / སྒོམ་ཐག་ – meditation belt or strap.

I remembered reading that Chögyam Trungpa Rinpoche had received the Dorje Tröllö empowerment from Dilgo Khyentsé Rinpoche in Bhutan, just before climbing to Taktsang to retreat there in 1968. It was during this stay at Taktsang that he received his seminal 'Sadhana of Mahamudra' gTérma.

"It's moving to think that Chögyam Trungpa Rinpoche most likely broke his journey and sat exactly here staring across at Tiger's Nest, just as we are now" I mused aloud. Rinpoche was quiet for a moment and then, smiling, said *"Indeed, yes – and of course… Chögyam Trungpa Rinpoche—as well as being an incarnation of Drukpa Künlegs* [5]*—was first an incarnation of Mahasiddha Dombhi Héruka – the tiger rider."*

"Ah yes… I'd forgotten that" I said. *"Doesn't Dombhi Héruka appear in Jomo Pema 'ö-Zér's gTérma of Mahasiddhas?"* I asked somewhat eagerly.

"Yes" Rinpoche grinned. *"I imagine… you might like me to relate that hagiography, whilst we wait for the others to join us?"*

As my gaze rested on Taktsang and the cliff face opposite, Rinpoche began the hagiography. Soon the chatter from tourists at tables around us, the clinks of cups and glasses, the distant shouts of horsemen, fell away and I was lost in the world of Dombhi Héruka, the Raja of Magadha. *"He was the Raja, but he was also secretly a Buddhist yogi who, as a young man, had become the disciple of Mahasiddha Virupa* [6]*…"*

From Virupa he had received transmission of Hévajra[7] and from that practice he had gained magical powers, yet he lacked nondual realisation.

---

[5] 'brug pa kun legs / འབྲུག་པ་ཀུན་ལེགས་ / 1455–1529.

[6] Virupa, son of King Suvarnachakra (gSer gyi 'khor lo / གསེར་གྱི་འཁོར་ལོ་) of Vesasa in eastern India. Court astrologers predicted his development of immense spiritual power. He was named Rupyachakra (dNgul gyi 'khor lo / དངུལ་གྱི་འཁོར་ལོ་) and entered Somapura monastery in Bengal as a child and received teachings from Vinitadeva and Jayakirti. He mastered the five major sciences and became a great scholar.

[7] The drüpthab or tantric method of Kya'i Dorje (dGyes rDo rJe rGyud kyi rGyal po / དགྱེས་རྡོ་རྗེ་རྒྱུད་ ཀྱི་རྒྱལ་པོ་ / Hevajratantraraja).

He was a good and just Raja but he kept his magical powers hidden, only using them for the benefit of his people. In spite of the fact that he was an excellent ruler, Magadha had deep and abiding social problems. Interpersonal disputes and feuds seemed unending. Larceny, burglary, and antisocial behaviour were common. Litigious disputes dragged on bringing poverty and despair. Dombhi Héruka attempted to ameliorate but his effort only seemed to keep the country from utter ruin.

Despite his wish to hide his magical powers, he decided that he could no longer keep them secret. He decided to have a great bell created which would stun the people into altered frames of mind. He designed the bell according to his knowledge of magical formulations and work began on casting the huge bronze bell. Once the bell was cast and burnished, he ordered it to be hung from the huge tree in the middle of his land. Through his magical powers he caused the bell to ring unexpectedly at various times throughout each day and gradually the people became peaceable and good natured. Feuds and disputes were amicably settled. Litigious suits ended and crime abated. Families learned to live harmoniously and trade began to flourish.

It was obvious to the people of Magadha that their Raja was a great yogi and their respect for him increased in proportion to the great benefit he brought them. More than this, they felt blessed to have such a ruler – as both prosperity and spirituality were served. The people had no doubt that their land was the most fortunate of any land anywhere.

Such was the growing affluence and fame of this marvellous land that it attracted wealth through trade with other lands. Soon many people made their way to Magadha: theatre companies, musicians, dance troupes, and all manner of artists. Amongst one troupe of wandering minstrels who performed at Dombhi Héruka's court, was a girl—by the name of Varuni—who attracted his attention. He recognised her immediately as a *natural dakini* [8] and asked her father for her hand in marriage.

---

[8] Tril-gyi Khandroma *(khril gyis mKha' 'gro ma* / ཁྲིལ་གྱིས་མཁའ་འགྲོ་མ་ / *akalpita dakini*).

Her father was shocked and confused, as a Raja could never marry an entertainer – a Dombhi. The social difference between them was so great that both the Raja and Varuni's father would be shamed. Had Varuni been of a higher class, it would have been a great honour and her father would have been overjoyed – but as it was, the proposition was impossible.

Dombhi Héruka considered the situation, and, knowing that money answers most problems, ordered that Varuni should be weighed and that her father should be given her exact weight in gold. He promised Varuni's father that the marriage with his daughter would be kept secret and thus no outrage or scandal would be experienced by the people of Magadha. At the prospect of such exorbitant wealth—and immunity from persecution—Varuni's father decided to accept the gold and leave Magadha with his troupe of minstrels as quickly as possible. Everything went well for Dombhi Héruka and Varuni accepted her new situation as entirely natural. As soon as they entered into kha-jor[9], Dombhi Héruka and Varuni attained nondual realisation, and they spent the following years in the experience of *spacious passion* in *passionate space*.

Their presence in Magadha made the magical bell superfluous. It ceased to ring and the people forgot that it had ever been installed in the great tree. Things being as they are however—by one means or another—someone espied Varuni in Dombhi Héruka's bedchamber and news of the Dombhi girl was bruited on every street corner. The people of Magadha—outraged and incensed—paid no thought to Dombhi Héruka's beneficent reign. They demanded that he abdicate as Raja. He acquiesced without argument and left Magadha with Varuni – enduring a hail of abuse as they left.

Rinpoche paused in the telling, and I commented how sad and tiresome it was to hear yet again about the problems caused by the restrictions of the varna system.

[9] *kha sByor* / ཁ་སྦྱོར་ – yoga of sexual union.

"Yes, but we still have varnas—or similar modalities—in the West today" Rinpoche responded. "We have our own version of Brahmins in the puritanical attitudes of the politically correct, spiritually correct, and those given to Nazi stances on dietary issues. The British class system is nowhere near as rigid as the varna system, but there are similarities which are useful to notice. As John Lennon sang 'Keep you doped with religion and sex and TV – and you think you're so clever and classless and free[10].' Although, today, religion hardly plays a part any more—in Britain at least—it has probably been replaced by sport. Sport is now more-or-less the religion of many people." Rinpoche shook his head sadly and shrugged. "Be that as it may, these hagiographies may seem part of an ancient Asiatic world, but aspects of an exclusionary class system still function in our lives. I lost a series of teenage lady-friends because I was working-class. Their parents forbade them to consort with me – one after another." Rinpoche gave a slight chuckle "I suppose it was my fault for choosing grammar school girls whose parents regarded me as a deranged long-haired working-class lout."

Khandro Déchen—laughing—continued "But you got your grammar school girl in the end!"

Ngak'chang Rinpoche smiled at Khandro Déchen "I certainly did!" and continued. "In terms of Vajrayana of course, a surprising percentage of Western spokespersons, authors, and teachers have private incomes."

"Do you resent that Rinpoche?"

"No" smiling and shaking his head "not in the least. I would never begrudge anyone their fortunate circumstances. If I were to suddenly inherit millions from a previously unknown relative, I'd be delighted. However, it's important—to me—to be able to show people that—anyone—can seek a Lama. Anyone can strive to access teachings and enter into practice. Anyone can manage time for retreats. You don't have to inherit money. My time on building sites, roadworks, and driving trucks was actually most helpful in terms of keeping my feet on the ground. It prevented me from creating a Himalayan dreamworld.

[10] John Lennon—*Working Class Hero*—1970

"It enabled me to converse with ordinary British people and deal with ordinary life in the West. It enables me now, to tell people that my life was not so different from theirs. I had no financial advantages. Being able to say that, of course, is a huge advantage because I can honestly say that there is no excuse for anyone *not to do more-or-less what I have done. The times have changed and Lamas such as Kyabjé Künzang Dorje Rinpoche are no longer as available as they were then – but anyone who endeavours, will be rewarded for their persistence."*

"Yes" chuckled Khandro Déchen *"…'endeavour to persevere'*[11] *has been an approach Rinpoche has often advocated."*

"Quite so." PAUSE *"You see… I'm not even intellectually gifted. In fact, I have a horribly low IQ. I failed most examinations at school other than English, Art, and History."* PAUSE *"I wasn't even allowed to take Mathematics 'O' Level, because it was deemed a waste of the school's money. So… you don't even need to be that bright."*

"You do need enthusiasm and devotion however" added Khandro Déchen *"and natural intelligence and insight grow from that."*

"Thus, have I heard" Rinpoche smiled. *"But to return to Dombhi Héruka, what is interesting about this hagiography is that Varuni belonged to an unusual varna."* PAUSE *"In all the translated hagiographies relating to Dombhi Héruka, Varuni is not given a name. She is merely described as a Dombhi which they interpret as a 'low caste woman' – that is to say, a Shudra. Dombhis however, were not Shudras. They were a varna of their own – a varna primarily of entertainers and musicians. As Shudras they would not have been allowed to perform in royal palaces. They were therefore evidently of higher varna than Shudras – possibly equating to Vaishyas. They were itinerant performers and travelled all over the Indian subcontinent and the Himalayas. They were, in fact, the origin of the Romani peoples who spread throughout the East and into Europe."*

---

[11] A quote from the Clint Eastwood movie *The Outlaw Josey Wales* – spoken by the character Lone Wattie, acted by Chief Dan George.

"And you said that Varuni was recognised by Dombhi Héruka as 'a natural dakini', Rinpoche. Can you say what's meant by that?"

"It means that she had a high propensity for realisation."

"But doesn't everybody have the potential for realisation?"

"Yes…" Rinpoche mused *"because we're all beginninglessly nondual. Occasionally however, there will be people who manifest this naturally – without practice. That phenomenon is bound to occur."*

After a moment of reflection, I said *"I've heard you talk about 'natural sages' before. I think you said that Chhi'mèd Rig'dzin Rinpoche used that term."*

"Yes" Rinpoche mused. *"In Tibetan the word for 'natural sage' is trang-trong[12] or 'rishi' in Sanskrit."*

"Ah… interesting – but you don't really hear people talking about 'natural dakas'. Dakinis, yes. Dakas, no."

"That is merely the cultural male bias" Rinpoche answered with a weary shake of his head. *"There is no other reason."* PAUSE *"There are many people who'd say otherwise – but that's the real reason. Our society accords a great deal of value to female beauty – far more than to male beauty. There are male pinups perhaps but nothing in comparison to the adoration of female pinups. There was the 'Miss World' competition but there wasn't a 'Mr. World' competition. There was 'Mr Universe', but it had nothing like the universal exposure of Miss World, and nothing like the same prestige. And so, we have something similar here. And it arises for the same reason."* PAUSE *"However, the Tibetan word for dakini is 'khandroma' but if you leave off 'ma'—the female suffix—as most people do, a khandro could be either male or female."*

"Yes" I responded. *"I remember Künzang Dorje Rinpoche saying that."*

"Indeed. Kyabjé Künzang Dorje Rinpoche often drew attention to the authentic meaning of Vajrayana.

[12] *drang srong* / དྲང་སྲོང་

"He was always extremely precise – and always pointed out the importance of gender equality. He said that we should not mistake culture for Vajrayana, and that we should not import cultural prejudice against women. Our female ordainees should wear the white robes even though it was culturally unacceptable in Tibet. 'In the West' he said 'you are free to wear whatever you like, and it is important that both men and women wear the gö kar chang lo. Here there are social restrictions – but they are not *Vajrayana.' Künzang Dorje Rinpoche made a strong point of that."* PAUSE *"So, anyhow… when the Raja and Varuni left Magadha"* Rinpoche continued *"the son of Dombhi Héruka's elderly cousin was made Raja and the people—idiots—appeared entirely satisfied…"*

On the point of Dombhi Héruka and Varuni leaving the palace, the great bell cracked with an ominous discordant clang, and from that point Magadha degenerated slowly into disharmony, disagreement, and discord. The erstwhile social problems re-emerged. The former interpersonal disputes and feuds erupted. The prior miseries of larceny, burglary, and antisocial behaviour again became common – as did the lengthy litigious disputes. Magadha was plunged into poverty, despair, and sundry dreadful debacles.

The people—stupid, narrow-minded, and bigoted as they were—had sufficient intelligence to realise what they had lost when Dombhi Héruka and Varuni had left the country. A search was soon instigated – but no trace of them could be found. They searched further and further into the remote areas beyond their borders and finally found them in a glorious glade surrounded by wild and dangerous creatures – all of whom appeared entirely peaceful. The closest creatures were two enormous tigers with eyes that glittered. On seeing the idiots from Magadha, the tigers roared with such violence that the people threw themselves on the ground in fear. There, prostrate, they were enveloped by huge snakes who coiled round them, imprisoning them in their reptilian coils. Dombhi Héruka and Varuni made a series of gesticulations with their hands, and the snakes withdrew and the tigers ceased to roar.

There was silence for a moment, so I asked *"What is the importance of the people from Magadha finding Dombhi Héruka and Varuni displaying this remarkable affinity with tigers – their ability to communicate so consummately with animals?"*

"It's more that they find them living in the natural world and able to exist in it without creating a superstructure" Rinpoche replied. *"There are no houses. There's nothing that people usually build or establish. Dombhi Héruka and Varuni have moved outside the parameters of situations where there have to be infrastructures, superstructures, and an array of organisational procedures. There is no trade, commerce, street lighting, or sewage system… This is in sharp contrast to the people of the town with their establishment, management, administration, government, and state. Dombhi Héruka and Varuni appear—from—the natural state."* Rinpoche smiled and continued. "

So the tigers roared and Dombhi Héruka asked *"Why have you come here? Do you wish to cast us from this glade as you cast us from Magadha?"*

At this the idiots of Magadha felt deeply ashamed and admitted their idiocy and the enormity of their ingratitude. *"Forgive us—for we are idiots—we beg you to return. The new Raja —although a good man—has no power to change our lives and Magadha has sunk into a state of poverty."*

"So you are idiots?" asked Dombhi Héruka.

"Yes, Lord and Lady, we are idiots, and… there is no help for us if you will not return."

"But if you are idiots…" asked Varuni *"… then for what reason should we not see your request as idiocy?"*

"We are not 'wicked idiots', Lady, we are 'well-meaning idiots' – and maybe you know what is best for us, despite our idiocy."

"That is a good answer, idiots of Magadha" laughed Dombhi Héruka. *"So… you wish us to return – but how will the new Raja feel about that? Will he not object?"*

"The new Raja is not an idiot. He himself is searching for you – to plead with you to return and be the Raja of the people of Magadha again, even though we are idiots."

"But isn't Varuni still a Dombhi? And will this not still be disgusting to you all?"

At this question the idiots of Magadha all wept and wrung their hands in shame about how they had acted.

"We did not know that Varuni was a Mahasiddha—that you were Mahasiddhas—because we are idiots."

"How is it… that idiots now know this?" asked Varuni.

"Because we saw what Magadha was before you left and we see what it has become."

"That is a good answer, idiots of Magadha" smiled Varuni.

"Very well then. We shall return" announced Dombhi Héruka in a strong commanding voice. It filled the idiots of Magadha with trepidation. *"But!"* he continued *"you should expect our return on the next night of the dark moon!"*

The idiots of Magadha returned to their homes. The search was called off. Everyone was delighted to have their Raja and Rani return. Goodwill began to return to the country, even though they had not yet returned. The people became able to release the tight bonds of idiocy and started to become more peaceable and good-natured with each other. Feuds and disputes began to be settled. Litigious suits ended and crime abated. Families learned to live harmoniously and trade began to grow again.

On the day of the dark moon the sky was so overcast that dawn arrived later than usual, and night drew in faster. As soon as evening dissolved into the night a thunder storm of violent proportions commenced.

The thunder was of such magnitude that people had to protect their ears. Then, suddenly—from out of the nearby jungle—Dombhi Héruka and Varuni appeared under a dazzling sky lit by lightning. They were each naked but for entwined serpents around their ankles, wrists, upper arms, throats, and waists. Each rode a tiger and each tiger roared louder than the thunder. They carried enormous snakes as living whips. The spectacle was so terrible that people covered their eyes and ears. Suddenly the storm abated. An eerie silence ensued, in which Dombhi Héruka announced *"You wanted us back! So now we have returned!"* Then again, the tigers roared and the lightning flashed in the sky.

Varuni laughed *"What do you have to say to us now, idiots of Magadha?"*

The idiots were shocked and replied *"We wished you back as you were before: peaceful, gentle, and wise."*

"Ha!" shouted Varuni. *"The peaceful, gentle, and wise Raja and Rani were the ones you banished from the land! Will you now banish them from the land again merely because they display their visionary nature?"*

The people, in spite of their fear, assured Dombhi Héruka and Varuni. *"No—please remember we are idiots—and do not be offended by our idiocy. We do not wish to banish you no matter how wrathful you appear – and even if you ride your tigers through the streets."*

"In that case… we shall stay" said Dombhi Héruka *"but… you must become tantrikas. You must accept the fourteen root vows, or else your presence will be incongruous – and eventually, when you have forgotten your previous misery, you will wish to banish us again."*

The idiots of Magadha were troubled and perplexed and begged for some other way of keeping Dombhi Héruka and Varuni with them. They claimed to be unable to become tantrikas.

Six: Dombhi Héruka – the tiger rider

They claimed to be merely members of the three varnas: Kshatriyas, Vaishyas, and Shudras – and even the Brahmins could not conceive of anything other than urbane priesthood.

"In that case…" said Dombhi Héruka in a gentler tone *"… we cannot stay amongst you."*

At this, the idiots wailed and some threw themselves on the ground in misery.

"Before we go…" Dombhi Héruka smiled *"… you must know that the knowledge of living in peace and harmony is already within you. Even before we returned you had improved your miserable lives. So our advice to you is simply this: continue as you were before the night of the dark moon arrived."*

The idiots looked utterly miserable – so, noticing this, Varuni said *"If it helps you – you may turn your minds to us and you will find that your minds are distanced from derangement."*

At that Dombhi Héruka and Varuni's tigers reared, span, and careered into the jungle with their terrifying riders laughing loudly on their backs. After that day, Magadha continued to improve. It never became as prosperous and harmonious as it was when Dombhi Héruka reigned – but it never degenerated as it had done before.

The hagiography ended. I became aware of the cafeteria bustle around us, but as the group and guides were not yet all gathered, I made the most of the time to ask more. *"This is the first of the hagiographies I've heard where the protagonist is actually a tantrika already. He's already attained relative siddhis – and although he lacks nondual realisation at the outset, he achieves that ultimate siddhi once he meets Varuni. And he doesn't meet a teacher, other than Varuni."*

"Yes!" Ngak'chang Rinpoche announced with a broad grin. *"This is important – although, of course, he had previously been the student of Virupa.*

"With regard to Varuni however, I should point out that it is often the consort— *of both yogis and yoginis—who provides the final impetus for realisation. I would say —personally—that it would be difficult to be a real vajra master without a consort – without a sangyum or sangyab."*

Rinpoche then indicated—with a movement of his hand and inclination of his head—that I should formulate a question. *"I'm wondering if the hagiography is therefore less about Dombhi Héruka himself and more about the rôle of the vajra master?"*

"I'd say that it concerns how people perceive Vajrayana" Rinpoche answered. *"If you compare this hagiography with Chögyam Trungpa Rinpoche's life, you will see a striking parallel. It was when Chögyam Trungpa Rinpoche took his consort* [13] *that his teaching life really blossomed. Whether the situation described is* 10th *century Kashmir or* 20th *or* 21st *century Britain, there is no difference in terms of there being those who are open to Vajrayana and those who are frightened by it. There are a fair few Western Buddhist teachers who are frightened by it and attempt to make it conform to Sutrayana. This is not new however – it was attempted at the beginning of the 'second spread' of Buddhism in Tibet."* PAUSE *"So, anyway – in the same way in which Dombhi Héruka—replete with consort—quits the royal court for the wilds of the forests, Chögyam Trungpa Rinpoche—replete with Lady Diana—quit the timorous company of the 'theosophically-oriented Buddhists' in Britain, for the relative freedom of America. So, how people perceive Vajrayana is important at this particular time, in terms of the fact that many don't really want it."* Rinpoche grinned *"Some* people really *don't* want it.*"*

---

[13] Lady Diana Mukpo—the Sakyong Wangmo *(sa sKyong dBang mo* / ས་སྐྱོང་དབང་མོ)—was born in Britain in 1953. She attended Benenden School until the age of sixteen when she left to marry Chögyam Trungpa Rinpoche. She moved to the United States in 1970, and remained with Trungpa Rinpoche until his Mahaparinirvana in 1987. During their marriage, she pursued intensive study of dressage. She is now the owner and director of *Windhorse Dressage*, and travels and teaches dressage throughout North America.

"Mainly" Khandro Déchen laughed *"it's the 'mindfulness' people*[14] *and 'Protestant Buddhists'* [15] *who don't want it."*

"Many Western Buddhists" added Rinpoche *"especially those with New Age tendencies, see Vajrayana merely as 'Sutrayana with pictures' or 'Sutrayana with magic' – and with the Lama who somehow acts as an ever-loving parent."* Rinpoche shook his head wearily. *"They don't want Vajrayana because it's disquieting. Vajrayana is politically, philosophically, and psychologically uncomfortable."*

"There are probably not many" continued Khandro Déchen *"who would have endured Kyabjé Künzang Dorje Rinpoche in his wrathful mode. People seem to love hearing about Rinpoche being shouted at every day…*[16] *but if it came to experiencing it themselves – they would run away."* PAUSE *"I feel that this is the important message of this account."*

"This is probably true of any religion" Ngak'chang Rinpoche continued. *"It's what confused me as a child. I was dragged to church and the vicar would say 'Love thy neighbour as thyself.' Then we'd go home and ignore it. The vicar would say 'Be decent to other people. Be like the Good Samaritan.' Everyone would listen. They'd agree that it was a good thing to hear – but apparently, they felt excused from living it. This confused me, I wanted to know why people didn't act on what the vicar told them. If that's what we were supposed to do, why didn't we do it? Why did we go to listen and ignore what we heard? I couldn't understand that. And no one could explain it to me – because they were all busy being evasive, dissembling, and prevaricating. I was never answered because the question was too embarrassing. So, this account highlights that problem."*

---

[14] 'Mindfulness' is a system conceived by Satya Narayana Goenka (1924–2013). The popularisation of mindfulness as a commodity has been criticised as a marketing strategy. Psychologist Thomas Joiner argues that mindfulness meditation has been corrupted for commercial gain by self-help celebrities, and suggests that it encourages unhealthy narcissistic and self-obsessed mindsets.

[15] Protestant trends in Buddhism date back to the late 19th century – inspired by modern movements in Japan and Thailand. This trend has developed in the West and led to an antipathy to religious forms, lineage, empowerment, transmission, and the rôle of the vajra master.

[16] See: Ngakpa Chögyam—*Wisdom Eccentrics*—Aro Books Inc.—2011

"And then all the local people want Dombhi Héruka to put things right for them, when it all goes wrong" I said *"but they can't really contend with how he is?"*

"Yes" Rinpoche smiled *"and they can't see that those two facts are interrelated."*

I had an immediate question *"Even when they say 'Oh, actually, we really want you to come back, and we'll cope with how you are' – they won't take the fourteen root vows. Which is—all—he says they have to do… isn't it?"*

"Yes" Rinpoche replied. *"Without that commitment he knows that they can always change their minds. Then the problem would be back where it began."*

"Is that saying that you can only really be a tantrika if you take the fourteen root vows?"

Khandro Déchen nodded.

"And is that something that you would say?"

"Certainly" Rinpoche nodded. *"So those ostensible Vajrayanists who have issues with the vajra master, are breaking the first and second root vows."*

At this point, all the students had been accounted for and we started to make our way down the mountain path. The coach awaited us in the valley below. Everyone walked at their own pace, in their own time. Conversations and mantra recitation occurred naturally, as we came together for stretches, or drifted apart. I was enjoying the pine trees with their lichen decorations. I enjoyed the copper-coloured path beneath my feet. I was still thinking about the hagiography, when I found myself walking alongside Rinpoche and Khandro Déchen. As we neared the stream on the lower slopes I said *"In all the other hagiographies from the gTérma that I've heard, there are men-ngag-dé instructions, either in the form of songs of realisation or they are obvious within the text. That doesn't seem to be the case here. There's just the instruction to take the fourteen root vows – take them, or don't take them. Take it or leave it, in fact. Is there no more instruction than that because there's not much else to say?"*

"*Yes*" Rinpoche replied. "*The idiots of Magadha are too consumed by their own neuroses for any more instruction than that to be useful. Any instruction has to be short, simple, straightforward. Either take on this practice, or not.*" PAUSE "*And, you know, that choice can be presented as me-ngag-dé. Take it or leave it. This or that. Here or there. Come or go. Yes or no.*"

"*We have found*" Khandro Déchen added "*that people often make themselves miserable by wanting 'this'—* **and** *'that'. No matter how many times we tell them. No matter how many times the world tells them 'You can either have 'this'—*or *—'that'; you can't have 'this'—*and*—'that.' They think there's a 'workaround'. We knew one woman who thought there was a workaround for everything – but it was always someone else who had to pick up the bill, or was otherwise, discommoded, inconvenienced, or discomforted.*"

Rinpoche and Khandro Déchen stopped walking for a moment and looked back up the track to see how the others were progressing. Khandro Déchen turned to me "*We even have students who struggle with understanding why they can't have 'this' and 'that'. They employ 'confusion' to avoid having to choose. Sometimes it's just to make themselves appear more 'interesting'. 'I'm confused, therefore I'm interesting.' And what we basically have to tell them, is 'Our main instruction to you is: stop being confused. If you can't decide between 'this' and 'that', toss a coin. It doesn't matter which way the coin falls, just do it, be it, take it or leave it – but get on with it. We're not interested in hearing lengthy discourses on self-created confusion'.*"

Rinpoche laughed "*That is—exactly—how it is.*"

On hearing that, I decided I might not voice any more confusion about the hagiography but Rinpoche continued "*So, this is what is happening with Dombhi Héruka and the idiots of Magadha. He tells them 'You have a problem. You can get over this problem, if you want – but you cannot hang on to what you want—and—get over the problem.' Dombhi Héruka presents the equation absolutely simply. They can escape from confusion by making a decision. If they don't like what the decision means, they have to ask themselves whether they like the opposite?*

"If the idiots say 'I want to escape from the problem, but I don't want 'this' to be the solution' – then there's no way out of that."

"And there's no negotiation" added Khandro Déchen. "Time to defæcate or dismount the commode."

Time to get on the bus, it seemed – as we had reached the vehicle park.

Seven: Saraha – consort of the fletcher's daughter

Saraha *(sa ra ha / ས་ར་ཧ)* / Da'nun *(mDa' bsNun / མདའ་བསྣུན)*
Disciple of: Khandira
Teacher of: Sarvaripa
Varna by birth: Brahmin

Yonphula in Trashigang, in the far east of Bhutan.

We had flown from Paro to Yonphula airport which comprises one room and a short runway carved out of the steep mountainside. At 9,000 feet it is enveloped in cloud and mist for most of the year. The precarious location and capricious weather mean that even on a clear sunny day there are only a few hours a day when landing or take-off are possible. The 45-minute flight in the small twin engine turboprop æroplane can be both breathtaking and hair-raising for most – other than Lamas. There were stunning views of the mountains and valleys below as we traversed the width of the country, and an arresting return to earth. We were heading towards Bartsham[1] to stay at Chador Lhakhang[2]. We took a detour however, to meet up with our friend Lama Dawa Zangpo and his ngakpa students in Bré-kha.

Bré-kha 'ö-Sel Chöling is known locally as the 'yogi gompa'. It is small and remote and was founded by Ngak'chang Rinpoche's first root Lama, Kyabjé Düd'jom Rinpoche Jig'drèl Yeshé Dorje and then developed by his son Dung-sré Thrin-lé Norbu Rinpoche. When Ngak'chang Rinpoche and Khandro Déchen's dear friend, Lama Tharchin Rinpoche, visited Bré-kha for the funeral of Thrinlé Norbu Rinpoche he declared that Bré-kha was the same as Bodhgaya in India. He said that it was the cradle of the Düd'jom gTérsar lineage.

---

[1] *bar tshams* / བར་ཚམས
[2] *phyag rDor lha khang* / བར་ཚམས་ཕྱག་རྡོར་ལྷ་ཁང

Bré-kha is currently under the care of Düd'jom Rinpoche's grandson, Dung-sré Garab Dorje Rinpoche, who was born and lived his early life there.

A small group of young ngakpas are in training at Bré-kha. It was wonderful to enjoy lunch with them in the shrine room. It was marvellous to receive transmission of Dung-sré Thrin-lé Norbu Rinpoche's gTérma melody of Dorje Tsig dün[3]. Shortly before we clambered aboard the coach, we were taken to visit the old inner gompa at Bré-kha where Düd'jom Rinpoche had practised and given transmission all those years ago. The shrine room is small and dark with worn wooden floorboards and walls, redolent of another age of the world. There is an old photograph of Düd'jom Rinpoche on the shrine. It was a moment of perfect poignancy watching Rinpoche, with tears in his eyes, bow and touch his forehead to the image of his root Lama. Then smiles and goodbyes – and we were back on the road to make Bartsham before nightfall.

The distance to be covered was not so great but the roads in this part of the country are only partly formed. The ground is uneven and the travelling slow. Landslides that block the way completely are common and bring journeys to a halt until a way through is cleared. But this time it was a burst tyre on the Toyota Landcruiser which brought Rinpoche and Khandro Déchen to a standstill. Our friend and driver, Ga-jé, embarked on repairing the tyre. Rinpoche and Khandro Déchen stood on the side of the road whilst he worked, gazing into the vast forested valley below. As I went to speak to them—and check on progress—I became aware of shouts and singing reaching us from a gap in the trees. Despite being in remote, seemingly uninhabited woodland, it appeared we had come upon an archery match.

---

[3] *tshig bDun gSol 'debs* / ཚིག་བདུན་གསོལ་འདེབས — the seven-line invocation of Guru Rinpoche.

Local mountain villagers had met up for a tournament on the most unlikely of archery fields – two hilltops on opposite sides of a deep valley. Archery was designated Bhutan's national sport in 1971, but their love of archery dates back two thousand years or more. For the Bhutanese archery is much more than a sport. The symbolic and religious significance of the bow and arrow are associated with both Drukpa Künlegs and with the legendary assassination of the apostate 10th century Tibetan king, Langdarma. Lhalung Pelgyi Dorje[4], a Buddhist yogi—performing the Black Hat Dance for Langdarma—used the occasion to whip out the bow and arrow secreted inside the large sleeves of his ceremonial dance costume. He then assassinated the apostate and made it possible for the religion of Vajrayana to be practised again. It is somewhat marvellous that the incarnation of Lhalung Palgyi Dorje—gTértön Drukdra Rinpoche[5]—is now a personal friend of Ngak'chang Rinpoche and Khandro Déchen. He is the son of Kharchen Rinzin Wangchuk Rinpoche[6] who is also a personal friend. Both Lamas are Bhutanese and Kharchen Rinpoche resides—at the time of writing—with his wife Déma Kèlsang[7] and daughter Ayu Kèlsang[8] in Colchester, England.

Village tournaments like the one we were watching now involve more than shooting arrows. Each team has their own group of dancers and singers who not only cheer and celebrate their archers' aim, but also taunt and distract their opponents as they take aim.

[4] *lha lung dPal gyi rDo rJe* / ཧླ་ལུང་དཔལ་གྱི་རྡོ་རྗེ — one of the 25 disciples of Guru Rinpoche.
[5] *gTer sTon 'brug dra rin po che* / གཏེར་སྟོན་འབྲུག་དྲ་རིན་པོ་ཆེ — the incarnation of Lhalung Pelgyi Dorje. His direct previous incarnation was Ögyen Dro'dül Thrin-lé Kunkhyab *(o rGyan gro 'dul phrin las kun khyab* / ཨོ་རྒྱན་གྲོ་འདུལ་ཕྲིན་ལས་ཀུན་ཁྱབ).
[6] *mKhar chen rin 'dzin dBang phyug* / མཁར་ཆེན་རིན་འཛིན་དབང་ཕྱུག) – the incarnation of Yeshé Tsogyel's brother, Kharchen Pelgyi Wangchuk *(mKhar chen dPal gyi dBang phyug* / མཁར་ཆེན་དཔལ་གྱི་དབང་ཕྱུག), who was also one of the 25 disciples.
[7] *bDe ma bsKal bZang* / བདེ་མ་བསྐལ་བཟང
[8] *A g.Yu bsKal bZang* / ཨ་གཡུ་བསྐལ་བཟང — who is the incarnation of Ayu Khandro Dechen dPaldrön *(A g.Yu mKha' 'gro bDe chen dPal gron* / ཨ་གཡུ་མཁའ་འགྲོ་བདེ་ཆེན་དཔལ་གྲོན), an important female Lama of Namkha'i Norbu Rinpoche.

They use wild songs and dances. Family members and friends join in too, so it's much more than a competition, it's a whole festive social event and can go on for many hours, or more often, days. We could hear the singing now and a kind of howling each time a target was hit.

The two wooden targets are traditionally placed almost 500 feet apart and the 13 archers of each team take it in turn to shoot pairs of arrows at the target at the opposite end of the range. In this match the arrows were being shot through the trees and right across the valley. It was remarkable to see them cover such a distance and still hit the small painted targets. Through the pine branches we caught glimpses of the colourful ghos[9] worn by the archers, and their bamboo bows and patterned quivers. The arrows appeared to be fletched with bird feathers which streaked colour across our vision with each arrow's flight. We couldn't help but laugh and join in with cheering when we heard the raucous singing celebration that ensued when the bullseye was hit.

At that point Ga-jé called that the tyre was fixed and as we turned away from the vista of the tournament below us Rinpoche said *"Of course, Düd'jom Rinpoche was an incarnation of Saraha the archer."* He paused. *"There's the hagiography of Mahasiddha Saraha—consort of the fletcher's daughter—from Jomo Pema ö-Zér's gTérma, if you'd like to hear it?"* Rinpoche raised his eyebrows in question. I felt that I certainly would like to hear it, so I joined them in the Landcruiser and settled to listen as we resumed our potholed way.

"Pal Da'nun[10]*—Saraha—was born in Bhadrak* [11] *in Orissa. That is called Odisha now. His mother was a natural dakini. He had many spiritual advantages and was imbued with the qualities of a dPa-wo*[12]*…"*

---

[9] *bGo* / བགོ་ – the gho is the traditional national dress for men in Bhutan.
[10] *dPal mDa' bsNun* / དཔལ་མདའ་བསྣུན་
[11] Bhadrak is an ancient area noted for Buddhist relics of the 7th and 8th centuries discovered in: Dipada and Solampur; the villages of Dhamnagar; Buddhist caves in Sarisua Hill, Kupari; and, the temple of Biranchinarayan in the village of Palia.
[12] *dPa' bo* / དཔའ་བོ་ / *daka* – warrior, hero.

Through his innate talents and assiduous practice, he attained all the relative siddhis. He lacked the ultimate siddhi however, and thus, although possessed of profound wisdom and unshakable equilibrium, he failed to remain in the nondual state.

This was no terrible problem, as he was a young man and had many years to attain the final fruit of practice. Unfortunately however, he was born into the Brahmin varna in a land that followed the Tirthika[13] persuasion. Like many Buddhists of that time—who lived in such areas—he was obliged to give the external appearance of a Hindu Brahmin priest, whilst practising Buddhism in secret – and internally in terms of his perceptual faculties. Although he gave no obvious external signs that he was not a Tirthika, the other Brahmin priests were suspicious of him. Somehow, his face didn't fit. His mien was slightly awry in ways which were not simple to describe. The Tirthikas[14] may have been deluded—ensnared in their own casuistry—but they were astute enough in their own way, to sense that all was not as it should be with Saraha. They discussed the matter together and decided to watch Saraha closely, in order to find out why he seemed alien.

After some months of spying on Saraha—via multifarious approaches—it was discovered that he partook of alcohol which he drank from a human skull bowl[15]. Of course, Saraha practised tsog'khorlo[16]. It is necessary to drink alcohol and eat meat—if only as tokens—if one is a tantrika. Even Buddhist monastics partake of alcohol within the context of tsog'khorlo, be it only a drop on the tip of the tongue, or a touch of a dipped finger on the top of the head. A gö kar chang lo practitioner however, may partake of alcohol every day as part of either their formal or informal practice.

---

[13] Sanskrit term referring to non-Buddhists.
[14] *mu sTegs can* / མུ་སྟེགས་ཅན་ or *mu sTegs pa* / མུ་སྟེགས་པ་ – those who adhere to the four denials: monism, dualism, nihilism and eternalism. Often mistranslated as 'heretic'.
[15] tödpa *(thod pa* / ཐོད་པ་ / *kapala)*.
[16] *(tshogs kyi 'khor lo* / ཚོགས་ཀྱི་འཁོར་ལོ་ / *gana puja)* – Vajrayana feast profferment.

Once the Tirthikas discovered that Saraha partook of alcohol, they sent a delegation to Raja Ratnapala demanding that Saraha should be made an outcast. *"We come to you as our Raja—because you are responsible for the purity of our religion—and this impious nonconformist pervert, Saraha, has dishonoured our varna by drinking alcohol. We therefore implore you to have him stripped of his fiefdom and exiled from your land."*

Ratnapala—although of the Tirthika persuasion—was only so at a social level. He was not keen therefore to banish Saraha. He also had some inkling that his accusers were envious of the thousand families of Saraha's fiefdom. Were he exiled, these accusers would stand to advance their own wealth and social standing. *"That is not such a simple matter. Saraha is a well-loved and widely respected lord of over a thousand households. To banish him would not be welcomed by those who look to his presence for their welfare. However, as it is my duty, I shall visit Saraha and bring your accusation to him – requiring him to desist."*

Ratnapala duly visited Saraha and asked him whether it was true that he drank intoxicants – because if it was, it was unacceptable.

"I have never imbibed any intoxicant" replied Saraha *"but I do not ask you to take my word for it. Gather those who have accused me and I shall prove that their accusation is false."*

The accusers, very many of them, gathered in the presence of Ratnapala, and Saraha proceeded to display a test or ordeal. *"If I am guilty as accused of imbibing intoxicants my hand will burn in this boiling oil. If I am innocent – it will not."* Saraha then plunged his hand into the boiling oil and when he retracted his hand it was untouched by the oil. *"If any of you would like to take the same test, you may maintain your accusation and I shall undergo another ordeal."*

None came forward. Seeing the ordeal and hearing Saraha's words, Ratnapala said *"Who still maintains that Saraha is guilty of drinking alcohol?"*

"*This was merely a conjuring trick!*" the accusers cried. "*We may not be able to emulate Saraha—because we are forbidden by our law's purity to perform conjuring tricks—so we still maintain our accusation. In any case this is only an external illusion – Saraha could not drink this boiling oil.*"

"*I could drink this boiling oil if you wished it*" replied Saraha "*but I can give a better proof than that.*" Saraha then took up a crucible of molten copper that he had prepared in a forge, and said "*If this molten copper kills me – then I am guilty. If it does not – then I am innocent.*" Then Saraha picked up the crucible—directly from the forge—and drank it in one gulp. He was unaffected by the molten metal and stood smiling at them all.

"*If any of you take this test – you may maintain your accusation and I shall undergo another ordeal.*"

None came forward and Ratnapala called out with some impatience "*Who can now maintain that Saraha is guilty of drinking alcohol?*"

"*This was black magic! We are pure and may never employ such evil arts! We know he drinks alcohol! This charade proves nothing!*"

"*If you say that was black magic…*" Saraha announced "*… I shall prove myself with ordinary engineering. Let the heavier on these scales be truthful – and the lighter, the liar.*"

The portliest, plumpest priest came forward but when he and Saraha sat side by side on the huge scales, Saraha sank to the floor. The priests gasped because they could see no trickery but their leader argued "*This proves nothing – because Saraha was heavier by virtue of the copper that is now in his belly. We maintain our position.*"

Saraha smiled. Ratnapala—impressed by Saraha's patience and equanimity and annoyed by the priests' intransigence—shouted "*How long will you weary me maintaining this ridiculous accusation against Saraha?*"

The priests looked nervous, aware that they were trying Ratnapala's patience. Their eyes were cast down but Saraha did not claim victory, he simply offered another ordeal. He opened a curtain and displayed a large tank of water, and said *"Let any liar sink immediately in this water – and let the one who speaks the truth be seen to float. It is pure water—as you may see—and so no Brahmanic rule will be broken. I will take the test last so that no one can claim that I have contaminated the water."* The accusers tested the water and it was indeed pure. This was a test they *were* willing to undergo – but each priest who entered the water sank like a stone and had to be pulled to the surface. Finally, Saraha plunged into the tank – but try as he would, he could not submerge himself.

"Enough already!" Ratnapala announced in a stentorian tone. He then decreed *"Even if Saraha does drink alcohol, he has power that not one of you can equal! Let him therefore drink or not drink as he pleases, and be satisfied that he is pure!"*

The priests could say nothing in support of their position and were sitting dejectedly in silence, when Saraha said *"Don't be downcast, my friends, for I have something I would like to offer you all."* Saraha then sang songs of teaching for the Raja, Rani, and the entire priesthood. They were so impressed by Saraha's teaching that they embraced Buddhism and the question of his drinking intoxicants or not was never again discussed.

Rinpoche paused as we bumped along and so I said *"I haven't yet heard any other hagiographies from Jomo Pema 'ö-Zér that have miracles like this."*

"No" Rinpoche replied. *"There are a few, but mainly the hagiographies in the gTérma don't particularly concern the overtly miraculous. This one is actually fairly similar to the commonly known hagiography of Saraha. What I'd say about that, is that the miraculous has always impressed people. That is the case now too. I hear it quite often when I'm listening to Radio 3. Some composer was basically an utter blaggard – but never mind, he created wonderful music. They ignore the fact that he was a vile, voracious, vicious, vituperate villain who brutalised his children.*

"That does—not—work for me. If I find out that someone wasn't pleasant, I immediately lose interest in their creativity. It always affects me in that way. I always liked a certain vocalist but when I started reading his biography I abandoned it after the first page because I wanted to continue liking him."

"Rinpoche is now attempting to forget that page" Khandro Déchen laughed. "He always prefers to think well of people."

"It's not always wise to think well of people" Rinpoche responded "but the alternative is unattractive." PAUSE "Be that as it may, for most people siddhis, magical powers, or capacities are more important than 'how they actually are'. So, because Saraha is able to accomplish these feats with molten copper, and vats of burning oil—and these other fellows can't—the Raja converts to Buddhism." Rinpoche shook his head. "This *is* not a good reason for becoming a Buddhist."

"It's interesting" continued Khandro Déchen "to see how we act in this way, just as much as they did in ancient India. You'll hear about Lama such-and-such, who must be realised because he can perform this, that, and the other miracle. But it doesn't really mean much, you know. Because someone can do something unusual doesn't necessarily mean that person has realisation. It's more miraculous to be kind and happy all the time. It's more miraculous to be a thoroughly decent, ethical, and honourable human being – sans remission. It's more miraculous to be an artist in every moment – and to witness the miraculous nature of the phenomenal world."

"You'll also hear" added Rinpoche "about Lama such-and-such, who must *be* realised because he has twenty or thirty thousand students – and has a book that sold three million copies in thirty-four languages—barring Inuit—in eighty countries. But that also means nothing. Because someone becomes an international celebrity doesn't mean that person has realisation. There have been world acclaimed pop stars who have almost disappeared without a trace – but that says nothing about their music, either good or bad."

I sat with the reality of that as I stared out of the window at the miraculous passing trees.

As I was musing on the tendency in people to be impressed by circus-trick miracles, Rinpoche said *"Of course, I should point out that Künzang Dorje Rinpoche was a Vajrayana prodigy. Kyabjé Düd'jom Rinpoche requested him to take part in an experiment with two scientists. In one he remained under water for a humanly impossible length of time. This account is not that well known – because he made nothing of it. Like Düd'jom Rinpoche he was primarily concerned with teaching and giving transmission, but both were clairvoyant and both had foresight. With them, it was merely part of the normal flow of life. I don't often mention their miraculous capacities – because it wasn't something they emphasised. They both said 'These powers: if you have them, it's good – if you don't have them, it's good. What matters is residing in the nondual state.'"*

"So, siddhis—to them—were not of any great importance?" I enquired.

"No – not to any great extent. Künzang Dorje Rinpoche said that powers were often a matter which obsessed poseurs, tricksters, frauds, and charlatans. They were the ones who liked to talk about miracles. 'Khordong gTérchen Tulku Chhi'mèd Rig'dzin Rinpoche quoted Lérab Lingpa[17] *as saying 'I am not impressed by someone who can turn the floor into the ceiling, or fire into water. The real miracle is someone being able to liberate even one negative emotion.' He quoted that on almost every occasion when someone expressed too much interest in the miraculous."*

"Who was Lérab Lingpa?" I enquired.

"He was the previous incarnation of Khenpo Jig'mèd Phüntsog Rinpoche[18]. *Lérab Lingpa is widely known in the West as gTértön Sogyal. Khenpo Jig'mèd Phüntsog Rinpoche was the one and only incarnation of gTértön Sogyal Lérab Lingpa.*

---

[17] gTer sTon bSod rGyal las rab gLing pa / ་་་་་ / 1856–1926) – previously appeared as Vajragarbha *(who received Dzogchen from Küntuzangpo)*; Prajapati Gotami *(Buddha Shakyamuni's aunt and founder of the order of nuns)*; Nanam Dorje Düd'jom *(sNa nam rDo rJe bDud joms / ་་་་་)*; Tro'phu Lotsawa *(khro phu lo tsA ba / ་་་་)*; and, Rig'dzin Gödem *(rig 'dzin rGod lDem / ་་་་ / 1337–1408* – founder of the Northern gTérma tradition). Lérab Lingpa was born in 1856 in Upper Nyarong in Kham. His father was Dar-gyé *(zhi ba dar rGyas / ་་་)* from the Zhi-pa *(zhi ba / ་)* family and his mother was Ögyen Drölma *(o rGyan sGrol ma / ་་་)*.

[18] *jigs med phun tshogs 'byung gNas* / ་་་་་ / 1933–2004

"I know about gTértön Sogyal from Chhi'mèd Rig'dzin Rinpoche because his Tsawa'i Lama—Tulku Tsorlo[19]—was a heart son of gTértön Sogyal. Sogyal Lakar[20]—according to Chhi'mèd Rig'dzin Rinpoche and various other Nyingma Lamas—was merely a nepotistic choice… a Tibetan entrepreneur and sociopath, as you know."

"Yes… it would have been valuable if more people had been aware of that in the 1970s… "

"Quite so." PAUSE "After his success with miracles, Saraha became disconsolate because, although he had triumphed, the victory had been won through a display of relative siddhis…"

Although Saraha's siddhis were neither conjuring tricks nor black magic, they were not a display of the nondual state. His songs of teaching spoke of the nondual state – but he knew that he did not dwell there. Considering this, Saraha realised, that although he had not been exiled, he was obliged to exile himself.

He went to Ratnapala and said "I once had accusers who wished to exile me – but now I am free of all accusations but one."

"And what is this accusation, Saraha? I cannot believe that a saint such as you can possibly be guilty of anything. Who accuses you? Let them be brought here and put to ordeal!"

"My accuser stands before you Raja – and I accuse myself of failing to integrate with the nondual state."

"But what of your powers? Are these not proof of your realisation?"

---

[19] sPrul sKu tshul lo / སྤྲུལ་སྐུ་ཚུལ་ལོ་ – also known as Tsültrim Zangpo (tshul khrims bZang po / ཚུལ་ཁྲིམས་བཟང་པོ་)

[20] Sogyal Lakar (bSod rGyal bLa dKar / བསོད་རྒྱལ་བླ་དཀར་ / 1947–2019) was born to the Lakar family in Kham. The family were tobacco traders and possibly the richest family in Tibet. For details on Sogyal Lakar, see: Mary Finnegan and Rob Hogendoorn—*Sex and Violence in Tibetan Buddhism: the rise and fall of Sogyal Rinpoche*—Jorvik Press—2019.

"No Raja – sadly not. These are merely proofs of a certain level of practice—merely relative siddhis—and I must attain the unlimited siddhi: nonduality. So let my fiefdom be divided amongst my former accusers. My accusers were not liars."

"How can this be? I saw them all sink in the tank of water – and I saw you float."

"That is simple to tell. It is true that I drank alcohol – but it is also true that I never imbibed intoxicants. They did not sink because they lied – they sank because of their delusory views. What I imbibed never clouded my mind – therefore I was never intoxicated, even though I drank alcohol. I shall leave your land now, to seek a vajra master who will enable me to recognise the nondual state."

Rinpoche noticed something in the trees and peered out of the window for a few moments before continuing. "Ratnapala was deeply saddened to lose Saraha from his land – but such was his respect for him, that he allowed him to leave and divided his fiefdom as he had asked."

"This is making me wonder…" I pondered "if there's any point pursuing relative siddhis as a practitioner. Is there any value in that at all?"

"I would say" Khandro Déchen replied "that siddhis, capacities, skills, only have value if you make them valuable for others – in terms of actual help."

"You know" continued Ngak'chang Rinpoche "it always occurred to me that the Beatles were disappointing in not realising that a reunion concert could have raised millions for charity. It wouldn't have cost them anything apart from having to perform with each other. Maybe some wanted it – I will not judge them." PAUSE "When you don't use capacities for good… that is something I find indefensible. There are siddhis obtained through effort – and siddhis with which you are born. Different people have different capacities and certain aptitudes arise more naturally for some. Whatever capacity one has however, one has the responsibility to use it for good. I've been lucky…" Rinpoche grinned "because I have no natural capacities apart from being an echt fresser [21]. I could eat most people under the table. But apart from that, everything else has been hard work – with not a great deal to show for it."

---

[21] Yiddish – a consummate eater or gourmand.

Rinpoche smiled. *"I can play sub-mediocre guitar, and adequate professional harp[22] – but that's about it."*

"So would you say that relative siddhis are actually quite meaningless if one doesn't have… maybe not necessarily realisation… but at least altruistic motivation?"

"Yes" Rinpoche nodded. *"With regard to mundane siddhis, the same goes for celibacy."*

"People revere celibacy" Khandro Déchen continued *"because they feel that they couldn't take that step. We tend to revere that of which we feel incapable – or revere those who chose to do what we would not choose to do, such as three year, three month, three day retreats."*

"Whatever it is" added Ngak'chang Rinpoche *"whether in the magical or mundane categories – they're all capacities. It's not having them that's important – it's how we employ them. We either use them for the benefit of others, or we do not."*

"So, you could have magical siddhis and use them for the benefit of others" I queried "but still not have the ultimate siddhi?" Rinpoche nodded agreement *"Yes… but, the chances are…"* PAUSE *"… that if you're using siddhis for the benefit of others – then the ultimate siddhi might not be more than a couple of inches away."*

There was a long pause as I let that hit home and then the hagiography recommenced.

Due to the strength of his intention, Saraha found his vajra master—after some wandering in the wilderness—in a cave at Edakkal[23]. His vajra master proved to be Khandira, the daughter of a fletcher—called Isukhara—who had been apprenticed to her father in his craft.

---

[22] Diatonic Blues harmonica.
[23] The Edakkal Caves are two natural caves at a remote location at Edakkal, 13 miles from Kalpetta in the Wayanad area of Kerala, India, in the western Ghats. They lie 4,000 feet above sea level on Ambukutty Mala, near an ancient trade route connecting the high mountains of Mysore to the ports of the Malabar Coast. Inside the caves are pictorial writings that date to 6,000 BC. The Stone Age carvings of Edakkal are rare and are the only known examples in southern India.

Isukhara was a Buddhist yogi and he therefore welcomed Saraha into his family as his daughter's husband. Marrying a Shudra girl violated Saraha's varna – but, being Buddhist tantrikas, neither father, daughter nor Saraha were concerned with societal convention. In taking this step however, Saraha sealed his banishment at the same time as sealing his ultimate realisation.

Khandira taught Saraha the essence of practice through the metaphor of archery and the flight of an arrow:

> "If you wish to recognise the nondual state – consider the moment at which an arrow is released from the bow.
> If you release the arrow with premeditation – emptiness and form remain as if they were divided.
> Where there is no premeditation – the point at which the arrow is released cannot be found.
> There is the form of holding the arrow and the emptiness of having let it loose – but the instant of release cannot be identified as either.
> That moment cannot be found by seeking – because all seeking is form, and that which is sought is empty."

And thus, Saraha practised in order to realise the nondual state. Khandira supported him in his practice and prepared his food in order that he could devote all his time to following Khandira's instruction. On one occasion—when asked by Khandira what dish he would enjoy—Saraha requested radish curry. By the time it was ready to eat however, Saraha had entered a state of absorption in emptiness. His absorption lasted eleven days – and when he emerged from the empty state, he immediately enquired about the radish curry.

"This is pathetic!" Khandira admonished him. *"You sit in absorption in emptiness for eleven days – and radish curry is the first thought to arise! What 'emptiness' is this that clings to the concept of radish curry for eleven days?"*

Saraha felt ashamed of himself *"Yes – you are right in abjuring me. I was once proud of my siddhis – but they are of no use to me in recognising the nondual state. Should I go into solitude in the hills to practise there?"*

"What use would that be, Saraha?" Then she gave him teaching and transmission as follows:

> *"Seeking conventional solitude will not avail you of authentic solitude.*
> *Real solitude is the freedom found in retirement from duality.*
> *Resign the creation of self-identity. Let go of reference points.*
> *Quit the domain of differentiation between: this and that;*
> *Here and there; arriving and departing; confidence and confusion.*
> *Only then will you discover the nondual state.*
> *What use is there in going to the hills to dwell on radish curry,*
> *When you could think about it just as well here?"*

Saraha understood Khandira's teaching perfectly and entered into practice; and, by the time Khandira had cooked another radish curry, Saraha had recognised the nondual state.

As the account ended, I said *"I love the ending and Khandira's admonishment – that you don't have to go to the hills to find realisation. It seems like a cogent endorsement of the non-monastic style of practice – that realisation is possible anywhere."*

"But then we do also engage in solitary retreats" commented Khandro Déchen.

"How do you assess whether practising in the world would be more useful for you at a given point in time or whether you need solitary practice?" I asked. *"Or is it simply that you just need both?"*

"You need both" Khandro Déchen laughed. *"If you discover that—for the sake of your health—it's necessary to defæcate, the answer is not to spend the rest of your life on the lavatory. You defæcate when you need to defæcate – and when you don't need to defæcate you get off the toilet. That's all there is to know about that."*

"*Let's look at being a musician*" Ngak'chang Rinpoche continued. "*I can't speak for classical musicians, but I know that there's a certain degree of practice with which one has to engage as a Blues musician. Some practice will be solitary. You have to practise scales for example – but it's also equally important to rehearse with others and to perform live. So, there's private solitary practice, there are rehearsals with the band, and then there's the live gig. The live gig is not really the end result; it's actually part of the process. I watched a teaching tape from Jack Bruce*[24] *once, where he demonstrated all the baselines from the most popular Cream songs – and showed how they're played. And the interviewer at the end asks him if he has any advice to give and he says 'Don't spend too much time practising. Get out there on stage and play. Play in a band and learn from that.' I've found that to be entirely true.*"

"*Similarly*" added Khandro Déchen "*you could engage in lengthy solitary practice—feel quite Buddha-like in your serenity—and then leave your retreat to find that everyone annoys you. There have been a few people, to our knowledge, who have completed these long retreats—in one case, two* three*-year retreats back-to-back—who have then gone on to… behave rather badly.*"

"*So only ever practising in solitude…*" I asked "*would make it quite hard to gauge where you'd got to with your practice?*"

"*Yes. One of the togdens*[25] *from Tashi Jong*" replied Rinpoche "*told Khandro Ten'dzin Drölkar that he'd become a 'placid vegetable' in retreat.*"

"*It's understood in the Tibetan tradition*" added Khandro Déchen "*that you can just end up not achieving anything, if there's nothing that you come up against as a challenge.*"

"*Exactly*" chimed in Ngak'chang Rinpoche. "*Jack Bruce's advice wasn't 'Buy yourself a bass guitar and get straight up on stage, before you can play it reasonably well'. There's obviously a period where you have to practise. So, solitary retreat is important. In terms of Dzogchen however, it's a training. It's not the end result.*

[24] John Symon Asher Bruce (1943–2014) was a Scottish musician. He gained popularity as the primary lead vocalist and bassist of the rock band Cream. After the group disbanded in 1968, he pursued a solo career and also played with several bands.

[25] *rTogs lDan* / རྟོགས་ལྡན — a yogi or yogini with nondual realisation.

"If you make it the end result, then something is lost. Kyabjé Künzang Dorje Rinpoche said that when he heard of someone who'd spent their whole life in retreat, he tended to think that they can't have been that successful."

"Success" concluded Khandro Déchen *"means coming out of retreat and living in the world to be of benefit."*

We gazed out of the windows as a few wooden buildings started to appear dotted on the hillside. The beauty of Trashigang Dzong loomed from the clouds above us. As we drew to a stop on the steep streets of the nearby town it seemed an opportune moment to change vehicles and rejoin the others in the bus. As I was clambering out of the Landcruiser, Rinpoche said *"If you were a great musician, and you spent your life in your room practising, and there was nothing you couldn't play… if everything you played was perfect – but no one ever heard you… if you never performed for anybody…"*

"What use would that be?" smiled Khandro Déchen.

"Thank you – the analogy of the musician makes it clear."

"It's always useful to look at other spheres of life" continued Ngak'chang Rinpoche *"and ask what sense does this make for a mountaineer, sky-diver, scuba-diver, spelunker* [26]*, spin doctor, jockey, taxidermist, restaurateur, raconteur, rapporteur, prosateur, saboteur, poet, sculptor, scientist, nudist, florist, cellist, flautist, flagellant, astronaut, argonaut, oneironaut* [27]*, vyomanaut* [28]*, taikonaut* [29]*, cosmonaut* [30]*, cybernaut* [31]*, busker, bosun, bellhop, botanist, barber, ballerina, butler, pulmonologist, ophthalmologist, wainwright, wheelwright, playwright, cartwright, cooper, tinker, tailor, soldier, espionage agent, farmer, lyricist, locksmith, or escape artist?"* PAUSE *"There is no 'great divide' between these things, you know.*

---

[26] Cave explorer.
[27] One who practises lucid dreaming.
[28] Indian astronaut.
[29] Chinese astronaut.
[30] Russian astronaut.
[31] One who uses computer technology to experience virtual reality; Robert Thurman's translation of 'yogi'.

"If you practise, you practise. Whatever you practise there's a result – and if the result can't be seen… then what benefit is it to anyone but yourself?"

"Then you would be practising pratyekabuddhayana [32] – the 'solitary realiser'…" added Khandro Déchen "and if no one witnesses your solitary realisation – then there's no value at all."

---

[32] rang gyalwa'i thepa *(rang rGyal ba'i theg pa* / རང་རྒྱལ་བའི་ཐེག་པ) – the vehicle of those who practice for their own realisation, rather than for the benefit of all beings.

Eight: Sarvaripa – the deer hunter

Sarvaripa *(sha wa ri pa /* ཤ་བ་རི་པ *)* / Sabara Wangchuk *(sa ba ra dBang phyug /* ས་བ་ར་དབང་ཕྱུག *)*
Disciple of: Saraha and Nagarjuna
Teacher of: Khadgapa
Varna by birth: Shudra

Long Ashton Estate, Bristol.

Bower Ashton was the location of Bristol Art School where Ngak'chang Rinpoche studied and received his first-class honours degree in 1975. It was an illustration degree, but with the kindly and inspired mentorship of Derek Crowe[1]—the Head of the Department—Rinpoche created his own degree course: a synthesis of Fine Art Printmaking, Painting, Photography, and Sculpture.

The Art School was built in 1969 on land adjacent to Ashton Court Mansion and its surrounding estate—850 acres of rolling countryside—just two miles from the centre of Bristol. It is placed in a tranquil setting, amidst the vast parkland designed by Humphry Repton, the last great English landscape designer of the 18th century. There are seven miles of high walls and majestic gatehouses around the edges of the estate, with access roads taking you past the School of Art to the Grade 1 listed, somewhat labyrinthine mansion. The manor house can be traced back to the 6th century. The current Great Hall exactly matches the dimensions of the original Saxon Hall. The manor may well be even older, as there is mosaic evidence that a Roman villa also stood on the site.

Long Ashton Estate and the manor are mentioned in the Domesday Book of 1086.

---

[1] See: Doc Togden—*an odd boy*, volume IV—Aro Books WORLDWIDE—2017

The settlement of Estune, as it was known then, was shared between three landowners, the chief of whom was Bishop Geoffrey of Coutances. By the 13th century the manor had been acquired by another Norman, Thomas de Lyon, who rebuilt the property in 1290. In 1392 the Lyons were granted a royal licence to enclose their lands and create a deer park, one of the first in the country. The deer park still exists as 200 of the 850 acres of estate land to this day. And that was where we were headed.

Rinpoche and Khandro Déchen were visiting for the day, and we had decided on an autumn afternoon walk to Rinpoche's old haunt, to enjoy the ancient oaks and the fallow and red deer that freely roam the parkland. There are more than a hundred red deer on the estate and almost as many fallow deer. Rinpoche looked entirely at home as we strolled across the open grassland towards the more wooded area where the deer are often to be found.

Rinpoche wore a Hebridean Marl Harris Tweed three-piece suit, the jacket of which was almost a coat, as this is always his preference. Beneath he wore a white shirt and a green double-length cravat tied in a 'four-in-hand' knot. With his impeccably polished brown Grenson brogues and brown Montana Crease hat, I was inspired to say *"Rinpoche, you look every inch, Lord of the Manor."*

"My apologies" he laughed. *"I was hoping I'd look like a mad scientist."*

"We will have to research the appropriate attire for a mad scientist" laughed Khandro Déchen *"or, perhaps, game keeper?"*

"Of course, that's what I meant. I always get those two confused."

Under a flawless, ice-blue sky, we came across a large herd of fallow deer bathing in a welcome wash of autumn sun on the edge of the wood. Although they also looked entirely at home, fallow deer are not native to Britain – they were introduced by the Normans in the 11th century.

Eight: Sarvaripa – the deer hunter

They are handsome creatures, some with spotted coats, others plain and paler. We watched a large buck, almost white in colour, with wide, palmate antlers, browsing the bushes beneath a magnificent old oak. Deer grazing is used to control scrub encroachment on the estate, enabling wildflower meadows and rare species of orchids and other plants to flourish.

After watching the fallow herd, and enjoying the vista of the city below us, we followed one of the paths through the woods emerging again on to open parkland with the majestic sight of the red deer herd grazing right in front of us. There were both hinds and stags in the group, their spiky antlers sharply silhouetted against the clear sky. We paused at a respectful distance. Red deer are Britain's largest land animals and although the Ashton Court herd may not be wild, they're not tame. A fully grown stag can weigh up to nearly thirty stone. They are an intimidating sight at close quarters. As the deer here are no longer hunted —and due to their winter diet being supplemented with hay and sugar-beet—they tend to be larger than their country cousins. The males have larger antlers, and with the red deer, it is antler size which determines the *rank* of the stag. Twelve tines on the antlers makes him a royal stag. Fourteen tines is an imperial stag – and sixteen tines makes him a monarch. We had heard that currently the largest stag in the Ashton Court herd had 21 tines—putting him beyond all categories—and he sounded an almost mythical beast. Our eyes searched for him – and suddenly, there he was, right at the centre of the herd feeding peacefully amidst a harem of hinds. He stopped for a moment and stared directly at us, chewing nonchalantly like a gunslinger in a Western saloon bar. He was a city stag and maybe not the monarch of the glen – but he too had the air of lord of the manor.

After minutes of watching with fascination, we turned and settled on two thoughtfully positioned park benches to continue enjoying the herd.

I commented *"Deer parks make me think of Shakyamuni Buddha and his first teaching."*

Rinpoche responded with a nod of agreement. Then, grinning, he suggested *"Gazing at deer brings to my mind Mahasiddha Sarvaripa – the deer hunter. Shall we have the hagiography – one that doesn't involve Vietnam and an insane colonel? Or was that* Apocalypse Now?*"*

"Yes" I laughed *"that was* Apocalypse Now *– Colonel Eddie Kurtz?"*[2]

Rinpoche nodded and said *"I met someone quite like him in America some years back. He was certainly psychopathic – but he was no deer hunter."*

So there, sitting on the wooden bench in the deer park, we listened as the remarkable account began. *"Sarvaripa was a deer hunter. He was of the Sabara tribe of hunter-gatherers from the Vindhya Hills and the Deccan, and one day whilst ranging the hills in search of game, Sarvaripa met Saraha…"*

Saraha greeted him with surprising hauteur *"Hey! What sort of hunter are you, my fine feathered friend?"*

The Sabaras wore peacock feathers woven into their clothing – and Saraha appeared as if he was making fun of Sarvaripa.

"I am probably the greatest hunter of this age" sneered Sarvaripa.

"You don't say – you don't say" laughed Saraha. *"Of course, you know that is impossible."*

"And why would that be? I warn you, I like a joke as much as the next man – but I'll brook no impertinence."

"Far be it from me to be impertinent – but I speak as I do because my bowmanship has no rival in any land."

---

[2] Colonel Walter E Kurtz, portrayed by Marlon Brando, is a character from Francis Ford Coppola's 1979 film *Apocalypse Now*. Colonel Kurtz is based on a 19th century ivory trader, also called Kurtz, from the 1899 novel *Heart of Darkness* by Joseph Conrad.

"Those are hollow words, my friend..." replied Sarvaripa *"... and a man who uses hollow words is safe to speak as he chooses – as long as he knows he is merely a fool."*

"Really?" smiled Saraha. *"And why would that be?"*

"Because I do not make a practice of taking the words of a fool as an insult."

"Then I would suggest that you may consider yourself insulted."

"You are a brave man, at least..." Sarvaripa laughed *"... because unless I now see you demonstrate your skill, your life will not extend beyond the next few minutes."*

"Then we must have a contest of skill" smiled Saraha.

"Tell me what you can do and I will better it."

"Certainly!" grinned Saraha *"but first tell me how many deer you can shoot with one arrow?"*

"That question makes no sense. With one arrow I can shoot one deer. Do you presume to tell me that you can shoot more than one deer with one arrow?"

"Without a doubt. I can shoot a hundred deer with one arrow."

At this Sarvaripa laughed *"You are a jester—and you are impertinent—so I shall certainly end your life if you cannot prove yourself."*

"We shall travel further into the hills together then – and I will be happy to show you as soon as we find some deer."

With that they walked on together into the distant hills in silence and finally they came upon a large herd of deer – over a hundred. Sarvaripa said *"Yours is the more outrageous boast – so you must begin. I could shoot any of these deer, even those standing furthest from us. If you can shoot one, I will be surprised."*

At that Saraha fitted his arrow to the string of his bow and let it fly – directly into the zenith. All but three of the deer fell to the ground.

Sarvaripa stood and stared for a moment, incapable of speech. Finally, he asked *"Why did you leave three standing?"*

"Because you need to show me that you can shoot the furthest deer. There were 111 deer on that hillside and I shot 108. I would now like to see you shoot the furthest deer of the three remaining – unless you think you can take them all down?"

Sarvaripa fitted his arrow to the string of his bow and let fly. The furthest deer fell to the ground and the other two ran away. Sarvaripa had done what he claimed he could do but he was completely in awe of Saraha.

As we all gazed at the deer ranging across our view, Rinpoche ceased in his narration – and, after a moment of quiet, he turned *"Of course, it takes someone with skill to recognise higher skill. So even though I never became any great horseman, I found that the better I became, the more I could see the greater achievements of others. I became increasingly astonished by the skill of other riders."*

"Watching riders in Western movies" said Khandro Déchen *"jumping up onto a horse from the ground, or being pulled up by another rider at full gallop – now, when we watch such spectacles, we're in complete awe of what such riders accomplish."*

"Before riding a horse" Rinpoche continued *"I watched people performing these stunts, and it simply didn't register. I couldn't understand the level of skill required. It's only when one has developed a little skill oneself that one becomes aware of what highly skilful riders are accomplishing. Then one marvels at their remarkable level of skill. If one has no capacity at all in an area then one doesn't even register what one sees."* PAUSE *"And so, in terms of Sarvaripa, he is open to being impressed by Saraha because he knows that Saraha is beyond him. And Sarvaripa is sufficiently skilled and expert himself to be able to acknowledge that. This is why Saraha had to impress him. This is an example of putting siddhis to good use: displaying capacities for a valuable end."* PAUSE *"Kyabjé Künzang Dorje Rinpoche had been a great horseman in Tibet, and an accomplished archer. He encouraged me to learn to ride if ever there was the opportunity and I have always been grateful for that encouragement. However, to get back to the hagiography…"*

Eight: Sarvaripa – the deer hunter

Sarvaripa had done what he claimed he could do but he was completely in awe of Saraha, who said *"I see that impertinence is not your only skill – but you are a man of your word. I respect that."*

"Well... you are a man of your word too, Sarvaripa. You shot the furthest deer – and I respect that. Anyhow, now we must carry our deer home. I will bring my catch back and you will bring yours. Is this possible?"

"Certainly..." replied Sarvaripa *"... but it is not possible, even for such a remarkable bowman as yourself, to bring all your catch home – you could carry two at the most, and they would be a heavy burden even for the strongest man."*

"What will you wager that I cannot bring all these deer back to your home tonight?"

"I have no money to speak of but I will accept any challenge you set me" replied Sarvaripa as proudly as he could, having been defeated as an archer in his contest with Saraha.

With that, Saraha and Sarvaripa strode off to the hillside where the deer lay. *"That is your deer"* remarked Saraha. *"Let me see you shoulder that deer."*

Without a word, Sarvaripa went to pick up the deer – but it proved too heavy for him to lift, no matter how hard he tried. In the end he sat on the ground exhausted by the effort.

"Well... I have failed – but now I must see how you keep your side of the wager. I shall try again to shoulder this deer – and as I do so, I shall see how you fare."

At that Saraha snapped his fingers and all the deer he had shot sprang to their feet and began to follow him down the hill – along with the two who had run away.

Whilst still visible to the Sabaran deer hunter, Saraha shouted back *"Follow me!"* He then snapped his fingers. As soon as he snapped his fingers, the deer which Sarvaripa had shot sprang to her feet. Sarvaripa—suddenly feeling full of life again—also jumped up and, accompanied by the deer, ran toward Saraha.

When Sarvaripa caught up, Saraha smiled *"Now we can send these deer away. We have no need of them."*

"But what shall we eat this evening if we bring back no game?"

"Have no fear of that!" laughed Saraha. *"I shall provide food sufficient for you and your wife this evening. I promise you the most excellent dining you have experienced in a good many years. I have a considerable array of ingredients for the preparation of a fine feast! It's all in this bag that I carry over my shoulder!"*

"So now…" grinned Sarvaripa rather wanly *"… you are telling me that you carry food for three hungry people in your haversack?"*

"Yes."

"Well… I have a feeling that it is unwise to doubt you. Any man who can fell 108 deer with one arrow and then bring them all back to life again could probably feed the same number of people from one haversack – and our party shall consist only of three."

"I see you are a man of intelligence and wit" smiled Saraha. *"We shall make a fine evening of it."*

In spite of his apprehension of this archer, who was obviously a sorcerer, Sarvaripa asked *"But… what of the wager – what challenge will you set me?"*

"Ah yes…" smiled Saraha *"it is honourable of you to remember our wager. I shall tell you after we have shared a feast together this evening with your wife."*

The deer Sarvaripa had shot, turned and ran into the distance. Saraha and Sarvaripa went on their way. When Sarvaripa's wife, Saradha, heard what had occurred, she became nervous – but Saraha put her at her ease. *"I am not a sorcerer as you and your good husband imagine. I am a Buddhist yogi and the siddhis I have shown your husband are the least of my capacity. We shall eat together first, and then I shall tell your husband of his challenge."*

Saraha opened his bag and brought out a substantial feast which Sarvaripa and Saradha heartily enjoyed. After the feast was over Saraha sang a song of realisation and both Sarvaripa and Saradha were astonished. They were astonished both by the profundity of the teaching and by the fact that they had no difficulty in understanding. *"And now for your challenge, Sarvaripa."*

Saradha made to leave the room in order for her husband to hear his challenge, but Saraha bade her stop with a motion of his hand, saying *"This challenge is for both of you."*

Overawed though he was, Sarvaripa revolted at this proposition. *"The challenge was for me because I lost the wager. The challenge is not for my wife – because she made no agreement with you."*

"That is true Sarvaripa – but maybe you should wait until you hear the nature of the challenge."

"We will hear your challenge…" replied Saradha.

"… but Saradha" insisted Sarvaripa *"must be free to accept it or reject it as she pleases."*

"As you please. You are an honourable man and a brave one to insist when you know me as you do. I have power enough to impel you, if I wished – but it would never be my wish to impel anyone. To impel is not the way of Dharma because one must learn directly from one's own experience. One who was impelled would lack the courage and independence to follow through."

Then Saraha began giving the couple instructions on how to practise. *"Whether you return to hunting after you have fulfilled my instruction is up to you, but unless you can make a connection with the deer you shoot—which will lead to their liberation—you should no longer shoot deer."*

Rinpoche paused for a moment for me to ask my question.

"*Saraha says that Sarvaripa has to stop hunting until he has the capacity to establish connection with the deer he shoots. Is that the same as saying that the connection would automatically be there in the nondual state, because there would be no separation between him and the animal?*"

"*Yes*" replied Khandro Déchen "*but it's also the recognition that one is already dead.*" PAUSE "*It is similar to being a warrior. One has to enter every battle without expectation of survival.*"

"*Death is what happens*" continued Rinpoche. "*One has to recognise that to think of oneself as doing nothing that causes harm or death – is fallacious.* Everyone *causes death – continually. You cannot walk across the grass without killing insects. If you take antibiotics—or put antiseptic on a wound—you're killing microbes. It's not possible to live without causing death. The only way you can attempt to disassociate from causing harm is by pretending that it is permissible to kill 'this' – but not permissible to kill 'that'.*"

I looked quizzical, so Khandro Déchen elaborated. "*We make the killing of microbes and insects acceptable by establishing arbitrary dividing lines. As soon as you establish that dividing line, you're on one side of it, and other people are on the other side of it.*"

"*Hitler had a dividing line*" Rinpoche commented grimly. "*He was on one side of the line with the Aryans – and the Jews were on the other. It's the same story. It's not that there's no value in vegetarianism, veganism, or fruitarianism – but they are not 'ultimate positions'. They are relative practices. They are not truth – they're methods. And so, anyone is free to engage in whatever method it is to which they relate in terms of what they eat and what they wear.*"

"*They have to realise*" added Khandro Déchen "*that methods are relative rather than ultimate.*"

"*I was vegetarian and abstemious for about thirteen years*" Rinpoche confided "*until Chhi'mèd Rig'dzin Rinpoche instructed me to change course.*"

"Was that because of the need to eat meat and drink alcohol in the tsog'khorlo?" I enquired.

"Partially – although I also ate meat and drank alcohol during those thirteen years when food was offered to me by Lamas." PAUSE "I was never a purist."

"There is no 'pure position' which can be reached" added Khandro Déchen.

"Chhi'mèd Rig'dzin Rinpoche was concerned with my life as a Lama in terms of Vajrayana" commented Rinpoche. "I had to show the example of creating links between myself and what I ate. When Vajrayana practitioners eat meat or wear leather, they establish connections for those animals in terms of their future lives." PAUSE "Of course, one has to have certainty about that. It can't be wishful thinking. It has to be based on determination to keep the root vows." PAUSE "And then, with alcohol, it is necessary to transform the experience and to maintain awareness."

Rinpoche smiled as he watched the deer. "So, Saraha continues, you may not be able to bring the deer you shoot back to life as I have done – but you must be able to establish a connection. First however, you must both retire to Danti Mountain and practise for three years according to the instructions I shall give you."

Both Sarvaripa and Saradha agreed and were surprised that the challenge seemed so convenient. "We are used to living in these hills, so what you ask is no problem to us – but how shall we eat?"

"I will provide what food you need just as I have provided it this evening. For your part you must simply practise."

Saraha then gave them pith instructions of the nondual nature of wisdom and method – the primordial bodhicitta.

> "Disparate rivers are no longer diverse when their waters unify with the water of the ocean.
> Yet the rivers remain rivers fed by the rain which is drawn from the sea.
> The darkness of a great web of lies is dispelled by a solitary genuine fact
> – and vanishes in the light of the sun.

> *Recognising that which is ineffable, it is neither pleasure nor pain.*
> *When there is nothing upon which to meditate – that in itself is the wisdom of bliss.*
> *Form and emptiness: neither is established – yet there is nothing aside from emptiness and form.*
> *There is no place to remain in the commencement, meridian, or culmination.*
> *For those obscured by concepts, emptiness and form are merely words or images appearing on the mirror's surface.*
> *Analyse appearances without the necessity of concept – seeing neither singularity nor multiplicity*
> *But do not become attached to the mirror's reflection – even though appearances are unborn and clear by nature.*
> *All appearances in their diversity are of the nature of the mirror.*
> *All the varieties of the seer and the seen are of this very nature.*
> *Aversion, indifference, and obsession—united in bodhicitta—also have this very nature.*
> *There is no negating, no constructing, and no apprehending. It is inconceivable."*

Then he taught them as Khandira had taught him – concerning the way in which one shoots an arrow. They were both skilled hunters with excellent marksmanship and so he presented them with the ideal teaching:

> *"To realise the nondual state – contemplate the instant at which the arrow is let loose.*
> *If you release the arrow with deliberation – emptiness and form remain as if separated.*
> *Where there is no calculation – the point in time at which the arrow is released cannot be determined.*
> *There is the form of retaining the arrow and the emptiness of letting it fly…*
> *But the point-instant of release cannot be ascertained as either.*

That point-instant cannot be located by pursuing it with conceptual mind. Because all scrutiny is form, and that which is scrutinised is empty."

They both understood, and the next day they left for the mountain hermitage at Danti. Within three years they had both gained experience of the nondual state.

They later met Mahasiddha Nagarjuna, from whom they received Mahamudra instruction. Sarvaripa and Saradha then passed these instructions on to their disciple Maitripa, who passed them on to the Tibetan translator Marpa. They spent their lives practising and passing on the teachings that Saraha and Nagarjuna had given them.

The autumn sun had sunk in the sky. A chill had crept into the air as we sat listening to the hagiography. It would soon be time to leave, so I asked *"That final teaching… about releasing the arrow – it reminds me of what you've taught before about handgun shooting. A description of the four naljors in fact?"*

"Indeed, whatever you can say of shooting an arrow, you can also say of firing a handgun. At first you need to be able to concentrate – but after that, you need to discover the empty space of effortless attention."

"Shi-nè" said Khandro Déchen *"is the practice of emptiness – the practice of letting disturbances fall away. I don't see how anyone without meditative ability achieves anything as a marksperson with a bow, or handgun, or anything else. You cannot engage in thought stories and maintain your aim."*

"Yes" continued Rinpoche. *"There's a certain empty point at which the trigger is squeezed, or the arrow released, and one has to know when that moment has arrived. One has to know it without knowing it – which means one has to know it without thought. So shi-nè is the moment of silence – the moment of stillness in which there is no distraction. Lhatong is the moment in which the practitioner integrates with movement – the movement in which the arrow is released or the trigger is squeezed. The two cannot be divided. If one waits for the perfect space, and then conceptualises about shooting – the shot will not be fired with awareness. Shi-nè and lhatong have to be unified; have to have the same taste."*

"Chögyam Trungpa Rinpoche encouraged interest in archery amongst his students, you know…" commented Khandro Déchen "dressage, ballroom dancing, Japanese flower arrangement too. All these activities have the same quality in terms of practice. But actually shi-nè and lhatong—stillness and change—are the two major considerations whatever the activity in which you engage."

"Emptiness and form must dance" concluded Rinpoche "in terms of what one is attempting to accomplish."

With that Rinpoche got up from the bench and we started the walk back through the gathering dusk to where we had left the cars.

Rinpoche suddenly laughed. "Of course, there's no difference whether you find nyi'mèd with a bow and arrow, a hand-gun, or whether you find it sitting in the shrine room – although nothing replaces silent sitting. But as an adjunct to silent sitting, archery, hand-gunning, or some similar form of hand-eye coordination is valuable in terms of integration – of integrating the meditative state with everyday activity." PAUSE "Now let us away – and practise hand-eye coordination with knives and forks…" PAUSE "integration with the consumption of pizza and Barolo."

Nine: Shatakshi – the mother of tigers

Shatakshi *(shar sTag shi' / ཤར་སྟག་ཤིའ་)* / Sa-tak Ama *(sa sTak a ma / ས་སྟག་ཨ་མ་)*
Disciple of: Saraha
Varna by birth: Shudra

Our first spring at Drala Jong.

Rinpoche and Khandro Déchen were staying for a few days to direct the plans and designs for developing the land and buildings. Plans were required to manifest their vision of what Drala Jong would become as a centre for the Aro gTér – and for re-establishing the Düd'jom gTér in Britain. We were planting the seeds of vision which might take many decades to bear fruit – fundraising being subject to fickle factors.

Rinpoche and Khandro Déchen translate Drala Jong as *'Sparkling Meadow of Primal Nondual Iridescence'*. 'Drala' is the life and vigour of the land. 'Jong' means mountain valley or meadow. They use this term to refer to a place where drala is more easily appreciated in terms of the elemental presence of the natural world. The practice of drala is a method of becoming aware of the sentient nature of phenomena. Enshrined in the idea of Drala Jong, is a sense of responsibility for the world. We had spent much time discussing the development of the shrine hall, farmhouse, and the two wings of outbuildings. The outer shrine hall— the 23 acres of land—was equally high on the agenda. Rinpoche and Khandro Déchen were keen to plant trees—particularly indigenous trees —and especially oaks and willows.

A temperate and unclouded March afternoon, we had taken chairs to the top field to sit and survey the view from the highest point of the land. Coming down the half mile long track to Drala Jong, the fields on either side are owned by Huw, the dairy farmer.

From the final sharp bend which leads down to the farmhouse and courtyard however, there are two fields which belong to Drala Jong. Sitting there—in the sparkling meadow of primal iridescence—we had a fine view over the rolling valleys to the distant shapes of the Black Mountains on the far horizon. Below, we could see the roof of the farmhouse, the pale viridian arch of the Dutch barn, and the line of silhouetted stately oak and ash not yet in leaf.

Rooks cawed overhead. In front of us grazed a flock of sheep, ranging along the bottom hedgerow of the field in the pleasant afternoon light. The sheep belonged to Gareth, Huw's son-in-law, whose long-standing arrangement to rent the fields for sheep grazing we had inherited with the property when Drala Jong was purchased.

We had also inherited a small flock of fowl: chickens, cockerels, ducks, and a goose, who all roamed freely around the central courtyard and surrounding barns. As we sat gazing at the view, we discussed the possible options for relocating the poultry housing when building work eventually started. The beings of the place, both animal and otherwise, both domesticated and wild, were now our responsibility too.

"At least we don't have to think about housing for Gareth's sheep" I commented *"but goats would need shelters – and I would love to have some goats."*

Khandro Déchen responded *"I didn't know you were fond of goats?"* and I explained that I had worked as the goat keeper on a city farm more than thirty years previously. I had fallen in love with the mischievous and intelligent characters I cared for. I still remembered their names, and had wanted to keep goats ever since.

Khandro Déchen smiled at that. *"If we had goats here, you would be like Shatakshi – other than the lack of tigers."*

"Tigers?" I enquired.

Nine: Shatakshi – the mother of tigers

"*Mahasiddha Shatakshi was a goatherd known as* the mother of tigers" Rinpoche explained. "*She doesn't appear in other collections of the* 84 *Mahasiddhas, but she's in Jomo Pema ö-Zér's gTérma. Would you like to hear more about her?*"

I was eager indeed, so Rinpoche continued "*She was the youngest of five daughters in a family who herded milking-goats. Being as she was the youngest daughter there was no money left to give her a dowry – so she was destined to tend the goats rather than marry…*"

Goat herding was a dangerous occupation because tigers sometimes came to take the goats. Shatakshi therefore often hid behind rocks—or in her small yet robust hut—feeling both sad and frightened. It was a miserable life for the poor young girl. She had no companionship and no hope of any in the future. Her father brought her food every three days but never stayed long, as he wanted to be back in his home before nightfall. The night was the dangerous time for tigers – and he had no wish to take unnecessary risks. He considered the hut, built of mud and stone, to be sufficient protection for his daughter but was never tempted to spend the night there, even occasionally, just to keep her company. Her sisters were all married and therefore felt their wifely duties did not permit them to visit her. Her mother claimed she was not hardy enough to manage the steep climb to her daughter's hut – so she only saw her at milking times when Shatakshi brought the goats down from the hills. At that time however, the milking precluded much conversation and so Shatakshi was more-or-less a recluse.

Shatakshi lived a desolate life: sad, because she knew she would never have children; frightened, because of the risk of being taken by a tiger; and lonely, through family neglect. Her one consolation was the beauty of the topography and the bird song. The birds in the area were quite accustomed to her presence and became tame as far as Shatakshi was concerned. The foxes too, visited her—along with other creatures—and, in this sense, there was pleasure and companionship in her life.

The pleasure she took in nature grew as the years went by, and she discovered that she could derive joy simply in seeing colours and hearing sounds.

The more curious sheep were moving up the field towards us. Rinpoche paused to gaze around him. *"This natural capacity that Shatakshi has, to be able to take pleasure in the sense fields"* I asked *"do you think that is always easier if you're out in nature? If you're out in the mountains for example, rather than sitting in an office in Milton Keynes?"*

"Yes" Rinpoche laughed *"there's less stratified, structured, systematic, administrative, bureaucratic concept in the wilds. Although… there's always concept. One can project anything onto anything."*

"There's not the sense of good and bad about it" added Khandro Déchen *"unless the weather's inclement. Whatever you're looking at, is just what you're looking at. There's not a lot of value judgement apart from enjoyment. That's about all that's possible under those circumstances. So, it's a simpler experience, even though it's highly variegated."*

"And" I asked immediately *"is that why people often find practice easier by the sea or in the mountains, because there's less concept?"*

"Yes" replied Rinpoche. *"Often people enjoy the sound of the wind; or the sound of the waves; or the sound of a fire crackling – but give them Avant Garde Jazz and many hate it. If they enjoy the sound of wind, sea, and fire however, why is the Avant Garde Jazz objectionable? Or why is Shostakovich, Schoenberg, or John Cage objectionable – or Benjamin Britten's Serenade for Tenor Horn and Strings?"*

"You can just enjoy a sound" added Khandro Déchen. *"The interesting thing is that you're allowed to enjoy the fire crackling. And you do so because there's no artificial limit on it. But when it's called 'music', then other factors come into play. There's far more concept – and you can judge it as 'not being music', merely because it doesn't conform to your criteria concerning music. It happens with painting too. It happens with all the Arts."*

"Some people are not keen on my poetry for that reason" Rinpoche grinned. *"They don't enjoy the interplay of: comprehensible and incomprehensible; coherent and incoherent; plausible and implausible; regularity and disarray; sequentiality and disjuncture; symmetry and asymmetry; order and chaos."*

"It's called 'nature' " laughed Khandro Déchen. *"You'll find all that there."*

"Kyabjé Künzang Dorje Rinpoche often alerted me to the sounds in the landscape when we walked together. He never switched anything off. Mainly people stop hearing when they speak – or stop seeing, savouring, et cetera. Künzang Dorje Rinpoche however, was awake in all the sense fields all the time. He'd spot a bird and hear the sound of a stream at the same time as giving an explanation; or at the same time as walking and looking in his bag for a piece of chu-ra [1] *or thud* [2] *– that's Tibetan cheese."* PAUSE *"We often ate cheese whilst walking up to the retreat caves above Tso Pema. Künzang Dorje Rinpoche could also detect my changing expression in peripheral vision whilst ostensibly looking at something else. He noticed everything – as far as I could ascertain."*

Rinpoche gave a protracted smile and continued the hagiography. *"One early evening, when the sound of tigers in the distance had driven her into her hut, Saraha appeared…"*

He knocked at her heavy wooden door and walked inside without explaining his appearance, asking her immediately *"Why are you both sad and frightened when you live amongst such beauty?"*

Shatakshi was surprised at the question, but replied *"I am sad, venerable sir, because my parents are too poor to provide a dowry, so I can never marry.*

---

[1] *phyur ba* / ཕྱུར་བ or *yu ra* / ཡུ་ར or *chur ba* / ཆུར་བ — cheese is a staple in Tibetan cuisine. Tibetan cheeses include soft cheese curds resembling cottage cheese made from buttermilk called chu-ra lönpa. Semi-hard cheese is called chu-ra kampo. Extra hard cheese, made from solidified yogurt, is called chur-pi, and is also found in Sikkim and Nepal. Another type of cheese is called sho-sha or chu-rul, made from cream and the skin of milk.

[2] *thud* / ཐུད

"I am sad, because I can never practise Dharma either – because I must stay and tend my parents' goats. I am frightened every day because I may be taken by tigers – and… one day I know it will happen no matter how cautious I am."

"Ah!" laughed Saraha *"Then I have a story to tell you about the Arhat Pindola. Is this something that would interest you?"*

"I am interested, venerable sir, in anything that might shed light on Dharma."

"Then I shall relate an account of him. Pindola was a soldier—a general—but because of his devotion to Buddha Shakyamuni he retired from military life and became a practitioner…"

Pindola went to live in a mountain hermitage with other practitioners but found them all to be afraid of the tiger that howled every day. It was not as calm as could be wished for a hermitage – but as it was merely the sound of the tiger, Pindola was not unduly perturbed. He spent his days in meditation or occupied with the simple tasks required of him by the hermitage. He proved to be an excellent sacristan[3], as his military background made him punctilious concerning cleanliness and order. The hermitage was never quite as neat and tidy as when it was his turn to clean and sweep. All seemed well, but one day the huge howling tiger appeared at the gates of the hermitage. This terrified the other hermits and caused the visiting laity to flee for their lives. Pindola was also frightened at first. *"Of course he was!"* laughed Saraha *"He'd been a general! He was brave – but he was not a fool. Only a fool would not feel fear concerning tigers. Anyhow…"*

Pindola sat with the problem – and, having dwelt on it for a while, began to wonder whether the huge howling tiger might not be ferocious by nature, but rather, that it might merely be driven to ferocity by hunger. It also seemed that no one else was prepared to deal with the situation.

---

[3] A person who has charge of the contents of a religious house, especially the sacred implements, robes, precious objects, and so on.

The other hermits had barricaded themselves into their rooms and would not come out, so Pindola—having been a military strategist—decided that a direct frontal assault was the only answer. He decided to feed the tiger. Every day he walked calmly to the gate and left food for the tiger. Each day the tiger came back—and each day Pindola provided food—until at last the tiger became tame as far as Pindola was concerned. Whilst this was continuing, Pindola saw to it that all the other hermits were fed. They kept to their rooms. He collected the 'night-soil' each morning—he cooked and swept alone—and generally lived as if he were in isolated retreat. The tiger no longer sought to intimidate him with its howling because it understood that Pindola was willingly sharing his own food. Eventually the tiger came to visit even when it did not want food. It came simply because it enjoyed Pindola's company.

"*So... in the end, they became friends...*" smiled Saraha "*... and Pindola came to be called 'the arhat who tamed tigers'. So that is my story. How does it sit with you?*"

"*I feel much better for having heard it – even though some fear remains.*"

"*That is to be expected, young lady – but yet... there is a sadness that lies below your fear. Please be forthright about its cause, so that I may help you.*"

She then explained her family situation and her loneliness.

"*How can you say that you cannot practise Dharma...*" Saraha smiled "*... when you live a life much like a hermit?*"

Shatakshi said that maybe she couldn't.

"*How can you say that you cannot practise Dharma when you appreciate the sense fields?*"

Shatakshi said that she did not know.

"*How can you say that you cannot practise Dharma, when you already have a sense of the one-taste of hope and fear?*"

Again, Shatakshi could not answer the question.

"How can you say that you cannot practise Dharma, when you live to benefit others?"

At this Shatakshi answered *"Yes… I do live to benefit my family – but not by any great intention. It is merely how things are for me and there is no other choice."*

"To benefit others with no intention is more natural than to have a specific plan because plans can always come to nothing. It is good to have no choice – because then one is not forever changing one's mind. I see every cause for happiness in your condition."

These statements bewildered Shatakshi *"But what of my lack of children?"*

Saraha smiled again *"That is simple. Many creatures are already your children. Can you say that you have not cared for fox cubs and fledgling birds?"*

"Yes, I have done all that—and much pleasure it gives me—but I have given birth to none of them."

"Even if you had given birth to them, space—the womb of pure potential—is the primordial mother of phenomena. When you recognise yourself as identical with the womb of pure potential you will become the mother of every being who recognises you as such."

Shatakshi was surprised to hear this. She was astonished to be receiving Dharma teachings – but astounded that she understood them. Still however, she had a question *"You have answered me well with regard to my lack of children… but I should have mentioned first that my lack of a dowry will prevent me from finding a husband."*

"There is no need for a dowry. There is no need to think, as yet, of a husband – human or otherwise. Your consorts will recognise you. First however, you must recognise the nondual state."

Shatakshi asked how she could accomplish that.

Saraha replied *"Simply recognise the one-taste of hope for a husband and children, and fear of being taken by tigers."* He then gave her detailed instructions on practice – along with transmission of the nature of Mind.

> *"Just as the wind lashes the mountain rains into ice,*
> *Conceptual mind multiplies 'illusory empty-unity' – and multifarious 'illusory forms' are seen.*
> *Seeing the many faces of Saraha, idiots will see them as separate.*
> *Cross-eyed idiots see one flame as two – but regular idiots think that 'sight' and 'that-which-is-seen' are separate.*
> *There may be many lighted lamps in the house – but the blind see only darkness.*
> *Awareness is all-pervasive – but idiots cannot see the forest for the trees.*
> *Idiots attempt to avoid suffering – but tantrikas celebrate the dance of pleasure and pain.*
> *We drink from the skull bowl of sky-nectar, whilst idiots hunger and thirst for fantasy.*
> *The nature of the beginning and the nature of the end are the same: they are both here and now.*
> *The former does not exist without the latter – and the latter does not exist without the former.*
> *Rationalistic idiots conceptualise the inconceivable in attempting to separate wisdom and compassion.*
> *Bees, from birth, know flowers are the source of honey – but idiots never know samsara and nirvana as the same.*
> *Idiots facing themselves in mirrors see merely unfamiliar configurations.*
> *The mind without awareness can only understand the figments of duality.*
> *When mind is absorbed in concept-free space, passion is pure immaculacy.*
> *Like a lotus rooted in the murk of a silted lake, reality is untouched by the pollution of duality.*
> *Reify vision of all phenomena as visionary dreams and you will attain transcendence.*

> *Instantaneous realisation and equanimity will bind the demons of darkness.*
> *Beyond thought and absence of thought your spontaneous nature is accomplished.*
> *Appearances have never been divided from their original radiance – so although we may wallow like pigs*
> *In what others describe as the sensual mire of putrescent swine – what can stain a pearlescent mind?"*

On having spoken, Saraha departed. When Saraha left, Shatakshi began practising immediately, and such was her fear—and her hope—that she recognised nonduality the following night.

As soon as darkness fell, the tigers came and Shatakshi left her hut to greet them. The first to arrive were two tiger cubs who had strayed from their mother. They were hungry and whimpering and as soon as they saw Shatakshi, they recognised her as a mother. As soon as Shatakshi saw them, she recognised them as her children – and, even though she had never conceived a child, she was spontaneously able to breastfeed them. Whilst feeding the cubs, their mother and father arrived. The father lay down and placed his head in her lap. The mother stood guard over them, as other tigers approached. The goats huddled together terrified, but the tigers left them in peace, understanding that they were Shatakshi's flock – and should therefore be left unmolested.

A year passed in this way, with the tiger family arriving every night. The goat herd grew in number. Forgetting their fear of tigers, they provided better and more plentiful milk. Shatakshi's parents found themselves with a growing goat herd. They became immensely proud of their daughter and even took to visiting her. Shatakshi made no mention of her relationship with the tigers and her parents never enquired as to how Shatakshi protected their goats. Due to their increasing herd, there was—after some years—sufficient wealth for her parents to put aside a dowry for Shatakshi.

When they told her however, she replied *"Due to Saraha's teaching I have no need of a dowry – nor do I need to live anywhere other than the hills. I am happy to spend my life as your goatherd."*

"But what of a husband?" they asked incredulously.

"I have no need of a husband."

"Then there will be no children..." her mother sighed, dismayed.

"I already have many children – they are tiger cubs. And as for husbands – I have tigers as my consorts."

Her parents were initially horrified. Her father blanched and her mother screamed – and both fled in fear of a daughter who had become a demonic sorceress.

Eventually however—things being as they are—they accepted the situation. Because, well... they could hardly cut themselves off from the source of their newfound wealth, could they... be their daughter a demonic sorceress or not. It was also evident—they reasoned with themselves—that their daughter had actually become a siddha through the transmission of a person they now knew to have been Mahasiddha Saraha. There was no pressing need to broadcast the nature of their daughter's siddhis – and, as no one ever asked, they found it easy to have nothing to say on the subject. They simply had a daughter who was not frightened of tigers – and who was also supremely skilled in protecting the flock. When asked how she protected the flock they would simply reply *"We don't know—we're afraid of tigers—but if you want to find out you can always go and visit Shatakshi."*

Shatakshi lived permanently in the hills where she gave transmission to any who were brave enough to visit her in the grove of tigers.

As Rinpoche concluded the hagiography, we had been sitting still long enough that the sheep were no longer wary of us.

They were now nibbling at the grass close to our feet. Enjoying watching their gentle faces it was a while before I asked *"I can imagine people reading this and thinking surely that couldn't happen, taking tigers as consorts, and breastfeeding tiger cubs?"*

"That would be the modern Western response." PAUSE *"I'm not sure—historically—when perceptions changed in Britain, but people used to believe such things. When I was a school boy, we were still taught to believe that Jesus walked on water, multiplied food, and raised people from the dead. It's all there in Christianity. So, these are phenomena which people used to believe."* PAUSE *"It's not that belief or faith is preferable to the scientific mindset – but there's a problem with 'inability to believe' having to manifest as 'active disbelief'."* PAUSE *"The alternative to active disbelief is agnosticism."* PAUSE *"It is better to say 'I don't know'. It's better to say 'I have no way of knowing – therefore I neither believe nor disbelieve.' Belief and disbelief are not the only available options – and disbelief is just another belief, merely a negative belief."*

"It can be that simple" said Khandro Déchen. *"The question can be left in space. Taking tigers as consorts—and breastfeeding tiger cubs—can be registered as one would register music or a painting. It is simply there. I feel this is preferable – and, actually, creatively mysterious. It is more interesting not to know – not to have a fixed idea."*

"If you hear the hagiography as an artist – it simply becomes poetry." Rinpoche perused the sheep nibbling around his feet. *"The hagiography itself creates an atmosphere and one can either enter into that atmosphere or not."* PAUSE *"Bestiality apart, there are certainly current examples in which people have remarkable relationships with animals – which seem impossible to some. They clearly aren't impossible because we can watch such interactions on film – human beings romping with tigers for example."*

"There was Francis of Assisi too, of course" added Khandro Déchen. *"He certainly had an unusually close connection with animals.*

"There are many Christian stories of that sort" Khandro Déchen grinned *"although maybe not about having sexual intercourse with large lethal felines."*

"I guess" I laughed *"that's something else that might create disbelief in a current audience – how impossibly dangerous it would be to get that close to tigers. But—as you said—I've also seen footage of people able to be physically close and affectionate with big cats."*

"And you know" Rinpoche nodded *"in terms of what's dangerous, a story comes to mind. I was in Seattle many years ago. I was being driven to a retreat by a young man called Andrew Bloomfield. He often ferried me 'round in those days. So, one evening we set off to a retreat venue and, after some time on the road, Andrew pulled into a gas station. It had a longshoreman's bar which the local loggers frequented. Andrew said 'I'm going to get a few things from the shop over there. No need to come with me, you can just stay comfortable in the car.' I didn't make anything of that, apart from the idea that he possibly wanted to do something on his own. He was gone for a while when I realised that I would be advantaged by using the facilities. In 1998 all I took to the USA was a rucksack. I wore my robes all the time. I had no room for secular street clothes. So I walked into the longshoreman's bar and said 'Excuse me, I wonder if I may use your toilet.' One of the loggers answered 'Yeah, feller, it's down there on the left.' He pointed down the corridor. So I went and used the toilet— came out, said 'Thank you very much'—and left. Meanwhile, Andrew had become frantic, looking for me. When I appeared, I apologised for causing him anxiety. He asked where I'd been and I said 'Well, I needed to use the loo' to which he replied 'You went in—**there**?' He had a frantic look on his face 'and no one threatened you?' That confused me. Why would anyone in there threaten me? Why would anyone wish to assault me for needing to use a toilet?' Andrew smiled at this point 'Because you're wearing a skirt?' The penny dropped 'Ah...' I replied 'I suppose I have never seen it as a skirt... and it's not the average transvestite garb – besides which, I have a rather fulsome beard.' Andrew's grin became broader and he said 'Maybe it's because you asked for the* **toilet** *rather than the* **rest room**.*'"*

"Americans think it's coarse to use the word 'toilet' so it's referred to as a rest room" smiled Khandro Déchen *"even though toilet is merely French for ablution."*

"And of course, 'toilet' replaced 'lavatory' in Britain when 'lavatory' became vulgar" added Rinpoche "but 'lavatory' is simply the Latin for ablution." PAUSE "The point of this story is that I wasn't expecting to be beaten up. I just walked into the longshoreman's bar. I therefore wasn't afraid. I addressed them civilly—used fairly polite language—got what I needed, and left. No one made anything of it. I think that's an important aspect in this hagiography vis-à-vis the tigers." PAUSE "We often take our danger with us – by adopting the mien of victims. We exude anxiety."

"Dogs interpret fear as aggression" added Khandro Déchen "which is why anxious people are more frequently bitten by dogs."

"Exactly" Rinpoche chuckled. "So that's the case with Shatakshi. Once she hears Mahasiddha Saraha's account of the tigers, she ceases to perceive herself as a potential victim."

After watching the sheep for a few minutes, Rinpoche queried "In terms of being in the wilds…" PAUSE "… you do know that drala is also available in London, Paris, or Manhattan? It doesn't have to be the countryside."

"Although the countryside is the best place to start with this practice" Khandro Déchen continued "one can eventually experience it everywhere – because ultimately 'natural' and 'fabricated' are not separate."

"So… we can also experience drala from everything?" I replied. "I was wondering —in terms of being able to perceive drala—if someone had that capacity, would all phenomena speak to them equally?"

"All phenomena would speak" responded Khandro Déchen "but not equally. There would still be differences in the experience of the phenomena communicating. This would be predicated on how individual appreciation functioned. If there wasn't differentiation, we would all be the same. There can sometimes be a tendency to monism in the way in which Sutrayana is understood – and 'equality' can be confused with 'homogeneity'."

"Ah yes" I laughed *"like the scene in Monty Python's 'Life of Brian' where Brian is telling his followers that they're all individuals and they reply in unison 'Yes Lord! We're all individuals!' and one solitary man says 'I'm not'…"*

"A valuable point" Rinpoche chuckled. *"So it's natural that everyone has an individual appreciation. If they didn't, we would be biological automatons. With phenomena therefore, connections will be there for some but not for others – depending on individual perception and appreciation. Of course, connection is a communication which develops as one becomes more intimate with whatever the phenomenon happens to be. It's quite well known by instrument makers, that an instrument has to learn how to be an instrument. You can't just make the perfect instrument – it needs to be played for a certain period of time."*

"That's scientifically based" added Khandro Déchen. *"The molecular structure of a violin changes, as it's played. The molecules readjust themselves. They begin to arrange themselves in relation to the sounds. You can't see that happening, unless you have an electron microscope – but if you did, you'd be able to see the activity. You'd see a new violin coming into being. The more it was played the better the violin would become."*

"That is also true of metal-bodied guitars like the National Tricone" Rinpoche added *"and even electric guitars."*

"Is that also why you hear about people who spend a lot of time together, getting more like each other, or even becoming like their pets?" I asked.

"Oh, yes, certainly. That definitely happens. People resonate with each other. Objects resonate with each other." PAUSE *"That is why* 12-string guitars stay in tune longer than 6-string guitars.*"* PAUSE *"It's because the strings 'prefer' to resonate with each other. It's in their physical nature to tend towards resonance."* PAUSE *"There's probably a scientific explanation for that – but I would not have the intelligence to understand it."* PAUSE *"With people however, that sometimes breaks down – and then they move in opposite directions. People can become increasingly resentful toward each other in the process of increasingly misunderstanding each other. They become 'out of tune' with each other."*

"They can, of course, also become increasingly attuned to each other." Khandro Déchen smiled and added. "Rinpoche and I have often got the same melody in mind at the same time – and either he starts singing it, or I do."

We sat in silence for a moment, the ewes milling round us, and then Rinpoche and Khandro Dechen simultaneously burst into a refrain from Händel's Messiah[4] *"All we, like sheep—all we, like sheep—have gone astray-ay-ay-ay-ay-ay-ay-ay-ay ay-ay-ay-ay-ay..."* We all burst into laughter. Even the sheep appeared to find it amusing.

---

[4] An English-language oratorio composed in 1741 by Georg Frideric Händel. The text was compiled from the King James Bible and the Coverdale Psalter by Charles Jennens.

Ten: Baruni – the surbdahar playing whore

Baruni *(ba ru' ni /* བ་རུའ་ནི *)* / Gyüdmang 'jud-thunma *(rGyud man 'jud mThun ma /* རྒྱུད་མན་འཇུད་མཐུན་མ *)*
Disciple of: Ghantapa
Teacher of: Bhagarvi
Varna by birth: Vaishya *(fallen to Harijan)*

The Lizard Peninsula, Cornwall.

The geology of the Lizard Peninsula is unique. The beaches and coves are strewn with red and green serpentine[1]. The Lizard is the only place on the planet where red serpentine can be found. We have found round pebbles of red serpentine over the years which have proved suitable for grinding and filing into spheres. These we have used for large Golok-style[2] 'end beads' in teng-ars. The cliffs and sea caves create spectacular rock formations which are vividly alive. There are a number of these remarkable formations close to Cadgwith. One of the most extraordinary is known as The Devil's Frying Pan. It can be found a quarter of a mile south of the fishing village – and is formed from the collapsed roof of a sea cave. The falling in of the cave roof has left a breath-taking arch of rock on the seaward side, and a two-hundred-foot plunge down to the sea below on the land side.

The sea cave collapsed in 1868 and the *Frying Pan* is now a crater of stone forming a vast boulder-strewn bowl of ocean. In high seas or fierce weather, the water appears to be boiling and spitting within the pan.

---

[1] Serpentine is a rock which is related to marble. The red variety only occurs on the Lizard Peninsula.
[2] Kham and Golok in Tibet were famous for brigands and so a style developed of employing end beads on mantra beads the size of a billiard ball or larger. This was intended as a means of self-defence against attack by robbers.

You can enter the cave from the sea, either by boat or by swimming round from Cadgwith cove – as Rinpoche and Khandro Déchen like to do each year.

It isn't quite possible to access the pool from the clifftop – the plunge down is too steep, and the sea too far below. Once many years ago, Rinpoche and Khandro Déchen were standing on the clifftop looking down into the Frying Pan with their son Düd'dül Dorje who was about two years old. Rinpoche asked him *"How many devils do you think there are in the Devil's Frying Pan?"* and he answered immediately *"Five! And they are all very happy!"*

I have always loved that story and thought of it as we headed up the steep path from Pink Cottage towards the Frying Pan for protector practice before dinner. There is a stone seat set into the clifftop hedgerow, overlooking the collapsed cave, and this is where we sat as the evening sun was setting and the sky starting to show shades of dusk.

The Frying Pan is always a marvellous environment for protector practice, drala, and riwo sang chod[3] juniper-smoke profferments. After we had practised for a while Rinpoche answered my unspoken question *"Yah… sa bDag*[4]*… they are—if you forgive the expression—transdimensional elemental personality-configurations. Their portal into accepted reality is the nature of the landscape itself. That portal is particularly accessible here. It's an interface, conduit, or doorway. So, it's also good to practise Dorje Legpa and Dorje Legma at the Frying Pan – and also Damçan Nod-jin 'Barwar Mé-zér."* PAUSE. *"Next time we should bring vajra hammers*[5]*."*

---

[3] *ri-wo bSang mChod* / རི་བོ་བསང་མཆོད་ — Mountain Smoke Profferment. It is a gTérma concealed by Guru Rinpoche and revealed in the 17th century by gTértön Lhatsün Namkha Jig'mèd (*lha bTsun nam mKha' 'jigs med* / ལྷ་བཙུན་ནམ་མཁའ་འཇིགས་མེད་ / 1597–1653), who brought it to Sikkim. From the many ways—elaborate or condensed—of performing this practice, Kyabjé Düd'jom Rinpoche composed an abbreviated version for daily practice. Khyungchen Aro Lingma did the same – and this is what is practised by the Aro gTér sangha.

[4] *sa bDag* / ས་བདག

[5] *jompa'i dorje thö-wa* (*joms pa'i rDo rJe tho ba* / འཇོམས་པའི་རྡོ་རྗེ་ཐོ་བ) – vajra hammer for destroying maliciousness.

Dorje Legpa—Benign Thunderbolt—is one of the ma gZa' dor sum[6] – the three main protectors of the Nyingma Tradition. He was oathbound by Guru Rinpoche to protect Vajrayana. He is found in different forms, either riding a snowlion or a goat. In the Aro gTér lineage there are a number of different forms of Dorje Legpa. There is also Dorje Legma, the female protectress. She is green and wields an iron vajra in one hand and a hammer in the other whilst riding on the back of a goat with long spirally entwined horns. The vajra hammer is particularly important in the Aro gTér as an association with blacksmithing is a symbol for the gö kar chang lo. Dorje Legma rides a goat[7] because goats fearlessly traverse the terrifying heights and dangers of precipitous mountain ridges. This is an analogy for the dangers of Vajrayana, and the spirally twisted horns of the goat are a symbol of nonduality.

"Kyabjé Künzang Dorje Rinpoche, when he was a child, saw Dorje Legpa in the sky – so he always had a close relationship with Dorje Legpa. He said that he was happy that Dorje Legpa held a prominent place in the Aro gTér."

"Was that when you told him about the Aro gTér?"

"Yes – but then Künzang Dorje Rinpoche also received the Aro gTér, directly from Khyungchen Aro Lingma. That is why he asked us to make him an Aro gTér Lineage Lama shawl."

"Ah! I wondered about that when I saw the photo of him wearing it" I beamed.

As we continued sitting, I mused aloud *"How very fortunate we are to belong to a lineage where we also have Dorje Legma, and where we have so many remarkable female yidams too – and so many powerful and inspiring female practitioners in fact."*

---

[6] *ma gZa' rDor gSum* / མ་གཟའ་རྡོར་གསུམ — **ma**: Mamo Ral gCigma *(ma mo ral gCig ma /* མ་མོ་རལ་གཅིག་མ) or Matari Ékajati; **gZa'**: Raksha gZa' Rahula *(ra kSha gZa' rA hu la /* ར་ཀྴ་གཟའ་རཱ་ཧུ་ལ); **dor**: Dorje Legpa / Vajra Sadhu; **sum**: these three, or triad *(gSum /* གསུམ).

[7] *the'u rang* / ཐེའུ་རང — protectors who ride goats and act as patrons of blacksmiths. They often carry bellows and a hammer. One such is the protector of Drala Jong – *Damçan Nod-jin 'Barwar Mé-zér*.

"There are certainly some splendidly powerful female Mahasiddhas in Jomo Pema 'ö-Zér's collection" Rinpoche responded. "It's true – one doesn't find so many in other compilations."

"Like Mahasiddha Baruni" Khandro Déchen offered "the surbdahar[8] playing whore. I have always liked her and her guileless demeanour. The way she talks with Mahasiddha Ghantapa[9] is so candid and ingenuous."

Rinpoche nodded as I asked if there was time to hear about her before we descended from the clifftop for dinner in the *Cadgwith Cove Inn*.

"Time? Maybe..." he turned to Khandro Déchen. "What do you think?"

"There's time – moules marinière[10] do not take long to cook."

"Mahasiddha Baruni then..." Rinpoche began. "She was a Vaishya by birth, the daughter of a mercantile family. The family however, fell on hard times and her parents regretfully cast Baruni adrift to make her own way in life at the age of fourteen..."

She had been a musically gifted girl, who loved to play the surbdahar but when her family was reduced to poverty everything had to be sold including Baruni's beloved surbdahar.

Being dispossessed, the only way Baruni could make a living was by prostitution. Because she was corpulent however, she was not popular enough to make more than a meagre income – and unlikely ever to be able to replace her cherished instrument.

When trade was slack, she would find somewhere out-of-the-way to practise scales, by vocalising the sounds of the surbdahar.

---

[8] The *Surbdahar* or *Surbahar* is sometimes known as the 'bass sitar' or 'baritone sitar'. It is a plucked string instrument used in Indian classical music. It is closely related to the sitar, but an octave, or half an octave, lower in pitch.

[9] Ghantapa (*gha nTa'pa* / རྒྱུད་པ་) / Drüpchen Drilbu Zhab (*grub chen dril bu zhabs* / གྲུབ་ཆེན་དྲིལ་བུ་ཞབས་). Ghantapa means *one who holds a bell*. Ghanta (*dril bu* / དྲིལ་བུ་) means bell in Sanskrit.

[10] A classic French shellfish recipe: mussels cooked in garlic and white wine.

After practising scales, she would vocalise extemporaneous compositions – but she was always shy of anyone hearing her. Whilst thus engaged, Ghantapa—the vajra campanologist—strolled through the town. He heard her voice—even at a distance—and recognised something in her tone. He hurried to speak with Baruni—strode up to her—and said *"Well met, fine lady of the streets! How immensely fortunate it is that I should encounter you. I find myself suddenly and momentously alive with desire for your remarkably ample favours. Are you currently available to spend some amorous time with me?"*

"Certainly sir" Baruni replied and informed him of her fee.

"That is most reasonable—most reasonable indeed—but... I am sorry to say... I cannot pay you with money. I am a yogi and I have no money at present. Alms are scant in this miserly town – however... I—could—offer you a teaching on music – if that would serve in place of money. Are you open to that idea?"

Baruni shook her head *"I am sorry, reverend sir – but I earn too little to use my time in that way. I need to find tricks that pay. I am sure your music lessons would be valuable, but without an instrument I could make no use of them"* and with that she went on her way.

"I shall be here tomorrow, young lady – should you change your mind" remarked Ghantapa as she walked away. Baruni turned and smiled at him before she disappeared into the tumult of the market place and called out *"Then I hope you find the townspeople more generous with alms before then."*

Baruni walked the streets for the rest of the day – but found no interest in her services. She saw other whores turning tricks – but they were all girls of far less girth than her. It was a worse day for trade than she had known in a long while and she became worried about what would happen the next day. Quite apart from not being able to save for a surbdahar, she began to worry how she would pay her rent. She continued to walk and to smile at passing men but eventually she returned to her room exhausted from walking. Her feet ached and her back ached.

It was a lonely life, as men never wanted conversation either before or after they had satisfied themselves. She found herself wishing that she had stayed longer in conversation with the strange yogi – as at least he seemed pleasantly disposed toward her.

The next day, as she was streetwalking and smiling in vain at passing men, she came across Ghantapa again. *"Well met—**again**—good lady – how fortunate I am to meet you once more! I had feared I might not find you. I would still very much like to avail myself of your plenteous partialities. I cannot, as before, offer financial remuneration being as yogis rarely have the wherewithal. However, as before… I could offer you a teaching on music."*

Baruni again, shook her head *"I am honestly sorry, reverend sir, that I must again decline. I am especially sorry, because you are so keen – and because you do not seem to mind my corpulence… but, as I said yesterday… I earn very little – and I simply cannot afford not to keep looking for tricks that pay. Under other circumstances your lessons would be of great value to me, but I have no instrument, and if I do not find paying tricks, I will never have one."*

"I see your problem" sighed Ghantapa. *"I really do see your problem – but tell me… did you find paying tricks after you left me yesterday?"*

Baruni had to admit that she had had no luck *"But it is sometimes like that. I could not have known that the day would turn out as it did."*

"I cannot argue with that – other than to say that today might work out the same way. I do not wish you bad luck, good lady, but if we meet again tomorrow you will be able to tell me how it went."

"I hope I will see you tomorrow, reverend sir, because you speak to me in a kindly manner – and it is good to see a friendly face."

"Then I wish you good luck with your day – and hope to see you tomorrow."

Baruni turned and smiled at him before vanishing into the hubbub of the bazaar.

Baruni walked the streets for the rest of the day – but found no takers for her services. Some men sneered at her – one even spat at her. It was even worse than the day before. Being ignored was bad enough – but being reviled made her cry. She sat weeping for a while in the shade of a wall on which some rather luxuriant creepers were growing, but decided that it was no use feeling sorry for herself. She would simply have to try harder the next day. But how? There was a limit to how little one could wear on the streets without risking punishment.

The twilight at the Devil's Frying Pan was becoming duskier by the moment. The cackling of gulls was fading. It seemed to me that their cries were becoming plaintive – but perhaps that was because I was feeling a little sad about Baruni's plight and the views to which she was subjected. *"Do you think all societies and cultures have got such conditioned ideas about body types?"* I asked.

"It changes depending on the society" Rinpoche answered *"but there's always some deranged notion of how people should be. In India there is a preference for larger ladies—and larger men too—in general. If you ever see Hindi film posters – there's most often a hero protecting a lady from an insane scar-faced bearded axe man. The lady is always rubenesque. The hero always has something of a double chin – and is plump by Western standards. The preference for emaciated ladies began in the 1960s with Twiggy* [11]*. A shift occurred — and suddenly everybody had to look anorexic. In Victorian times, what was thought to be attractive was definitely larger. So, the view shifts with the times. It shifts with income too – because now the overweight tend to be poor. The wealthier tend to be lean because they avoid fast food, having access to better education in terms of nutrition. They also tend to exercise. It used to be thought that if you were thin, you were poor. These shifts keep occurring. People were keen on suntans not so long ago – and now that's shifting. Eventually perhaps we'll revert to the rich and educated keeping out of the sun.*

---

[11] Dame Lesley Lawson (b.1949) – English model, actress, and singer known as 'Twiggy'. She was a British cultural icon and a prominent teenage model in 1960's London. Twiggy was famed for her emaciated androgynous appearance.

"In Jane Austen's time if you were tanned you were a fieldworker, a manual labourer. These conditioned views of body types and appearances are often inextricably linked with social status."

"It's worth bearing in mind" added Khandro Déchen *"that the Vajrayana perspective values the three body types in terms of the three demeanours of the yidams: peaceful, joyous, and wrathful, Peaceful equates with being slim or thin. Joyous equates with being voluptuous. Wrathful equates with being powerfully prodigious... obese or bariatric."*

"Strange isn't it..." Rinpoche continued. *"Words other than 'slim' are derogatory – even 'voluptuous' is a little double-edged these days."* PAUSE *"Be that as it may, the next day Baruni was in wretchedly low spirits – and, as she was walking in yet another part of the town, she espied Ghantapa at a distance..."*

On immediate impulse, she hurried towards Ghantapa, eager for a friendly word. She found herself keen to converse with him, even at the risk of missing a trick.

*"Well met **yet again**, my good lady! This is now the third time we have met. I feel we are almost friends at this point. How fortunate it is that we keep chancing upon one another. It occurred to me last night that the chances of meeting you a third time were quite remote. I feel we should at least know each other's names. My name is Ghantapa – and I am called Ghantapa... because of the bell that I ring. I naturally also have a vajra – but there is no need to speak of that at present."*

"My name is Baruni – but most people call me 'the fat whore'... there is little kindness in the world."

"Well, Baruni, I must tell you that I still earnestly desire the concupiscent pleasure of your conspicuously copious corporality. Are you still set against taking my teaching on music as recompense?"

Baruni's eyes filled with tears, simply in response to Ghantapa's kindly words.

"My dear young woman – what makes you so sad?" he asked – and Baruni told him of the contempt that she had been offered and of her entire failure to turn a single trick on the previous day.

"I am so sorry to hear this" Ghantapa responded gravely. *"Most sorry indeed… and, I am sorry to hear of the gross stupidity of the men in this miserable town. But for you, I would have left this accursed place soon after I had entered it. A more loathsome excuse for a town I have never seen. Those who are not fools are idiots, and those who are not idiots are imbeciles."*

Baruni was surprised by this remark. *"Can you explain your low opinion of this place, reverend sir?"*

"Certainly, my bounteously pulchritudinous friend. I see no reason why you should not turn as many tricks as the other ladies of the demi-monde – therefore this place must be inhabited by fools, idiots, and imbeciles—as far as the men go, that is—but the women cannot be much better because they endure staying in the same town with the men."

"… but am I not fat, extremely callipygous, exceptionally bathykolpian – and… therefore, obviously undesirable?"

"You are indeed rotund, callipygous, and bathykolpian – but this is only undesirable to fools, idiots, and imbeciles. It is true however, that I am a yogi and that my perception will therefore not be like that of most other men. But if you lived in a town of yogis you would never want for trade."

Rinpoche paused to cover his knees with his denim duster[12].

"Ghantapa certainly makes that clear!" laughed Khandro Déchen.

"The idiocy of buying into prevalent conditioned perception" added Rinpoche *"and relating to arbitrary ideas as if they were truth – is that we can make no sense of the world as it is. We relate to the world more-or-less as an hallucination."*

---

[12] A duster in an ankle-length coat worn on horseback in desert conditions. They are usually made of cotton or linen. Ngak'chang Rinpoche's was made from five pairs of his old Levi Strauss 501 Serge de Nîmes trousers.

"*Yes, unfortunately people just believe what they want to believe*" Khandro Déchen added.

"*And what they believe…*" Rinpoche emitted a slight yawn "*is based on evidence which is often dubious at best.*"

"*People don't tend to question*" continued Khandro Déchen "*whatever is currently deemed attractive, what people like.*"

"*Yes*" laughed Rinpoche. "*Everyone liked flared trousers at one time – then, ten years later, they considered them risible. One needs to consider the implications of that. How is it that I once thought flared trousers were desirable and now I think they're ludicrous? What does that mean about my appreciative sense? Is my appreciation actually personal to me? Or am I simply programmed by society to like what I like.*" PAUSE "*Most people are conditioned.*"

"*They accept societal programming – and never question it*" added Khandro Déchen. "*They then issue proclamations about it – as if it were commonly accepted fact.*"

"*I remember back in the late 1970s*" continued Rinpoche "*I used to attend a counselling training course which was held in the Methodist Church Hall in Penarth – which was some five miles from Cardiff, where I lived at the time. I used to cycle there and become quite hot on the journey. When I arrived, I'd sit in the outer entrance lobby in the dark. I found it rather soothing after becoming hot from the exercise. Almost every time one or other of the ladies on the course would come into the room on the way to the hall and say 'Oh! You're sitting in the dark – you can't do that!' and switch the light on. I'd reply 'Actually I find it quite pleasant to sit in the dark and rest after cycling from Cardiff.' The lady would then look aghast and exclaim 'Oh, no-no-no. You can't do that'.*" We all laughed at this juncture. "*Then I'd say 'Oh yes-yes-yes. I find it most pleasant to sit in the dark'.*" More laughter. "*Then she'd say 'Oh no-no-no-no, not in the dark' and I'd reply 'Well, I respect your personal point of view – but would you be so kind as to turn the light off, when you've passed through the room.'*"

"It's peculiar, isn't it?" Khandro Déchen commented. "These ideas of what human preferences are supposed to be."

"Quite so…" replied Rinpoche "such as it's better when it's not overcast. Certainly, it would be better if it were not raining, had one planned to go for a walk – but whether the sun is visible or not doesn't detract from enjoying a walk. It's pleasant when it's sunny and it's pleasant when it's grey – it's just a different kind of pleasant. People act as if coming out of the winter is coming out of a period of penance and misery, into the glorious spring. 'Oh, spring is here at last!' they exclaim – and everyone agrees. I sometimes feel moved to say 'What do you mean 'at last'? I've not been waiting for the spring. It didn't occur to me that there was anything wrong with the winter."

"And now I'm going to start crying because it'll soon be autumn" laughed Khandro Déchen "and winter's next, oh how miserable…!"

"Quite so" added Rinpoche. "That is actually somewhat farcical – but people live with that as if it were normal." There were a few minutes of companionable silence before Rinpoche continued the hagiography.

Baruni gazed incredulously at Ghantapa. "So…" Baruni mused "you would really not rather have a lithe, slim young woman?"

"No more than the other forms of manifest realisation. It is in fact rare to find a young woman so gloriously plump, callipygous—and—bathykolpian. You have a 'wrathful body' – but that is no less an expression of realisation than 'joyous bodies' or 'peaceful bodies'. Each of the three body types can be found amongst the many yidams. The five Simhavaktras[13] represent all body types and the Green Simhavaktra is more copious even than you."

"Really?" Baruni looked astounded to hear these words – so Ghantapa continued "A yogi or yogini must admire peaceful, joyous, and wrathful bodies alike – or they would break their vows."

---

[13] Seng-gé Dongma (seng ge gDongs ma / སེང་གེ་གདོངས་མ་) – lion-headed khandro.

"This..." Baruni began with some strange uncertainty "*I have never heard anything like this before.*"

"*Have you never spoken with a yogi or yogini before?*"

"Never... 'til I met you..."

"*Have you never—seen—yogis or yoginis in your life?*"

"Yes, I have... but I have never approached holy people – because... well, I'm a whore and... holy people are... pure – and I am impure."

"*Pure and impure...*" Ghantapa mused, shaking his head as if the very thought of the subject wearied him "*... whilst that may be true for Tirthikas, the conventionally pious, and the morally constipated – it is not true for Buddhist yogis and yoginis, immersed as they are, in the ocean of the Inner Tantras. Buddhist tantrikas—you see—are not bound by codes which dictate pure and impure. In fact, such ideas constitute vow-breakage in themselves. So, for me, there is nothing impure about you or your profession. You are beginninglessly possessed of nondual being and that which appears either pure or impure is a delusion of samsara.*"

"I am astonished..." Baruni wept with a sudden flooding of joy. "I knew nothing of this teaching. Is the teaching you give on music also of this nature?"

"*Everything a yogi or yogini teaches, is of this nature.*" Ghantapa smiled. "*So, what do you say now to receiving my teaching on the nature of music?*"

"I would dearly love to hear it, reverend sir. I love music—so I agree—but... how will I make use of your teaching without an instrument? I rather fear that your teaching will be wasted on me if I am not able to replace my lost surbdahar – and that now causes me even greater sadness."

"*The absence of an instrument is not something I can change. If I had money, I would buy you the instrument of your desire – but alas that is not within my power. As far as relative truth goes, an instrument could be said to be necessary – but ultimately you are never separate from sound or from music.*"

"I believe that is true for you—because you are a yogi—but I miss playing my surbdahar – and my failure to turn tricks means that obtaining another one remains as far away as it was when I lost it through my parents' decline into poverty."

"You're right" Ghantapa replied. "I speak as a yogi – but there is no need for you to speak as if you could never be a yogini."

"Even if I could become a yogini – I would still desire a surbdahar. The surbdahar was my greatest pleasure in life."

"What you don't understand…" Ghantapa replied "is that the pleasure you—give others—through plying your trade and the pleasure you could—derive yourself—through playing a surbdahar – have one-taste."

"If I was a yogini, I might realise the reality of what you teach – but what can I do in my position? I have no time to learn Dharma beyond what you will teach me today, of music – so… I cannot become a yogini." Then Baruni wept. "I must continue my life as a whore – but that is useless as I am too fat to be a beautiful courtesan with wealthy clients. Unless by some miracle there is a town with many yogis who have money to pay for a fat whore's services – I will never have a surbdahar again in this life. What is worse, is that after some years have passed, I will become old and then no one will want me – not even those who do not object too much to a fat whore."

"From what you tell me, it seems you have no choice other than Dharma – but there you are fortunate, because I can help you. You need no more time than you already have – so there is no need to abandon your profession. There is also no need to imagine that your desirability will remain limited. Nothing in the phenomenal world is fixed and all possibilities are naturally inherent in every situation. I shall remain here in this town and give you instructions until you are able to realise the goal – and then we shall see whether my music lesson will be valuable or not."

Baruni felt cheered by Ghantapa's speech and said that she would favour him whenever he wished.

"There is no need or requirement—at this moment—to unite with you, because we must first establish the bedrock of our union.

"I must first give you the instructions that will allow you to live the life of a yogini – and then you will be the judge of whether uniting with me would be valuable or not."

"Shall I go with you now to receive your teaching?" asked Baruni – but Ghantapa shook his head and said *"Here is where the teaching shall be given – in the bazaar where we have always met."*

"But is it not noisy here?"

"There is sound here – and I shall speak of sound. What is music other than sound? Where is beauty other than in every form – wrathful, joyous or peaceful? The sounds of the bazaar were peaceful when we met – but now they have become joyous, and soon they will be wrathful. What better ambience for you to receive this teaching?"

Baruni understood Ghantapa's words—although the sense of them was highly unusual to her—so she sat and prepared to listen attentively to Ghantapa, whilst the bazaar became increasingly busy. Ghantapa seemed to pay no attention to the increasing noise of the bazaar and taught as if he and Baruni were sitting in a private room. Ghantapa instructed Baruni:

> *"Pay attention equally to the sound of my voice and the sound of the bazaar – and take all sound as equal.*
> *When you realise the one-taste of the music of my words and the music of the bazaar,*
> *Your body will be no different from the surbdahar.*
> *The vibration of the strings of the surbdahar and the resonance of the body of the surbdahar*
> *Are the same as the vibration of my voice and the resonance of the bazaar.*
> *Together they compose the music of reality and of the transmission of reality.*
> *If you realise the meaning of my words, you will be a musician with or without a musical instrument."*

Baruni understood the teaching and immediately asked Ghantapa to unite with her.

Ghantapa returned to Baruni's room where they practised kha-jor – Ghantapa ringing his bell as they consummated their union; announcing:

> *"The play of the bell and the play of sensation are indivisible.*
> *The sonorous sounds of the surbdahar and the sonority of sensuality are*
> *also indivisible.*
> *If you recognise this you will recognise the nondual state."*

From that moment Baruni practised as she had been taught – singing the sounds of the surbdahar with passionate abandon. She sang regardless of the reactions of people in the bazaar, and before three days had passed, men found themselves intrigued by her voice. Before a week had passed, men found themselves fascinated, engrossed, enchanted, captivated, and enthralled. Her voice and her form informed each other and described each other, and it became impossible to lasciviate over her voice without being stirred to lasciviousness by her form. Both were hugely voluptuous. As fascination grew, Baruni's obesity presented an incrementally diminishing problem for the townsmen given to whoring. Within a comparatively short time the men who formerly derided her, found that they desired her.

Thereafter she was sought out as the most desirable of whores. Soon she had money sufficient to purchase a surbdahar of extremely high quality. It was a far better instrument than she had previously owned – and had an additional gourd at the top of the neck. She was then able to live so well from the offerings she was given simply for playing music that she had no need to ply her trade as a whore. Knowing however, that playing her surbdahar and the play of sexual sensation were indivisible – she offered her favours freely to all those who authentically desired music. By this means she gave transmission to many students.

As the hagiography concluded, the dusk had turned to dark and the sounds of the clifftop day had ended.

As I listened to the last cries of the gulls, I was still thinking about the process of deciding whether we like or dislike something. It prompted the question *"What about noise? Is there such a thing as noise in fact, or is it all just sound and how we're interpreting it?"*

"Well, there is a level of sound which is damaging to the ears" answered Khandro Déchen. *"But that's volume. The rest is interpretation. Some people don't like the sound of seagulls. I enjoy them. Especially when they laugh. People got upset with Rinpoche one year because he was feeding a seagull. They're nasty, vicious, violent vermin apparently."*

"I know seagulls may defæcate on one's car – but it can be washed off."

"One doesn't have to get so upset about everything that happens" continued Khandro Déchen. *"I don't object to snails and slugs eating our plants either. They're not eating them with malice aforethought. If you have a garden that's what you get: slugs and snails; greenfly and blackfly. You don't have to be enraged by it. You don't have to try to control everything. Something I've seen more in America than Britain, is people buying leather settees and leaving them covered with the protective plastic in which they were purchased – in case they get marked. It inclines me to ask 'Why not save money and buy a plastic settee?' "*

"People want a perfect world – a perfect world that doesn't exist." Rinpoche sighed. *"This means they can't really enjoy the world. It's always becoming creased or threadbare. It's always becoming verdigrised or rusted. It's always getting dented or breaking down. There's always some pest or vexatious vermin perpetrating some horror. Moth and rust are busy corrupting*[14] *their garden furniture."*

"It seems we have such fixed ideas about what we should like or dislike, and we want everyone else to agree with our ideas" I commented.

"Yes" Rinpoche grinned *"but… there's also the possibility of liking, or not liking – without concept."*

---

[14] Ngak'chang Rinpoche is referencing the Gospel of Matthew, 6:19–21 *(which he studied at school)* in which Christ says *'Lay not up for yourselves treasures upon earth, where moth and rust doth corrupt, and where thieves break through and steal.'*

That boggled me and Rinpoche could tell by the expression on my face. *"Yes! One can like or dislike without inflicting it on anyone else"* Rinpoche chuckled. *"It's happened more than once that people have assumed I should like Picasso's Guernica. Personally… I find it almost engenders ennui. It does not interest me – unless I simply concentrate on the colours. People have wanted to educate me into what Guernica means – because 'If you knew what it meant, you'd like it.' I listened to their explanation of what the painting meant – and it made no difference. My loss. Of course."* PAUSE *"Of course, I knew what it meant—I went to Art School—but that didn't help me like it. I knew Picasso was an excellent draughtsman. I'd seen his drawings. He didn't paint Guernica as he did because he couldn't draw. So, I know it was a choice on his part to paint in the Cubist style. Obviously, it was meaningful to him. It is also meaningful to others – but that does not translate in terms of my enjoying it. It's not that I dislike looking at it – it doesn't revolt me or incense me"* Rinpoche grinned. *"It's just that I look at it – and I'm unmoved by it. I'm indifferent. That's not a problem. Guernica doesn't communicate anything to me – but I don't have to be upset by that. No one else needs to be upset by that either. I don't tell other people that they shouldn't like it. If people like Guernica, then that's perfect. I don't like it, and that's perfect too."*

"There is no problem with not liking a thing" added Khandro Déchen. *"There's only a problem with actively disliking—being self-righteously indignant—and feeling that the painting shouldn't exist. It's true—mostly—that people only start liking things when they understand them – but whether you understand or not, can have little to do with liking or not liking. Liking and not liking are subjective – and therefore empty."*

"That's interesting…" I responded *"to think of 'indifference' as a 'lack of communication'. I guess that's what it is. Everything that we're indifferent to, just isn't communicating to us – or we're not receiving the communication. So, why is that the case with 'something' for me"* I asked *"but not for someone else?"*

"Part of what makes us individual" Khandro Déchen responded *"is that attraction, aversion, and indifference have to function in terms of free dispositions.*

"Indifference is not ignorance. You're not blanking it out, it's just something that is not registering."

I must have had a question written in my expression because Rinpoche commented *"It's necessary to have attraction, aversion, and indifference in a free dimension — where aversion is* not *seen as objective. You need to understand that your personal aversion is* subjective. *Then, it can be amusing."* PAUSE *"I find it highly amusing to watch people eating porridge, rice pudding, tapioca, or semolina. I would vomit if I attempted to eat those substances — especially with hot milk. Hot sugared milk produces an immediate gag reflex — so observing people enjoying such things— from a safe distance—is amusing."*

"*Rachel always likes Rinpoche to make her porridge for her, because she thinks he makes the best porridge. She likes his porridge because he uses more milk, which makes it creamier. He starts it off the night before. He brings it to simmer and then lets it stand overnight. Then in the morning—when it's congealed—he adds more milk."*

"I can thoroughly enjoy making Rachel's porridge" Rinpoche added. *"It's a pleasure — but that doesn't mean I have to want to eat it."* Rinpoche laughed, and then added *"Whereas give me cod, chips, and tartar sauce and I'll devour it with unwithheld glee."* My stomach agreed. It was time to head to the *Cadgwith Cove Inn* where we had booked a table. Rinpoche always opted for the Betty Stogs[15] battered cod.

---

[15] 'Betty Stogs' is a copper-coloured bitter beer, brewed since 1997 using: Cornish water; whole-flower Celeia, Northdown and Aurora hops; malted barley, wheat, and Skinner's yeast.

Eleven: Bhagarvi – the terrifying wanton

Bhagarvi *(bha ga' bi /* ཥ་གའ་བི*)* / Trul-chèd Tröma *('khrul byed khro ma /* འཁྲུལ་བྱེད་ཁྲོ་མ*)*

Disciple of: Baruni
Teacher of: Vinapa and Khalapa
Varna by birth: Vaishya

Pembrokeshire Coastal Path, Wales.

Another summer. Another summer's afternoon on a fabulously wrinkled coastline. This time it was Pembrokeshire. We were not far from Drala Jong, walking a section of the coastal path, in order to visit another collapsed sea cave with Rinpoche and Khandro Déchen. The Pembrokeshire coastal path is almost two hundred miles in length and takes in some of the most breathtaking shoreside scenery in Britain. It displays almost every kind of maritime landscape – from steep limestone cliffs and undulating red sandstone bays; to volcanic headlands, beaches, estuaries, and flooded glacial valleys. It is also home to the wonder that is *The Witch's Cauldron.*

We parked at Ceibwr Bay and walked a mile or so south along the path, passing great folds of contorted rock which shelved into glittering seas. There are deep caves and sea tunnels which punctuate this stretch too, and despite the glorious sunshine we were the only ones enjoying this stunning scenery. The vista became entirely spectacular as we rounded the final headland and *The Witch's Cauldron* hove into view. As with the Cadgwith *Frying Pan*, the collapse of the cave where sea waters have eroded soft rocks along a fault, has left a remarkable arch of rock. Here at *The Witch's Cauldron,* the path teeters along the top of the arch itself, with steep and long drops on either side. As we edged downwards, we had the turquoise sea below us to the right and to the left the iridescent green pool of The Cauldron's lagoon.

After crossing the arch, we turned off the path and took our seats on the grassy clifftop overlooking the yawning crater of The Cauldron and facing out to sea. Rinpoche was clad all in Levis: shirt, waistcoat, and duster, with a green raw silk double-length cravat and blue Montana Crease hat. He made an arresting sight perched above us on the cliff. We took our vajra hammers out of their custom-made leather cases and began to practise. The *dorje chak-tö* [1]—vajra hammers of Dorje Legpa and Dorje Legma—were made in Finland. They have octagonal hafts of Finnish oak, with iron nine-pronged wrathful vajra terminals. The hammerheads are exact copies, in iron, of a Neolithic hammerhead in the Helsinki Museum. They have been case-hardened[2] to produce a dark rainbow appearance – as produced by oil or petroleum spillage in road gutters in the rain. These hammers are weighty implements, in every sense of the word.

As I sat with the hammer in my lap, the loud cackling of the gulls, and the chee-ow calls of the choughs filled my sense fields. I fell into a *pool* outside time and place where *The Frying Pan* and *The Cauldron* merged. We sat for some time in silence. At a certain point, Rinpoche wielded the hammer above his head whilst reciting mantra. The vivid red, blue, and white of Rinpoche and Khandro Déchen's lineage shawls were radiant against the gold-viridian grass and acetylene-azure sky. The colour saturation seemed to have been turned up to eleven on everything in my field of vision, as Rinpoche and Khandro Déchen sounded the primordial syllable **A**.

We continued sitting, gazing across the arch to the pellucid sea beyond.

---

[1] *rDo rJe lCags tho* / རྡོ་རྗེ་ལྕགས་ཐོ་

[2] Case-hardening is a process of hardening iron or steel. The traditional method involves packing the metal in a mixture of ground bone and charcoal or a combination of leather, hooves, and salt – inside a sealed case. This is then heated to a high temperature *(under melting point)* and left at that temperature for a length of time. The steel darkens, showing a dappled pattern of black, blue, green, and violet caused by the impurities in the bone and charcoal. This is seen now mostly as a decorative finish to firearms.

"According to local folklore" I commented *"The Cauldron is alleged to be the lair of a sea witch who will lure in and consume anyone who trespasses on her land or enters her pool."*

Khandro Déchen laughed and said *"Well, there's more than one way to consume someone. Which reminds me of Bhagarvi and her insatiable consumption of any young man who entered her bedroom."* She paused a moment and then continued *"Bhagarvi—the terrifying wanton—was in fact a disciple of Baruni – of whom Rinpoche spoke at the Devil's Frying Pan last month."*

"Perhaps we could have Bhagarvi's hagiography here at The Cauldron before we leave?" I requested.

"Certainly" replied Rinpoche. *"This seems an ideal confluence of circumstances."*

So, we relaxed on the tussocky cushions of sea grass and Rinpoche commenced *"Bhagarvi is a name in Sanskrit which relates to the terrible goddess Durga – but also to Laxmi and Parvati, so it can mean 'beautiful' or 'courageous'. Bhagarvi was born to a rich merchant family in Sitanagaram near Bezawada on the banks of the Krishna River on the east coast of India…"*

She was a beautiful young girl, perhaps slightly enamoured of her own attractiveness – but not to the degree of vanity. She realised at an early age that she had a certain power over the young lads who sometimes arrived—with their parents—to visit her family. When playing with boys she held court and they were all keen to perform whatever exploits of which they were capable at her behest. Her family entertained quite often and was widely known for their generous and gracious hospitality. There were many dinners replete with marvellous entertainments at which Bhagarvi often heard highly talented singers and musicians. As a young girl she would sing along with them – and in this she was indulged by her parents. It was a pursuit in which they saw no harm as long as she developed no desire to become a performer herself. Bhagarvi was destined to marry well and bring increased prosperity to the family.

Bhagarvi was as highly intelligent as she was desirable – and soon perceived that the only power a woman had lay *before* her marriage. Once married, a woman was entirely subject to her husband. Before her marriage however, she was entirely subject to her parents. The margin of freedom allowed to a woman therefore, such as it was, was negligible. Bhagarvi found this both detestable and depressing – and this feeling increased as she approached her fourteenth year. The idea of a lifetime of subjection appalled Bhagarvi – and yet, as she was enamoured of men, the idea of becoming a nun held no appeal to her at all.

As Bhagarvi grew older she became aware that she had great powers of seduction and could captivate the young men who came to pay her court simply by her smiles and tone of voice. Her parents were initially happy that their daughter was deemed so desirable, but as time passed, they became concerned that Bhagarvi had no interest in accepting any of her suitors as a husband. No young man ever came to them to ask for her hand in marriage – but rather, at some point, they simply ceased to visit.

Bhagarvi's parents asked her why none of the eminently suitable and wealthy young men of good families appealed to her as a husband. She dissembled in any way she could, in order to avoid a direct answer. Her parents told her that she had three months to make up her mind and then she would have to accept one of her suitors. It was beginning to prove an embarrassment to them that the worthy sons of worthy associates were deemed unworthy. It was beginning to crimp their social circle somewhat and they knew that something had to be done or they would become social pariahs.

Horrified by both her current and impending captivity, Bhagarvi decided that her last three months of freedom should be spent experiencing whatever was possible of romance, where she had the upper hand. Inevitably this led to amorous assignations in which the sexual dimension of romance changed her life in a surprising manner.

Bhagarvi was inordinately skilled at avoiding detection. She found she could mislead her chaperone and meet with a prospective lover in her bedroom on the pretext that the young man was leaving the house. Sadly, she found little joy in the aftermath of sexual encounters. Her libido and unwithheld enthusiasm were so powerful that the young men—who imagined they would like nothing better than to couple with the beautiful Bhagarvi—were frightened away by her adventurousness and the sheer ferocity of her lovemaking. One young man after another departed, never to return, until she had no more suitors.

"Somehow, Rinpoche, Bhagarvi brings to mind Anelie Mandelbaum, the twenty-two year old Swiss au pair girl you write about in Volume I of an odd boy[3]*. It seems though, that she didn't frighten you even though you were only fourteen."*

"I never was much use at being a child or teenager" Rinpoche laughed. *"I never really saw myself as being anyone other than an adult – but I imagine that might not be so uncommon. Most young people don't understand the nature of their immaturity."*

"But she caused you no anxiety?"

"No… maybe a certain degree of apprehension blended with the excitement – but she was an extremely kindly and considerate 'educator', as it were. I was grateful to her in many different ways, the most important being that I learnt to relate to ladies in terms of equality. Anelie was highly intelligent and cultured. I was her inferior in many ways, but she never took advantage of that. It was clear that she was more educated and worldly wise, but I seemed to hold the secret to understanding Rock lyrics. She often got me to explain Bob Dylan lyrics to her – which, although not always straightforward, was not difficult for me because of my understanding of Blues culture. I knew what Highway 61 signified. I knew what several hundred words and phrases, such as: mojo, hoodoo, juke joint, barrel house, crawdad, nation sack, riding the blinds, spoonful, canned heat, jelly roll, high yeller and bigleg mamma meant.

---

[3] Doc Togden—*an odd boy*—Volume I—Aro Books WORLDWIDE—2011

"So that gave me some equality with her – along with the fact that I could draw and play harp."

Bhagarvi's parents were troubled by the changes that were occurring in the life of the household, and in the distance they experienced in their relationship with other mercantile families. They questioned Bhagarvi – but to no avail. They did not know how they should approach the families of the former suitors without embarrassment – but one day they met one of Bhagarvi's former suitors in the bazaar and asked him why he no longer came to visit their house. The young man—obviously extremely embarrassed by the question—was unable to explain himself – other than mumbling something to the effect that Bhagarvi was somewhat frightening. Before they could ask him what such a statement could mean, the young man found himself having to keep an urgent appointment – and disappeared into the crowd like a greased weasel.

Time passed. Sporadically Bhagarvi's parents met other suitors who had paid court to their daughter – but each time the result was the same. Finally, they concluded they would have to confront their daughter with their findings.

"Bhagarvi" her mother asked *"we have met with several young men who were previously your suitors and each one has seemed deeply embarrassed to meet us. Each one—when pressed—has admitted to being frightened of you. They then found excuses to escape from our company. You will now explain this to us."*

Bhagarvi was unable to explain—dissembling as before—but her mother was too wise to believe Bhagarvi's prevarication. She called for her husband, who in his turn, questioned Bhagarvi as to the meaning of what they had been told. Again, Bhagarvi dissembled further – telling her parents that she could not understand what they were saying or why they were asking such questions of her.

At this her father became angry and said *"If you cannot explain, you will be locked in a room with no comforts of any kind, and there you will stay until you give us an explanation which we will be able to believe."*

Days became weeks. Weeks became a month. Bhagarvi said nothing even though she became utterly miserable for want of company or any of the things that gave her pleasure. Early one overcast morning during Bhagarvi's incarceration, Baruni—the surbdahar playing whore—happened to walk below Bhagarvi's window. She looked up and saw the young lady weeping.

"What is your sadness, young woman?" she asked.

Bhagarvi was shocked and retreated into her room. Baruni was obviously a low varna woman—and one of obvious loose morality—and she had no wish to speak with her. The next morning however, Baruni returned and asked the same question. Again, Bhagarvi retreated into her room without a word. On the third morning however, Bhagarvi felt so desolate that she decided to speak. What did it matter that the rubenesque, callipygous, bathykolpian figure below her window was of a low varna? She would prefer to speak to anyone at all – rather than no one.

"I am sorry that I rejected you before – and so rudely ignored you" Bhagarvi wept *"but… you are of a low varna and I know that I should not speak with you. Yet I am so lonely here in this room that I now welcome whatever words may pass between us."*

"You are quite right, young lady – but I entered a low varna on becoming a whore. I was once as you were—born to a rich mercantile family—and I loved to play the surbdahar when I was young. But my father's business fell on hard times and I was cast adrift to make my own way in life at the age of fourteen. The only way I could make a living was by prostitution."

"Could you not have been a musician?" asked Bhagarvi *"…rather than taking to prostitution?"*

"Possibly… but my beloved surbdahar had to be sold – and I had no way of replacing it."

"Could you not have used the money you gained from prostitution to buy a new instrument?"

"Alas, no…" sighed Baruni "because—as you see—I am rather corpulent. I could only make a meagre living – and could not buy another surbdahar."

"That is very sad!" cried Bhagarvi and wept with pity.

"You are kind…" smiled Baruni "…but my story is not yet over. Are you interested to listen further?"

"Yes – I am most keen to listen further, if there is a happier ending to your story."

"There is indeed a happier ending."

"But… you are still a prostitute…?"

"Yes" laughed Baruni "but I no longer ask for any fee. I no longer seek business – because it seeks me." Baruni noticed Bhagarvi's expression and continued 'No – not in the way that you think. It is not that I have become so popular. It is not that I have become a courtesan. It is because there are people who seek freedom from the self-defeating cycle of dualistic experience. But I will not speak more of that now – first I will tell you of the happy ending. One day—when I was singing the sounds of the surbdahar—there appeared Mahasiddha Ghantapa – the vajra campanologist. He heard me sing and recognised something in my voice. He approached me and said that he would like to avail himself of my favours. He said 'I cannot pay you with money—as I am a yogi—but I could give you teachings on music instead.' "

Bhagarvi was now intrigued. This singularly rotund, callipygous, bathykolpian woman may well be a whore – but she had met with the Mahasiddha Ghantapa and he had given her teachings. "What did Mahasiddha Ghantapa say to you? What teachings did he give on music?"

"That must be all for today" Baruni smiled. *"I have some visits to make in this town – but I shall come at the same time tomorrow and tell you more of my story. In the meantime, I would like you to contemplate the price you are willing to pay for freedom. I know that you have already paid a price for freedom – but the freedom you have gained is captivity. Tomorrow I may be able to tell you something of real freedom – but that will depend on your mind. Just consider that the secrets you keep from your parents will not remain a secret forever."*

Rinpoche paused, as the first coastal walkers we had seen, breasted the rise of The Cauldron's arch and stopped to take in the view before them.

"These interweaving aspects of freedom and captivity are fascinating" I commented.

"Yes. With Bhagarvi, we have the idea of freedom and how it interacts with a lack of freedom in others" Rinpoche replied. *"You can't expect your own freedom to be reciprocated. You have these young men here, who are dreadfully keen. Then they become frightened because the situation is outside their notions of what ought to happen. So, they get what they want – but as soon as they get what they want, they're horrified that they got what they wanted."* PAUSE *"That should be incomprehensible."* PAUSE *"One of the interesting factors here is that going outside of social norms is possible – but you have to be prepared for the consequences."*

"May I ask whether there were any consequences from your liaison with Anelie Mandelbaum?"

"Yes… the consequences were that I became her age in relation to the girls of my own age – and they seemed like children. I'd taken a trip in a time machine – and there was no turning back. Well… until I met Lindie Dale.[4] That is why I was always attracted to grammar school girls." PAUSE *"Anyhow, in terms of consequences…"* PAUSE *"…if I decide that I'm going to wear this Montana Crease hat in Cardiff, yet become terribly upset when people whistle the theme music to 'The Good, The Bad, and The Ugly' at me – then whose problem is that? It's mine, naturally. I was not compelled to wear such a hat.*

---

[4] Doc Togden—*an odd boy*—Volume II—Chapter 1—*easy rider*—Aro Books WORLDWIDE—2012

"I could say 'I didn't know people would try to make fun of me, but now I know.' So, I could choose to stop wearing it. As it is, people may as well whistle 'til their teeth protest – it makes no difference to me. In fact – I am happy to cause them amusement."

"So, there are choices to be made when you go beyond social convention" added Khandro Déchen. "To a certain extent—where it only affects you personally—any consequence of going beyond social convention is fine. But when it upsets other people, then it's not really freedom any more – not in the sense of compassionate activity."

"Freedom is also responsibility" added Rinpoche. "That is the principle of anarchism: freedom with responsibility."

"And we're all captive in the prison of dualism" I commented "where dualistic conventions seem real."

"Yes" replied Rinpoche. "We imprison ourselves. We're imprisoned by our own machinations in which societal acceptance is a security blanket."

"That is samsara" added Khandro Déchen. "We do it to ourselves."

The coastal walkers had continued on their way past us, chatting cheerfully in German. "Guten Spaziergang [5]" Rinpoche offered as they walked away. They were slightly startled to be addressed in German – but smiled. "Vielen Dank – Ihnen auch[6]." Once they were out of earshot Rinpoche said "People from other countries never expect the English to understand what they are saying." PAUSE "It's my way of giving them a surprise – hopefully a pleasant surprise."

Rinpoche stretched his legs and continued the hagiography.

As Baruni left, Bhagarvi retreated from the window and sat alone in her room thinking about the strange portentous, callipygous, bathykolpian whore who had met Mahasiddha Ghantapa.

---

[5] Enjoy your walk.
[6] Many thanks – you too.

It became clear to her that her situation was worsening. It became clear to her that her secrets could one day be revealed.

The next day at the appointed time Baruni appeared below Bhagarvi's window *"So... have you considered freedom, young lady?"*

"I have... and I have also considered the price I have paid. It has been too much and I fear that I will have much more to pay – but how is it that you have some knowledge of the secrets I keep from my parents. Are you clairvoyant?"

"I may have received transmission from Mahasiddha Ghantapa, but it does not require clairvoyance to know your secrets. Whores know everything there is to know in a town. The young men who met with you in your bedchamber visit whores and whores tell each other whatever there is to tell that may be of interest – but do not be alarmed. Although it is public knowledge amongst whores – your parents and their associates do not mingle with whores."

Bhagarvi was simultaneously relieved and anxious: relieved because her secrets were still secret from her parents – and anxious because others knew those secrets.

"I shall not betray your secrets, young lady – besides which... I know a lot about you, because we are similar in some ways."

Bhagarvi was shocked and Baruni laughed at her expression. *"No-no-no, dear girl! Dear me, do not be so faint-hearted and prissy. You were not so faint-hearted with your lovers. You are no shy, retiring model of chastity. I know you love sexuality as much as I love my surbdahar – but it was through entering into kha-jor with Mahasiddha Ghantapa that I learnt the nature of music. It was through entering into kha-jor with Mahasiddha Ghantapa that I regained my surbdahar. So maybe you will be honest enough to admit that we are similar?"*

Bhagarvi—although still a little shocked—nodded her head. She could not deny it. *"No... there is not such a great difference between us.*

"You became a whore through poverty, and although I did not sell my favours – I gave them with great enthusiasm. I gave them with such enthusiasm that I frightened all my suitors away."

"That..." Baruni laughed "... was the foolishness and vanity of your suitors. Any young man worth his salt would be glad to have met a young woman like you! Such a man would understand your extraordinary qualities! Such a young man would not imprison you as his domestic chattel!"

Bhagarvi was surprised by these words. "This is the first time I have ever heard a woman speak of freedom in such a way. Is this what you learned from Mahasiddha Ghantapa?"

"No, young lady—not specifically—but would you like now to hear what he taught me?"

Bhagarvi nodded.

"Mahasiddha Ghantapa told me that, ultimately, I was never separate from music – because I was never separate from sound. He said that the pleasure I give through plying my trade, and the pleasure I could derive through playing my surbdahar, are of one-taste."

Bhagarvi pondered "How then would you experience this one-taste, if... you had no surbdahar?"

"Ah... this is where the story takes a brighter turn – as you wish your story to take a brighter turn. Mahasiddha Ghantapa said 'There is also no need to imagine that your desirability will remain limited. There is no reason to imagine that you will not be able to obtain a surbdahar again – but first you must learn the indivisible nature of music and pleasure. Nothing in the phenomenal world is fixed – and all possibilities are naturally inherent in every situation.' He told me then that he would remain and give me instructions until I realised the goal. Then I would see whether his music lesson was valuable or not. I was cheered by Mahasiddha Ghantapa's speech and told him that I would favour him whenever he wished."

Bhagarvi was now quite fascinated. *"Tell me what happened next? Did you favour him?"*

"Mahasiddha Ghantapa said 'There is no need or requirement—at this moment—to unite with you, because we must first establish the bedrock of our union. I must first give you the instructions that will allow you to live the life of a yogini – and then you will be the judge of whether uniting with me would be valuable or not.' So, I agreed."

Baruni stood silently for a while but Bhagarvi could not contain her curiosity *"What happened next? Please go on with your story."*

"That must be all for today" Baruni smiled. *"I have yet more visits to make in this town – but I shall come at the same time tomorrow and tell you the rest of the story. In the meantime, I would like you to contemplate the price you are willing to pay for freedom. I know that you have already paid a price for freedom – but the freedom you have gained is captivity. When I return tomorrow, I shall offer you more than freedom from captivity – I shall offer you the chance of real freedom."*

Bhagarvi sat alone in her room thinking about the extraordinary callipygous bathykolpian voluptuary who had received teachings from Mahasiddha Ghantapa. It became clear to her that her situation was horrendous. It became clear that her secrets would be revealed – and that this could occur at almost any time. Her parents would discover the truth and it was likely that she would be beaten. It was even possible that she might be put to death. She had heard of such things and it terrified her.

The next day at the appointed time Baruni appeared below Bhagarvi's window. *"Have you considered freedom, young lady?"*

"I have considered my life…" Bhagarvi sighed in a low, flat, dejected voice *"and I have considered my death. I have also considered freedom."*

"I know life and death and what they represent in your situation – but what of freedom?"

"I do not wish to die or even to be beaten – but I know now that avoiding either fate is meaningless without freedom. I no longer desire the freedom I once desired – because that freedom held no joy for me. I thought there would be great joy in uniting with a lover… but, one after another had no joy in me, and in the end I lost them all. I felt that I could have been happy with any one of them – but now I realise that I would have been happy with none. They thought they wanted me – but they were afraid of me and ran away."

Rinpoche was silent for a moment and then said *"It's interesting to look at what people want. Mainly people want what other people want."*

Khandro Déchen laughed and said *"If you shop on the internet, it will suggest you buy what everyone else is buying. It tells you what is 'trending'. A lot of people are buying this – so you will obviously want to buy it."*

"Eat fæces – one hundred thousand billion flies can't be wrong" laughed Rinpoche. *"If I see people putting their heads in doorways and slamming the door repeatedly, I should say 'This is what is 'trending'! How marvellous!!' "*

"As it's 'trending' I'd better do the same – and as soon as I can!" added Khandro Déchen. *"But… why should anyone want something merely because many other people want it? How does something become the good or the right thing just because a lot of people want it, or do it?"*

"A few too many people wanted Hitler at one time" Rinpoche sighed.

"Just because a lot of people want something doesn't mean it's good" Khandro Déchen continued. *"It doesn't mean it's bad either. It doesn't mean anything. It just means that it's 'caught the public imagination' or the public have been coaxed into thinking it's a good thing by the media and advertising."*

"Many say they seek freedom" added Rinpoche *"but… few have any real desire to leave their prisons."* He laughed and continued with the hagiography.

"Many say they seek the nondual state" stated Baruni *"but few have any real desire to throw off the chains of duality.*

"Many young men are excited by the idea of sexual embrace—especially with a beautiful girl such as yourself—but few have the courage to meet with a woman who has any power of her own. The problem—in relation to your power—is that it lacks relationship with wisdom and compassion."

"Is that something you can teach me?"

"Certainly – but before I do that, I shall complete the account of my meeting with Mahasiddha Ghantapa. He said 'When you realise the indivisibility of sound and sensation, your body will be no different from the surbdahar and you will be a musician with or without a musical instrument.' I understood the teaching immediately and Ghantapa united with me, ringing his bell as we were thus embroiled. He gave me symbolic transmission, saying 'The play of the bell and the play of sensation are indivisible – if you recognise this you will recognise the nondual state.' From that moment I practised as I had been taught – and was sought out as the most desirable whore. I soon had sufficient money to purchase a surbdahar of extremely high quality and was able to live off the offerings I was given simply for playing. But—knowing that playing my surbdahar and the play of sexual sensation are indivisible—I now offer my favours freely to anyone who authentically desires to know the nature of music."

"…and of freedom?" asked Bhagarvi.

"There is no difference – music and freedom know no boundaries" replied Baruni. "But, freedom in our immediate case requires that you leave home tonight. You can stay here no longer because your secret is no longer secret. Your parents will not know before tomorrow evening, but if you are not gone from your home this evening – your life will not extend beyond the following night."

Bhagarvi blanched. Harrowing moments of silence ensued. She opened her mouth in the form of a question but was unable to speak.

'No' Baruni replied to Bhagarvi's wordless enquiry. "I have not revealed your secret, nor has any whore in this town – but your secret will become known tomorrow night."

The young men who had been Bhagarvi's suitors had sought each other out—one by one—as their anxiety had grown. Their parents had become aware that all was not well. They sensed distance between themselves and Bhagarvi's parents and had questioned their sons as to why they no longer paid court to Bhagarvi. The young men dissembled, not knowing what to say – as their own behaviour would be deemed disgraceful. An agreement was made between the young men that they would all give the same account to their parents. Bhagarvi had made trysts with them. They had agreed to meet in her bedchamber – just to steal a kiss and spend time in intimate conversation. They had gone to her room only to find her naked and wild with lascivious desire. They had fled saying nothing to anyone for fear of the consequences for themselves and for Bhagarvi.

"This is a lie!" stated Bhagarvi with some force. *"These young men were as enthusiastic as I was at first – and after some moments just as naked."*

"I have no doubt of it" Baruni replied *"but your denial will mean nothing to their parents or yours. You will be tied up in a sack with live cats and thrown into the river – there to die in agony."*

Bhagarvi almost fainted – but held onto the balcony to steady herself. *"I shall be ready to leave tonight and will go anywhere you take me."*

Baruni left and returned late that night, as she had promised. She flung up a rope and Bhagarvi climbed down. Baruni threw the rope back into the room to make the escape less obvious and they made their way to the edge of the town where they slept the night in a convenient brothel where Baruni was known. They left the town the next morning with a caravan headed west. Baruni taught Bhagarvi the way to play the surbdahar – and how to sing in accompaniment of the surbdahar. They then proceeded in the guise of travelling musicians. Bhagarvi had always had a fine voice and had always sung – so this proved no great challenge. Learning to play the surbdahar was more difficult but she had a natural talent with music, so she advanced rapidly.

Eleven: Bhagarvi – the terrifying wanton

Baruni had rubbed Bhagarvi's face with red-brown vegetable dye in order that she could not be recognised and they escaped without difficulty.

Once they had travelled to a safe distance—some leagues beyond the town—Baruni asked *"Bhagarvi—now you are free of fear and free of your parents—have you any real need of any further freedom?"*

Bhagarvi had considered this question quite intensely as they had travelled and had come to the conclusion that although she was glad of her escape from death – that this was not the answer in terms of freedom. She was free of many things – but she was still not free. *"I can no longer hope for joy with men in the normal way that such joy is found. There is no joy there for me. I do not wish to marry – and there is no hope for me in any case, as I have now lost my varna. I do have a need for freedom beyond the freedom you have already given me – and, if you will be so kind as to consent to my request, I would beg to be your disciple. You are clearly a siddha – and I could do no better than to devote my life to realising the freedom that is to be found by following your instructions."*

"Then this is my instruction. Contemplate the nature of desire and discover the spacious passion of passionate space. Realise that you are the space in which form moves – just as you have the space in which the form of lovemaking moves. When you realise the nature of this space you will meet with travelling yogis with whom you may consort – should they provide you with signs of their realisation. I shall remain with you as you practise – and we shall continue as itinerant musicians until the point when you have realisation adequate to leaving my company."

Bhagarvi agreed, and travelled with Baruni—singing to the accompaniment of her surbdahar—until she gained realisation. Every day Baruni gave Dharma teachings and practice instructions. Within a year Baruni said *"Now you know what I know apart from the final recognition of the nondual state. You will be recognised as a yogini wherever you go and you will have no difficulties in the world. Simply continue in your practice—singing for alms if necessary—and giving teachings to anyone who sincerely makes a request.*

"There may be times when you recognise others who need the assistance you needed – and at such times you will know exactly what to do."

Bhagarvi and Baruni parted company and did not meet again in that life. Within three years Bhagarvi had gained nondual realisation and was known as Mahasiddha Bhagarvi – the terrifying wanton. She gave transmission through kha-jor to many yogis—living with them for differing periods of time—and they all gained nondual realisation.

As Rinpoche concluded, I mentioned *"It seems as if it was often the parameters of social convention in these Mahasiddha stories that highlight the nature of duality."*

"Yes" Rinpoche nodded. *"Social convention – and what happens if you stand against it."* PAUSE *"The fact is that people actually like to live within fixed parameters. Of course, it's partially useful in terms of people being able to understand each other's behaviour. We need to know how to bid each other 'Good morning'. If we observe social graces – then social interactions are pleasant."* PAUSE *"However, there needs to be latitude in which people can deviate to a certain extent. Without that, interactions would become mechanical."*

"We knew an Englishwoman" Khandro Déchen grinned *"who moved to Italy and suddenly had to have a football team she supported. Why? Because all the expatriates had a team they supported. So, she felt she had to start supporting a British football team—as an expatriate—where she had had no interest at all in football before."*

"You find that all the time" Rinpoche added. *"People actually need to fit in – and they're uncomfortable with people who don't seem to fit in. That was even true of hippies. I remember sitting on a park bench in Bristol, having purchased a Ravi Shankar album. That was entirely kosher for a hippy. I had long hair. I was wearing some kind of an Afghani embroidered smock – so I looked the part.*

"Then —as I sat reading the sleeve notes of the album—a hippy loped past, with the loping hippie stride: the 'Mister Natural" walk. Noticing the album I was holding he said 'Hey man, whaddya score?' I replied 'It's a Ravi Shankar album.' He looked startled—said 'Yeah man cool'—and hurried away. It was my voice. I spoke in a fairly normal Home Counties English. He must have thought that I was an undercover narcotics agent. If I'd adopted the pseudo-Californian accent that was popular in Britain at that time – he would have understood me as a kindred spirit. Almost everyone who looked like a hippie was talking in a soft quasi-West Coast drawl. I didn't. I washed, ironed, and starched my Levi's too. That was not comprehensible to the mindset. Hippies were supposed to be free – but apparently not free to starch their Levi's or speak everyday English. That kind of 'free' was prohibited. So, I'd placed myself outside the social group." PAUSE "Later that day I was leaving Lloyd's Bank and held the door open for a conservatively dressed businessman. He looked utterly surprised and said 'Thank you very much indeed.' Then I crossed the street and entered a gentleman's outfitters. They eyed me with undisguised suspicion until they heard me speak. I said 'Good afternoon—I wonder if you could help me—I'm looking for a pair of lightweight grey woollen socks.' The man behind the counter changed his expression immediately and replied 'Certainly sir – there are a variety from which you could choose.'"

"So, the hippie saw you as a hippie until he heard you speak – and concluded you were to be avoided. Then the conservatives saw you as a hippie until you acted and spoke politely – and concluded that you were acceptable."

"Exactly – but, I was misunderstood in both perspectives, in both directions." PAUSE "None of them understood who I was – they simply took me out of one box and placed me in another, as if I'd been miscatalogued."

"If you're not understood in appearance or speech" added Khandro Déchen "people are suspicious of you. In whatever society it is – you can be free within dictated parameters.

---

[7] *Mister Natural* is a character created and drawn by 1960s counterculture and underground comic artist Robert Crumb. The character gained a following during the emergence of underground comics in the 1960s and 1970s.

"As a hippie you would not be free to like Winston Churchill. Every society has a set of subtle social rules – and you either abide by them or become ostracised."

"It's interesting. Any degree of freedom immediately gives you choices" Rinpoche added "and when you start making choices – it can be that they jar with social convention." PAUSE "Deliberately going counter to social convention—of course—is just another convention." PAUSE "That's because you're not doing what you want to do as a free individual making choices – you're just deciding to oppose everything."

"Then there's going outside of social convention in an acceptable way…" Khandro Déchen laughed "… like the 'English eccentric'. Being eccentric is fine if you're wealthy enough – or if you're a Rock Star."

"I remember when I went to visit my mother in hospital" Rinpoche added. "I was wearing my usual clothes and I apparently looked sufficiently unconventional that a lady asked me 'Are you a Rock Star?' I was caught off guard and replied 'No, I'm just visiting my mother.'"

"I imagine that really confused her" I smiled.

"I think it may have done – but I smiled at her and so she did not take it amiss" Rinpoche replied. "You see… Rock Stars, Film Stars, and other celebrities are allowed to dress unusually or unconventionally. The lumpen proletariat are not supposed to do that. Artists are allowed to go outside social convention to some degree too – because they're artists and that is the social convention. It's allowed by the rest of society. 'Oh, of course he's a poet, that's why he dresses like that.' You wouldn't hear anyone say 'Oh, of course he's an accountant, that's why he dresses weirdly.' As soon as the 'artist' or 'celebrity' label is appended – one's eccentricities of appearance are excused. That however, is just another convention. I'm the artist therefore I break conventions."

"So, playing with social conventions in this way" Khandro Déchen added "has to come from a genuine and authentic exploration rather than from breaking conventions for the sake of it. There's nothing intrinsically wrong with any convention, as long as it's not mandatory or unkind.

"So Bhagarvi was stuck in a situation and was not acting intelligently. She should have seen that it was going to play out in the same way every time. She should have seen it wasn't really the way to go about anything. Free though it seemed—it actually wasn't really free—and it wasn't going to get her what she wanted."

"It makes me wonder" I asked "if circumstances hadn't become so dire for Bhagarvi, whether she would have made that move or not?"

"Well, a choice becomes far clearer, when the other option is an agonising death." Rinpoche partially grinned. "Quite probably she wouldn't have taken the chance without the extremity of the situation."

"People often turn their lives around after a heart attack or some other brush with death" added Khandro Déchen. "But they have to have the heart attack first, or have someone close to them die of lung cancer before they think 'This is serious! I'd better lose weight, or exercise more, or give up smoking.' Then, of course, they tend to lapse, when the immediate horror has subsided."

"The prospect of imminent death can be most useful" Ngak'chang Rinpoche concluded.

With that we started gathering our things – and as I packed away my hammer, I mused about the nature of power. "Baruni says that the problem with the power that Bhagarvi wielded over the young men, was that it was divorced from wisdom and compassion. I guess that's always the case when power becomes problematic?"

"It's always a problem when it's the 'power over' rather than the 'power to' " Rinpoche replied. "It's a problem also of wanting power. Anybody who wants power has a problem, immediately." PAUSE "You see – power is not something to want for itself. Unless it has a function and it's operative in terms of helping somebody – there's no point in having it."

"Being able to pick a car up at one end as Rinpoche did, with Ngakma Shardröl, in India" smiled Khandro Déchen *"so that someone could change the wheel, is only good because someone needed to change the wheel. If nobody needs that capacity, there would have been no point in lifting the front end of a car off the ground."*

"It's the same" continued Rinpoche *"with physical power as with any kind of power or capacity. It's whether it serves a good purpose that matters. If it's power in terms of charisma and you can persuade people to do things…"* PAUSE *"… why would you want to persuade anyone to do anything apart from what was going to be beneficial? It would be deranged. With the realised protectors, we have the example of terrific power being controlled in such a way as to serve practitioners."*

"We have mundane examples around us of that as well…" added Khandro Déchen *"… how we harness the power of water, of wind, steam, and fire. Whether the power of water is contained within pipes or held back by dams, it is the nature of what's containing the power which makes that power both accessible and valuable."*

Food for thought on powerful forces. We strolled slowly back towards the car in the sunset. The giant ball of radiant gases coloured the entire sky as it sank dramatically into the vast ocean deeps to our left.

Twelve: Vinapa – the vajra vainika

Vinapa *(bi' na' pa* / བི་ནའ་པ་) / Dorje Dranyenpa *(rDo rJe sGra sNyan pa* / རྡོ་རྗེ་སྒྲ་སྙན་པ་)

Disciple of: Baruni
Teacher of: Chamaripa
Varna by birth: Kshatriya

A Sunday in late November, Penarth, South Wales.

Ja'gyür and I were visiting Rinpoche and Khandro Déchen for dinner at Frogs' Leap in Penarth. We had arrived early during the afternoon, and were called over to the coach house where they were both working. The coach house sits on the other side of the small brick-paved courtyard across from the house. It has three rooms on the ground floor: a storage room, bathroom, and a general-purpose room which contains a sofa bed for overnight guests – and Rinpoche's cross trainer. He uses this between four and five each morning when there is no one staying. He then returns to sleep a little longer *'able to consider that hour of exercise as merely a bad dream.'* Rinpoche is not that keen on exercise but keeps it up to keep his weight down.

A carpeted wooden staircase leads from there to the first floor – their open-plan art studio and writing space. Rinpoche has a large wooden headmaster's desk in one corner surrounded by shelves containing some seven to eight hundred books on Vajrayana and Himalayan culture. He has been collecting these reference materials since 1964 and fifty or more are ancient out-of-print editions.

The shelves were built as an extension of a huge old bookcase – extended with recycled pitch-pine floor boards. It completely fills the wall space up to the apex of the roof.

The desk is commodious enough to hold two large computer screens which Rinpoche uses for writing and for PhotoShop[1] work. Khandro Déchen has both a small wooden desk in the window for computer work, and a large drawing desk under the skylight. This is where she produces the images of yidams, lineage Lamas, and protectors of the Aro gTér. Behind her drawing desk is a pine planning chest holding completed drawings, works in progress, and references. On the far side of the room there is a photograph of Kyabjé Künzang Dorje Rinpoche on the wall – above two Victorian armchairs and a two-seater sofa inherited from Khandro Déchen's parents. This is where Rinpoche and Khandro Déchen often talk with their students when they come to visit.

The first thing you notice on arrival in the coach house however, is the array of guitars and amplifiers. Next to Rinpoche's desk there is a stack of old Marshall bass amplifiers, a 1960s Fender Princeton Deluxe Reverb tube amplifier, a music stand, guitar stands, and microphone stands with three microphones. Six guitars appear to be suspended precariously over the stairwell on brackets affixed to the original wooden roof beam – but Rinpoche assures us that the brackets are capable of carrying the weight of a rhinoceros. One guitar is Rinpoche's 1961 Gibson EB3 bass[2], which he played from 1966 to 1970 with the Savage Cabbage Blues band. This and the other four National ResoPhonic 12-string guitars wait to be picked up and played whenever Rinpoche takes a break from his desk. They make a beautiful and striking collection, including a rare 12-string Fender Telecaster with a narrow 6-string-width neck and two metal-bodied Tricones. One of the Tricones was made as a present for Ripoche, by his friend Don Young—the founder of National ResoPhonic Guitars —and has the name 'Doc Togden' in abalone as fret markers.

On this Sunday afternoon as we crossed from the house, we could hear Rinpoche singing and playing his version of *Sitting On Top of The World*.[3]

---

[1] Adobe Photoshop™.
[2] The Gibson EB3 was introduced in 1961 and discontinued in 1979.
[3] Walter Vinson / Lonnie Chatmon—The Mississippi Sheiks—*Sitting On Top of The World*—a Country Blues song—first recorded in 1930.

Twelve: Vinapa – the vajra vainika

It would have been difficult not to hear him in fact as he was belting it out in a fine baritone voice, which—although not entirely Mississippi Delta—was not English, with its Southern States vowels. The sound filled the courtyard. As we climbed the stairs, he was standing next to his desk, in front of the microphones – looking every inch the Bluesman in his father's sun-faded beige linen suit, made in Egypt in the 1920s.

Khandro Déchen was perched on the tall stool at her drawing desk bent over her work. She was humming along to Rinpoche's song, with Tashi the tiger-striped ginger cat winding around her legs.

After Rinpoche finished playing, we settled on the chairs and sofa to talk. Conversation turned to the current incarnation of the *Savage Cabbage Blues Band* who had been rehearsing in the coach house on the previous day. The original *Savage Cabbage* was the Blues band that Rinpoche fronted as vocalist and harp player back in his late teens. Now fifty years have passed and there are new generations of the *Savage Cabbage Blues Band* in Britain, the US, and Finland. The members are all Lineage disciples and students. In Britain, the three vocalists are called the Jellyroll Bakers – and Khandro Déchen is one of them. There are two lead guitarists, bass, percussion, and Rinpoche on harp and occasional vocals. I was sitting on the sofa, the guitars hanging to one side of me. As Rinpoche talked about the rehearsal, I commented *"It's a shame there wasn't a guitar-playing Mahasiddha – an antiquarian Jimi Hendrix."*

"It would certainly be preferable to the guitar-playing Vicar of Vajrayana" Rinpoche laughed. *"But—actually—there are a number of Mahasiddha musicians in Jomo Pema 'ö-Zér's gTérma, like Baruni and Ghantapa. And there's also Vinapa, of course. He played 12 -string – like Lead Belly, Blind Willie McTell, and Barbecue Bob"* he smiled.

Somewhat shocked I asked *"He played a guitar?"*

"No" Rinpoche grinned *"not a guitar – but a Vina, which has 12 sympathetic strings, as well as main strings and drone strings."*

"And is there teaching about music and being a musician in his hagiography?" I asked.

"Oh yes" he grinned. *"It's an exciting account. It may not have the drugs part of the triad – but it does feature 'sex' and 'Rock & Roll' of a kind"* Rinpoche laughed. That of course made me even more eager to hear it. *"Although I jest in relation to Ian Dury's song 'Sex and Drugs and Rock & Roll'* [4] *– I am also serious in terms of not dividing these hagiographies from the present-day world. The principles within these hagiographies are still entirely alive."*

As dinner was an hour or so away, Rinpoche agreed to relate the account. *"In terms of being a musician, I would say that Vinapa became a musician from the time he first heard music being played…"*

He sat mesmerised as an infant whenever he heard music and so his parents made sure that he heard as much music as time would allow. When he was barely old enough to support the instrument with his tiny arms, his Kshatriya parents provided him with a five stringed tambura – the drone instrument which accompanies other instruments such as the vina, sitar, surbdahar, saród, and sarangi.

"Can you describe the tambura, Rinpoche?"

"Certainly. The body of the tambura resembles that of the sitar – but it is fretless, the strings all being plucked without stopping them to create different pitches on the strings. It has four to six metal strings, which are plucked consecutively in repeating patterns to create an harmonic resonance with the basic key. The tambura forms the root of all Classical Indian ensembles, as it creates an acoustic reference chord from which ragas derive their distinctive character. The tambura does not engage with the melodic aspect of music – but supports and sustains the melody by providing a dynamic harmonic resonance field according to the key in which the raga is played.

---

[4] Ian Dury / Chaz Jankel—Ian Dury and The Blockheads—*Sex & Drugs & Rock & Roll*— 1977. It was released under the name Ian Dury – but *The Blockheads* also feature: the co-writer and guitarist Chaz Jankel, Norman Watt-Roy on bass, and drummer Charlie Charles.

"Rhythmically, it is not played in tandem with the melody instrument – but the timing of the plucking cycle provides a continuous loop which determines the overall ambience. The sound of the tambura is rich in overtones and the audible movements in the inner resonances of tone are achieved by the jiwari bridge, which creates a sustained whirring sound from which harmonics emerge. The principle by which the jiwari bridge functions is like the sonic equivalent of the prismatic refraction of white light into rainbow colours. The acoustic correlate of the prism amplifies the sonic spectrum of a tone to reveal its subtle harmonics. The strings pass over a wide curved bridge, which slopes incrementally away from the strings. When strings are plucked, an intermittent glancing of the bridge results. This glancing of strings on the curved bridge moves, as the points of contact with the bridge gradually shift. When a string is plucked, its amplitude gradually diminishes – and the contact of string and bridge slowly ascends the slope of the bridge creating an ethereal sonic falling-away."

This explanation was somewhat more than I could take in – but I enjoyed it nonetheless. Sometimes a welter of information—if well delivered—is like looking at a painting.

"So" Rinpoche returned to the hagiography *"Vinapa became entirely obsessed with playing the tambura and was occupied by it for most of his waking life…"*

As he grew older, he requested his parents to allow him to be instructed in the vina. They agreed and he began his training on a majestic Padma Sarasvati Vina, one of the most ancient string instruments of India.

"And… what was that like?" I dared to ask.

"The Padma Sarasvati Vina" Rinpoche launched – but kept the explanation shorter *"has one huge gourd as a sound box at the upper end of the instrument and a kudam—a larger resonating chamber—carved and hollowed from a jackwood log. It had 12 sympathetic strings—tuned to the chromatic scale—which vibrate in sympathy with the main strings. In addition, it has three chikari or drone strings. It has a tapering hollow dandi neck which carries bell-metal frets set in scalloped hardened bees-wax, mixed with charcoal powder on hardwood tracks – and a tuning box culminating in the downward curve of a yali or dragon's head…"*

Vinapa loved the instrument and learnt to name every part of it. He learnt of its construction and every skill by which the instrument was made. Due to his obsession, he learnt every technique rapidly and mastered the instrument by the age of fourteen years. At first Vinapa's joy in music was unbridled and he revelled in his mastery. He gave lessons to musicians far older than himself. He loved to teach – and the older musicians who came to him enjoyed his instructions. To those who lacked the financial resources to make large offerings for tuition he gave his lessons without any requirement for recompense. Simply the joy of seeing musicians advance in their skills was his major reward and he soon became widely respected as a master vainika.

This wonderful life continued until Vinapa was eighteen – when he started to become slightly jaded with his own accomplishment. Vinapa's disappointment with music lay in the fact that he believed there to be a further dimension of music to which he had no access. He travelled widely and asked many music teachers about the existence of another dimension of music – but none could answer his question. He had learnt the scales and rhythms. He had learnt all the intricate subtleties of which the vina was capable. He was acknowledged as the preëminent vainika of his day—at least within the land in which he lived—but he remained dissatisfied with himself.

After some years he became disconsolate. He played less and less until he ceased playing and became depressed. At this time, he began mooching around the town – not knowing what he was doing or for what he might be searching. He returned home each day, jaded and ill at ease. Sometimes he listened to itinerant musicians, who—although far less talented—seemed to derive joy from the music they played. He asked each one he met if they could tell him the secret of joy in playing music – but none could answer him. None saw it as a secret and simply answered that they did not understand his question.

On one occasion however, he heard a strange deep-pitched instrument. He followed the sound until he saw an obese, callipygous, bathykolpian woman playing a surbdahar for a throng of people who were clearly captivated by her playing. He stood at the back of the crowd—equally captivated—listening to her play. This was clearly music from some other sphere of experience. It was not that she was a faster or more intricate player than Vinapa – but her phrasing was utterly exquisite. It was not that she was playing anything he could not play—note for note—but, there was something unusual in her playing which he knew he could not replicate. He could not name it – but he could hear it. As he stood entranced, the strange half naked surbdahar player caught his eye and held his gaze – but only for a moment. Vinapa backed away and left the vicinity of the buxom behemoth with some urgency. The woman was obviously of the lowest varna and probably a whore – so even though her musicianship was sublime, he needed to distance himself.

That night however, as he lay in bed, he found that sleep did not come as quickly as it usually did. Memories of the music he had heard returned to him in an eerie manner – fragments of phrases emerged and subsided before he could connect them in any comprehensible manner. He sat up and attempted to piece together the phrases, but found it difficult to reconstruct the patterns he had heard – or the mood in which they were delivered. He decided that the next day he would play his vina again – and see whether the strings would help his memory of the wonderful cadences he had heard. There was, after all, nothing she had played that was beyond his technical capabilities. Much of what she had played was actually fairly simple – even though the time signatures were subtly different in ways that he could not describe.

The next day he tuned his vina for the first time in months. He played for several hours – but somehow, the more he played the further away his memories were driven. At this he became dejected.

How could it be that an alarmingly rotund street musician, of evidently loose morals, could play music that was beyond him? It made no sense. He'd had the finest tutors – and he'd had all the time in the world to practice. How could a low varna woman have received instruction that compared with his?

He toyed with the idea of simply never playing again—of giving his instrument away—but somehow, he knew this to be impossible. His parents, now deceased, had given all they could to promote his genius – and now to throw it all away would be the vilest and basest ingratitude.

Later that day he decided to walk around the town as he had done on so many previous occasions. He told himself that he had no intention of trying to find the mysterious surbdahar player – but it was simultaneously clear that he was lying to himself. He kept catching himself listening whenever he heard anything that might have been a distant musical refrain. After an hour he had to admit to the fact that he was searching for the woman. He did not know what he would do when he found her – he simply wanted to hear her playing again in order that he could return to his vina and emulate what she had played. As night fell, he gave up and returned home highly frustrated.

The next day—he assured himself—he would set out earlier and search for the surbdahar player as actively as he could. He would surreptitiously enquire of the townspeople. His enquiries would have to be surreptitious because he could not let it be known that he wished to discover the whereabouts of a low varna musician – who was, in all probability, a whore. Several bazaar merchants had seen her – but when he arrived at the last place she had been seen, she had always already left that place and moved on. After three days of searching, he came across her by accident not long after he had set out.

He was again repulsed by her. She was corpulent, callipygous, bathykolpian and half naked.

She did indeed have all the appearance of a whore and he knew that someone of his class should not approach such a woman. The Mahasiddha Baruni however, was aware of his mind and called out to him *"What do you want of me?"* As she spoke, she played deep yet delicate patterns on her surbdahar. The patterns she played moved in counterpoint to her voice – almost as if she were singing a song accompanied by her instrument.

Vinapa—although delighted by the sounds he heard—dissembled. *"I'm merely walking through the streets and lanes of the town in order to consider certain difficulties I've been experiencing – what could I possibly want of you?"*

"You are an excellent musician…" Baruni laughed *"… but a pitifully poor liar."*

Vinapa—amazed and thrown off guard by Baruni's clarity—replied *"How do you know I am a musician?"*

"I know that…" Baruni laughed, with such mirth that her wobbling disturbed Vinapa *"… because of the way you listen. You listen like a musician."*

Vinapa could not deny that he had great gifts of listening. He could remember and replicate any sequence of notes played by another musician. *"Yes… I can listen… and I can remember music – but that wasn't difficult for you to know. What else do you know?"*

"I also know the answer to your question…" smiled Baruni *"… but I will say nothing unless you ask me politely and from a good wholesome enquiring state of mind."*

Vinapa was now beset with philosophical difficulties. If he asked Baruni his question, he would have to make social contact with her – and that would offend against his varna protocol. He stood for a while in silence – goaded by the possibility that this woman might be able to answer the question that had tormented him for some years. After some moments of tortured confusion, he blurted out *"I have no question that you could answer"* and left hurriedly before anyone saw him speaking with her.

That night Vinapa was agitated and confused. His mind was a disorientated tangle of apprehension and perplexity. He found himself torn between the visceral need to hear Baruni's unearthly music – and the fear of what would happen to his life if he ever met the slatternly baggage again. He realised it would be an act of extreme foolishness ever to be seen to have any connection with her – and also, in terms of musical creativity, a self-destructive act of insanity to miss the opportunity. He seemed to have two options – either to seek her out or forget about music entirely for the remainder of his life. By the early hours of the morning, he realised he would have to seek her out. There was no way out other than dreary years of abject misery – and with that he finally fell asleep.

The next day Vinapa went in search of Baruni but for three days could find no trace of her. As the days passed, he found himself gripped by a rising terror. He might never find her again. He castigated himself for his imbecility in losing such a rare opportunity – and promised himself that, should he find her again, he would immediately beg for instruction no matter what the social consequences would be.

Moments after this conviction was established in his mind, he chanced upon Baruni. She was sitting under a large tree in a small town square where a group of people were listening avidly to her surbdahar recital. Vinapa took his seat amongst them and listened. He had never experienced such pleasure in listening in his life – apart from the previous two occasions he had heard Baruni play. Once her performance had come to an end, she called to him *"Hey, mister vainika man, play a song for me – I'm not sleepy and there is no place I'm going to."*

Suddenly all eyes were on Vinapa – and he froze, unable to move under the vast weight of the silence that suddenly engulfed the square. After some moments of silence, Baruni spoke again *"Go and fetch your vina and play for the people."* This was entirely unexpected. Vinapa did not know what to say.

Twelve: Vinapa – the vajra vainika

He had been prepared to speak with her – but he had never played on the public street before. Such a thing was unthinkable for a person of his varna. Baruni gazed at him for a considerable time as he sat in silence. Baruni's audience—aware of the strangeness of the situation—gradually left until only Baruni and Vinapa remained.

Finally, he asked *"How do you know I play the vina?"*

"That is simply answered, young man" Baruni smiled *"... because you sit like a vainika. You rest your hands on your knees like a vainika. When you move your hands, you move them like a vainika – and, when you look at me, your eyes travel like a vainika's."* Then Baruni looked as if she was sad – and gave the slightest frown *"That would all be good – but—and it saddens me to tell you this —you... are a dead vainika."*

Vinapa knew the truth of this statement – but still felt the need to defend and justify himself. *"Do you say this merely because I will not perform on the public street? You must realise that for a person of my varna it is not possible to perform on the street. It is problem enough that I am here talking with you – but if you want to hear me play, you will see for yourself that I am no dead performer. You may come to my house and hear. You may enter by the way for Shudras – and no one will think it a problem."*

Baruni shrieked with laughter at this proposition. *"My dear young fellow! You are a clown... I have—never—met a person more entirely ridiculous than you appear to be. You claim you are not a dead vainika – but you seek me out every day on the streets of this town just to hear me play. You lie awake at night embroiled in self-torture as to how you will learn from me without losing the purity of your varna. Why would you act in such a way if you did not know in your heart that you were dead as a vainika?"*

Vinapa knew that Baruni's statement was indisputable – but, chagrined that she had seen through his bogus rationalisations, he stood up and left without a further word. He walked back to his house stung by Baruni's remarks – and bewildered by the impossibility of his situation.

Before he was half way home he turned on an impulse and ran back to find Baruni – but there was no sign of her. He sought for her until the night fell before giving up. He decided that on the next day he would seek for her again, carrying his vina. She was obviously a yogini and obviously the very person to unlock the secret of music for him. Siddhas were known to hail from every varna. Varnas were of no consequence to them. He knew that as varnas counted for nothing amongst siddhas, that varnas could count for nothing amongst their disciples.

He set out in the morning as planned – but he was not used to carrying his vina further than from one room to another. He soon became tired as the enterprise became increasingly taxing. The days passed with wearying trudging – and on the third day he expected to see Baruni. He had always found her after three days – and it seemed to him that this was part of her method. A week went by however, and she could not be found. Some thought that Baruni had left the town and others thought otherwise. At least now he knew her name – and was able to enquire after her more directly. He no longer cared whether his search for a low varna woman brought him into disrepute. He was committed to finding her. After nine days he reached a point where he could walk no further with his burden – and so he sat down in the shade of a tree. He would wait a while until he felt capable of walking further – but after an hour he felt little different and decided to tune his vina. He did not notice—as he tuned his instrument—that a group of people had formed. When he looked up he was somewhat surprised. He was more surprised when a young girl asked *"Your vina is now in tune – so will you play for us soon?"*

To refuse would have been churlish to say the least – so he found himself with no choice but to play. The group of people increased as he played and by the end of his piece a large throng had assembled. They had been delighted by his playing and expressed their appreciation quite excessively. They laid offerings at his feet which caused him great embarrassment *"Please give me no offerings"* he pleaded – but they would not listen.

Twelve: Vinapa – the vajra vainika

Then, finally *"If you must give offerings – please give them to Baruni the surbdahar player because she is a far better musician than I will ever be. The only reason I am here is because I have been seeking her for instruction for nine days – and now, I am too weary to walk further."*

At that moment Vinapa saw Baruni amongst the crowd and stood up immediately to greet her – and beg her forgiveness for his previous foolishness and discourtesy. Baruni smiled at him *"Your apologies are for yourself, mister vainika—I do not need them—but it is valuable that you begin to see your foolishness."*

Vinapa was disquieted by Baruni's words. The idea that he had simply begun to see his foolishness—rather than having seen it in its entirety—was disturbing. *"So… may I now beg you to listen to the question that has tortured me for these last few years?"*

"Certainly…" replied Baruni *"but I do not wish to hear the question in words. You need to explain your question to me through playing your vina."*

This was bewildering and Vinapa replied *"…but you must have heard me play when you were amongst the people who were listening to my raga."*

"Yes—I was listening—but I want you to ask me your question through your vina – not by merely playing your vina."

"But I do not know how to do that" answered Vinapa, entirely bewildered. *"I would not even know how to begin."*

"Then let me provide you with inspiration" Baruni smiled. *"Simply fix your eyes on me – and begin to play."*

Vinapa prepared to do as he was instructed – but before his fingers touched the strings, Baruni removed her upper garment, exposed her breasts and caused them to sway. Vinapa's fingers froze. He looked down quickly, so as not to be seen gawping at the brazen bare-breasted trollop who stood before him.

After some moments Vinapa realised that he was alone in the square. Baruni had gone and his erstwhile audience was also gone.

Vinapa began weeping uncontrollably as soon as the reality of his situation crystallised. He had spent days trudging around the town looking for Baruni after having lost his opportunity twice before. Was he incapable of knowing what he really wanted from life? If he wanted the secret of music as much as he insisted to himself that he wanted it – why did other factors dominate his desire? Was he incapable of learning from mistakes? What would happen now? Would there be another nine days of searching – or would it now take longer? Nine weeks? Nine months? Nine years? Would his search take him beyond the town, to other towns, and other countries? He knew at this point that he might have to spend the rest of his life in search of Baruni. She was clearly a siddha – and he had squandered precious opportunities one after another.

A strange certainty began to form in Vinapa's mind, as he realised the weight of the commitment he was making with himself. He was committing to seek for Baruni until he found her—however long that might take—and he had to begin his journey the way he meant to continue it. He would not go home again – but sleep in the street like a beggar in the last place he had seen Baruni. He fell asleep next to his vina and awoke covered with dust. His vina had been stolen – but this didn't worry him. At least he would not be forced to carry it. He obtained some water to wash himself and was about to set out in search of Baruni – when she appeared. *"Ah, mister vina man – it seems you have lost your instrument but found me instead. Maybe you will have to ask me your question in words?"*

Vinapa began with tears in his eyes *"I thought I would have to search the world for you, reverend lady. I have been a fool. I have fooled myself into believing that I was serious in my quest for music, but in my foolishness I have come to understand that my desire for music was real – it was merely my conditioning that was not real.*

"I now see that I continually misled myself with distorted ideas of my real motivation – that merely obscured that motivation."

"Yes…" smiled Baruni *"… but I would rather hear your question than hear your philosophising about your confusion."*

Vinapa nodded and began *"I have studied and practised for many years—and I was acknowledged as having reached the peak of my art in playing the vina—but I was left dissatisfied and frustrated. I believed there was a further dimension of music which I could not find. I walked the streets of this town—before meeting you—and there I heard many travelling musicians. I noticed that although they were below me in technique – they seemed to radiate with a joy of playing that I could no longer find. That joy was there when I was young—when I simply played my tambura—but as I advanced in technique and skill, I lost what was there naturally when I was an infant."*

"Mister vainika—skilled as you are—you have never lain with a woman and therefore you have no capacity to play any instrument. If you lack the capacity to admire my prodigiously pendulous breasts – it is little wonder that the secret of music escapes you. If you wish to learn the further dimension of playing music you must first learn to play with me."

Rinpoche paused in his account and I asked *"Why is she saying that experience of sexual intimacy is necessary to be a musician?"* I asked. *"Is it because he lacks the capacity to feel the music? That he's just a technician with no capacity for sensation?"*

"In terms of sexuality" replied Khandro Déchen *"it's an arena where there is loss of control. And that was something outside Vinapa's experience."*

"When you're a young musician" added Rinpoche *"and you're learning – you can make mistakes. You lose control. But if you become totally proficient, then loss of control becomes rare. If there's never any mistake – there's never a challenge, either.*

"If you become perfect, there's no challenge – because you know you're not going to make a mistake. When learning, if you perform perfectly, there's great joy. There's joy because you could have made a mistake – because you're still capable of mistakes."

"When you're no longer capable of making mistakes" added Khandro Déchen "interesting accidents cease to occur. So, sexuality becomes part of the equation in terms of loss of control."

"You need something that moves you outside of that state of having to control everything." Rinpoche smiled "Shall I continue?"

I nodded. Rinpoche placed his National Resolectric across his knees – and slid a note up to the twelfth fret—with the chromium tube in his hand—before continuing.

Vinapa sat staring at Baruni as she removed her clothing. He had no response to make. He was still torn between contradictory concepts – but he knew that he now had no choice but to follow his resolution. He knew that the rest of his life would be worthless if he retreated yet again – so he simply sat and gaped.

"If you enter into union with me, I shall teach you the further dimension of music."

Vinapa, horrified as he was, replied "I shall commit to whatever is needed, reverend lady. I would do anything to learn the secret of such mastery."

Baruni replaced her clothing—the square would soon be peopled, as the day began—and sat down with her surbdahar. She began to play and the music swelled and spiralled: majestically, ætherically, rhapsodically, plaintively, joyously, exuberantly, jubilantly, enigmatically, and mysteriously. There was no doubt left in Vinapa's mind that he had made the right choice. It seemed also to him that the horror that previously accompanied the prospect of union with an obese, callipygous, bathykolpian strumpet had faded into an overarching sense of awe in which music and Baruni could not be divided into separate entities.

Vinapa came to Baruni at night as she instructed him – and before entering into union she said *"To be a musician is partial unless you are also a tantrika – because tantrikas are the masters of all the Arts."*

"But… how can I become a tantrika? I have no religious training…"

"Religious training is not entirely necessary. I had no religious training when the Mahasiddha Ghantapa gave me transmission – and I shall give you the same transmission as he gave me. First you must shed your clothing – the clothing of your body and the conceptual clothing of your perception."

Vinapa did as he was requested and Baruni instructed *"Now, allow your mind to be tuned like the strings of your vina: too loose and they will not resonate; too tight and they will not ring."* Baruni then enquired whether Vinapa understood what she had said. He replied that he did. *"Then…"* continued Baruni *"I shall explain further:*

> *"The secret lotus: if it is too loose there is no sensation;*
> *If it is too tight there is no pleasure.*
> *The secret vajra: if there is no movement there is no sensation;*
> *If it is frenetic there is no pleasure.*
> *Where there is no sensation or pleasure,*
> *There is no possibility of realisation*
> *Through empty sensation and empty pleasure."*

With that Baruni and Vinapa entered into kha-jor and Vinapa received transmission of the nondual nature of sound and silence. Whilst in union Baruni sang:

> *"Leave mind in its own space as you pluck the seven strings of the vina.*
> *When you recognise that sounds and the hearers of sound are not separate,*
> *The music of your vina will resemble our union – your fingers moving of themselves*
> *As they traverse the callipygous bathykolpian contours of my manifest form.*

Your fingers know the vina but they are trapped in the lifeless patterns of expertise.
Release mind from musical patterning, societal patterning, and personal patterning
And you will know the innermost heart of music as the nondual state."

Baruni then commanded him to play the vina which she had removed when she found him asleep in the small town square. As soon as his fingers touched the strings, he experienced the sphere of nondual play where form and emptiness resound as the ornaments of reality. Baruni then instructed him in the essential aspects of Vajrayana and advised him in terms of how he should proceed to live the life of a tantrika.

The next morning Vinapa awoke to find Baruni gone. He practised as he was instructed for three years – but the nondual state eluded him. This did not worry him greatly because Baruni had advised him not to chase the nondual state in the same way that he had chased for the essence of music. *"The nondual state"* she had told him *"is not as easily found and integrated as your new knowledge of music – so be content to play your vina without hope of realisation or fear that it will elude you."* Vinapa was repossessed by the joy of music – and so he was more than content to continue without anticipation or expectations. He resumed his rôle as a teacher of vina – but gave free performances on the street, so that even the poorest people would have access to music. This earned him disfavour in certain quarters – but it no longer concerned him. He taught everyone who approached him and asked nothing in return.

One evening whilst teaching a group of young musicians he was told that there was a fat, morally dubious, low varna woman at the back door carrying a surbdahar. Vinapa was overjoyed and asked that she be invited in by the front door as an honoured guest. *"This is Mahasiddha Baruni – we are greatly honoured that she has come to visit us. Now you will hear music the like of which you have never heard before."*

Some of Vinapa's Tirthika students were shocked and left immediately in order that they would have no contact with Baruni – but those who remained found themselves as a small audience for the most exquisite raga they had ever heard: a raga for the early hours of the morning. Vinapa prepared a room for Baruni and she remained with him for nine days in which she imparted her final teaching.

On the day before she departed, Vinapa and Baruni entered kha-jor together and Vinapa realised the nondual state. His association with Baruni however, became common knowledge in the town—due to her residence at his home—and those who were fixated with ideas of varna purity had nothing more to do with him. He was ostracised by many – but all those to whom music was more important than societal sanction, became his students. Mahasiddha Vinapa taught many disciples through the Art of the vina – and many of those realised the nondual state.

After almost a minute of silent pondering, I said *"It's an interesting statement that to be a musician is partial unless you're also a tantrika, because tantrikas are the masters of all the Arts."*

"Yes" Rinpoche interjected. *"That is what both Kyabjé Düd'jom Rinpoche Jig'drèl Yeshé Dorje and Kyabjé Künzang Dorje Rinpoche told me, several times. They were adamant. This is why Düd'jom Rinpoche insisted that I return to Britain to take my Art degree rather than returning immediately to Nepal. This is also why Düd'jom Rinpoche told me never to abandon Blues or any of the Western Arts with which I'd engaged before I met him."*

"That will be important for artists and musicians to know" I replied. *"Presumably —with regard to what you said previously—it's not saying that in order to be a great musician you need to practise Vajrayana?"*

"Yes and no" replied Rinpoche. *"The 'no' would relate to not having to practise what would be recognisable as Vajrayana. The 'yes' would relate to naturally entering into a sphere of experience which would not be entirely dissimilar to the essential dynamic of Vajrayana."*

"So…" I mused *"to be a real musician, your artistry needs to extend into other spheres – and that is what a tantrika does?"*

"Yes, it is just natural" Rinpoche responded. *"If you push any skill far enough, it takes you into the sphere of Vajrayana. It has to – because although Vajrayana is a religion, it's also natural."*

"It's something that anyone can discover" added Khandro Déchen *"anyone who is willing to move outside conditioned constraints, that is."*

"Think of William Blake for example" continued Rinpoche.

"Yes" I replied. *"He was nominally Christian – but he went outside the parameters of conventional Christianity quite considerably."*

It then started raining heavily: *'raining old women and sticks'* as they say in Wales – and, for some minutes, we all sat and listened to those crones and their staves pounding on the skylights.

"I think it comes down to—everyone—being an artist" Rinpoche continued. *"When everyone's an artist – people make artistic choices. If you recognise yourself as an artist then you make those choices about everything: the clothes you wear, the colour you paint your home… You don't just go for magnolia—or 'not-quite-white'—because that's the current fashion. We like white to be white."*

"Our house, for example" continued Khandro Déchen *"is natural wood and white walls. A certain woman confided to us 'Wood and white were fashionable in the 1970s – but it's now strictly démodé"* Khandro Déchen laughed. *"It hadn't occurred to her that we were not trying to be fashionable. We were simply following our own æsthetics and were entirely unconcerned with the possibility of being seen as démodé or passé."*

"Whenever you talk about liking, it always makes me wonder where 'disliking' comes from?" I asked. *"What's going on when we dislike something?"*

"We may have addressed this before… ?"

"Yes, we have – but I feel it's well worth looking at it again, if you don't mind?"

"Not at all – but maybe this time it should be a more formal exposition" Rinpoche replied with some sense of gravitas. *"I feel that it is vital for Vajrayana students to know how to relate to the apparent 'likes' and 'dislikes' of their Lamas – especially their strongly expressed 'likes' and 'dislikes'. If students cannot relate to these as empty displays, they end up trying to adopt the 'likes' and 'dislikes' of their Lamas – as if these 'likes' and 'dislikes' represent absolute reality. That is the first point. The second point is that Lamas—in terms of Inner Tantra—must, of necessity, manifest these 'empty displays' to illustrate the nature of transformation. In terms of Sutrayana, the 'personality of the Lama' should not be apparent – it should reflect emptiness. This is because the principle of Sutra is* renunciation.*"* PAUSE *"With Inner Tantra however, the principle is* transformation *– and therefore, the Lama's personality is a mode of teaching."* PAUSE *"This does not mean that the vajra master is central to a 'cult of the personality'. This could easily become the case – but the student's personality is a vital part of the equation. It is the rôle of the Lama to conjure with the personality of the student. Chhi'mèd Rig'dzin Rinpoche certainly worked with me in that way. He never sought to negate my personality – but rather to enable me to discover the potential of my personality."*

"Then" added Khandro Déchen *"a dance can occur in terms of the personalities of Lama and student."*

"Quite so" Rinpoche continued. *"The third point—returning to your question about 'disliking'—is that 'disliking' is simply another form of 'liking'. One can relish 'disliking' as much as 'liking'. One's 'disliking' however, does not have to be competitive, embattled, or bellicose. There is a difference between 'dislike' seen as 'objectivity' – and 'dislike' seen as 'subjectivity'. If you* know *that your 'dislike' is subjective – you do not have to be hostile. I do not have to take issue with* you *because of what you* like*. What I* like *does not have to upset or anger* you*. We do not need to correct each other – because our likes and dislikes are subjective, and therefore empty. We do not need to look down on* each other *for liking whatever it might be that we like or dislike."*

Rinpoche smiled. *"The Lama's subjective likes and dislikes are not religious truths – and the student's contradictory likes and dislikes are not heresy."*

"What is interesting here" added Khandro Déchen *"is the incongruity. That someone likes something that you don't like, could simply be intriguing – but it can only be intriguing, when both views are seen as subjective, as empty. If both views are seen as objective – then you have to argue."* Khandro Déchen laughed *"You may even have to fight to the death over it."*

"Exactly" laughed Rinpoche. *"There is a common misunderstanding in the arena of Western Buddhism, in which one has to like everything. Everything—is—primordially equal – but 'objective equality' does not preclude 'subjective liking' and 'subjective disliking'. That all form is empty, does not mean that form can no longer arise. In terms of Vajrayana – one has to consider 'authentic individuality' and 'authentic appreciation'. One has moved beyond the emptiness bias of Sutrayana into the sphere in which form arises from emptiness. When form arises, it is multifarious. All forms are equal in terms of their* empty nature *– but the form aspect is* individual *and therefore* different. *Where there is* difference *there is the possibility of 'like' and 'dislike' – but, 'like' and 'dislike' must be seen as* equally subjective.*"* PAUSE *"This is why individuality is not a problem in terms of Vajrayana."*

"You have to be able to subjectively 'dislike' as well as subjectively 'like' " continued Khandro Déchen. *"I think—in general—that Western Buddhists tend to find this difficult. An entirely free 'dislike' is the same as 'liking'. When you know your 'liking' and 'disliking' are subjective – there's no discord. You don't have to attach anything to it."*

"Sometimes" I commented *"it seems that, not only are Buddhists* not *supposed to dislike anything – but they're not supposed to like anything* that *much, either."*

"This would seem to come from the somewhat puritanical Western take on Sutrayana – in which enjoyment equates with lust, one of the deadly sins" responded Rinpoche.

"People with this view are probably influenced—albeit unconsciously—by Calvinistic[5] austerity and rigorous severity of self-censure and self-denial. This is not the same as the Buddhist denial of the existence of a 'self'—where the self[6] that is denied is the solid, permanent, separate, continuous, and defined identity—it's the self-denial or doing without, abstinence, flagellation, sack-cloth and ashes, et cetera. Some Western Buddhists seem to take pride in absence of appreciation; absence of enjoyment, admiration, delight, animation, exhilaration, or excitement. With Vajrayana however – liking, lust, passion are all aspects of changchub sem[7] and of the nondual state."

"That sounds much more enjoyable" I commented. "What's not so much fun is hearing how jaded Vinapa is at the beginning of the story. It's sad to think how even the pursuit of something creative and artistic can still lead to a dead end."

"Yes… but Vinapa needs to reach that point in order to break out of his varna restrictions. He also needs to hit that barrier – the barrier of virtuosity." Rinpoche paused for a moment and then said "I'm reminded—with Vinapa—of an album called 'The London Howlin' Wolf Sessions'. Howlin' Wolf came to London and made an album with Steve Winwood, Eric Clapton, and other British Rock and Blues musicians. Howlin' Wolf is mainly on vocals but when they play Little Red Rooster, Eric Clapton says 'You should play guitar on this.' That was because it required slide-guitar[8]. Howlin' Wolf tells Eric Clapton that he should play it – and teaches him how to play the slide. Eric Clapton is a little tentative – so Howlin' Wolf says 'No, man. It's like this, you gotta do it like this.' Eric Clapton gets it quite quickly. He replicates Howlin' Wolf exactly – but something is missing. I couldn't say—musically—what the difference was; apart from the lack of something that one might term mojo[9]. So, this is similar to the way Vinapa reached a point of sterility.

---

[5] The theological system of Calvin has a strong emphasis on the depravity of humanity.
[6] dag (bDag / བདག / atman)
[7] byang chub sems / བྱང་ཆུབ་སེམས་ / bodhicitta – active compassion; empathetic appreciation in Dzogchen – the nondual state of the individual.
[8] Slide-guitar is a technique often used in Blues. It involves holding a glass or metal tube—a slide—fitted on one of the fingers and held against the strings, to create glissandos and extended vibrato.
[9] Magic.

"There was nothing wrong with Eric Clapton's guitar playing, he could play the notes perfectly – but there was somehow a lack of emotion in the notes. Howlin' Wolf couldn't match Eric Clapton's technical virtuosity as a guitarist – but he could play Blues as naturally as breathing. That's the interesting point. Howlin' Wolf couldn't generally play with the virtuosity of Eric Clapton—he was a fairly primitive guitarist —but, he could play Blues with utter aplomb."

"So, Vinapa hears Baruni in the marketplace" added Khandro Déchen "and he hears something which is missing in his own music. And he wants to know how to play as Baruni plays. That is what is fascinating."

"And knowing that something is missing" Rinpoche chuckled and offered 'because the thrill is gone' [10]."

"Yes" responded Khandro Déchen. "When you become utterly expert at something—and there's nowhere to go—the only place there is to go is somewhere so subtle that it seems inaccessible. It seems inaccessible because perfect is perfect and it is not possible to be more perfect than perfect." PAUSE "There's no way forward from perfect – because to go beyond perfect, requires a sideways step into somewhere else."

"Is it that 'advanced skill and technique' is just increasing the 'form' aspect" I pondered "and that the 'emptiness' aspect is lost?"

"Yes" Khandro Déchen responded. "The process of playing becomes rigid and confining – because perfection doesn't open itself to anything else. The more perfect you become, the more perfect the cage becomes – and, if you don't realise it's a cage, then of course, you'll lose enthusiasm. Enthusiasm dwindles, because you're in a cage – not knowing it's a cage. That's the effect of the 'cage of musical perfection'. It cramps enthusiasm. It cramps the emotion. It stultifies everything."

"But Vinapa knows there's something wrong, doesn't he?" I asked. "He hasn't identified the nature of the cage maybe – but he knows that there's something outside of it. He's got this sense of something missing."

---

[10] Roy Hawkins / Rick Darnell—BB King—*The Thrill Is Gone*—*Completely Well*—1951. This slow Blues song became a major success for BB King – and his rendition made the song a Blues standard.

"Yes. That *is because he has the musical prowess to hear it*" Rinpoche added. "*He hears itinerant players, and he knows that he's hearing something he doesn't have even though the itinerant musicians are nowhere near as technically proficient as he is. He might have been an 'Eric Clapton' – with those itinerant musicians as Howlin' Wolves.*"

With that Rinpoche picked up his slide from by the chair and played the riff from 'Little Red Rooster'. He then paused "*I'm a primitive musician – but, because I'm a primitive musician and don't understand certain things, it gives me a certain latitude which could be described as freedom*" Rinpoche smiled. "*My cage is not perfect.*"

"*Someone once told Rinpoche that he couldn't keep time*" Khandro Déchen chuckled "*and he just accepted that. Then one day he was playing with others in New York and Ngakpa Seng-gé said 'I thought you said that you couldn't keep time? You were keeping time with us—all—through that.' The opinion as to Rinpoche's time keeping was, of course, based on his solo performances in which he performed songs in multiple time signatures. The person who expressed the idea was more familiar with Pop music – where the beat is unvarying. With Classical Music however, multiple time signatures are standard.*"

"*Avant Garde Jazz too*" Rinpoche added. "*Not so much with Blues – but Blues is decidedly relaxed in terms of time signatures.*" PAUSE "*It takes me a while to discover how to make a song my own. I have to experiment until it becomes something I can sing with conviction – and my way of doing that is to change time signatures within the song. So, I may start in 4:4 shuffle but change to 5:4, standard 4:4, 5:8, and back to 4:4 shuffle.*"

"*Rinpoche does that consistently however*" explained Khandro Déchen. "*Although the timing is unusual, it's the same each time he plays the song.*"

"*I just play a song in the way it feels best to me – and so changing time signatures just happens. But I didn't know about time signatures – I had to be told what the time signatures were that I was using.*" Rinpoche laughed. "*I was glad to have my education improved.*"

"That, Rinpoche" I smiled "is a wonderfully great example of 'lack of technical knowledge' being more creative than the result of study."

"Possibly – but the little I have learned concerning time signatures has been most helpful to me."

I knew it would soon be time to get the dinner ready but wanted to ask about the final line of Baruni's transmission to Vinapa. "That phrase about knowing the innermost heart of music as the nondual state…" I commented "… it's made me think about seed syllables, and whether you can say there is a sound of the nondual state?"

"No, not a particular sound other than the primordial A – which again, is a symbol, rather than the nondual state. It's a symbol for the nondual state."

"Is it A rather than Om, A'a:, or Hung—or any other seed syllable—because they are all more complex?"

"Yes, you could say that. A is the first and last sound that one makes as a human being. It's the outbreath."

"So are all seed syllables only symbolic?" I asked. "You sometimes hear people talk of Om being the humming of the universe?"

"That sounds like something you'd hear in terms of Hinduism or other forms of eternalist monism" responded Khandro Déchen. "It's making something meaningful in an artificial way. Because it's all sound. It's not one specific sound. You can find presence of awareness in any sound."

"Whenever you find a reliance on symbol" added Rinpoche "you are moving more towards Mahayoga."

Rinpoche ran his slide up the top string creating an unearthly wailing echo of the Mississippi Delta – adding *"but right now…"* a slide-note *"we need to be moving…"* another slide-note *"toward the kitchen…"* PAUSE *"to prepare the lobster fondue."* Then he sang *"When a woman got trouble, ever'body throws her down – lookin' for a good friend, who can't be found. You gotta come on— in my kitchen—because it gonna be raining, out there*[11]*."*

---

[11] Robert Johnson—Robert Johnson—*Come On in My Kitchen*—1936. Robert Johnson (1911–1938) was a Blues musician and songwriter. His recordings from 1936 to 1937 display a combination of singing, guitar skills, and songwriting talent which influenced later generations of musicians. His recording career spanned a mere seven months – but he is recognised as a master of Blues, particularly Delta Blues style, and as one of the most influential musicians of the 20th century.

Thirteen: Lu'ipa – the piscatorial viscera epicurean

Lu'ipa *(lu'i pa /* སུའི་པ *) /* Nya-to Zhab *(nya lTo zhabs /* ཉ་ལྟོ་ཞབས *)*
Disciple of: Bhagarvi
Varna by birth: Kshatriya

An August morning in Cadgwith.

We had risen early to take a boat trip with Nigel Legge before breakfast. Rinpoche and Khandro Déchen have been taking boat trips with Nigel every year since 1990. The trip had been planned for the day before. The weather however, had proved just slightly too inclement for a boat the size of the *Razorbill* – and Nigel postponed the jaunt until today. He had promised, with his fisherman's knowledge, that today would be perfect weather. And, of course it was. The sea out in the bay was entirely calm and the sky clear and early-morning-blue as we made our way down to the fishing cove where Nigel and the *Razorbill* awaited.

Nigel Legge, *'fisherman, oil-painting artist, and traditional willow lobster pot maker'*, as he is known, has been fishing from Cadgwith since he was sixteen years old. Although now past retirement age, he has not yet retired from the sea and is a well-known and well-loved part of the Lizard fishing community. He seems *of the sea* himself. It's hard to imagine that he will ever stop taking his boat out of the cove to catch crab and lobster as he does each fine day during the summer months. Nigel hauls his catch from lobster pots which are left out in the ocean overnight with lines attached to buoys. Many of those pots Nigel has handcrafted himself from willow as his father taught him half a century ago. The pots are things of beauty and he now also sells them to television and film companies, design shops, and the passing public. He spends the winter months making the withy pots for sale, and for his own use the following summer.

He also paints in oils, and when not out at sea, he can usually be found in his tiny studio hidden away up a cobbled side alley in the cove[1]. Like everything else about him, Nigel's Art is inspired by the ocean. He produces paintings of traditional fishing boats set against the changing moods of the sea, some on canvas but many on irregular-shaped pieces of driftwood washed up on local beaches. His paintings grace the inn and café of the cove, and hang in most of the cottages that are rented out to holidaymakers. Nigel is a good friend of the Togden family and they always venture out to sea with him at least once during each Cadgwith holiday.

On this morning we clambered across the shingle of the cove to where *Razorbill* was gently rocking on the edge of the sea. With an upturned fish crate to stand on, and a hand from Nigel, we were all soon aboard. It's a small open wooden boat, painted white with a bright blue trim, two flags at the rear and a large fog horn in the prow. Nigel cut the perfect fisherman figure, standing in the stern of *Razorbill*, hand on the tiller, in yellow Wellington boots and a dark blue fisherman's jumper. He fired up *Razorbill* and we ranged ourselves against the gunwales as we headed out from the bay to the open sea.

We had a marvellous trip, following along the coastline, checking Nigel's pots as we went. As Nigel hauled on the rope from one of his buoys, a large bundle of willow withies rose to the surface with the pot. Nigel explained that he needed to make a pot that afternoon and so had left the sticks soaking in the sea the day before. If left to soak in a bucket of water on land it could take three days to reach the required saturation for weaving. The pressure of the water at thirty feet was sufficient to reach that saturation overnight. We headed south towards Lizard Point passing the Devil's Frying Pan and Church Cove. The craggy coastline to our right was spectacular, but the open sparkling sea to our left was equally mesmerising.

---

[1] Now in a yellow wooden shed at the entrance to the Todden.

Thirteen: Lu'ipa – the piscatorial viscera epicurean

We came to the lifeboat station at Kilcobben Cove with its long precipitous launching ramp that plummets into the sea from the station perched high on the cliff above. Then Nigel turned *Razorbill* in a sweeping arc and we were heading back towards Cadgwith. There were the antics of gulls, cormorants, and terns to entertain us – and, as we neared The Devil's Frying Pan, we spotted the sleek head of a seal only feet from the boat. We sailed under the arch of the Frying Pan and Nigel switched the engine off as we all silently enjoyed the stillness of the water in the lagoon. Robert's[2] ashes were scattered here from Nigel's boat years ago and this part of the trip was always powerful—poignant—and Nigel was visibly moved.

After some minutes in the Frying Pan, we passed back under the arch and headed towards the cove. Nigel sailed *Razorbill* right up on to the shingle and we disembarked as elegantly as we could. It was still early and the cove filled with fascinating fishing activity, so we settled on the long wooden bench outside the winch house to watch. Breakfast could wait a while longer. Nigel used the communal motorised winch to pull *Razorbill* high up the beach and started unloading his pots. Then one of the larger boats of the returning fishing fleet was also winched aground and the crew threw crates of catch onto the shingle. There was a strong smell of fish, the pleasing aromas of the ocean from the fresh catch, and a less pleasant background odour of old fish heads and rotting guts from a plastic bucket near our feet. As I caught a strong draught of fœtid fish I asked *"This would be a perfect place to hear about Lu'ipa, the fish gut eater – although it might put me off my breakfast. I know his story from other collections but I think he appears in the Jomo Pema 'ö-Zér gTérma too?"*

"Ah yes, he certainly does" **Rinpoche** smiled. *"Mahasiddha Lu'ipa – the connoisseur of piscatorial entrails. The hagiography however, might not be quite in the style to which you're accustomed. I could start telling it now – and we'll see how far we get before breakfast beckons?"* We all nodded eagerly.

[2] Ngakpa Düd'dül Dorje—Robert E Lee Togden—died in 2011 at the age of 17.

"He didn't eat piscatorial intestines as a child, of course" Rinpoche began *"Lu'ipa was the second son of a Raja of the Land of Lions."*

I asked where that was located in India and Rinpoche answered *"It bordered on the eastern frontier of Ögyen. Ögyen is more-or-less north-eastern Afghanistan…"*

As a second son he had no expectation of succeeding his father as Raja of the Land of Lions. He turned his mind instead to other considerations: philosophy, the Arts, and Sciences. He became an exponent of all the Arts and was keen to absorb as much knowledge of the world as he could. He was a young man who thought in depth about the nature of experience and existence – and of the nature of reality. His studies and internal enquiries eventually led him to understand that although his exploration of the Arts and Sciences within the palace were rewarding – they were not as rewarding as they could be, if he were free to roam the wider world. On reaching this conclusion he determined to leave the palace, seek a teacher, and become a wandering yogi. As a prince of the Land of Lions, Lu'ipa had been raised to think of himself as Mi'i Seng-gé—a human-lion—and so, as a yogi, he intended to roam the snow ranges as a lion amongst yogis.

Unfortunately for Lu'ipa, his father died on the cusp of his decision to set off on what he imagined to be a great journey of adventure and discovery. The court astrologers added to his woe by determining that he should succeed his father as Raja, rather than his elder brother. His elder brother was naturally indignant – but Lu'ipa went to him with a plan. *"Do not be angry with me or be resentful, brother – because I like this idea no better than you. I do not wish to take your place as Raja – and, I need not take your place if you can help me escape from the palace."* His brother was deeply touched by Lu'ipa's lack of self-interest. He threw himself into the creation of an elaborate plan to aid Lu'ipa in his escape.

Lu'ipa told his immediate family that he intended to remain in his apartments fasting for a week, in order to prepare for the ceremonies at which he would be installed as Raja. His family was naturally pleased at his familial piety—knowing that he did not relish the idea of becoming Raja—and left him to prepare. That night, with the assistance of his elder brother, Lu'ipa escaped from the palace dressed in the white rags of a yogi. By the time his supposed week-long seclusion was over, he was both a sea voyage and a week's hard horseback ride away. Despite searches Lu'ipa was lost to his family and country – and eventually his elder brother became Raja. He became a good and just ruler – because he never forgot the lack of self-interest of Lu'ipa. The court astrologers—seeing what a fine ruler Lu'ipa's brother turned out to be—soon determined that there were sound astrological reasons why he turned out to be the best ruler after all.

Lu'ipa sought out Vajrayana teachings from the wandering yogis and yoginis he met – but, although they all gave him valuable teachings, none of them turned out to be his vajra master. Somehow all he ever received was information. There was no sense of transmission – and without the experience of transmission Lu'ipa could not dedicate himself to becoming a disciple. Although frustrating, this was not too severe a problem to Lu'ipa as he was young and had many years ahead of him. He was thus confident that, in time, he would find his vajra master. He was never in want—or in need of sustenance—because his courtly manners won him the respect of everyone who encountered him. Thus, although he never sought luxury, his life was extremely easy. He ate the best of food and wore the finest cloth because everyone felt moved to present him with the best. It seemed natural – because Lu'ipa was so evidently cultured, well mannered, and well spoken. He never sought the best—but the best always came to him—and he was too polite, courteous, and gracious to refuse.

He was used to life at court and even though he had the character and strength to endure a far harsher life than he had experienced in the palace – his life was still far removed from that of most tantric itinerants.

Eventually however, the situation of other tantrikas began to worry Lu'ipa – as he saw how much better his life was than theirs. He started to feel as if he was some kind of pseud – a tantric pretender, trivial poseur in the world of those to whom comfort was irrelevant. *'I've left the palace'* he thought *'but I've brought the palace with me. I thought I had escaped – but I'm actually still more-or-less where I always was. I'm just a prince in disguise.'*

The loud grating of the winch pulling another boat up the beach interrupted the story and Rinpoche paused as we all watched the busyness before us. My attention was caught by the sight of two fishermen engaged in untangling hundreds of feet of net. *"It's interesting that everything being easy can be an obstacle to practice too…"* I mused *"not just difficult circumstances."*

Rinpoche was watching the net untanglers. *"Yes, having any kind of safety net can be a problem"* he smiled. *"Kyabjé Künzang Dorje Rinpoche lived without any kind of safety net. He never had an attendant and always travelled as the general public travelled. He had no home when I first knew him – but an unknown number of people had rooms he could occupy when he happened to arrive in whatever place it was. The room in Tso Pema was lovely – but lovely in terms of our concepts: whitewashed walls and wood. There was no shrine to speak of other than a photograph of Kyabjé Düd'jom Rinpoche and a statue of Guru Rinpoche. I do remember a cabinet with texts in it and a drawer in which he kept certain Vajrayana implements – but in Himalayan Vajrayana terms this was almost alarmingly sparse for a Lama of his eminence."* PAUSE *"So… Lu'ipa always had a safety net. Not that he had any real insurance against privation – but in behaving like a prince, he received far better treatment than other religious mendicants. He unconsciously comported himself in an aristocratic manner. He didn't really know that he was acting in that way but people could tell he was probably a Kshatriya."*

"It's the same today" explained Khandro Déchen. "We've seen it. When people can tell if you're upper class – then they don't respond to you in the same way. That can be an obstacle. Some high ranking tulkus aren't cognisant of that. They don't see that they are being treated in a special way because of how they are perceived. They are never pushed or tested in terms of their capacity for explanation."

"In our case however" Rinpoche added "if people don't like what we say, they're not inhibited about saying so. They ask 'How so?' or 'Why should that have to be?' or 'What do you mean by that?' or 'That doesn't make sense' or 'Why d'you have to use all these technical words?' or 'Why do there have to be so many foreign words?' As if veranda, palanquin, cashmere, swastika, musk, mango, mongoose, jungle, pyjamas, bungalow, shampoo, and juggernaut were not Indian. They are all of Indian origin and were therefore once foreign words. Then" added Rinpoche "there's Blighty, dekko, bandana, dinghy, cushy, pepper, dungarees, khaki, thug, sugar, typhoon, opal, catamaran, and loot." PAUSE "People often push us for answers – which we regard as valuable. It made for an excellent training because Khandro Déchen and I had to work hard to answer people in ways that helped them understand." PAUSE "That no longer seems to happen. Maybe because of our age – or maybe because of some other reason. We have no idea." PAUSE "If we'd been important tulkus and people hadn't understood our answers, it would have been seen as their fault, not ours. They'd either have thought themselves unworthy, or that what we'd said was ineffably profound. No one would have said 'You didn't explain that very well.' That – is a sociological issue which every Lama needs to examine."

"Yes" Khandro Déchen continued. "The fact that people can be inhibited, can become an obstacle to the Lama in terms of improving communication skills."

"Could you say" I asked "that in similar vein, the situation Lu'ipa finds himself in is also an example of why the human realm is the only mind state that works for practice? I mean, that the god realm is as problematic as the hell realm?"

"Yes, if life is continually too easy, or too hard, one never experiences disparity" responded Khandro Déchen.

"*Life has to be a fluctuating situation in which there's pleasure and pain, and you see the difference. If it's all pain, you can't see anything beyond the pain. If it's all pleasure there's no motivation to look beyond anything.*"

Rinpoche continued with the hagiography. "*Lu'ipa decided that the only way to live the life of a real yogi would be to destroy his reputation as a genteel, refined, socially polished vajrayanist…*"

Shortly after these ruminations, he came upon a brothel – and, rather than wait for darkness, he made something of a show of entering the place. He waited until the street was thronged with people and there were some who would recognise him. He then entered the brothel with the broadest grin he could muster. This was difficult for him because even though he believed in the sincerity of his action, the level of discomfort generated by his background and upbringing made him highly anxious. As he walked through the door, he realised that he had no idea at all of what would happen once he had entered the brothel. What he would say to those who dwelt there to account for his presence? He had no idea of actually taking advantage of the service the brothel had to offer – he merely wished to ruin his reputation.

Sitting inside the brothel, close to the entrance, was a naked whore by the name of Bhagarvi. As soon as she saw Lu'ipa she yelled "*Look who's come to see me! How—very—very—funny! Look girls! Here's a prissy young virgin – eager for pussy. I think he needs to be fucked senseless!*[3] *What do you think? Who wants him first?*" Lu'ipa was horrified and started to back out of the brothel. "*Too late for that, young lad*" Bhagarvi laughed. "*You'll need a key to unlock that door. We have to make sure our customers pay up before they leave – so there's no way out of here, unless a whore unlocks the door.*"

At that moment four other naked whores appeared each brandishing a cudgel and grinning. One guarded the front door with a yellowed ivory skull-tipped cudgel.

---

[3] Ngak'chang Rinpoche is known for almost never swearing or using profanities. This account was therefore all the more shocking – and therefore all the more effective.

Thirteen: Lu'ipa – the piscatorial viscera epicurean

One guarded the rear door with a cudgel surmounted by a verdigrised copper skull. One stood by the eastern side window with a cudgel surmounted by a crystal skull. One stood by the western side window with a cudgel surmounted by a coral skull. There was no way out of the situation. The four whores made no response in ordinary speech. They roared like lions and waved their cudgels as they danced with powerful movements.

The whore bearing the yellowed ivory skull-tipped cudgel was slim yet curvaceous and her movements made her breasts flail. She approached Lu'ipa in a menacing manner – but pulled away and returned to the door.

The whore bearing the cudgel surmounted by a verdigrised copper skull was outrageously obese, callipygous, and bathykolpian. Her movements were erratic and unpredictable. She gyrated—moving no closer to Lu'ipa —and finally sneered at him from the rear door.

The whore bearing the cudgel surmounted by a crystal skull was thin and sinuous and her movements were precise and intricate. She leapt at Lu'ipa – but stopped short of colliding with him. She then returned to the eastern window.

The whore bearing the cudgel surmounted by a coral skull was muscular and voluptuous. Her movements were wild and capricious. She swayed and swooped – sweeping her arms and fanning her fingers as she circled Lu'ipa. Finally, she laughed at him and glided back to the western window.

Bhagarvi—with her legs spread wide—sat with regal hauteur. She cradled a cudgel surmounted by a lapis lazuli skull in the crook of her left arm. She stared at him with wide wrathful eyes and laughed. *"It seems that the girls aren't interested in you – so it will be down to me."*

Lu'ipa stood rooted to the spot in a cold sweat – but finally he said *"I… I have no money – so… maybe… could you… just let me leave?"*

Bhagarvi laughed loudly. *"No one enters this place and leaves without having had a thoroughly good fuck—it would be bad for business—so, money or not, a thoroughly good fuck is what you're going to get."*

"But I have no money – I am a yogi."

"You're a yogi, are you?" she laughed. *"That seems hard to believe. I can believe you are a prince from the Land of Lions because you have the torso of a lion and the stride of a lion – but… in reality you are a fake lion—a lion from the taxidermist —a fictional lion."*

"Yes…" sighed Lu'ipa *"… I admit to that. I was to have been a Raja – but I wanted to be a yogi and in that I have failed."*

"Yes, I know that – but it is good that you are honest. You know, of course—or maybe you don't—that you had no need to leave your palace to be a yogi. A yogi can be a yogi wherever he lives – but you sought to be an itinerant yogi and ended up in an itinerant palace…" PAUSE *"Still… you came in here to demolish your palace – and that you have done."*

Lu'ipa wept with shame. *"So now, may I leave – and learn to live as other yogis live?"*

"No, no, no, dear boy – there's no need for that. You have sought for a teacher and you will not find a teacher by leaving here without a game of hide-the-salami. However… as you have no money, I'd better take my fee in services: we'll start with cunnilingus – and see where we go from there."

Lu'ipa, again, was utterly horrified – and Bhagarvi had to give him the lowdown on what was expected of him in terms of oral sex. Lu'ipa saw no way out of the situation and obliged Bhagarvi as best he could – but, rather than sounds of pleasure, Bhagarvi began to sing a song of realisation that climaxed in a quintessential explosion of the nondual state. Lu'ipa had studied and practised sufficiently to understand that Bhagarvi was a siddha and that he had received the most profound transmission. Lu'ipa then requested Bhagarvi to be his teacher.

Thirteen: Lu'ipa – the piscatorial viscera epicurean

She accepted him as a matter of course. *"This is however, not the time for kha-jor. That must await a later time – a time when you have experienced the result of the transmission you've received. You will now be hungry – and, as you have gained an appetite for the flavour and fragrance of fish, you may take this to eat."* She handed him a bowl. *"You may leave now – and I will find you when you are ready."*

Lu'ipa thanked Bhagarvi for her transmission and teaching and for the food she had given him. One of the cudgel-bearing whores unlocked the door – and Lu'ipa took his leave.

When he examined the contents of his bowl however, he found some disgusting shreds of rotten fish. Considering it to be a jest on the part of Bhagarvi, he threw it into the gutter – but as soon as he did so Bhagarvi appeared. *"I see you're still a daintily refined delicate gourmet at heart. You won't find realisation this way, my prim little prince."* At that she vanished – and Lu'ipa immediately remembered Bhagarvi's words *"There's no way out of here, unless a whore unlocks the door."* He broke down and wept at his lost opportunity.

I laughed and said *"I love that line 'There's no way out of here, unless a whore unlocks the door.' I guess it's also a statement about the khandro being necessary for realisation?"*

Rinpoche laughed too *"Yes – but it also rhymes, at least in Shakespearean dialect."* Then he returned to the hagiography.

Lu'ipa returned to the brothel but no one had heard of Bhagarvi. He spent the rest of the night looking everywhere for her but no one knew of a whore called Bhagarvi. He sought her for the whole of the next day and the following night, without discovering a trace of her. By the morning he was exhausted and fell asleep on the fishing beach. When he awoke, he was ravenous – not having eaten for almost three days. He sat up and looked around him at the fishers gutting the catch.

Piles of raw fish guts lay in small heaps around the fishermen – and, somehow knowing what he had to do, he enquired of the fishermen *"Would you allow me to eat the fish guts as I am starving – and must eat something?"* The fishermen told him to help himself – and laughed at him. As he sat there eating fish guts however, Bhagarvi appeared—invisible to the fishermen—and silently motioned Lu'ipa to follow her. She led him to a remote stretch of the dunes far from the fishermen where she seemed to become conventionally visible. Her mien was entirely different from that of the Bhagarvi he had encountered in the brothel – and her speech had nothing of the lewd linguistics Bhagarvi the whore had employed.

"May I ask a question, reverend lady?" Bhagarvi nodded her assent. *"You are entirely different – from the…"*

"… whore?" Bhagarvi supplied the word.

"…from the lady I met in the brothel."

"Yes" replied Bhagarvi. *"That is because you are different – but not yet entirely different."*

"And… who were the other four…"

"… whores?" Bhagarvi supplied the word.

"… the ones who danced and approached me in symbolic ways?"

At that moment—having reached a spot far from the eyes of the fishermen—Bhagarvi removed her clothes and began to teach. *"They did not exist as such – they were all mind emanations. I simply showed you the kyil'khor of the five Seng-gé Dongmas. This is why they roared like lions and waved their cudgels as they danced. The whore bearing the yellowed ivory skull-tipped cudgel who made her breasts flail was the Yellow Seng-gé Dongma. The whore bearing the cudgel surmounted by a verdigrised copper skull—whose movements were erratic and unpredictable—was the Green Seng-gé Dongma.*

"The whore bearing the cudgel surmounted by a crystal skull—who was precise and intricate—was the White Seng-gé Dongma. The whore bearing the cudgel surmounted by a coral skull—whose movements were wild and capricious—was the Red Seng-gé Dongma. I manifested these Seng-gé Dongmas as the Blue Seng-gé Dongma of Space – bearing a cudgel surmounted by a lapis lazuli skull."

Lu'ipa understood Bhagarvi's teaching and—experiencing it as empowerment—asked *"Please give me teachings in order that I may comprehend the human body."*

"The view of the human body changes according to the vehicle, Lu'ipa. In terms of Sutra, a view is cultivated in which the body is seen as a morass of defilements. The body is seen as being a potentially festering mass of disease. One considers the waste products of the body and develops revulsion for one's gross physical form. One trains according to the path of renunciation in terms of freeing oneself from attachment with regard to one's self-orientation. This has been your view until now – and this is what caused you such great shock in what you understood to be a brothel."

Lu'ipa was startled by Bhagarvi's teaching and—experiencing it as oral transmission—asked *"Please give me teachings in order that I may realise the wisdom manifested by the human body."*

"In the Outer Tantras, although human bodies are not regarded as a pure phenomenon – they are regarded with respect as the basis of the vajra body of the rTsa rLung system. From the point of view of Outer Tantra therefore, disparaging the body is seen as a breakage of vows. In the Inner Tantras we pass beyond the pure-impure dichotomy, and no need is seen for any form of purification with regard to the body."

Lu'ipa was magnetised by Bhagarvi's teaching and—experiencing it as symbolic transmission—asked *"Please give me teachings in order that I may understand the primordial nature as it is displayed by the human body."*

"According to Dzogchen, the body is ultimately identical to the body of a Buddha. The physical body itself is regarded as the self-perfected dimension. When one views one's partner's body – one views the actual body of a Buddha."

Lu'ipa was ecstatically disoriented by Bhagarvi's teaching and—experiencing it as direct transmission—asked *"Please give me the conclusion of your teaching in order that I may integrate what I have received into each moment."*

"To gaze upon the self-perfected kyil'khors of the body of one's partner—chagtèn[4]—is in itself a profound cause of liberation if you authentically enter into that view with co-emergent awareness and devotion. It is extremely important to be in awe of the body of one's partner – because if this enthralled appreciation is lacking, the practice will become degraded. If you engage in the outer form of kha-jor without pure view, one merely imitates a practice and descends into nihilistic depravity."

On the conclusion of Bhagarvi's teaching they entered into kha-jor – and Lu'ipa attained nondual realisation. From that time on he lived on the offal thrown out by the fishermen and was known as Mahasiddha Lu'ipa – the piscatorial viscera epicurean; the consummate connoisseur of fish entrails.

After a moment's pause Rinpoche stated *"Right now, I'd like to be the avid ingestant of a perfectly boiled egg with heavily buttered granary toast."*

We all stood up and headed up the hill towards Pink Cottage. As we walked, I commented *"That whole teaching from Bhagarvi on the changing view of the body through the yanas is fantastic, Rinpoche. The Sutrayana and Outer Tantra view of the body really seem to dominate Buddhism. There seem to be a lot of ideas about needing to purify something?"*

"Yes. I think that can be a problem, particularly with Western Buddhists" Rinpoche replied. *"There aren't many people who know whence these different perspectives originate, in terms of the yanas. So, certain ideas from the Outer Tantras —like purification—tend to become pervasive."*

---

[4] *phyag rTen* / ཕྱག་རྟེན་ – mudra or gestural support.

"That idea seems to be prevalent across the world" I commented *"and not just the Buddhist world. So many people seem hooked on wanting a pure diet."*

"It's even got a name now" added Khandro Déchen *"… 'Orthorexia Nervosa'. This is the obsessive preoccupation with eating healthily – or trying to become sufficiently pure. However, we would categorise it along with every other neurosis. The underlying problem is the same – the* world *and the* body *are reviled as if the* world *and the* body *were samsara in themselves."* PAUSE *"That's not true in Vajrayana. There, phenomena and the body aren't reviled. With Dzogchen, samsara and nirvana are nondual. The two ideas are not polarised. In almost every religion however, there's this polarisation – and one has to regard oneself as 'impure'. Then there's the work of becoming pure."*

"In terms of the yanas" added Rinpoche *"the emphasis on purification is found in the Outer Tantras. The Inner Tantras transcend the 'pure-impure dichotomy'. The sutric principle of 'renunciation' and the outer tantric principle of 'purification', have become understood as the generalised pervasive aspects of Buddhism. The principals of 'renunciation' and 'purification' should not be employed therefore, as if they applied to every vehicle of Buddhism. They should be employed in context. Out of context, these principles become problematic. That is why people become bewildered. Having received Dzogchen teaching people ask 'What about renunciation and purification? How do you renounce and purify in Dzogchen?' Of course—from the perspective of Dzogchen —there isn't anything to renounce or purify. This is because the principle of Dzogchen is 'self-liberation' – not 'renunciation' or 'purification'."*

"So, it depends where you're coming from whether there is something to purify or not" explained Khandro Déchen. *"It depends on the vehicle. Western people rarely have an understanding of that, which is why they're often confused. It's often difficult for people to understand. There seems to be something about the yana system that doesn't register with people. They don't remember it. We have been talking to people— and writing books—about the difference between the yanas for over forty years – and there are still some who lose the plot. It doesn't occur to people to think about the yanas when they don't understand some aspect of what is being taught.*

"The first question to ask if you're confused by conflicting aspects of the teachings is 'What are the yanas involved with these seemingly opposing views?'... If you understand the principles of the yanas, then nothing will ever be confusing. If you don't understand the principles of the yanas – it can appear to become a morass of conflicting ideas."

"I sometimes don't find it so straightforward to identify the yana though" I commented. "It sometimes seems like something is a bit of a hybrid between two yanas?"

"Yes, there—is—crossover. Certainly. It could not be otherwise" Rinpoche replied. "What you must bear in mind, is that one can speak of every vehicle, in the language of every other vehicle – so there are at least eighty-one modes of presenting Dharma. This means that Lamas who are fluent with the yanas—such as Chögyam Trungpa Rinpoche—can create beautiful formulations tailored to be of value to different audiences."

"This will tend to function—in the moment—as transmission" commented Khandro Déchen. "But to take it away—in terms of long-term understanding—one has to be able to unpack what has been taught, in terms of the individual yanas."

We paused on breasting the hill. "Because the yanas are not understood" laughed Rinpoche "people make up stories to try to make contradictions fit. I heard about one teacher—who shall remain nameless—who concocted an explanation about celibacy. It involved outer celibacy, inner celibacy, secret celibacy, and ultimate celibacy" Rinpoche laughed. "Outer celibacy was celibacy as it is commonly understood. Inner celibacy was being able to be physically close. Secret celibacy was kissing and caressing. Ultimate celibacy was sexual coitus."

"We've never heard a reference to this anywhere else" commented Khandro Déchen.

"These ideas tend to be devised because people don't understand the yanas" continued Rinpoche. "Knowing the 'outer, inner, secret, ultimate' framework, this absurd stratification of celibacy sounds kosher, even though it isn't."

"*You have to ask*" added Khandro Déchen *'What is the purpose of this inner, secret, and ultimate celibacy – what is the principle and function of 'cuddling' as a practice?' You have to provide the principle and function – or it cannot be a practice. You can tell that it's a bogus concoction when you take it apart and ask 'What comes out of these different phases?'*"

For a moment I was laughing too much to talk, then I managed *"The whole idea of using the word 'celibacy' to describe a practice of sex is pretty damn confusing too."*

We had reached Pink Cottage and it was definitely time to make breakfast. Sitting at the table a short while later the conversation over eggs and toast returned to the tale of Lu'ipa. I said *"I'm not entirely certain what was being referred to by the words 'self-perfected kyil'khors of the body'"*

"The energetic display of what are known in the West as the erogenous zones" Khandro Déchen answered.

"Yes" continued Rinpoche. *"A subtle interaction occurs whilst gazing with present-attention. There are different experiences which are available with present open-ended observation. Lust is the most obvious experience – but there is also a hypnotic state which is of no great value. The nonconceptual state which is 'erotic'— but not dominated by any need to act sexually—is entirely different."*

"Can you elaborate" asked Ja'gyür *"on what you mean by 'erotic' in terms of not being dominated by the need to act sexually?"*

"We are severely limited by the conditioned understanding of sexuality" Rinpoche replied. *"The word 'erotic' is not a useful word really – it's linked too closely with sexuality as it's commonly understood. When entering into the nonconceptual state of gazing – there is the unification of 'seeing' and 'what is seen'. This unified experience manifests in terms of reciprocal communication – but this has nothing to do with conventional sexuality."*

"*This comes into play with tögal*⁵ *– and dark retreat*" added Khandro Déchen "*in terms of Dzogchen long-dé – which approaches realisation through the nondual dimension of physical sensation.*"

"*There's the visual aspect of it*" continued Rinpoche "*of the body 'becoming light' – and perceiving that in a person. This functions because every person has 'light potential' which can be unlocked through nondual vision. So, you focus on your partner, simply as an 'amazement' of shape, and colour, and luminosity. This is the practice. I suppose you could call it 'sexual', because clothes are not worn – but it doesn't fit with any conventional idea of sexuality, as it is non-coital.*"

"*Is that a practice from the Zér-tsal Thugthig gTérma, Rinpoche?*" I asked.

"*Yes*" Rinpoche replied. "*I don't want to say too much here because tögal is highly reserved – but the form of tögal in the Zér-tsal Thugthig concerns the perception of one's partner in gradually decreasing light conditions, so that one becomes gradually more aware of the innate luminosity of one's partner.*" PAUSE "*There is obviously much more to know – but this gives a vague idea, at least.*"

"*So, although it's visual*" I queried "*are all the other sense fields also involved in terms of the perception of your partner?*"

"*Yes, all the sense fields remain open.*"

"*The sexual aspect of arousal is the energy which fuels the vision*" continued Khandro Déchen "*but it's not 'erotic' in the common understanding of the word. There is no physical involvement. Using the word 'erotic' is necessary—because there is no other word—but it can confuse the issue. It's simply that this is a practice which is approached from a 'state of arousal' – but which involves all of the sense fields, due to the fact that they're indivisible.*"

With that, it was time for a swim in the sea and some hunting for serpentine in the cove below.

---

⁵ *thod rGal* / ཐོད་རྒལ་ – direct crossing, or leap-over. This is the practise which leads to ja'lü *(ja' lus* / འཇའ་ལུས་) – the rainbow body. The practice of tögal brings the realisation of lhundrüp *(lhun grub* / ལྷུན་གྲུབ་) – spontaneous presence.

Fourteen: Chamaripa – the nondual cordwainer

Chamaripa *(tsa' ma' ri pa /* རྩ་སུ་རི་པ *)* / Lham Khan Drüpthob *(lham mKhan sGrub thobs /* ལྷམ་མཁན་སྒྲུབ་ཐོབས *)*
Disciple of: Vinapa
Varna by birth: Shudra

Frogs' Leap, Penarth, South Wales.

It was eight o'clock and the dining table was laid for breakfast at Frogs' Leap, with silver cutlery and white linen napkins in silver rings – all inherited from Rinpoche's German grandmother and great grandmother. There were white reproduction Georgian egg cups in the shape of geese, ducks, and chicken made by a young woman who once had a shop in Lizard, Cornwall. There were blue and white mugs celebrating the Queen's Diamond Jubilee. A wooden fruit bowl filled with peaches, nectarines, cherries, plums, and figs was sitting in the centre of the table – posing, as if for a still life painting. Music from Radio 3 played pleasingly in the background and the aroma of exceedingly strong espresso permeated the room. Rinpoche was in the kitchen overseeing the boiling of eggs whilst Khandro Déchen made the toast. 'The Vicar of Bray'[1] rang out from Rinpoche's iPhone[2], signalling that the eggs were cooked to their *five-minutes and thirty-three seconds* perfection. Rinpoche sang along *"And this be law, I will maintain until my dying day, sir – that whatsoever King may reign, still I'll be the Vicar of Bray, sir."* We gathered eggs and toast —grilled just short of black for Rinpoche—and carried them through to the dining room.

"The amusing thing about that song" commented Rinpoche *"is that I entirely misunderstood it when I was young."*
He laughed *"I thought that the Vicar of Bray was a fine honourable character. I only discovered recently—when I had the chance to read the words—that the song was satirical and the Vicar of Bray ran with the fox and chased with the hounds.*

---

[1] *The Vicar of Bray* is an 18th century satirical song recounting the career of The Vicar of Bray and his contortions of principle in order to retain his ecclesiastic office despite the changes in the Established Church of England through the course of several English monarchs.
[2] Apple® iPhone®

"He changed his religious orientation according to whatever epistemological leaning prevailed. Now I simply love the melody and refrain from identification with the Vicar of Bray."

"But are you still the 'Convivial Vicars' of Vajrayana'? Is that connected with the song?" I enquired.

"No" replied Khandro Déchen. "It's connected with how we see our rôles. We're no 'grand' figures. We prohibit prostration in our direction. Not that we do not offer them to our Lamas – but we don't see ourselves in that way."

"I thought" I enquired "that prostrations were for the benefit of the students, though?"

"Yes, they are" Rinpoche responded "but we would rather people benefited themselves through study, practice, and retreat – and we would rather people were genuine. We'd rather they listened carefully and lived the view."

The dining table and chairs are all from house clearance auctions accessed by their friend Gareth Luckwell, the cabinet maker. Some of the floor-to-ceiling built-in cupboards are original and some are made by Gareth. These have been made from reclaimed wood from the early 1800s – older in fact than the house, which was built in 1849. The walls are painted with brilliant white emulsion. On one wall there is a large photograph of Robert grinning down at us. It always makes me smile.

Rinpoche brought in his old wooden Tibetan bowl, from which he drinks his pint of espresso each morning. Each morning the same coffee: eight double espressos pressed in succession from his La Pavoni espresso machine. The coffee is freshly ground, from particularly strong, fiercely roasted beans called *New Extra-Espresso* which he brings back from Christopher Street in the West Village of New York.

It was an early winter's day with smoky overcast skies promising later rain. As we chatted over breakfast, we decided it was perfect weather for a walk down to the seafront esplanade.

Fourteen: Chamaripa – the nondual cordwainer

A stroll along the Penarth pier would be a fine way to spend the morning. The cast iron and wooden pier has jutted out 700 feet into the Bristol Channel since the time of Queen Victoria. It was opened in 1898 and now houses a café and gallery in the Art Deco pavilion which was added in 1929.

As we prepared to depart, Rinpoche said he would require a few minutes to polish his boots. He was changing from his elderly dark brown leather slippers made by Church's of Northampton in the 1920s, to his green leather boots—made in Wien[3]—perfectly matching his dark green carpenters' lederhosen and six-pocket leather waistcoat. Having noticed a few marks on the toes of his boots, he opened the shoe-cleaning cupboard and took out a brush. This cupboard has been cleverly constructed to utilise the triangular space formed under the staircase, and above the broom closet. The shoe-cleaning cupboard has the bottom of one of the stairs intruding – and this is used as a surface from which shoe-brushes hang. The cupboard contents look and smell marvellous. There's an array of hanging brushes, an assortment of shoe-cleaning tools, shoe creams and hard-wax polishes of many colours, bottles of Lexol, and the now discontinued *original* Liquid Nikwax.

Rinpoche proceeded to buff his boots telling me, as he did so, of their provenance. They had been made for him by Herrn Béla Balint the Schuhmacher, as a copy of the Beatle Boots once worn by John Lennon. Beatle Boots were Chelsea Boots with Cuban heels – but John Lennon's were made several inches higher than the ankle and therefore had to have a zip on one side where the other elasticated gusset would have been. Rinpoche spoke of Herrn Béla Balint's remarkable expertise and skill and his extraordinary hour-long foot measuring process. Herr Béla Balint had made them especially as a token of appreciation.

---

[3] Vienna, Austria.

I remembered that there was a shoemaker amongst the usual collections of Mahasiddhas. *"Herr Balint sounds as if he's in the same league as Mahasiddha Chamaripa"* I commented – and then, laughing, told Rinpoche about the company 'Chamaripa Shoes' that I'd come across online. They are the foremost manufacturers of 'elevator shoes' designed to give the wearer added height. When the mirth had subsided, I asked Rinpoche if Chamaripa also appeared in the Jomo Pema 'ö-Zér gTérma, and nodding he answered *"Oh yes, Mahasiddha Chamaripa – the nondual cordwainer."*

"Would his hagiography be possible this morning?" I enquired. *"Recounting that whilst walking along in a fine pair of Beatle Boots would be wonderfully appropriate."*

"Quite so" Rinpoche smiled as we donned coats and hats and headed out of the door. As we were nearing the corner of Salop Street he commenced. *"Chamaripa lived in Visundnagar – which is in the east of India. He belonged to a reputable guild of cordwainers and was well respected for his extremely fine shoes...."*

He took great pride in his craft – repairing all the old shoes he had made for his customers in such a way as to make them almost as good as new. His customers valued his work and he was largely happy with his profession and with his much-loved family.

Although Chamaripa worked hard—and was always fully absorbed in his craft—he became increasingly dissatisfied by his lowly position in society. Although he was respected and valued by his customers, his varna gave him no position and he was unable to mix socially with those for whom he made his best shoes. Even Kshatriyas had no self-imposed barrier to having him measure their feet. They would speak with him most cordially —almost as an equal—but it never extended beyond the immediate milieu of the cordwainer's craft.

Chamaripa had no exalted ideas of himself—nor did he desire great wealth—but he was displeased with a life that was so artificially limited.

He made the best shoes in the land and no one was his equal but he was not equal to those of higher varnas – whether they had skills or not. There was no way he could better himself – and this thought troubled him. Eventually his disappointment with his life stole the joy he found in the perfection of his craft. His friends advised him not to make himself miserable about a situation that could not be changed – but although he saw the sense of their arguments, he remained chagrined by the fact that, not only was he doomed to his low societal status but so were his children and their children. In fact – it was not really for himself that he was concerned. It was for his children and for his wife. Surely his skill was worth more for them than he had been able to achieve.

One day as he sat in the sun repairing shoes, a shadow fell on him and did not move. He was used to the shadows of passers-by – but they never lingered. Curious as to who had halted to look at him for so long, Chamaripa looked up and saw a yogi—the Mahasiddha Vinapa—gazing at him intently. Chamaripa had seen yogis and other ascetics before – but he had never had any contact with them other than in giving alms. *"May I help you, reverend sir? It would please me to make an offering of my services if your shoes are in need of repair."*

"It is kind of you to offer – but I would not wish to give you the extra work."

"It is no difficulty for me" replied Chamaripa.

"But it would be for me. You see, I perceive that you have lost heart in your work – and because of that, the joy of wearing shoes you had skilfully repaired would be lessened."

Chamaripa was surprised that the yogi knew his mind – and, looking a little startled, replied *"How do you know this of me?"*

"I know it from your face as you work. I can see that you have great skill—and that you still give full attention to every detail—but there is no pleasure in what you do."

"Yes..." replied Chamaripa *"that is my situation. You have read it exactly. I am a craftsman but I am a Shudra—rather than a Vaishya—and my children can rise no higher than my wife and myself. I would wish a better life for them – but it is beyond all possibility. That is why I am no longer happy in my craft."*

We paused to cross Albert Road. *"Vinapa seems the perfect teacher for him"* I commented *"because he can spot that Chamaripa has lost his enthusiasm for his craft. He knows what that feels like – but it's not the stultification of expertise that's the problem here, is it?"*

"No, it's like The Jungle Book – as presented by Walt Disney, at least." Rinpoche burst into song *"Well, I'm the king of the swingers, the jungle VIP I reached the top, and I had to stop and that's what's bothering me*[4]...*"* PAUSE *"He's reached the top of his profession but he sees that 'the top' is not where he is, socially. He makes shoes for 'the top'—the Kshatriyas—but he's not at 'the top' – or even one rung up. The important factor in his case, is his care for his family. It's more for them than for himself that he would like his social station to be different. He would like to do something for them that he can't achieve. He can't move beyond his varna to help them. He's aware that whatever expertise he has—however skilled he is—he's locked into his varna."*

"And if Vinapa hadn't come along, he wouldn't have changed" I commented. *"It doesn't seem as if he was looking to change anything, he was just dissatisfied. That makes him pretty fortunate that Vinapa appeared, doesn't it?"* to which Rinpoche nodded and made a gesture which signified that what I'd stated was entirely obvious.

We headed down the gully to Church Road. *"This was the situation in Ancient India"* said Khandro Déchen. *"For Mahasiddhas, the rôle was to wander around looking for people they could help – people who could be nudged into practice. It's not so unusual."*

---

[4] Sherman / Sherman—*I Wanna Be Like You*—Louis Prima—The Jungle Book (film)—Walt Disney Productions—1967

"All kinds of people like to help each other" Rinpoche added. *"John Martyn—for example—gave me an outrageously wonderful introduction to the audience in Newquay Folk and Blues Club. He was supportive to me when I was faced with an indifferent audience who had only come to see him. I was the third-rate warm up act – but he made me out to be the next great wonder on the British Blues scene.*[5]*"*

"So, he was like a Mahasiddha giving you a nudge?" asked Ja'gyür.

"Very much so" Rinpoche replied. *"John Martyn was a musical genius. He never achieved great fame – but Jeff Beck, Jack Bruce, Eric Clapton, and Johnny Winter all spoke highly of him."* PAUSE *"Bob Dylan and Leonard Cohen also respected his music."* PAUSE *"As it happens… I had another nudge which was taking me in another direction."*

"Being the incarnation of Aro Yeshé?" suggested Ja'gyür.

"No… I can't say that I knew this at the time" replied Rinpoche. *"I had to wait until I met Kyabjé Düd'jom Rinpoche Jig'drèl Yeshé Dorje before that was made plain."* PAUSE *"The nudge to which I was referring however, was the Himalayas. They had been acting like a magnet for me from the first time I saw photographs of Tibet."* PAUSE *"At that point in my life it simply became necessary to go where I could immerse myself in Vajrayana."* Rinpoche smiled *"Kyabjé Düd'jom Rinpoche was a superlative musician. This is not widely known, but he was a brilliant exponent of dramnyen*[6] *– the Himalayan lute."* Rinpoche smiled again and continued with the hagiography.

As Chamaripa explained the problem—and why he was no longer happy in his craft—Vinapa responded with a look of consternation. *"I see that you are not possessed of the best information concerning status."*

"Really?" Chamaripa replied with some surprise.

---

[5] See: Doc Togden—*an odd boy*—Volume II—chapter 6—*John Martyn*—Aro Books WORLDWIDE —2012. Also see: Ngakpa Chögyam—*Goodbye Forever – the Miscellaneous Memoirs of an English Lama*—Volume I—chapter 13—*Diminutive Demon*—Aro Books WORLDWIDE—2020
[6] *sGra sNyan* / སྒྲ་སྙན་

"Really. You see, you have probably been told that status is created by society and religion."

"Yes, that is true – so tell me, what is the real nature of status if it is not that which is ordained by society and religion?"

"The real nature of status…" smiled Vinapa "is beyond both society and codified religion."

"Really?" Chamaripa replied with even greater surprise.

"Really" replied Vinapa. "Shakyamuni Buddha did not teach the system of the varnas. He spoke against it. There are those however, whose addiction to mundane status has led them to maintain the Tirthika system of varnas – but they cannot authentically describe themselves as adherents of Shakyamuni Buddha's teaching."

"I did not know this, venerable sir. Can you explain how I should understand my situation in the world?"

"Certainly, my good fellow. Firstly, I should tell you that I was a Kshatriya by birth but I became a Harijan when I took instructions in music from Mahasiddha Baruni – the surbdahar playing whore. I was prosperous as a teacher of the vina but when Mahasiddha Baruni paid me an unexpected visit at the end of an evening's music lesson – most of my clientele abandoned me and I was thenceforth shunned in the town."

"But was this not a tragedy?" gasped Chamaripa.

"No, my dear fellow – not in the slightest way. It merely destroyed the last vestiges of my varna-clinging neurosis. At the moment I was abandoned and shunned I became liberated from the need to comply with stupidity. I was free to wander and to play my vina wherever I wished. Of course, now I have the status of a 'holy man' and so no one questions my varna. A 'holy man' you see, belongs to no varna – and yet, is not a Harijan. Those who abandon the world of limited appearances rise above all varnas and gain the respect of all simply through being alive. Status, you see, can only arise from realisation.

"The highest status is the primordial state – and that is the birthright of everyone. It is not given by birth as varnas are given by birth – it can only be given by the birth of awareness."

Chamaripa had never heard such things before. He knew that siddhas existed and that they possessed profound realisation – but he had never imagined that he would understand a teaching if he should hear one.

"You must be a Mahasiddha to speak as you do. How have I deserved such good fortune!" cried Chamaripa with delight.

"Well… Baruni—the surbdahar playing whore—is a Mahasiddha – but I am simply a Buddhist yogi. I have tasted the nondual state – but I am deserving of no grand titles."

"Then, as you have tasted the nondual state, how may I come to give birth to this awareness? How may I realise the primordial state?"

"You must practise Dharma."

"Yes…" sighed Chamaripa *"but how can I do that when I am a cordwainer – and must support my family? I cannot leave my family and become a monk or wander homeless as a yogi. My wife and children would suffer terribly if I did not continue in my craft."*

Vinapa considered Chamaripa for some moments and said *"Dharma is not the religion of society. Dharma is uncreated and accords to no fixed form. To become a monk—or wandering yogi—are outer forms. Anyone can dress like a monk and give the appearance of living like a monk—and anyone can dress like a yogi and give the appearance of living like a yogi—but these appearances are not necessarily Dharma. There is no reason why you cannot practise Dharma as a cordwainer – apart from the need for transmission and teaching. If you wish for transmission and teaching, you may repair my shoes – and then I shall give you all that is required to be a cordwainer yogi."*

Chamaripa was overwhelmed by what he heard. He was both shocked and delighted. This was a possibility he had never expected.

"Whatever your varna" continued Vinapa *"to become a tantrika means that you no longer belong to the varnas of samsara – and the children of a yogi are free to be what they wish to be."*

"Then please be seated, reverend sir…" smiled Chamaripa, knowing the first real pleasure he had experienced for a year *"and it shall be my pleasure to repair your shoes – and make them better than they have ever been."*

Vinapa sat down, removed his shoes and watched Chamaripa work. As he did so, he explained:

> *"The yogi cordwainer must mould the leather of preconception—of misperception and addiction to concepts—around the empty last of nondual wisdom and method.*
> *The yogi cordwainer must take the awl of empty insight and sew—with the thread of existence and nonexistence—the eight worldly dharmas into the seamless fabric of completion.*
> *By this means the yogi cordwainer repairs the division of emptiness and form and manifests the shoes which traverse the three spheres of being[7]."*

When the repair was completed, the teaching and transmission were completed – and Vinapa said *"Now I shall repay you for your skill with an offering of my skill."* He then opened the large bag that he carried—took out his vina—and commenced to play. Chamaripa—already being in a heightened state of awareness—heard Vinapa's music as simply a further dimension of transmission. Others who heard the music gradually thronged the thoroughfare until there was no room to move. Vinapa played for an hour before packing away his vina.

---

[7] chö-ku *(chos sKu / ཆོས་སྐུ / dharmakaya)* – the sphere of unconditioned potentiality; long-ku *(longs sKu / ལོངས་སྐུ / sambhogakaya)* – the sphere of intangible realised appearances; trül-ku *(sPrul sKu / སྤྲུལ་སྐུ / nirmanakaya)* – the sphere of realised corporeal manifestation.

Fourteen: Chamaripa – the nondual cordwainer

The local people begged him to stay – but he replied *"There is only room for one siddha in this town – and he is your cordwainer. Treat him with friendship and respect as a siddha and your lives will prosper. Ill-use him and misery will attend you."* Then Vinapa left, never to be seen again in that land.

"Goodbye forever…" I said.

Rinpoche laughed. *"Quite so. There's no need to be anywhere if you cannot be of use."* Then Rinpoche sang *'I was born by the river, just like this river, I been moving ever since, Ain't got no place to call my own, You know, I been moving since the day I was born.' Or something along those lines.*[8]*"*

By this time, we had reached the bottom of Alexandra Park and Rinpoche paused the telling as we turned right to walk along the esplanade, heading for the pier. It was a sufficiently cool and grey day that there were few others promenading on the pier – and we had it almost to ourselves as we strolled its length. We paused to gaze first at Robert's brass memorial plaque set into the wooden decking, and then over the rail to the channel beyond. Rinpoche returned to the hagiography.

"Chamaripa continued to practise as he'd been instructed…"

He regained the happiness of his youth and the joyful pride in his craft. As he continued to practise, each pair of shoes or slippers he made became an expression of Vinapa's teaching – and those who wore them began to gain a sense of well-being that they had not felt before. At first, they did not attribute their well-being to Chamaripa's shoes – but they found that when they wore the gold inlaid shoes and slippers they wore at court, the same sense of well-being was lost.

---

[8] Fraser/Rodgers—Free—*I'm a Mover*—*Tons of Sobs*—1968. *Free* were one of the definitive bands of the British Blues Boom of the late 1960s. Ngak'chang Rinpoche's band *Savage Cabbage* once played support for *Free* at *Colonel Barefoot's Rock Garden* on Eel Pie Island, Twickenham, London.

After nine days, those who wore Chamaripa's shoes and slippers found that they recovered from illnesses – and within a short time it became public knowledge that Chamaripa was a siddha whose shoes bestowed health and vitality. The Raja offered Chamaripa a place in his palace to make shoes exclusively for his family – but Chamaripa replied *"My shoes are for everyone. Although I respect you as the Raja of this land – I cannot make them only for you as this would be to disobey the teaching of my vajra master, Mahasiddha Vinapa. He told me that I must make shoes for anyone who comes to me wishing for footwear."*

"This I understand" replied the Raja *"but would you not be more comfortable in superior living conditions?"*

"I thank you for your consideration – but Mahasiddha Vinapa also told me that I should never live where poor people cannot approach me – for I am now a yogi. Even if he had not instructed me as I have explained, I am most content to live where I have always lived – because, the place in which I live was the place where I received transmission from Mahasiddha Vinapa. To me, it is therefore a palace and beyond all other residences."

"So will you also not make shoes for me and my family?" enquired the Raja, expecting yet another refusal.

"I will—certainly—make shoes for you and your family and make them as gorgeous as you could wish, but for those who cannot afford them, I must continue to make shoes and repair them for whatever they can afford – or for no payment at all. My cobbling craft is my practice – and so I must make shoes and slippers in the house where I first met the Mahasiddha Vinapa."

The Raja was content with Chamaripa's refusal. He knew of the Mahasiddha Vinapa and recognised that Chamaripa was a yogi of the same calibre. From that time on, Chamaripa's children received a royal education and his wife wore the finest clothes and somehow, highly discreetly, they came to be regarded as Vaishyas rather than Shudras – as it was impossible that Shudras should be seen in the palace precincts.

Chamaripa dressed as he had always dressed and lived as he had always lived. He was, of course, always given access to the palace precincts because he was a Mahasiddha and therefore no longer a Shudra.

His friends—though they were in awe of him—asked *'Why, when you no longer need to remain a Shudra, do you choose to do so?'* to which Chamaripa replied *'I was born a Shudra—and am happy to remain a Shudra to all who would see me as a Shudra—but I am not bound by the Shudra varna.'*

'Were we to be offered release from the Shudra varna…' they replied *'… we would all seize the opportunity as the world's greatest gift!'*

'As I would once have done, my friends – but I am no longer who I once was. I am a Buddhist yogi and a disciple of Mahasiddha Vinapa – and so varnas have no meaning to me.'

'How can that be…' they asked, perplexed *'when you now make shoes for the royal family?'*

'Would you have me look down upon you, my old friends?' Chamaripa laughed. *'If I were to take the system of varnas as reality I would assuredly have to act as if I was superior to you – and that would not please me. There is no superior or inferior in my mind apart from the superior who is my vajra master.'*

Chamaripa's friends considered this speech and, although amazed by his erudition and fluency, questioned him further on his new circumstances. *'Can you explain why, even when your wife and children move freely within the higher circles of society and dress accordingly – that you remain here wearing the clothes you have always worn?'*

'Yes. Most certainly. These are the clothes in which I received transmission and teaching from the Mahasiddha Vinapa!' Chamaripa laughed. *'There is no style of dress superior to this. There is no activity superior to the craft of cobbling. To those who understand Dharma – these rough and simple clothes are the clothes of the highest varna. I used to be concerned about my status in society and the status of my children – but varnas mean nothing to me now. They mean nothing to my wife either.*

"She simply wears what she wears for the sake of our children – in order that they may have a better life as Vaishyas, even though they may not be drawn to Dharma."

All those who were sick or dispirited came to Chamaripa to be rid of the sickness or malaise – and those who wished for realisation came to receive instruction. Chamaripa was known for teachings which employed the imagery of his craft – and gave pointing-out instructions with the question *"Why cover the land with leather when you could wear sandals?"* This meant: why attempt to understand reality by studying everything – when you could know everything there is to know through single-pointed absorption?

Rinpoche finished the hagiography, and as we stood looking out across the slate grey channel to the islands of Flat Holm and Steep Holm I mused *"That's a theme in a fair few of the Mahasiddha stories. They found imagery within the occupations or crafts of their disciples to employ in their teaching. It made me think of all the analogies that you use, that come from your personal experience – and also from movies."*

"Someone once asked me why I watched movies" Rinpoche replied *"or why I read novels – books other than Buddhist texts. I replied 'There's no movie I've ever watched —or book I've read—which I haven't quoted when teaching.' That came as a surprise to the questioner."* PAUSE *"People seem to imagine that Dharma is only found in books with* DHARMA *in block capitals on the cover in Gill Sans Ultra Bold."*

"If your mind is geared towards Vajrayana" added Khandro Déchen *"then whatever you hear, whatever you read, whatever you see, is going to be available to bring into teaching when necessary. There are always scenes in movies that offer interesting reflections in terms of Vajrayana."*

"I remember passing a Flamenco club in London once when I was in my twenties" continued Rinpoche. *"I'd gone to London to visit with James Low* [9].

---

[9] Tibetan translator and disciple of 'Khordong gTérchen Tulku Chhi'mèd Rig'dzin Rinpoche.. Author/co-author of a series of books published by 'Simply Being' in 2021: *Simply Being: Texts in the Dzogchen tradition; Being Guru Rinpoche: A Commentary on Nuden Dorje's Terma Vidyadhara Guru Sadhana; Longing for Limitless Light;* and *Lotus Source: Becoming Lotus Born* – amongst others.

"It was after midnight—he likes to stay up into the early hours of the morning—and there was no one there, apart from one couple who were practising Flamenco. I was fascinated to see the difference between the man's style and the woman's style. There was a marked difference. With the man the movement was all from the hips down – feet clattering. With the woman the movement was mainly in the torso, arms, and the swaying of her head. It struck me immediately that they were the dPa'wo and khandro. They were the dance-display of method and wisdom. It was phenomenal." PAUSE *"You always see these reflections of Vajrayana. If you're open to seeing them, they are everywhere. They're in Spanish Flamenco dance. They're there in all forms of dance – and all forms of every Art."*

"They are there in anything you see" added Khandro Déchen. *"If you have the 'mind of Vajrayana', then you'll see Vajrayana."*

After more minutes of silent gazing from the pier out to sea, we turned to head back up the hill towards Frogs' Leap. As we walked, I asked *"The final statement of the hagiography—that you could know everything there is to know through one-pointed absorption—is interesting. If all you need to 'understand reality' is meditation experience, why bother with other study, studying history, psychology etc…"*

"Well, this isn't your question – is it?" chuckled Khandro Déchen. *"This is a question you're asking for people who would ask this kind of question."*

"Guilty as charged" I smiled sheepishly.

"In that case" continued Khandro Déchen *"when it comes to one-pointed absorption, you have to arrive at the point at which you're primed. The study of history is valuable for other reasons. It's necessary if you are to teach. You have to understand the context of Vajrayana. The study of Vajrayana psychology gives you the framework which makes sense of practice experience – and enables you to discuss practice with the Lama."*

"If you look at history" added Rinpoche *"you will see how conditioning functions.*

"*Then, you become increasingly suspicious of the conditioning – of the way that most people, youself included, are swayed by passing fashions, of the fashion of the period, or epoch.*" PAUSE "*There was a time a few years back when everyone suddenly started answering 'yeah-yeah' rapidly, in agreement to statements made. I'd point it out—when students did it—and they'd almost always reply that they'd always said 'yeah-yeah'. I'd reply 'No. You started saying 'yeah-yeah' this year – along with all the others who started saying 'yeah-yeah' this year.'*"

"*How did they respond to that?*"

"*Well…*" Rinpoche laughed. "*As I'm their Lama, they're more-or-less obliged to believe me – but they're shocked by it. They realise they've picked up the 'yeah-yeah' speech habit unconsciously.*" PAUSE "*Now, of course, the trend has faded away. These speech trends, like all trends, are always coming and going – and it's just a matter of catching yourself falling in with them.*"

"*So, you have always shunned fashion?*"

"*No… I wouldn't say that. If I authentically appreciate something that happens to have become fashionable – then I might buy it or go along with it in some way. The answer isn't to abjure fashion – that's just another form of incarceration. The answer is to become an authentic individual – and* know *what you authentically appreciate. The* problem *is liking whatever-it-is because it is fashionable rather than because you authentically appreciate whatever-it-is.*"

"*So…*" I ruminated "*how d'you come to know what you authentically appreciate?*"

"*Trial and error.*" Pause with a grin. "*You have to start young, maybe.*" PAUSE "*You have to see how long appreciation lasts. Maybe this can only occur once one is an adult – because childhood is typically peppered with passing fancies. When one continues to have passing fancies however – one should take that as an indication that one has no sense of authentic appreciation.*"

"*So, it is when appreciation endures…?*"

"Yes. For example, I desired a William Morris [10] jacket—like the ones George Harrison, Steve Marriot, and Jimi Hendrix had back in 1966/1967. They could not be purchased then – because they were all personally tailored and would have cost a fortune. I now have one, made for me by our disciple Naljorma Kha'drön in Sweden. So, as you can see, my appreciation for the jacket has lasted for more than fifty years. In fact—when I'm not wearing robes—I dress more-or-less the same way I dressed from 1966 onward. I've worn Levi Strauss 501 Serge de Nîmes trousers since I was five years old – but that was not because they were fashionable. They weren't even available in Britain in 1957. They only became available by the early 1960s. My first three pairs were purchased at the American Air Base in Reading, Hampshire by my half sister Monica from Santa Monica. She was a daughter from my father's first family. She had married an American Airman, and she was thus able to take us all to the Airbase for lunch on her special pass. She wanted me to have something 'American' and so she chose Levis. I was highly intrigued by them because they had a French seam on the outside leg. They also had a button fly which I naïvely considered to be ultra-modern – because I'd never seen a button fly before. I have been wearing Levis ever since." Rinpoche laughed "Not the same ones, you understand." PAUSE "So, with fashion… you have to be present. You have to have a sense of suspicion or scepticism concerning what 'seems' attractive – and this applies to clothing, music, Art, social conventions, politics, and every other area of life. Almost every aspect of life has 'fashions which pass'. You have to be aware of that."

"And—that—is the point at which you become a full-time practitioner" added Khandro Déchen. "Once you become a full-time practitioner, you continue to study yourself, as well as the texts. Even when you fully understand the texts you continue to study them to enjoy the beauty of Vajrayana. This is what Kyabjé Dilgo Khyentsé Rinpoche said when asked why he was still reading texts. At this point you're not studying to 'get anywhere' – but to enjoy the wealth of phenomenal reality. This, of course, feeds into the Art of teaching."

---

[10] William Morris (1834–1896) – British textile designer, poet, artist, author, and socialist activist associated with the British Arts and Crafts movement. He was a major contributor to the revival of traditional British textile Arts.

"In terms of movies and literature, if you don't understand enough about the world in respect of social mores, styles, and conventions" added Rinpoche "you can't teach people. You can't teach people because you're not conversant with their world."

The conversation continued as we sauntered upwards through Alexandra Park. "So" I asked "does that mean if you're a great realised yogi or yogini—sitting in your cave—you might not be able to help anybody else because you don't know about the world?"

"No" replied Khandro Déchen. "The fact that there's some yogi or yogini in a cave—and they've been there for twenty years—is greatly inspiring for everybody else. Such anchorites offer the inspiration of the appearance of their lives."

"Just as it is with the gTummo [11] masters at Tashi Jong" added Rinpoche. "They simply practise continually. That's what's inspiring. This works best in a culture where people understand that, of course. If I lock myself up in a room in Huddersfield for twenty years" Rinpoche laughed "that's not going to inspire anyone. No one would know I was there, or what I was doing. So, it depends where one is – in terms of what value one's seclusion might offer others."

"And with those gTummo yogis" I enquired "is that what makes it different to pratyekabuddha yana... that they're not just doing it for themselves because they're doing it to inspire others?"

"Yes – but there are several answers to this question" began Rinpoche. "They are practising with the motivation which wishes for the realisation of everyone and everything everywhere. That would not be the case with pratyekabuddha yana. They are also offering their accomplishment to show that the result of gTummo is real."
PAUSE "With gTummo you cannot retain the capacity unless you maintain the physical practices. So, to be a gTummo yogi or yogini—as an example to others—means you have to practise all the time. You cannot stop – which means you cannot take time out to teach. Or rather, you can't teach internationally or have many disciples. You've got to stay in one place – and people have to come to you if they want to learn gTummo.

---

[11] gTum mo / གཏུམ་མོ་ / candali – yoga of spatial heat.

"So that limits the number of people you can teach. Of course, the only people you teach then are the people who are absolutely serious. You don't take on anybody else."

"I read somewhere that as a serious practitioner, you can either teach or take rainbow body. You can't do both? Is that how it is?"

"That's the tendency, yes" replied Rinpoche. "When you have a religious culture – then people practise in many different ways. It makes sense as a whole. That's why it's a religion. You have hermits; gTummo yogis and yoginis; people who practise 'phowa; and, itinerants who practise gČod. There will be a network of people engaged in different practices, including ngakpas and ngakmas, monks and nuns – and also, devout lay people."

"It's an incredibly rich situation" added Khandro Déchen. "It's open to anybody being able to do anything, because they tend to find themselves where they need to be. You can only find that however, with a religion which is part of a society."

"Because the religion and the society will be interconnected and feed each other?" I asked.

"Yes, everybody is part of a whole—of something bigger—rather than being the big **I Am**' " Khandro Déchen responded. "That's a colossal cul-de-sac."

"This is why our students specialise in different areas" added Rinpoche. "Although we have a core practice—in which we engage when we gather in the morning—everyone practises individually: Vajrayana craft, yidam drüpthab, yogic song, sKu-mNyé, trül'khor, A-tri, Dzogchen long-dé or the 21 sem'dzin of Dzogchen men-ngag-dé, et cetera. It's important that there is this diversity. In that way we can replicate the rich situation of the Himalayas."

"Is that why you advocate calling Buddhism a 'religion' – because it has the potential to provide that rich situation?"

"Yes, certainly" Rinpoche nodded emphatically. "Otherwise you merely have 'self'-development – a person merely employing a technique.

"Perhaps people mean well when they talk about 'removing the religion from Buddhism' – but they haven't actually understood that 'religion' has a broad range of functions which are supportive to the core practice." PAUSE "It's a problem if you decide to do away with something—without looking at what function it serves—merely because it doesn't suit your social-philosophical point of view."

"That lesson was learnt with willow bark and aspirin" added Khandro Déchen. "The salicin in willow bark converts to salicylic acid – which is the same chemical which forms the basis of aspirin. Willow bark however, has other properties—along with the salicin—which make it gentler to the stomach." PAUSE "So, you can isolate the active ingredient. Then, you forgo what seems 'inactive' – but which fulfils a vital purpose. The Western Buddhist teachers who want to strip Buddhism of religion should consider this more carefully. Isolating the active ingredient of a religion is not a sensible idea."

"Governments need to look at this too" added Rinpoche. "Why is there vandalism? Why do people leave their rubbish in the countryside? Where does 'disrespect for the environment' originate?" PAUSE "Preventing it is not just a matter of imposing fines. We need to find out why people have become degraded in this way." PAUSE "Personally, I feel it's the decline of religion in society. There are churches closing everywhere. The Methodist Church at the end of our street has been converted into expensive apartments." We had reached the corner of Salop Street, and Rinpoche gestured to the church. "This was a functioning church when we moved here – now it's apartments. Whatever one might feel about Christianity – it serves a valuable function. There's the tendency to demolish the past without looking at what might be lost. Take patriotism for example. There's obviously an extremely negative aspect to it – but there are also worthy features. Being proud of one's country doesn't have to exist at the expense of other countries. It's touching to see the Bhutanese being proud of where they live. Whereas if you wave a union jack flag in Britain it's assumed you're a card-carrying fascist – unless it's the Last Night of the Proms."

Fourteen: Chamaripa – the nondual cordwainer

"Rinpoche's looking forward to receiving his Union Jacket" smiled Khandro Déchen. *"Kha'drön in Sweden is making it – from two linen Union Jacks made by Khyungtsal in Bavaria.*[12]*"*

"I've fancied one of those since Pete Townsend of The Who wore one, back in 1966" smiled Rinpoche *"but this one will be longer and made with period-weave linen in the colours typical of the late 1700s."* PAUSE *"It will have twin ticket pockets and wide lapels."* PAUSE *"I shall have a Welsh Dragon pin, of course—as I've lived in Wales since 1976—and a Cornish Flag pin too."*

We had reached Frogs' Leap and as Rinpoche opened the door Khandro Déchen grinned *"You know, perhaps it's time we had a flagpole in our garden."*

---

[12] Ngak'chang Rinpoche's Union jacket arrived for his 70th birthday and the celebration of Queen Elizabeth II's Platinum Jubilee in June 2022.

Fifteen: Lila Vajra – the regal hedonist

Lila Vajra *(li'i la badzra / ལིའི་ལ་བཛྲ)* / Gègpa'i Dorje *(sGegs pa'i rDo rJe / སྒེགས་པའི་རྡོ་རྗེ)*

Disciple of: Mékopa
Varna by birth: Kshatriya

A Saturday morning in June at Frogs' Leap for the celebration of three birthdays – Rinpoche's, Khandro Déchen's and their daughter's, Ræchel[1]*.*

There is a tradition of Rinpoche and Khandro Déchen hosting a dGa'tön[2] in June each year, as a summer garden party. Although *party* is the closest English word we have, the Vajrayana term dGa'tön suggests more than a secular social gathering. *dGa'* means joy, happiness, or pleasure and *tön* relates to feasting – but also, to *that which displays, or reveals teachings*. Rinpoche and Khandro Déchen therefore describe dGa'tön as a mode of *informal symbolic transmission* where joy is experienced through celebration and appreciation – a delightful Vajrayana exploration of the non-separation of sacred and secular.

We had arrived early in the morning to help prepare the house and garden and lend our hands to the making of the traditional salad sandwiches and homemade sausage rolls. The salad sandwiches are made according to Rinpoche's father's recipe: granary bread with lashings of salted butter, crisp lettuce leaves, sliced unpeeled cucumber, tomatoes, and spring onions – and all with a generous shaking of salt and black pepper.

With the sandwiches made, Rinpoche, Khandro Déchen and Ræchel had changed into their dGa'tön outfits for the day – Farnham Girls' Grammar School Blazers.

---

[1] Ræchel was given the name Künzang Tsodrön *(kun bZang mTsho gron / ཀུན་བཟང་མཚོ་སྒྲོན)* by Kyabjé Künzang Dorje Rinpoche and Jomo Sam'phel Déchen Rinpoche.
[2] *dGa' sTon / དགའ་སྟོན*

This was an ensemble devised by Rinpoche in 1970 when he first saw girls' grammar school blazers worn by fellow male Art students. They were very much desired by Art students in the late 1960s. It was difficult to find them large enough and Rinpoche could never find one to fit. Those that could be obtained in the charity shops were usually far too small for adult males.

Four decades or so later, Rinpoche had procured the necessary vestiary elements and now sported his Farnham Girls' Grammar School Blazer; Levi Strauß 501 Serge de Nîmes trousers and Levi shirt; red socks, white plimsolls, and a red & white polka-dot Ascot[3]. There would be other guests in Farnham Girls' Grammar School Blazers too – as an order had been placed with a *Club Blazer* company. All it took was 20 people to make the commission possible. Rinpoche provided the pattern of stripes —deep red, deep yellow and emerald green—and their respective widths. Other guests would wear different kinds of striped boating jackets, complete with straw boaters. All the guests for the dGa'tön put considerable thought and effort into their attire. There would be authentic period clothing and sartorial displays of all manner of interesting costume. We already knew that Queen Victoria, Boadicea, Jimi Hendrix, Cleopatra, Harald Hardrada, Charlie Chaplin, Doc Holiday, Oscar Wilde, and Mae West would be appearing for the occasion.

All the dGa'tön preparation was completed – chairs and small tables were gathered outside in the courtyard, the parasols open, and the cushions assembled. The dining table had been arranged to display the impending banquet. The salad sandwiches and sausage rolls were there, waiting to be joined by the culinary offerings of the dGa'tön guests.

---

[3] An ascot is a type of necktie that is usually made of silk. It is characterised by its wide, flat base, and narrow pointed ends.

Jugs of Pimm's full of fruit and mint were in the refrigerator and the glasses set on trays ready for the recitation of the Drinking Song of Kyabjé Düd'jom Rinpoche[4].

It was approaching 'High Noon', the designated time for dGa'tön commencement. We sat conversing in the shaded part of the garden courtyard as we awaited the guests. *"You have orchestrated a number of dGa'töns over the years. It seems like you're creating 'group situations' in which informal symbolic transmission can occur"* I commented. *"Am I accurate in that idea?"*

"Yes" responded Rinpoche. *"It's an important aspect of Dzogchen long-dé – all Dzogchen in fact."*

"It facilitates integration with the texture of experience in everyday life. It shows the mode in which every moment of existence is dGa'tön: the party of duality and nonduality" Khandro Déchen smiled.

"… and what would you say" I asked *"is the principle here?"*

"The principle is awareness – in terms of spacious appreciation" Khandro Déchen smiled *"and finding the presence of awareness in the sense fields."*

"In effect, it's a participatory Art event" Rinpoche added. *"In terms of Vajrayana, Art is life and life is Art. Kyabjé Düd'jom Rinpoche told me that the Arts are the efflorescence of the senses as they dance within the fields of the senses. In the 1960s they would have been called 'happenings' perhaps."* Rinpoche grimaced slightly at the use of the word – then laughed. *"These 'happenings' weren't always meaningful of course – but sometimes there were brilliant moments, when the natural goodness and creativity of certain people created a wave which carried others along with it. No doubt there will be such brilliant moments today. We do have Queen Victoria gracing us with her presence after all"* Rinpoche grinned.

---

[4] A recitation composed by Düd'jom Rinpoche for oration before imbibing. This is read aloud by a member of the Aro gTér sangha in one of the 17 languages into which it has been translated by students of Ngak'chang Rinpoche and Khandro Déchen.

"Actually, as we're about to have a celebration and we're expecting royal company, perhaps we could have the hagiography of Lila Vajra – the regal hedonist, whilst we await the arrival of the Sovereign?" Rinpoche asked, raising his eyebrows in question.

I said that this sounded like a delightful idea, so he began. *"Lila Vajra was a Raja, the Maharaja of Thiruvananthapuram in southern India – and he was exceedingly wealthy even by the Indian standards of the day…"*

In fact, his wealth was so inordinate that he was not touched by greed. He was devoted to sensual enjoyment – but such enjoyment did not serve as a reassurance of his status. He surrounded himself with that which was beautiful to see, hear, taste, smell, and touch. He had no idea of measuring himself against other Rajas—in terms of the extent of enjoyment—and therefore what was simple was equal to that which was lavish. He was an expert in the Art of enjoyment and never tired of that which he enjoyed. Beyond these pleasures, Lila Vajra had a taste for intellectual gratification which led him to seek out interesting people: spiritual seekers, philosophers, alchemists, astronomers, astrologers, and travellers who had visited strange and distant lands. He gave generous gifts – and they all accepted them, even the soi-disant[5] renunciate sadhus.

He continually sent emissaries out into his own lands and beyond to find new cognoscenti with whom he could converse. On one such foray—as far as Bengal—one of Lila Vajra's emissaries met Mahasiddha Mékopa and prevailed upon him to visit Lila Vajra. *"If I can be of value I will travel anywhere—there is no need for me to be in one place any more than another—but will your Raja listen seriously to what I say? I know about Rajas and so you must excuse my doubt that he would have any interest in Vajrayana – or, especially, a man like me."* The emissary assured Mékopa that his Raja had a great thirst for knowledge and would listen with unprecedented concentration to Mékopa's words.

---

[5] French, meaning 'saying oneself'.

They travelled back to southern India and the emissary began to discuss how Mékopa would be presented to Lila Vajra. *"I will make sure that you are well dressed for the occasion – as it would be wrong to come before our Raja in the white rags that you wear."*

"Ah…" replied Mékopa *"… then I must walk back to Bengal. Thank you for accompanying me here, it was a pleasant journey."*

The emissary was aghast – because he had already told Lila Vajra of the astonishing tantric yogi he had found in Bengal. He had explained how nothing worried this man. He spoke kindly no matter what anyone said. He was utterly generous with whatever he had – and, above all else, he could stare without blinking no matter how bright the sun. *"Please do not leave, good sir – I have told the Raja about you already and it would be extremely bad for me if you were to leave without having an audience."*

"Certainly, I will stay – but your Raja must see me as I am. If I dress in the beautiful clothes you want to give me, I will not be who I am – and that would be a deception. How can I meet your Raja as a deceiver who lies to his face?"

The emissary was perplexed by this. What Mékopa said was true; yet – it was also disrespectful to present the Raja with a man dressed in rags. He explained this to Mékopa and he replied *"Ah… I see your problem. What you do not understand about my rags is that they are priceless. No one but a tantrika could afford rags like these. All your Raja's wealth would not buy a shred snipped from clothes like these. When I explain this to your Raja, I am sure he will understand. You have told me that he is wise and perceptive. You have told me that he has listened to many sages and philosophers. As this is the case – he will not be offended by my appearance. He will understand the limitless wealth they represent."*

The emissary was far from stupid and could find no fault with Mékopa's words. The lesser of the two evils therefore, seemed to be to take Mékopa to meet Lila Vajra dressed in the ragged white robes he wore. *"If it would make things easier…"* Mékopa suggested *"my robes could be washed and I could bathe. Would that make you more relaxed?"*

The emissary was heartily relieved. Mékopa's robes were washed and Mékopa bathed. Thus—slightly improved in appearance and odour—he appeared before the Raja Lila Vajra. The two conversed for an hour or more and Lila Vajra was evidently deeply fascinated by Mékopa's teaching. The emissary who sat nearby was relieved that Mékopa's appearance had caused no displeasure – but eventually the question of Mékopa's ragged robes became part of the conversation. *"It must be hard for a man of such profound knowledge and wisdom to wander from place to place as you do."*

"Not at all. Wherever I go is the palace of the yidam – so I never leave that royal court."

"You would—really—be as happy anywhere as here?" asked Lila Vajra with some incredulity.

"Yes."

"So, if I were to offer you your own apartments here – you would refuse them?"

"No. I would not refuse them—that would be unappreciative and discourteous—but I could only accept them for a few weeks. I would not stay for long. If I stayed, I would neglect the many other palaces of my yidam – and that would be a great discourtesy."

"But a few weeks is such a short time – could you not stay longer?"

"However long I stayed I would eventually die – and so my residence is limited whatever my choice. What is more important than the duration of my stay, is the benefit I might be whilst I remain, and a few days might be enough for that."

"I see" replied Lila Vajra, somewhat overawed by the answer. *"But please allow me to clothe you according to your stature as a vajra master."*

"Thank you…" Mékopa smiled at Lila Vajra *"for your generous offer – but what I must explain is that these rags are priceless. No one but a tantrika could afford rags like these.*

"One cannot buy them with money or with gold and jewels – one can only buy them with experience. All your wealth would not buy a shred snipped from clothes such as these. You are wise and perceptive. You have listened to many sages and philosophers, so I have no doubt that you will comprehend the meaning of my words – and not be offended by my appearance. You will understand the limitless wealth they represent."

Hearing this, made the emissary agitated – but Lila Vajra understood immediately. *"You are the first yogi to come before me who is truly disinterested in appearances. It is true, I cannot afford raiment such as yours. I would dearly love to embrace your teaching wholeheartedly – but I know that I enjoy my situation too much to give it up. Is there nothing I could do to practise Vajrayana as a Raja?"*

"Certainly" replied Mékopa *"if you are not jaded by your enjoyments."*

"No… I am far from jaded. I never tire of my sensory pleasures – but is it not the case that I should be weary of samsara?"

"Certainly…" responded Mékopa *"but being jaded by the sense fields and being weary of samsara are entirely different. The sense fields are not necessarily 'samsara' – and being weary of samsara may not be what you take it to be."*

Rinpoche paused as Tashi the cat nonchalantly approached across the courtyard, jumped on to Rinpoche's lap, and started to purr with apparent pleasure. *"It's making me wonder"* I asked *"what's going on when we become jaded. Is it always a dulling of the sense fields?"*

"Yes" Rinpoche replied. *"People tend to become jaded when 'what was exciting or interesting' is no longer 'new'. You see… what was exciting, was not 'the thing itself' – but merely that it was new."* PAUSE *"So, people become jaded when they didn't really appreciate 'whatever it was' in the first place. They merely appreciated the 'newness'. That is why fashion exists. Fashion is in everything – and everything has to be new and exciting."* PAUSE *"There was a time—particularly on the West Coast—when people would say 'Hi, what's new and different?'… I'd then answer 'Nothing—it's all the same—and it's perfect!' New and different is not interesting per se."*

"*It's what makes things uninteresting in fact*" added Khandro Déchen "*because what's 'new and different' today is 'old and highly similar' tomorrow. That never ends. We chase our tails – and even Tashi hardly ever does that. That's how we become jaded.*"

"*So not to become jaded*" continued Rinpoche "*is simply to appreciate what is there. Kyabjé Künzang Dorje Rinpoche said that when you appreciate what is there —you find that it's inexhaustible. You cannot become jaded when you authentically enjoy anything – as you will see as I continue with the hagiography…*"

Lila Vajra asked "*Tell me then, what does it mean to be weary of samsara and yet open to the enjoyment of the sense fields?*"

"*To be weary of samsara is to see samsara for what it is – in what one is. Samsara is a cycle which never ends, until one ends it through seeing the moment in which one created it.*"

"*It is merely 'habit' then?*" suggested Lila Vajra.

"*Yes. Merely habit. It is empty – and vanishes without a trace as soon as it is gone.*"

"*So, what does this habit look like…*" asked Lila Vajra "*and… how do I recognise it?*"

"*You will recognise samsara in the imaginary belief that the 'fulfilment of desire' is desirable.*"

"*… and desire is undesirable because?*"

"*Because the movement of thought around the fulfilment of desire comes to a standstill. There is nowhere further to go after consummation – other than appreciation. However, because we have no respect for—or enjoyment in —'consummate appreciation free of subject and object' we become jaded. There is nowhere to go after consummation – other than to attempt consummation elsewhere with some new focus of desire.*"

"*And that…*" said Lila Vajra "*is why samsara never ends until one ends it.*"

"Precisely" smiled Mékopa. *"And to end samsara, you simply need to realise that appreciation has neither inception nor culmination."*

Rinpoche paused and I asked *"Can you describe appreciation as communication too?"*

"Certainly. Appreciation—authentic desire—is what exists in terms of connecting directly with phenomena. Authentic connection is based on appreciation. The statement 'I desire that'—even at the level of neurosis—is a statement of communication. Changchub sem is always communication. It's the energy which exists between everything." PAUSE *"At this moment, I'm looking at the redness of Ja'gyür's shirt against the huge green leaves of the castor oil tree. I detect the breeze from the sea. I smell the mint we picked for the Pimm's. That confluence of sensations is essentially enjoyable. Everything is enjoyable – just as it is. Colours and sounds are enjoyable – just as they are."*

"Mark Darcy likes Bridget Jones[6] *'just as she is'"* laughed Khandro Déchen *"and she's very pleased about that, even though they both repeatedly ruin their relationship with indignance, petulance, irritation, and narrow-minded judgementality."* PAUSE *"That's the crucial issue – that you have to* stay *with liking whatever it is, just as it is."*

"Phenomena don't have to 'do' anything for us" Rinpoche grinned. *"Phenomena don't have to provide us with any kind of reference point to substantiate the form qualities of our existence. Red is simply beautiful because it is red. Green is simply beautiful because it is green. Blue is simply beautiful because it is blue – and likewise with white, yellow and every colour, hue and shade. The five colours continuously speak of what they are. That is communication. Recognising it, is* appreciation *– changchub sem."* Rinpoche smiled and continued with the hagiography.

"So with appreciation…" pondered Lila Vajra.

---

[6] *Bridget Jones's Diary* is a 2001 romantic comedy film starring Renée Zellweger as Bridget Jones, a 32-year-old British single woman, who writes a diary focusing on her wishes in life. Two men vie for her affections, portrayed by Colin Firth and Hugh Grant.

"With appreciation there is nothing to lose – and nothing to gain" replied Mékopa. "There is nothing to gain because everything is already possessed – as self-possessed. There is nothing to lose – because the entire phenomenal universe is always there. The enjoyment of the sense fields is simply 'what it is' without need of acquisition. So, because you are not jaded by your enjoyments – you are already at the base of practice. If you are prepared to experience empty-enjoyment, you can attain the nondual state." Mékopa paused and asked *"And once you dwell in the nondual state... ?"*

"... I will have sufficient wealth to wear what you wear?"

"Yes. Then you will have sufficient wealth to wear what I wear."

"How do I begin?" enquired Lila Vajra.

"Begin with the impressive diamond on your ring."

"Shall I give it away?" asked Lila Vajra.

"No" smiled Mékopa. *"I do not wish you to emulate the ascetics – even to the extent of one ring."*

"But I may be generous to the poor, may I not?"

"Certainly, you may – but not with the thought that this makes you more like a yogi. You must never approach generosity with the thought that: there is a giver; there is a gift; and, there is one to whom the gift is given."

Lila Vajra understood the meaning of this. He bowed his head in acceptance. Mékopa then asked Lila Vajra to gaze at the stone set into the ring.

> *"Mind is a jewel – but a jewel of immeasurable worth.*
> *This diamond – though it may be the largest in this world is merely a small reflection of a partial facet of Mind.*

*Gaze into this diamond with one-pointed awareness
And you will realise the empty-enjoyment in which possession and
possessor are indivisible.
Whatever you enjoy is both emptiness and form.
Whatever you enjoy you can give away – because you can never lose it.
You can never lose it because it was always empty
And because it was always empty it always provided you with form to
enjoy."*

Lila Vajra was so inspired by Mékopa's teaching that he was determined to practise every day for several hours. Once he had begun however, he derived so much pleasure from his absorption that his practice became ceaseless and flooded the rest of his experience. Once his practice was firmly established Mékopa took his leave and returned to his life of wandering. Lila Vajra continued his life as a hedonist – but his appreciation transformed his hedonism into the nondual efflorescence of hedonism and asceticism. He gave teachings to his court – and from then on, the Arts, music, poetry, dancing, sculpture, theatre, sartorial display, and feasting became rolpa.

The two tantrikas only met once more in their lives, when Mékopa happened to wander in the south of India. Lila Vajra had robes made that were exactly like those of Mékopa: white and made of rags – and when he went wandering incognito in the backlands of his domain he wore these robes. Whilst dressed as a ragged tantrika he gave jewels to those who needed help – but no one ever knew that the mysterious yogi was their own ruler. When Lila Vajra and Mékopa met – they both offered each other prostrations and Lila Vajra asked *"Now at last it feels as if I am wealthy enough to dress in emulation of my vajra master."*

"You are not mistaken in that feeling" Mékopa replied *"and now I will wear the clothes you offered me years ago and live in the apartments you put at my disposal – but only for a month. Then I must leave and we will not meet again in this life."*

During the month at Lila Vajra's palace, Mékopa shared his disciple's life of empty-hedonism and wore gorgeous royal raiment. He then gave Lila Vajra final transmissions, reassumed his ragged white raiment, and set out north for the Himalayas.

I sat smiling somewhat vacantly for a moment and then asked *"Would you explain what 'empty-hedonism' might look like?"*

"Hedonism without the idea of obtaining anything special" Rinpoche replied. *"Hedonism is often predicated on indulging in whatever other people lack or what they can't have. It can be predicated on what is too expensive."*

"It can be predicated on giving you rewards" added Khandro Déchen *"without the effort required to reap a reward."*

"So, hedonists will usually consume without authentic appreciation" Rinpoche emphasised. *"Their appreciation will often be predicated on rarity, scarcity, or expense. They don't often appreciate anything which requires work – so the appreciation is incredibly limited."* PAUSE *"So, for 'empty-hedonism' you could read 'unlimited hedonism' – whereas, 'ordinary hedonism' is highly limited and specific to certain things. With 'empty-hedonism', 'empty' means 'without boundary' – whereas 'form-hedonism' has boundaries."*

"There are people who drink expensive champagne—who eat caviar and oysters—but who don't actually enjoy it as much as they express" added Khandro Déchen. *"It's just that they're expensive, and they can feel good about themselves by indulging in them because other people can't afford such things. There is all that ungainly concept around it."* PAUSE *"When Rinpoche and I first got together he very kindly brought champagne for our picnic on the beach at Monknash. I asked him whether he could tell the difference between champagne and sparkling dry white wine. He said that he didn't know – but would be interested to try. He did – and concluded that he couldn't tell the difference. Since then, we have never bought champagne."* PAUSE *"A 'form-hedonist' would have had to continue drinking Moët et Chandon."*

Fifteen: Lila Vajra – the regal hedonist

"*Or take it further*" said Rinpoche "*to Bollinger or Dom Perignon, for which you can pay over £3,000 a bottle. A nondual hedonist in contradistinction, would enjoy sparkling water with a healthy squeeze of lemon. Or enjoy the texture of a piece of driftwood on the beach, or a piece of broken bottle which had been turned into a translucent pebble by the tide. A nondual hedonist would enjoy observing a snail as much as an albatross, eagle, beagle, rhinoceros, rhinestone, or diamond. A nondual hedonist would enjoy cheese-on-toast as much as a steak.*"

"*Rinpoche used to eat pretty miserable cheese on toast when he was poor*" Khandro Déchen laughed.

"*Oh yes*" Rinpoche chuckled. "*I once came back from seeing Chhi'mèd Rig'dzin Rinpoche in the Netherlands. I had no money left and no food worth speaking of in the larder – just some stale bread and a piece of cheese which had become rock hard. Fortunately, there was a tub of frozen milk in the freezer – so I grated the cheese with the finest side of the grater and mixed some milk with the cheese-powder. This turned it into a cheese paste. I ran the stale bread under the tap—spread the cheese paste on it with some garlic—and popped it under the grill. It was surprisingly good.*"

"*I might have to try that one day*" I laughed.

"*Speaking of hedonism – I'd like to indulge in some of those salad sandwiches soon*" Rinpoche added. "*High Noon is upon us.*"

"*I expect folk will start arriving shortly*" I answered. "*Can I just ask about rolpa before they do?*" Rinpoche nodded, so I continued "*The hagiography relates that after Lila Vajra has gained realisation, then all that goes on at his court—all the music, poetry, dancing, and feasting—becomes rolpa. Is that simply because everything becomes rolpa once you're in the nondual state?*"

"*Yes*" Rinpoche answered. "*Everything.*"

"*In terms of Dzogchen long-dé*" continued Khandro Déchen "*it is crucial to avoid sensory dullness and flatness of affect.*

"So, rolpa is a principal means for those who have the capacity to enter into the play of experience without gravitating to banality, or bestial indulgence."

"Let's say there was a gathering – a dGa'tön as we have today" Rinpoche smiled. "Say that this splendid food had been prepared – and we're all sitting there enjoying it." PAUSE "Then... someone asks 'This is good – but wouldn't it be marvelous if we were at Buckingham Palace, eating this with the Queen, and having this, that, and the other as well?'" PAUSE "If asked such a question, I would have to answer 'Not particularly. It would naturally be marvellous to be at Buckingham Palace with the Queen – but I wouldn't wish this situation to be other than exactly as it is.' In terms of rolpa, everything needs to be perfect just as it is. "

"So, rolpa..." I asked "... would be the 'actual enjoyment' rather than the 'concept of enjoyment' and any reference point it provided? That sounds synonymous with empty-hedonism?"

Before Rinpoche could answer, the doorbell rang heralding the arrival of the first guests. Rinpoche smiled "Yes, it's the same."

"And now it seems it's time to continue our practice of appreciation" added Khandro Déchen. They rose from their seats. "Appreciation is the key to enjoyment – and, to delighting in the enjoyment of others, so let's let the others in." Khandro Déchen grinned and went with Rinpoche to answer the door.

Ngakma Lé-kyi appeared dressed as Queen Victoria, accompanied by her husband Naresh, dressed as a Bollywood movie star.

"Queen Elizabeth was unable to attend" smiled Khandro Déchen "but..."

Sixteen: Tantipa – the vacuous carpet-weaver

Tantipa *(ta nTi pa /* ཏནྟི་པ *)* / Gé'khyom Thagapa *(rGas 'khyoms tha ga pa /* རྒས་འཁྱོམས་ཐ་ག་པ *)*

Disciple of: Jalandhara
Teacher of: Kanhapa
Varna by birth: Vaishya

A damp and misty March morning at Drala Jong during our second winter of residence.

Ngak'chang Rinpoche and Khandro Déchen were staying for a few days to oversee the display of statuary and practice implements in the evolving shrine hall. Over breakfast in the farmhouse Khandro Déchen said *"I would like to pay some attention to the outer shrine hall too. Maybe we could take advantage of the rain easing up and spend the morning clearing weeds from the vegetable beds."* The flower and vegetable garden abuts the shrine hall to the south, and is an abundance of colours in the spring and summer. One day a *Himalayan medicinal garden*[1] will also flourish there. As Khandro Déchen headed off with a wheelbarrow, spade, and secateurs, we accompanied Rinpoche to the shrine hall to commence the arrangement of the statues and artefacts.

The shrine hall lies in a partly converted barn. It was once the milking parlour for the dairy farm. It has a high, beamed roof and foot-thick stone walls. We had plastered most of the walls and spent some weeks the previous summer painting them with the Aro gTér traditional pattern of stripes. They were originally the Düd'jom gTér colours – but they only ever existed in the London and Paris Düd'jom gTér centres. After these centres were appropriated by Sogyal Lakar the colour scheme was changed to a ubiquitous yellow – incongruously the colour of morality.

The Düd'jom gTér colours represent the phenomenal universe. The bottom sections of the walls are the deep red of earth. Then there's a hands-width emerald green stripe representing all the flora and fauna on the surface of the earth.

---

[1] tswa'i ga'tshal *(rTswa'i dGa' tshal /* རྩྭའི་དགའ་ཚལ *)*

Next there is an orange hands-width stripe representing the sphere of the sun and moon – followed by a wide band of golden yellow, for the light of the sun and moon. The final sections of the walls and the entire ceiling are painted deep blue, for space. The effect of the colour scheme is remarkably dramatic – simultaneously startling and warmly welcoming.

There is already a unique and eclectic collection of zo'i rigné[2]—Vajrayana Arts—on display in the shrine hall. There are rare antique pieces and extremely rare pieces of ancient origin – some dating to the 8th century. These items were collected by Ngak'chang Rinpoche and Khandro Déchen from the 1970s onward. Some are priceless ritual objects given to Ngak'chang Rinpoche by Kyabjé Düd'jom Rinpoche Jig'drèl Yeshé Dorje.

"I heard that one of these is a meteorite iron phurba made for Guru Rinpoche by Dorje Legpa. Is that correct?" I asked.

"Yes. Kyabjé Düd'jom Rinpoche was fantastically generous. I have kept these items secret until now – and only talk about them now because of the establishment of Drala Jong."

"Did he ask you to keep it secret?"

"No – but I didn't want to act stupidly in relation to these wonders. It would have been too much like playground boasting to mention the provenance of these phurbas and dorjes – let alone display them. Now however, is a good time as we are concerned with establishing a retreat centre. I never thought I would establish a retreat centre but Kyabjé Künzang Dorje Rinpoche expressly commanded it." PAUSE *"It seemed impossible – but both Düd'jom Rinpoche and Künzang Dorje Rinpoche were adept at making the impossible possible."*

Other items were given by Künzang Dorje Rinpoche, Kyabjé Dilgo Khyentsé Rinpoche, and 'Khordong gTérchen Tulku Chhi'mèd Rig'dzin Rinpoche.

---

[2] *bZo'i rig gNas* / བཟོའི་རིག་གནས

Then there is the recent work produced by the talented Aro gTér bZo-pas³ and bZo-mas⁴ – the artists and craftspeople of the Aro gTér sangha.

The Drala Jong development plans include extending the seating area of the shrine hall by fifteen feet and by adding an entrance porch to the side. There is also to be a separate gön-khang⁵. When the building work is completed, we can start work on the bespoke shrine cabinets to house the lineage statues and treasures. Until then, Rinpoche and Khandro Déchen wanted to ensure that we were displaying everything as sensibly —comprehensibly—as possible with the extant erratic shelving. As Rinpoche adjusted the arrangement of the Lineage Lama figures, talk turned to his vision for the finished shrine hall. *"We will need efficient lighting, of course. Maybe spotlights for the shrine cabinets and appliqué thangkas. Then, there's the rather considerable matter of the floor. I had this idea – which is probably out of the question financially…"* Rinpoche grinned *"but it would be rather splendid to commission a garuda-patterned carpet, using our design for the garuda brocade which we had made in Varanasi."*

"Now wouldn't—that—be something!" added Khandro Déchen who had overheard what was said through one of the open windows.

"Actually, Rinpoche" I grimaced *"I investigated a little about having a Drala Jong carpet design produced… and the cost, particularly for such a large area, would be well out of our league unless a millionaire patron appeared."*

"Oy—oy veh—oy gewaldt ⁶…*"* Rinpoche sighed in mock chagrin – then grinned *"What we need in this sangha—as well as an architect, builder, and millionaire—is Mahasiddha Tantipa."*

Ja'gyür laughed *"He was the carpet-weaver, Rinpoche, wasn't he?"*

³ *bZo pa* / བཟོ་པ
⁴ *bZo ma* / བཟོ་མ
⁵ *mGon khang* / མགོན་ཁང – protector house, room, shrine, or cabinet.
⁶ 'Oy veh' is a Yiddish phrase expressing dismay or exasperation. It can be translated as 'woe is me', but literally it means 'oh pain' from its Germanic origin 'weh' meaning 'pain'. 'Oy' stems from Biblical Hebrew. *Gewaldt* pertains to violent expression. Ngak'chang Rinpoche often uses Yiddish words and phrases he has garnered from Jewish students in New York.

"*Exactly*" Rinpoche nodded. "*I could recount his hagiography when we've arranged everything – as far as we can with this outstandingly abysmal shelving.*"

Once we'd placed as many items as possible in reasonably coherent order, we settled on the shrine room chairs to listen.

"*So, yes, Ja'gyür. Tantipa was indeed a carpet-weaver – but more than that, he was a highly skilled and exceptionally luminary loomster. He was a genius in the Art…*"

He lived in Zahor[7]. That's near the town now known as Mandi. It is not far from Tso Pema[8]. Be that as it may, his carpets were highly prized and sought after. Being so gifted his reputation grew – and his wealth increased. He married Vibhuti—a beautiful girl of a good family—and as his five sons reached an appropriate age he taught them all his skills and trade secrets. The family became increasingly wealthy, and recognising his good fortune, Tantipa gave generously to the poor. He became known for his generosity and relative wisdom. He worked hard and the pride in his work extended to his sons – so the quality of their carpets remained exceptional.

All went well with his family but, sadly, he advanced in years so far that finally Vibhuti predeceased him. Although Vibhuti was elderly when she died—and although they had had an ideal life together—Vibhuti's death shocked Tantipa. His sons had all married – and, observing their conjugal felicity, he became so saddened by his loss that he lost heart in his work as a carpet-weaver.

Considering that he was now old, Tantipa decided that it was best that he hand over the carpet-weaving business to his sons.

---

[7] *za hor* / ཟ་ཧོར་ – the birthplace of Shantarakshita (725–788) and Tilopa (988–1069); centre for study and practice of medicine; and location of one of the eight great charnel grounds, durtrö chenpo gyèd *(dur khrod chen po brGyad* / དུར་ཁྲོད་ཆེན་པོ་བརྒྱད་ / *astamahasmasana)* – the Lanka Mound *(lang ka brTsegs* / ལང་ཀ་བརྩེགས་). Zahor is best known as the country in which the Vajrayana teachings first appeared.
[8] Rewalsar on Indian maps.

They felt that it was only right and fitting that, at his age, Tantipa should retire. He would be well looked after and given the respect he deserved in his twilight years.

Tantipa however—after a life of committed industry—found idleness disquieting. He soon fell to sitting for protracted periods staring into space. He recovered, as much as he could, from grief at his wife's demise – but had nothing to say to anyone. He had no conversation if anyone attempted to converse with him. Tantipa's sons gradually became uncomfortable with Tantipa's presence in the house – especially when discussing business with those who came to order carpets. It became increasingly difficult to explain the old man who sat staring like an owl – at nothing. He was not depressed exactly – but he was far from contented. He was purely a preoccupied pensive presence, who was absent.

The daughters-in-law pleaded for tolerance from their husbands – but eventually it was decided that Tantipa would have to be removed from the main house. A hut was built for him in the garden – and there he lived in solitary gloom. The daughters-in-law brought him food—and took care of his simple needs—but otherwise he was left in isolation. The daughters-in-law would sometimes comment on how sad it was, that the dear old man who had founded the great wealth of their family was relegated to a garden shed with only a bed and a chair. One daughter-in-law commented that Tantipa even lacked one of his own fine carpets beneath his feet – but her husband replied that their father was beyond noticing. A fine carpet would be wasted on him. Nonetheless the kind-hearted daughter-in-law insisted, and an old carpet was given to him. Tantipa's sons noticed no degree of appreciation in their father—on being supplied with a carpet—and expressed themselves to have been in the right when they told their wives that their father would not notice. The daughters-in-law maintained their care of the old man – but in time the sons failed even to call in on him.

I interrupted the hagiographic account as Rinpoche had encouraged me always to ask questions as soon as they arose. *"This vacuousness seems like he's retracted from his sense fields, almost like sleepy shi-nè – no thought, but no presence either?"*

Rinpoche assumed a questioning expression *"Yes…?"*

I continued *"Do you feel that grief is, in part, about not feeling useful anymore?"*

"Well, it's a question… What is this pizza if I cannot share it with the person with whom I used to share it?' When one's husband or wife dies the pizza loses value. It becomes a 'wifeless pizza' or a 'husbandless pizza'. This is because part of the value of the pizza was sharing it with someone else. Now that person is no longer there, the pizza is just the aggregate of its ingredients. This applies to everything. What is this object I'm observing? What is this that I'm hearing, smelling, tasting, touching? These foci of attention can become meaningless – if they're no longer experienced in connection with someone highly significant. Everything was invested in the presence of someone being there. It's a wonderful thing to be able to share enjoyments with others – and that sharing certainly enhances life. Enjoyment however, has got to exist independently. It can't be dependent on anything else. Otherwise, when whatever the circumstances on which you're dependent dissolve – intrinsic enjoyment also dissolves."

"In terms of value" I suggested *"Tantipa's not valued by his sons either, is he?"*

"Indeed not – because he's no longer a carpet-weaver. Whenever we invest value—in terms of expecting a return—there's necessarily a problem. You see, Tantipa's children didn't actually value him as a person. They only valued his world-class skill as the legendary lustrous laudably lambent loomster. When he ceased weaving, he no longer had a function in their lives. Tantipa then became an embarrassment. Because he had no function, they parked him in the shed at the bottom of the garden." Rinpoche looked sombre for a moment. *"Sadly, such situations are not uncommon."* PAUSE *"But then…"* he visibly cheered *"One—**Fine**—Day!"* he almost yelled *"Mahasiddha Jalandhara arrived in Zahor! He called at the carpet-weavers' establishment for alms – and everything changed!"* PAUSE *"That, you see, is why Mahasiddhas need to wander!"*

The daughters-in-law invited Jalandhara in to partake of a meal and he accepted their kind invitation. On realising that he was the Mahasiddha, Jalandhara, they begged him to accept their accommodation – but Jalandhara told them that he was used to sleeping rough. A bed would not suit his lifestyle. They then asked him if he would deign to sleep in the garden and he agreed.

After giving the family some simple teachings—as requested—Jalandhara went to take his rest in the garden. He went to sleep – but, awareness of someone moving in the garden shed in the early hours of the morning, roused him from the mi-lam bardo. He got up immediately to see who was there as he was curious to see who was awake at such a time. Jalandhara entered the garden shed and saw Tantipa sitting in his chair staring vacantly at the night. *"Hello, old gentleman – what are you doing… sitting in this garden shed in the middle of the night? Can't you sleep?"*

Tantipa explained himself, even though it was the first time he had spoken for some years. There was something in the presence of Jalandhara that necessitated a response.

"I see… I see…" Jalandhara pondered. *"This is a sad story – but a sad story isn't over until it's over."*

"I cannot argue with that, good sir."

"No indeed – and your story…" Jalandhara chuckled *"is by no means over."*

"But I am old" Tantipa sighed.

"Yes – and I am Jalandhara. Further to that fact – I have only just appeared in the story of your life. Let me ask you a question. Had I not appeared in your garden – would your life merely have continued to its conclusion in the same way?"

"Yes, good sir – that is what I would have expected."

"Exactly!" laughed Jalandhara. *"But now all expectations are thrown to the wind, are they not?"*

"Who are you, good sir, if I may ask?"

"I am a Buddhist yogi. My name, as I have told you, is Jalandhara – or that is how I am known in many places. I am also known as Wakhjir, Wakhan, Aror, Viratnagar, or Oddiyana. I travel from place to place, you see..."

"Why sir, if you do not mind me asking, do you have so many names?"

"Well... when I arrive at some place and people ask others 'Who is he' they just tell them where I came from. They say 'Oh, he's Wakhjir' because that is where they first ran into me. That is how it seems to work – and when anyone calls out 'Hey Wakhjir – may I speak with you about my camel?' I reply 'Certainly, good sir – what ails your camel?' Does this answer your question?"

"Yes... but I thought you said you were a Buddhist yogi?"

"I did not lie to you – but I was not always a Buddhist yogi, just as you will not always be a neglected old gentleman in a hut."

"May I ask what brought you here?"

"Why – my camel, good sir, my camel![9]" laughed Jalandhara. "My apologies. I knew what you meant. Your family has given me food and shelter for the night – and that is why I am here conversing with you."

"So, you too have been sent to sleep in the garden – this is not proper. They should have offered you a bed."

"I was offered a bed – but I prefer to sleep here" replied Jalandhara. "This is a fine place to sleep. It is also a fine place to die – if you are well prepared for death. Are you – well prepared for death?"

"No, reverend sir – I am not prepared."

"Do you fear death?"

---

[9] Ngak'chang Rinpoche is referring to Shakespeare's *Henry IV, Part I* (act II, scene iii) in which Lady Percy asks *"What is it that carries you away?"* to which Hotspur (Henry Percy) replies *"Why – my horse, my love, my horse."*

"No…" sighed Tantipa. "I do not fear death – but then I have no attachment to life since my wife died. I was sent to live in this shed since I had no conversation for anyone and my sons assumed I was senile. It is simply that I have no interest in life any longer – and have nothing to say to anyone about anything."

"Well… you would seem to have had a conversation with me… would you like to be prepared for death?"

"Yes, reverend sir. If you would be so good as to instruct me – I will give you all my attention."

"You have sat staring at nothing for years – but your mind has been dull. When you sit and stare, your mind must shine with presence. You must see reality. You must hear reality – and you must touch, taste, and smell the nature of reality. If you remain alert and without concept—even as you enter into the sleep state—you will understand the experience of death before you die."

Jalandhara then gave Tantipa transmission – and specific instructions before leaving the next morning. As Jalandhara made his farewells to the family he said *"I have spent many hours in conversation with your father. He is a most interesting old gentleman! You are most fortunate that he chooses to live in your garden shed. There can be no other family in the land with such a marvellous guest."*

The daughters and the husbands were dumbfounded by this statement – but said nothing to contradict Jalandhara. Once Jalandhara had departed however, they tentatively ventured into the garden to see how they could best understand Jalandhara's words. *"Good morning, my sons and daughters, I hope you have slept well. I want to thank you for your kindness and for introducing me to the Mahasiddha, Jalandhara."*

Tantipa's speech amazed them – because they had not heard their father speak for several years. *"How is it now father, that you speak? We are very pleased to hear you speak – but why have you not spoken before?"*

"I did not speak before because I had nothing to say – but now I am preparing to die and there are things I need to tell you."

The daughters-in-law wept to hear Tantipa speak of death – but he waved his hand to indicate that there was no need for tears. *"I do not say that my death is imminent – simply that I am practising to prepare myself in order that my life will not have been wasted. I taught my sons to weave – but I have not taught them of the warp and weft of existence. To do so I must spend my life in meditation."*

The sons and their wives welcomed Tantipa back into their house – but he declined. *"This garden is the best place for me. It is where I met my vajra master and I do not wish to leave this sacred spot."*

Tantipa always received his sons and their wives when they came to him – and he became part of their family once more. Even though he had nothing to do with the business – he returned to weaving and made carpets which surpassed anything he had ever made in his life before.

One morning—before dawn—a blaze of light bathed the household. The households roundabout thought that dawn had come unusually early – but they discovered that it was not the dawn, as it became dim again soon afterwards. It had been a strong light that emanated from Tantipa's garden dwelling. First Tantipa's family—then their neighbours—came to see what had happened. They all saw different things according to the nature of their perception. Some saw Tantipa seated in the air. Some saw him emanating rainbows. Some saw him surrounded by apparitional dakinis. And some saw Tantipa as a mass of inchoate light. Once these visions subsided, they found Tantipa weaving wondrous designs and singing songs of realisation. Many people gathered to be in his presence, and rather than an embarrassment to his sons, Tantipa became a cause of great family pride.

When the people finally dispersed, Tantipa called his sons and their families to him. *"My dear children, as you see, I am no longer an old man – but although I have woven a few carpets, I do not intend to return to weaving or to living in one place. The time has come for me to leave and enter a life of wandering."*

"How shall you live, dear father?" they remonstrated with some dread. *"How shall you not suffer discomfort and privation?"*

"I shall live as other yogis live. As for discomfort and privation, I shall only experience what they experience – and I did not hear Jalandhara complain of his life. He was happier to stay in this garden than in the house – so what have I to fear? In any case – I was so much older then, I'm younger than that now[10]*. I shall live by teaching Dharma through the Art of weaving."*

I laughed at Rinpoche's Bob Dylan quote.

"It's one of my plethoric idiosyncrasies" Rinpoche smiled. *"I like to insert the words of Rock or Blues lyrics where I can, whether people notice them, or not. I do the same with Shakespeare and the various poets I have studied. I do this, not merely to amuse – but to encourage people to look at the world. To hear the world – and to experience it through each sense field. To prompt sensory exploration, one sometimes needs to surprise people. One wouldn't expect a quote from Bob Dylan, Leonard Cohen, or John Lennon to suddenly appear in a hagiography. It could create a certain frisson. It's deliberately incongruous. It could make people think 'Oh, so you can listen to a song, you can read a piece of poetry, you can look at a painting – and there'll be something which suddenly speaks of something.' I don't employ such references every time I recount a hagiography, of course. I only do so on the inspiration of the moment."*

At that moment Khandro Déchen passed by the shrine hall window pushing a wheelbarrow laden with weeds, heading for the compost pile. She paused and waved, and Rinpoche smiled and waved back. She called out *"Tantipa, the geriatric weaver – as told by he who describes himself as 'the senile delinquent'!"*

"Yes indeed" Rinpoche replied. *"It's the fruitional stage – from having been a juvenile delinquent and a maladroit middle-aged maniac…"* and continued the hagiography.

---

[10] Bob Dylan—*My Back Pages*—Another Side of Bob Dylan—1964

Tantipa's family was astonished by Tantipa's sudden youthfulness – but nonetheless implored him to stay. He told them however *"That is now impossible. I have taken transmission and teaching from Mahasiddha Jalandhara – and so, I must now live as he lives. Before I leave however, I must tell you of the real nature of weaving – and entrust this carpet to your care. It is a pair of saddle-carpets, which I have made for Mahasiddha Jalandhara. He will pass this way again in some years – and I would ask you to remember to give these to him as an offering from the whole family."*

His family looked at the saddle-carpets in speechless admiration. They were finely woven to a point where not even young eyes could see how they were woven. They seemed to sparkle with light – whilst being superbly dense. They were wonderfully soft – yet remarkably robust. They were saddle-carpets which would last many lifetimes. His sons wondered at them and asked whether the secret could be taught.

"No..." he laughed *"but not because I will not tell you. This kind of weaving is only possible for a yogi. If one of you ever tires of mundane existence—and wishes to find me—I shall be happy to teach you to weave the fabric of existence and non-existence on the loom of nonduality. Then you will understand everything."*

Then, with his family assembled, Tantipa sang a song of realisation:

> *"The warp and weft of existence is strung of emptiness and form;*
> *When the warp is form, the weft is emptiness;*
> *When the weft is form, the warp is emptiness;*
> *With the empty thread of space, I weave the patterns of the five elements and the five displays of awareness;*
> *The shuttle is the transmission of Jalandhara;*
> *The loom is built of his teachings;*
> *And from this spacious loom of light I weave the seamless fabric of the three dimensions of being."*

Tantipa's family all understood his teaching according to their own capacities – and from that time their family, down through many generations, attended to their craft as a religious observance, giving generous alms to the poor and presenting carpets to those who deserved them by virtue of their kindness.

Tantipa wandered throughout India manifesting prodigies for the benefit of ordinary people. Through his powers of non-discrimination[11], he was able to eat as wolves and jackals eat. He accomplished much to rid the country of Tirthika animal sacrifice – on one occasion transforming a thousand goats into jackals so they would not be slaughtered for the sake of a Tirthika deity whose worship demanded blood.

The hagiography ended and I asked *"Why do some of the Mahasiddhas go off wandering in order to teach, like Tantipa does? Why couldn't he have just sat in his shed and had people come to him?"*

"I think that's largely cultural" Rinpoche replied. *"It's what one did as a yogi or yogini. One wandered. This, of course, provides the possibility of meeting unexpected people. In wandering, one encounters diverse situations – and observes whatever there is to be apprehended. Whereas getting known as a Mahasiddha in a particular place could attract certain inauspicious persons – such as those attracted by high renown. If you simply wander unrecognised however – then you see ordinary life. Then, in the case of Tantipa, he's emulating his teacher. Jalandhara wanders, so Tantipa wanders. That is quite natural."*

"Do you think that the ease of communication in terms of the online availability of teachings we have now is taking the place of the wandering yogi or yogini?" I asked.

Rinpoche grimaced *"I don't think I'm a skilled social commentator… but I'll attempt to venture* something. *I don't really know how 'online teaching' would function, realistically. There could be no transmission. For transmission to occur there have to be visceral teachers and visceral students. One has to be able to see the eyes of those hearing the oral transmission."*

[11] nampar mi-togpa *(rNam par mi rTog pa /* རྣམ་པར་མི་རྟོག་པ */ nirvikalpa)*

There was obviously still a question in mind, and Rinpoche continued *"If Ja'gyür was in Sweden and you were here at Drala Jong – how would you make love? You could be creative and have a video meeting. You could remove your clothing – and let the situation take its course. What would transpire however, could only be described as masturbation. For it to be anything else, you would both have to be in the same physical location."* PAUSE *"I am not saying that online transmission would not be possible for a Mahasiddha – but Khandro Déchen and I are not Mahasiddhas. I am not saying that those Lamas who give online transmissions are* **not** *Mahasiddhas – but if they are not, then there could be no transmission."*

"One could teach Sutrayana perhaps" Khandro Déchen offered through the window *"but it would not be possible to teach Vajrayana on the internet – because teaching is not merely informational."*

"So, back to the business of roaming through the Indian subcontinent…" PAUSE *"In terms of being a wandering yogi or yogini… I don't think one could realistically live that way now, in the West. Ancient India was a land where people had heard of Mahasiddhas. Maybe there weren't many of them – but, people* had *heard of them. Anyone could say therefore 'Oh, this is somebody interesting – maybe he or she is a Mahasiddha'. But almost nobody is going to come to that conclusion now – or at least not in the contemporary Western world."* Rinpoche chuckled. *"So there's no point in wandering off to Milton Keynes just in case. It wouldn't work. It wouldn't function. In Ancient India it was likely that you'd be useful to people if you wandered. That wouldn't be the case now. It wasn't the case in the Himalayan lands quite as much as it was in Ancient India."*

There was a moment of quiet as we watched Khandro Déchen pass by the window again, this time heading back to the vegetable garden with her empty wheelbarrow. I asked *"The neighbours… they see the light emanating from the shed when Tantipa achieves realisation. I'm wondering why that was visible? Was it simply that it was useful for them to see a sign?"*

"Well…" Rinpoche smiled *"the simple answer is that—that—is the hagiography."* PAUSE *"And again, in part, it's cultural.*

"*It's what would be expected. Culturally—in any country—what happens, happens according to what is expected. There was a time in the early 60s where you knew you were 'successful as a Rock musician' if the young women in the audience screamed from the beginning to the end – and had to be carried away by the St. John's Ambulance medics. That was how it was at that time. Now, people find it really hard to understand why they didn't want to listen to the music. Or who started it? Why did it catch on? No one knows. It just happened. So, with these stories, there are aspects which speak of the times in which they occurred.*"

"*There's actually more of that kind of thing in the other collections of Mahasiddha hagiographies*" I commented and Rinpoche agreed. "*So, emanating light, or something like that…*" I continued "*… that's the usual presentation in the hagiographies – or some kind of transcendent or beatific experience?*" Again, Rinpoche agreed and I continued "*But… that doesn't seem to be the way in these hagiographies so much. It's not often—in Jomo Pema 'ö-Zér's hagiographies— that there's any outward sign of realisation occurring. So maybe that's why it struck me – because it doesn't happen that often?*"

Rinpoche nodded again and said "*Light can manifest however. It's our nature – but the manifestation of light depends on contributary circumstances. With some people, in some places, light will manifest. With other people, in other places, it will not – and, that doesn't necessarily mean anything. Of course, if it can be of benefit to others. There's a reason for light to be manifested. That would be the case with this hagiography. I feel that is the rôle it plays here. There are the sons, who feel Tantipa to be an embarrassment. Then suddenly they 'see the light' – and suddenly he's the cause of endless pride! The situation switches completely.*" PAUSE "*I suppose it would be interesting to know what happened to the children – but that's not contained in the hagiography.*"

"*Yes, is there any particular reason why Jalandhara doesn't teach the whole family? Is it just because he only sees potential in Tantipa?*"

"*Yes. The family—although inspired by Tantipa—are still fundamentally 'lay people' who wish to continue as carpet-weavers in mainstream society.*

"And, of course, there's never enough time. Jalandhara has to spend his time where he can be of most benefit. He would have been of limited benefit to Tantipa's family." Rinpoche noticed Khandro Déchen passing the window yet again with her wheelbarrow. *"Mind you"* he smiled. *"I think it's now probably time for me to join Khandro Déchen – and be of limited benefit in the garden."*

Seventeen: Khadgapa – the lord of larceny

Khadgapa *(ka dGa pa* / ཀ་དགའ་པ་) / Ku-chèd Gyalpo *(rKu byed rGyal po* / རྐུ་བྱེད་རྒྱལ་པོ་)

Disciple of: Sarvaripa

Varna by birth: Harijan

On pilgrimage with Ngak'chang Rinpoche and Khandro Déchen in the far-east of Bhutan.

We were staying for a week at Chador Lhakhang near the village of Bartsham. The Lhakhang—which had been established in the 12th century—sits in a striking position on the crest of a prodigious incline. Surrounding it, there are open vistas of sky and mountains. The tiny villages of North Trashigang dot the sloping valleys below. The Lhakhang was formerly known as Gompa Ringbu. Now however, it is called Chador Lhakhang – after the gTérma statue of Chana Dorje which was retrieved from Yu-tso[1] by gTértön Pema Lingpa[2] in the 15th century. The gTérma is housed in the Lhakhang and many Bhutanese travel across the country to practise there and receive Chana Dorje's benefaction from the statue. Its reputation as a protective relic has extended omnidirectionally.

Although originally built in the 12th century, the present-day Lhakhang was founded in the 1970s by Lama Nagpo[3]. He was a close disciple of Kyabjé Düd'jom Rinpoche Jig'drèl Yeshé Dorje.

---

[1] *g.Yu mTsho* / གཡུ་མཚོ་ — Turquoise Lake.
[2] *pa dma gLing pa* / པདྨ་གླིང་པ་ / 1450–1521 – the great Bhutanese gTértön. The 4th of the five sovereign gTértöns and last of the five tulkus of Princess Pema Sal *(lha lCam padma gSal* / ལྷ་ལྕམ་ པདྨ་གསལ་ / 8th century)*, the daughter of Trisong Détsen and Dro gZa' Changchub, who died at the age of eight. Guru Rinpoche drew the syllable **Nri** on her heart, restored her to life, and gave her the Nyingthig transmissions. Yeshé Tsogyel concealed these as gTérma.
[3] Lama Pema Wangchen Rinpoche *(bLa ma padma dBang chen* / བླ་མ་པདྨ་དབང་ཆེན་)

Lama Nagpo established Chador as a Gomchen Dratsang[4] and after he passed away his work was continued by Lama Nyingkula Rinpoche[5] who took over the running of the Lhakhang adding an adjoining shèdra[6] to further support the training of Düd'jom gTérsar practitioners. The Lhakhang is on the second floor accessed up a rickety wooden ladder. It is also small, so a new, much larger, five-storied Lhakhang has recently been built across the courtyard from the old one. As the only guests staying at Chador Lhakhang, we were able to roam between the two Lhakhangs, practising in both.

The old gompa is my favourite of all those we visited in Bhutan. It has sculpted three-dimensional walls with little 'caves' set into them containing figures of practising yogis. It also houses a slightly over-life-sized statue of Kyabjé Düd'jom Rinpoche Jig'drèl Yeshé Dorje. The statue is both mesmerising and extremely moving. Ngak'chang Rinpoche —on seeing it—set in motion the project of building a matching statue for Drala Jong[7]. The whole site at Chador Lhakhang is imbued with the presence of Kyabjé Düd'jom Rinpoche, with the top floor of the new Lhakhang being illustrated with scenes from his life which are marvellous to behold. One scene struck Rinpoche in particular. It was one in which Düd'jom Rinpoche is shown being interrogated in an Indian prison. Rinpoche has explained the story behind this picture in *Goodbye Forever*. It is the shocking account of how Kyabjé Düd'jom Rinpoche was accused of being a spy in the pay of the Chinese.

---

[4] *sGom chen grwa tshang* / སྒོམ་ཆེན་གྲྭ་ཚང་ – a practice-residence for ngakpas.
[5] Lopön Nyingkula Lama Künzang Wangdü *(sLob dPon sNying ku la bLa ma kun bZang dBang 'dus* / སློབ་དཔོན་སྙིང་ཀུ་ལ་བླ་མ་ཀུན་བཟང་དབང་འདུས་ / d. 2018) – was a disciple of Kyabjé Düd'jom Rinpoche Jig'drèl Yeshé Dorje and re-established Bartsham Chador Lhakhang for the Düd'jom gTérsar. Ngak'chang Rinpoche met him with Düd'jom Rinpoche in 1975 in Bodhanath, Nepal.
[6] *bShad grwa* / བཤད་གྲྭ་ – ngakpa college.
[7] The statue was designed by Dung-sré Thrin-lé Norbu Rinpoche. The body was made in Bhutan, but the entirely lifelike head was made in the USA by two of his students. They have made another head sculpture for Drala Jong.

The accusation was apparently made by persons in the Tibetan Government in Exile who were antagonistic to Düd'jom Rinpoche's rising popularity amongst the Tibetan people[8].

Rinpoche gazed at the depiction for some time – shaking his head wearily in perplexity at the nature of human folly. *"Mark Twain said 'When we remember we are all mad, the mysteries disappear and life stands explained…'*[9]*"*

I then showed Rinpoche a scene in which Düd'jom Rinpoche is giving an empowerment to an evidently Western young man – and exclaimed *"Look! This might be you!"*

Rinpoche smiled *"Maybe. Maybe not. Kyabjé Düd'jom Rinpoche had other Western students who were—and are still—far better known than Ngakpa Chögyam'. In any case, this young man is wearing a chuba. I always wore the gö kar chang lo costume which Düd'jom Rinpoche designated."* PAUSE *"You know, some people used to ask me 'Why do you* have *to wear those robes?' It was a question with a built-in statement. I always replied 'Because Kyabjé Düd'jom Rinpoche told me to. He told me always to wear them whenever I was in a Buddhist context.' A few would then ask 'And you always do as you're told?' to which I'd answer 'When Kyabjé Düd'jom Rinpoche gave the instruction – yes. Why would I do otherwise?' They'd then look confused, confounded, or confusticated – and I'd tell them that I felt highly fortunate that Kyabjé Düd'jom Rinpoche had made my life so simple. These were people, of course, who had never met Düd'jom Rinpoche and so they had no idea why I found him so easy to obey. Although 'obey' sounds peculiar—awkward—as a word. Düd'jom Rinpoche simply explained and I implemented what he explained. I never thought about it in terms of obedience, submission, or compliance."* PAUSE *"I sometimes continued by saying that I was not naturally obedient. If anything I had tended to be insubordinate at school and rebellious to a certain degree."*

---

[8] Ngakpa Chögyam—*Goodbye Forever – the Miscellaneous Memoirs of an English Lama*—volume I—*born in a dragon year*—Aro Books WORLDWIDE—2020
[9] Mark Twain's Notebook, 1898.

It had been an utterly remarkable day. Rinpoche, Khandro Déchen and their students had spent the morning practising kora[10] around the old gompa wearing the iron chain-link shawl. This is left hanging over the rails for any passing pilgrims to put on and practise kora. The weighty shawl was made in Pemaköd[11] on the instruction of Kyabjé Düd'jom Rinpoche. It contains links of iron made by both Thangtong Gyalpo and Pema Lingpa. Ngak'chang Rinpoche—having seen the shawl and performed kora wearing it—had a dream of clarity in which Kyabjé Düd'jom Rinpoche instructed him to make such a shawl for Drala Jong. It was to contain a link from Pema Lingpa and one from Thangtong Gyalpo – just as the original did[12]. This dream inaugurated the project of creating a matching shawl for Drala Jong. This has now been forged by Naljorma Charog – and assembled and burnished by students in Finland.

The remarkableness of the morning had continued into the afternoon when we were honoured by an extraordinary three-hour performance of Dramé-tsé Nga-cham[13] – a particular sacred, masked dance. The cham was an astonishing spectacle for all the sense fields with vivid panchromatic brocade costumes, full tantric orchestra, and breathtakingly proficient choreography. The dancers wore animal-head masks and seemed to become the animals themselves as they whirled and swirled before us. There were the four protector animals of Bhutan—the snow lion[14], khyung[15], dragon[16] and tiger[17].

---

[10] *sKor ba* / སྐོར་བ / *vivartana*) – circumambulation.
[11] *padma bKod* / པདྨ་བཀོད – the most famous of the hidden lands, is located in south-eastern Tibet.
[12] Ngak'chang Rinpoche was able to obtain iron chain links made by Pema Lingpa and Thangtong Gyalpo in Nepal in 2022.
[13] *dGra med tse rNga 'cham* / དགྲ་མེད་རྩེ་རྔ་འཆམ
[14] *seng ge* / སེང་གེ
[15] *khyung* / ཁྱུང – garuda
[16] *'brug* / འབྲུག
[17] *sTag* / སྟག

There were also yak[18], leopard[19], goat[20], snake[21], raven[22], horse[23], owl[24], stag[25], boar[26], dog[27], bear[28] and ox[29]. The surround-sound orchestra merged with the thuds of the dancers—barefoot on the wooden floor—and the complex rhythm of the stick drums.

Chöten Zangmo[30] was the daughter of Pema Lingpa. She had been pursued as a potential bride by the ruler of Chö'khor valley — and made her journey to Dramé-tsé, in eastern Bhutan, to escape him. Dramé-tsé means 'Peak without Enemy', because she settled there to continue her practice without enemies. The Dramé-tsé Nga-cham originated in Dramé-tsé. Chöten Zangmo's brother, Künga Gyaltsen[31], had many visions and during a dream of clarity, he visited the copper-coloured mountain of Guru Rinpoche, where he witnessed a dance performed by animal-headed dPa'wos. When he awoke, he remembered the costumes, choreography, and visualisations of the dance. Aware of the liberative power of the dance, he wrote down the details of the performance and enacted the dance in Dramé-tsé – and thus it gained its name. In the 19th century, two consecutive tulkus of Zhabdrung Ngawang Namgyal[32]—the founder of Bhutan—took incarnation in Dramé-tsé. Zhabdrung Jigmé Chögyal from Dramé-tsé, introduced the dance at Ta-lö Sang-ngak Chöling.

---

[18] *g.Yag* / གཡག
[19] *gZig* / གཟིག
[20] *ra* / ར
[21] *sBrul* / སྦྲུལ
[22] *bya rog* / བྱ་རོག
[23] *rTa* / རྟ
[24] *'ug pa* / འུག་པ
[25] *sha wa* / ཤ་བ
[26] *phag pa* / ཕག་པ
[27] *khyi* / ཁྱི
[28] *dom* / དོམ
[29] *gLang* / གླང
[30] *mChod rTen bZang mo* / མཆོད་རྟེན་བཟང་མོ
[31] *kun dGa' rGyal mTshan* / ཀུན་དགའ་རྒྱལ་མཚན
[32] *zhabs drung ngag dBang rNam rGyal* / ཞབས་དྲུང་ངག་དབང་རྣམ་རྒྱལ /1594–1651) – an immediate incarnation of Pema Karpo.

In the middle of the 20th century, the dance was further introduced at the Paro and Trongsa Dzongs, and Gangten and Ura. By the end of the 20th century, the Dramé-tsé Nga-cham was performed in many state festivals and gompas.

The cham was followed by dinner with many of the locals who had come to receive blessings from Rinpoche and Khandro Déchen. Consequent to the festive dinner, they proceeded to entertain us with the joyful, exuberant singing of local folk songs. As this remarkable day drew to a close, we stood on the wooden walkway outside the dining room and gazed into the evening sky. The last of the day's sunlight caught the golden top of the Lhakhang below us. *"These golden gyaltsens[33] on the gompa roofs"* I said *"always make me think of that Dza Paltrül story about the thief which Kyabjé Künzang Dorje Rinpoche told you. Can you remind me of the details, Rinpoche?"*

"Certainly" Rinpoche smiled *"It's a favourite."* PAUSE *"So… Paltrül was staying as a guest at a small gompa – as we are here. I don't know the name of the gompa, but Paltrül was staying in the labrang[34] – the visiting Lama's apartments on the top floor. One night, strange noises were heard issuing from his room. An attendant monk became aware that Paltrül was talking either to himself or someone else. The attendant's curiosity overcame him and he crept closer to make out what was being said. When he was close enough, he heard the most extraordinary speech: 'Yes—yes—yes!'* PAUSE *'Go on – you can make it!'* PAUSE *'Just a bit further now and you will be there!'* PAUSE *'Yes! Now you are there and it's within your reach!'* PAUSE *'Grab it quickly!'* PAUSE *'Be swift now!'* PAUSE *'Yes! Now you have it—now you have it!'* PAUSE *'Quickly now! Make your escape!'* PAUSE *'Good—good—good! Run away—run away—run away!' The attendant was perplexed because there was no sense in the words. The next morning a theft was discovered. The golden gyaltsen had been stolen from the roof of the gompa.*

---

[33] *rGyal mTshan* / རྒྱལ་མཚན་ — victory banner.
[34] *bLa brang* / བླ་བྲང་ — Lama house.

Seventeen: Khadgapa – the lord of larceny

"The abbot decided that it would be best to inform Paltrül as soon as possible in case Paltrül could give some indication as to the identity of the thief and what direction he had taken. When asked, Paltrül replied with great delight 'Yes! He wanted it—so—much!'"

We all burst out laughing as Rinpoche finished the story and Khandro Déchen commented *"Such a fabulous teaching on happiness arising from appreciation rather than possession. Paltrül appreciates the thief's appreciation and even enjoys the thief's possession."* We all laughed again. *"If you enjoyed that story, you would probably also enjoy hearing about Mahasiddha Khadgapa. He was a thief too"* Rinpoche grinned. *"He was—in fact—the lord of larceny."* As we were all keen to hear the hagiography, we arranged ourselves on chairs along the walkway, gazing into the gathering dusk.

"Well, Khadgapa was the son of a prostitute" Rinpoche began *"who had died when he was barely old enough to look after himself. And so being an orphan, he became a thief as a matter of course…"*

The city in which he lived had other orphans like himself who survived through stealing – and so the morality of his means of livelihood never came under question. He had no choice – and, what was more, there were enough other children who kept themselves fed and clothed by the same means, and so his occupation was merely a fact of life. He had no sense of morality or immorality – it was simply a fact of life, that the deprived, dispossessed, and homeless had to steal.

Khadgapa began by roaming the streets in search of food and clothing. He also had to find relatively safe places to sleep and seek shelter in inclement weather. He began by sharing quarters with other young thieves – but by the time he reached the age of thirteen, he had established his own apartment in a ruined house which still had several habitable rooms.

He had begun as a scavenger of items which had not-quite-been-thrown-away – and gradually advanced to proficient pick-pocketry.

He was thin, agile, nimble, dexterous, and ultra light-fingered, and—aware of his talent—developed it to an extraordinary degree. He found that if he were able to relax—and proceed in an unhurried manner—he could avoid the anxious clumsiness which proved the undoing of other less confident pick-pockets. His sense of calm evolved, along with his presence of mind and circumspect awareness. He gained a sense of his environment and those who occupied it – always knowing the right moment and the right person's pocket to pick.

Being a brave and resourceful young lad, Khadgapa worked assiduously at his methods of criminal appropriation – and when pick-pocketry began to prove limiting, his next step was to investigate the realm of burglary. Burglary was more dangerous by far than picking pockets – but his mind was finely attuned to the surveillance of prospective houses. He took note of the comings and goings and of the times at which lights appeared and disappeared in rooms. He took his time – because there was no need for hurry. He developed mental plans of each house he burgled – and as time went on, he became increasingly professional in his approach.

Khadgapa lived a marginal existence – becoming skilled in negotiating those margins: the twilight zones of existence. He hid his growing wealth – becoming highly adept at camouflaging his various hoards, in order that no one would suspect the wealth he had hidden. He had plans to gather greater wealth – wealth which would enable him to retire from his life of crime and live as others lived. He decided that once he had sufficient wealth he would escape to some distant land where he could establish himself as a wealthy man, not of the highest varna – but maybe as a member of the merchant varna.

The problem with Khadgapa's plan was that his interest in settling down to a life of ease in a distant land became less attractive to him as the thrill of burglary increased. He began to glory in his expertise – and, as he developed his skills, he became increasingly adventurous.

He revelled in the pleasure afforded by the sheer danger of his pursuit. The greater the risk, the more delighted he was.

Rinpoche paused momentarily – and so I took the chance to ask *"That makes me think about risk-taking generally. Why do some people find it exciting – and some find it horrifying? Why do some people want to jump off bridges attached to bungee ropes and others would never dream of it?"*

"Well, there's nothing right or wrong with risk taking, in particular" Rinpoche stated. *"It only becomes problematic when you want to keep doing it in order to provide major reference points. It's useful for a practitioner to experience as much of life as possible – in terms of acquiring familiarity with 'the edge'. It's not useful to be afraid of life. The other side to 'throwing yourself off bridges', is fear of taking any sort of risk. Never taking risks... never trying anything new, not even food. That is not viable for a practitioner. With risk-taking – there are two ends of the spectrum. Buddhism, as always, is the Middle Way. It's important that 'what you do' involves authentic enjoyment of the sense fields – rather than trying to prove that you're solid, separate, permanent, continuous, and defined."*

"And that's interesting too, that some people seem to be fearful and some seem to be fearless. But you can be brave and still fearful?" I queried.

"Fearlessness can be simply foolhardiness or banal bravado" Khandro Déchen nodded. *"Bravery is knowing what your limits are – and being willing to push them. Pushing your limits too far however, is foolhardy – so having some sense of fear is useful."*

"You know" Rinpoche added *"it's similar to bodily strength. You need to know where your limits are so you can say 'No, I can't do that. I can't hang off that bar over a thousand-foot chasm for half an hour – my arms would give out.' That would not be anxiety or trepidation. That would not be fearfulness or dread. That would be common sense. If you know the limits of your body – you can push yourself reasonably. You shouldn't push yourself unreasonably – because you have a body which has limitations. You have to know the limitations of any tool you choose to use.*

"You can only push an electric drill so far before it burns out. So, you let it cool down every once in a while. You work within the known limits."

"Of course" Khandro Déchen smiled *"there's also the problem of inventing artificial limits, and cramping your life with anxiety. But that wasn't Khadgapa's problem. He was just enjoying the risk too much…"*

Khadgapa was never aware of the exact point when his former retirement plan changed – and when he began to live solely for the joy of stealing from increasingly wealthy people. For a time, he pretended to himself that he simply needed more wealth than he'd previously imagined in order to retire – but as time went on his former plan seemed lacklustre in comparison with the life of abundantly ambitious arrogation. Where would be the excitement in retirement? Where would be the thrill of merely being wealthy?

It was not long after he gave up the idea of retirement, that he came to hear that the wealthiest man in the city owned a prized ruby of immense size and astronomical worth. The ruby was well guarded and the idea of stealing it caught Khadgapa's imagination. It would be his most dangerous exploit – and one which had so many chances of failure that it besotted him. It was a burglary to outstrip all other burglaries and no matter how perilous it seemed, Khadgapa felt unable to resist the temptation. Of course, this burglary proved to be one step too far. Khadgapa was caught off guard whilst escaping down the back stairs. He had failed in his caution – and, smiling to himself about his success, he slipped and fell on a pool of oil that had been spilled from a lamp by one of the household servants.

"Was it his self-satisfaction…" I asked *"his smugness about his success, which caused the accident?"*

"That would make a good 'moral tale' perhaps" Rinpoche grinned *"but no, it was the oil on the stairs which caught him out."*

"Of course" Khandro Déchen laughed *"there's—always—going to be oil on the stairs in accounts such as these."* I looked quizzical so Khandro Déchen continued *"If there wasn't oil on the stairs – there's got to be something else. He'd have to trip, bang his head on a suspended plant, be alarmed by a pipistrelle – or, as he got older, his knee might give way."*

"So, why is there always going to—be—something?" I queried *"Why is there—always—oil on the stairs?"*

"Emptiness?" asked Rinpoche rhetorically. *"At some point in any sequence of 'forms' – 'emptiness' will happen. If this was not the case, everything would be predictable – everything would be 'form'. There's going to be some point in any evolving scenario, where the pattern breaks down."*

"When I said there's always going to be oil on the stairs" added Khandro Déchen *"there's always going to be the* possibility *of oil on the stairs – or the possibility of something or other."*

"A burglar" Rinpoche continued *"relies on routines being followed – but people don't always follow their own set routines. A housemaid sneezes and spills oil without noticing it. Emptiness happens."*

"The 'emptiness of oil happened' for Khadgapa" Khandro Déchen continued. *"He then had to flee with the ruby in his pocket – chased by household servants…"*

"…armed with all manner of interesting 'forms' in the shape of batons, cudgels, bludgeons, truncheons – and shillelaghs… although…" Rinpoche concluded *"Irish immigrants were not thick on the ground in India at that time…"*

Fortunately, a funeral procession was passing just before dawn – and Khadgapa slipped into the ranks of the mourners. Being a cunning fellow Khadgapa emulated those around him in their grief and by that means escaped. Several of the household servants had seen his face however, so Khadgapa decided to remain in the charnel ground where the body from the funeral had been cremated.

This was not unusual—being taken as a sign of piety to remain after all others had left—so no one questioned him and no one mentioned that they did not know him as a relative of the deceased.

Khadgapa sat by what remained of the funeral pyre for an hour or so before he decided he had better go in search of food. As he was walking, he came across the Mahasiddha Sarvaripa—the deer hunter—and was startled by his sudden appearance. Taken aback and not knowing what to say, he asked *"What is your purpose in being here?"*

"Me?" Sarvaripa laughed. *"I'm here to fulfil my potential – by stealing as much as I can."*

This was a strange answer. It bewildered Khadgapa. *"What is there to steal here?"* he asked, just to display some sort of nonchalance. *"This is a charnel ground. There's nothing of value here."*

"You say that…" Sarvaripa laughed again *"because you do not understand what is of value and what is not of value."*

"What is of value in a charnel ground?"

"What is—not—of value in a charnel ground?"

"What sort of question is that?" asked Khadgapa, now a little annoyed with the stranger and his apparent non-sequiturs.

"That—my friend—is the sort of question which can be expected from me" he laughed. *"Anyway, enough of this polite polished parlour conversation. It's all very well in divans, drawing rooms, lounges, salons, soirées and the like – but it's not suitable for a charnel ground. Let me tell you something. You are here because you failed at your last burglary – but I am here because I never fail in what I set out to steal."*

"*Ha!*" exclaimed Khadgapa. "*I used to think that. That was before I foolishly became so sure of myself that I walked carelessly down some marble stairs and slipped in a pool of oil. We all think we're invincible until we make a mistake. Now I'm a hunted man.*"

"*That is as it should be!*" laughed Sarvaripa "*because I was once a great hunter.*" PAUSE "*Now, however, I prefer to be a thief – and I can assure you that I can— never—make a mistake.*"

"*Yes—yes—yes*" retorted Khadgapa with a shrug. "*And I would have said the same yesterday.*"

"*That is true*" laughed Sarvaripa "*but I will say the same both today and tomorrow.*"

"*You boast rather well—I must say—but what makes you so different?*" jibed Khadgapa with an insolent sneer. "*Please tell me, I'm—**all**—ears.*"

"*I am different because my theft is without limits. I give away everything I steal, immediately it is stolen. I steal whatever arises in mind – and bank it in the dimension of space. Likewise, with everything I perceive in the phenomenal world. Everything that enters my sense fields is my possession – and therefore I am free to give it away to everyone else without impoverishing myself to the slightest degree.*"

Khadgapa had not heard this kind of speech before. He was therefore both intrigued and somewhat pacified. "*Well… I too, would give much away if I could steal everything that came into my sense fields. I may be a thief – but I am not avaricious or ungenerous.*"

That much was true – because Khadgapa had always looked after younger thieves and allowed them to share his food and ambiguous accommodation.

"*Tell me more, young man*" Sarvaripa asked in a far kindlier tone than he had adopted before. "*I would enjoy hearing of this side of your character.*"

"*For me…*" Khadgapa began, somewhat more at ease "*it's the risk and danger of stealing that I love, rather than hoarding wealth. I already have many caches of wealth in different places – and to be frank, it means very little to me.*"

"*This is a far better account. Is there more to tell?*"

"*Yes… there is… if you would like to hear it.*"

"*I consider it well worth the hearing*" smiled Sarvaripa – now seemingly unusually benevolent.

"*Well… having lived on the streets as an orphan my needs are actually few – and… I do not desire luxury in particular.*" Then Khadgapa remembered what Sarvaripa had said about his once having been a hunter "*… but… before I say much more about my past… can I ask you… why did you say 'That is as it should be' when I told you I was a hunted man? What does a hunter want with a hunted man – presumably you hunted for food and skins, or…*" added Khadgapa feeling for his knife and backing off "*… were you a bounty hunter?*"

"*No—no—no, my friend – I was never a bounty hunter. I was a deer hunter – but a dangerous man, nonetheless.*"

At that Khadgapa drew his knife and took a defensive posture. "*Keep your distance – if you know what's good for you. I have a knife!*"

"*Call—that—a knife?*" laughed Sarvaripa. "**This** *– is a knife!*" And he pulled out his long hunting knife, threw it into the air, and caught it with his other hand without even looking to check whether he would catch it by the haft or by the blade.

I burst out laughing at this point and asked "*Isn't that from the film… Crocodile Dundee*[35]*?*"

"*Yes*" grinned Ngak'chang Rinpoche. "*Bob Dylan is not my sole source of quotations.*

---

[35] *Crocodile Dundee*—Paramount Pictures—1986 – an action-comedy film set in Australia and New York; starring Paul Hogan and Linda Kozlowski; inspired by the exploits of Rod Ansell.

"I like to quote from anything in the popular media or literature, because these hagiographies concern everyday life – albeit a millennium distant. It could destroy the magic of these hagiographies for some people – but these accounts are colourful antiquarian legends." Then Rinpoche continued.

Sarvaripa, with a kindly smile suggested *"Be a good fellow and put that little cooking knife away – it will not avail you, as you see."* He then replaced his immense blade in its scabbard and said *"I now hunt for those who could practise the kind of Dharma I am best at teaching. And I can see that—you—are definitely such a man."*

"Am I?" asked Khadgapa, now feeling entirely bemused *"Why…?"*

"Because you are fearless. I am larger, stronger, and older than you. I also have great experience in weaponry—as I am sure you must know by now—and yet you are valiant enough to try to hold your own against me. One needs to be fearless to practise Vajrayana – and I take you to be fearless. Is this not the case?"

"Yes… I have no anxiety, it's true – and, I could be said to be fearless. However, I have no interest in Dharma."

"No one does – until they do" laughed Sarvaripa. *"I had no interest in Dharma until Mahasiddha Saraha showed me the error of my ways."*

"And how, may I ask, did he do that?"

"He began by shooting one hundred and eight deer with a single arrow."

"That's a ripping yarn…" scoffed Khadgapa. *"Can you do that too?"*

"No. Not every Buddhist yogi can do what a Mahasiddha can do."

"So why should I be interested in Dharma? I see no advantage in living as you do. Where's the pay-off?"

"Would you see an advantage in being invincible?" asked Sarvaripa.

"Yes. If Dharma can make me invincible—then I will practise Dharma—but how do I know you are not stringing me a line?"

"That is simple to answer..." laughed Sarvaripa. *"I am a better thief than you are – and I am not addicted to theft. To prove this to you, I shall return the ruby I stole from your pocket."*

Khadgapa reached into his pocket but the ruby was gone. Just as he realised it was gone, Sarvaripa held out the great jewel and returned it to him, saying *"I do not want this ruby. I would have no use for it – and in any case, I am not here to take advantage of you or deceive you. I would not waste my time in such a way."*

"How is it that you were able to steal this ruby..." gasped Khadgapa in sheer amazement *"... when I have never come near enough for you to reach it?!"*

"Because I can steal the whole phenomenal world in my mind. My ability to steal is beyond limits. Whatever I steal, I bank in the dimension of space – from whence it is immediately credited to the accounts of everyone who needs it. Everything I perceive in the phenomenal world belongs to me – and therefore, simultaneously to everyone else."

At this point Khadgapa started to understand something of what Sarvaripa was teaching and realised that Sarvaripa was evidently a siddha, even though he claimed not to be able to shoot one hundred and eight deer with a single arrow. Khadgapa had only ever heard of siddhas – he had never yet met with one, or even seen one. He had not even met a yogi. Siddhas were said to be capable of supernormal feats – and this was certainly true of the person who had just removed and returned the ruby he had stolen. *"Tell me, reverend sir, how I should practise to become invincible – and I shall carry out your instructions, whatever they may be."*

"First you must learn to steal as I steal. You must sit silently, as calmly, and with the same stillness of mind you had when you were engaged in pick-pocketry and burglary.

"You must have the same non-conceptual awareness of space—and immediacy of presence—which previously assured you of the exact time to make your felonious move."

Khadgapa nodded his agreement. He could do that.

"Then—piece by piece—you must try to steal the phenomenal universe – placing each piece in the vault of space. You must continue until you have emptied the phenomenal universe and completely filled space."

Khadgapa agreed to try as best he could to accomplish that end.

"You have a month to do this. I shall make sure you are provided with food – as Mahasiddha Saraha provided me with food when he sent my wife Saradha and I into retreat. Then, when your task is accomplished, return to me and I shall give you the teaching on invincibility."

Khadgapa nodded his agreement. He needed to stay in the charnel ground in any case – because there would be people searching for him in order to recover the ruby. The charnel ground was the only place he would be safe from capture. After the month, Sarvaripa returned and with him was Saradha.

"Greetings, Lord of Larceny!" laughed Saradha. "Tell me how you proceeded with the practice my husband gave you."

Saradha looked quite like Sarvaripa in the manner of her dress – as she had almost the same Sabara costume, threaded with peacock feathers. Apart from being evidently facially and vocally female, it was not easy to tell them apart.

"I failed... no matter how hard I tried... I failed" replied Khadgapa shamefacedly.

"Tell me how you failed" asked Sarvaripa.

"I failed to steal the entire phenomenal universe – because, no matter how much I stole, there was always just as much as there was before. And no matter how much I placed in the vault of space – it remained as empty as when I began to make deposits of my spoils there."

"This is a great success!" laughed Saradha.

"How can this possibly be a success?" asked Khadgapa in bemused incomprehension.

"Because there's no success like failure – and failure's no success at all [36]."

"I am sorry, venerable sir – but I do not understand your words."

"The meaning is clear. You have learned that form and emptiness are the same. You cannot take from one and give to the other. That is why success is failure and failure is success. They are both the same. You cannot steal from phenomenal reality because you are part of phenomenal reality and whatever you steal simply remains where it is – as part of phenomenal reality. It is like stealing from one part of a river and placing it in another part of the same river. Nothing will have changed."

Khadgapa was stunned by this realisation – and Sarvaripa continued "Now you will experientially understand what I said of myself, when we first met. My theft is without limits. Everything I steal is immediately given away by virtue of its own nature. I steal whatever arises in mind – and bank it in the dimension of space. And likewise, the phenomenal world. Everything that enters your sense fields is your possession – but only insofar as you are free to give it away.' Now you understand."

Khadgapa bowed before both vajra masters and said "I now have no need of invincibility – and more than that, I have no desire for it."

"But nonetheless, others will have need of it—in you—so you must proceed to gain this siddhi" replied Saradha.

---

[36] Bob Dylan—*Love Minus Zero/No Limit*—*Bringing it All back Home*—1965.

"It will not be difficult for you – for one who has no desire for that which he pursues, will not be distracted by compulsion, or by hope of success and fear of failure."

Khadgapa agreed.

"There is a chörten in the middle of the charnel ground" explained Sarvaripa. *"You must circumambulate this chörten one hundred and eleven thousand, one hundred and eleven times with perfect concentration reciting the mantra of Chenrézigs*[37] *one hundred and eleven times with each kora – without faltering. If you accomplish this, a black snake will spring at you from the sphere of the chörten and you must grab it fearlessly just behind the head. If you accomplish this – you will become invincible. If you fail – that snake will bite you and you will die in agony."*

Khadgapa agreed and went in search of the chörten. He accomplished the practice just as Sarvaripa had instructed – and the great black snake leapt out of the chörten. Khadgapa seized the snake immediately just behind its head – and as soon as he did so, the snake became a sword. As soon as the sword appeared in Khadgapa's hand, he realised the nature of emptiness – and, although he had become invincible, any idea of making use of that siddhi left his mind. He returned to Sarvaripa and Saradha and requested teaching and transmission on how to return everything he had ever stolen in this life and all previous lives. As soon as he made this aspiration, he gained nondual awareness and spent the rest of his life assuaging the lives of the poor – saying *"Whatever I give to help others has been stolen from space – where it resides, secure from being stolen, because it can only be given away by the one who steals it."*

"One of the most interesting things I find about this hagiography" Khandro Déchen commented at its conclusion *"is the discussion they have in the charnel ground. Khadgapa meets a greater thief than himself. He's confronted with somebody whose mastery of everything is greater than his. He knows that he's out of his depth – so he's got two possibilities. He can either run away – or he can conclude that he could learn something."*

---

[37] sPyan ras gZigs / སྤྱན་རས་གཟིགས་ / *Avalokiteshvara*

"Sarvaripa has trounced Khadgapa in every possible direction" added Rinpoche. "This interested Khadgapa – and Khadgapa is brave enough to recognise that there is an opportunity in this. It's because he is no ordinary thief. So, when someone appears who is superior to him – he's able to see it as an opportunity rather than a threat."

"Sarvaripa had to challenge him on his own terms at first" continued Khandro Déchen. "He had to impress Khadgapa in the context of his own game. Then—Khadgapa being thoroughly impressed—has nowhere to go. He is then naturally open to transmission."

"Which is almost exactly what happened to Sarvaripa with Saraha!" Ja'gyür laughed. "So is he passing on the transmission in the same kind of way, where you have to challenge the disciple first?"

"Exactly" replied Rinpoche. "Not that 'challenge' would necessarily be the method required with every student – but it was with Khadgapa."

"And if you know the story of Sarvaripa with Saraha" added Khandro Déchen "you can see how he knows how to do that with Khadgapa – at just the right time."

"Sarvaripa also talks about hunting out prospective students" I commented. "I've not heard it talked of in that way with any other of the Mahasiddhas. They usually come across their prospective students, or come upon them, or hear about them…"

"Well, Sarvaripa and Saradha are hunters" Rinpoche replied "so that's what they do. They hunt students."

We all laughed at how obvious that was. Once the laughter had subsided, I asked about the practice Sarvaripa and Saradha had given Khadgapa: to attempt to steal the phenomenal universe and bank it in the vault of space. "The way he finds it impossible because there's no end to the form" I began "and then there's no limit to the space… this reminded me of the two practices you've talked about – where an instruction is being given by a master to an aspiring disciple. It's the one where the yogi tells the student first to go and sit for a day and have no thoughts – and then, to go and sit and think continuously."

"It made me wonder if the teaching is always going to be some version of that, some emptiness and form experience?"

"Yes, in that situation you find having 'no thought' impossible" Khandro Déchen replied. "And then you're told to 'have thoughts' – and you think 'Oh, this is good, I'm good at this', but then realise you're not good at that either. What you're good at is sitting there daydreaming and having occasional thoughts – but as soon as thought has to be continuous, you find it difficult. Then the thoughts become somehow uninteresting – whereas before they were fascinating."

"You know" Rinpoche added "it's like my early experiences at Art School—in the first term at Bristol—when I was told I could do whatever I wanted. Suddenly I had no creative ideas." PAUSE "But when I was given a set project that I didn't like – creativity welled up in terms of how I could twist the project in order to make it personally interesting. And then it became fascinating – because I would be turning the project into something it wasn't intended to be. I'd found a loophole. Then it became interesting. Suddenly I was doing what I wanted – which I could have done when I was told I could do whatever I liked. But before there was nothing I wanted to do. As soon as I found something with which I could tussle, wrangle, juggle, or manœuvre in some way, it became fascinating."

"That kind of logic could make you suspicious, as a practitioner" Khandro Déchen grinned.

"Fortunately for me, my previous Buddhist studies—primitive though they were—had made it possible for me to see that" Rinpoche laughed. "But that didn't take the fun out of manipulating the assignment." Then, looking out at the sky which was now an inky darkness—salted and peppered with piquant stars—Rinpoche said "Time for bed – and we'll see if that golden gyaltsen is still there in the morning."

Eighteen: Shyama – the cloud-weaver

Shyama *(shya' ma /* ཤྱ་མ *)* / Kha'du Tha-gama *(mKha' du tha ga ma /* མཁའ་དུ་ཐ་ག་མ *)*

Disciple of: Ishani
Teacher of: Sarvagjna
Varna by birth: Vaishya

A clear August morning in Cadgwith.

After breakfast we decided to walk the South West Coast Path to the hamlet and cove of Poltesco[1], on the Lizard Peninsula. The Lizard Peninsula was formed some 375 million years ago when enormous pressures within the Earth forced molten rock some seven miles through the Earth's crust. In its passage to the surface, the magma brought with it the full range of the rocks it passed along the way. This included the beautiful red and green serpentines for which the area is famous. Serpentine is fairly soft, making it easy to work, and after Queen Victoria visited Penzance in 1846 and ordered several serpentine ornaments for her house on the Isle of Wight, the local serpentine business became a boom industry. The rock was quarried in several locations around the Lizard including the site at Poltesco.

Prior to the serpentine factory, the cove had been an important pilchard fishery since way back in the 14th century. Now the only visible evidence of the fishing industry is the round, roofless building in the cove, housing the capstan which was used to haul boats out of the water. The fishery buildings were repurposed by the serpentine manufacturers but those buildings were also abandoned with the demise of the stone industry.

---

[1] The Poltesco stream drains from the Goonhilly Downs and reaches the sea at Carleon Cove on the eastern Lizard coast. The walls of three or four large buildings, including an engine house, can still be seen. The lower part of the valley is owned by the National Trust and was once the site of a serpentine industry.

Today there is just the wheel pit of the twenty-five-foot water wheel which once provided the power, and the stone ruins of the warehouse and machine shops.

Toads hop around the fringes of the old millpond and gulls and cormorants gather on the stone remains. The stream that fed the mill leat[2] still empties onto the beach of the tiny cove and seeps into the colourful shingle. There's pink granite, banded gneiss, and red and green serpentines here, and sitting by the sea in Poltesco picking over the pebbles was a favourite part of each holiday. So too was the walk there from Cadgwith. As well as following the coastal path, the track crosses a wonderful open area of clifftop heathland which brilliantly displays the abundant varieties of wildflowers for which the Lizard has been designated a Special Area of Conservation. There are cliff flowers such as sea campion, thrift, and spring squill here and Ræchel talked about maybe drawing some of the flowers we'd see as she packed her leather drawing bag. We knew we would be stopping for practice along the way, so gomthags were packed too, and as Khandro Déchen was keen to watch the birds, she added her binoculars to the backpack.

We set off down the steep lane from Pink Cottage, through Cadgwith village, past the *Cadgwith Cove Inn* and up the other side of the cove. Then we turned right onto the coastal path which took us up past Sharkey's Cottage[3] and out onto the headland. The narrow stone path climbs up and down through gorse bushes—and scrubby low sloe-bearing blackthorn—with the sea glittering to the right, below. There was the vivid turquoise of the sea, the deep greens of the bushes with bright splashes of yellow from the flowers of gorse and fragrant Lady's bedstraw.

---

[2] A leat is an artificial watercourse supplying water to a watermill. *Leat* is the name commonly used in south-west England and Wales. Other names include *fleam* in northern England, and *goit* in Sheffield.
[3] *Sharkey's Cottage*—owned by Sheila Stevens, a friend of Ngak'chang Rinpoche and Khandro Déchen—can be found on the coastal footpath above Cadgwith heading east. It was the home of one of the most characterful fishermen in Cadgwith.

Eighteen: Shyama – the cloud-weaver

There was St John's Wort too – about which Rinpoche commented *"That's called John the Conqueror Root in the southern States of the USA. It is mentioned in various Blues numbers – but pronounced Johnny Conqueroo."* Then Rinpoche sang *"Gotta black-cat bone and a mojo too, Got the Johnny Conqueroo – Gonna mess with you. An' all-a-you girls, wanna take my hand, Then the world gonna know, I'm the Hoochie Coochie Man."*

"Isn't that the song you sang Kyabjé Düd'jom Rinpoche?" I asked, and Rinpoche concurred. *"How long ago was that now?"*

"1971" Rinpoche replied *"… and yes, Kyabjé Düd'jom Rinpoche Jig'drèl Yeshé Dorje asked me to sing him a Blues number so that he would know how it sounded."* PAUSE *"He had asked me about my life and I'd told him about having been the vocalist for the Savage Cabbage Blues Band – and it all led from there[4]. Düd'jom Rinpoche was the most astonishing catalyst in so many ways."*

My eyes kept being drawn to the pinks amongst the greens and yellows. There was the darker pink of betony and the delicate pink flowers of the lesser centaury. We came to the more open piece of headland where the gorse becomes sparser and the ground is covered in thick springy tufts of cliff grass. We often stopped here to sit for practice. This day was no exception. We climbed over the low fence marking the edge of the path so that we could reach the very edge of the cliff with its dramatic drop to crags and waves below. We spread out over the patch of clifftop, Khandro Déchen moving further down to a perfect perch for perusing passing birds. As Ræchel got out her sketch pad and pencils we sat silently gazing at the sky. The sky was a perfect summer cornflower-blue, entirely different in depth and hue to the blue sea below. Drifting across the sky were threaded wisps of white cloud.

As I sat gazing at the cloud movements, I became aware that there were two distinct layers moving in different directions.

---

[4] See: Ngakpa Chögyam—*Goodbye Forever – the Miscellaneous Memoirs of an English Lama*—Volume I—Aro Books WORLDWIDE—2020.

There were individual *cauliflowers* of cumulus closer to me – moving from right to left across my field of vision. The bases of these clouds were not so white, but the tops of them were brilliant white tufts lit by the sun. At a higher altitude were delicate streaks of cirrus moving at a different speed and in the opposite direction. They had an almost silky sheen and were the whitest of all the clouds I could see. The mesmerising movement and shifting patterns became the entirety of my experience and I was unsure how much time had passed when Rinpoche said *"The highest clouds you can see are at an altitude of around twenty thousand feet. Up there, at the moment, what you can see are cirrus and cirrostratus. The lower-level clouds are around six to seven thousand feet and they're stratocumulus and cumulus."* PAUSE *"I could tell you about Mahasiddha Shyama – the cloud-weaver, if you would like to hear her hagiography?"* I looked across the cliff to see Rinpoche smiling, and nodded keenly.

"Shyama was the youngest daughter of a Vaishya mercantile family from Sakala— bordering on Ögyen—in the far north-west of India" Rinpoche began. *"Although she was beautiful – she was a disappointment to her parents in being vague to the point of uselessness…"*

Shyama would never make anyone a wife – nor was she of any real use around the house, were she to stay at home. She was not mentally subnormal or moronic – but she was unable to concentrate on any task in order to take it to a satisfactory conclusion. Whatever task she was given, she would set out with the full intention of doing as she had been asked – but would simply forget what the task was if anything else more fascinating caught her notice. If a butterfly entered the window she would sit and watch the butterfly with rapt attention and when it flew away, she would move to the next focus of intrigue – without any sense that a task had been left uncompleted. Shyama was not lazy. She would work hard and was eager to please her parents – but whatever she tried to do, merely led to disarray and disorder.

Eighteen: Shyama – the cloud-weaver

Shyama could never keep track of the time or remember the day of the week. She knew night and day—because the difference was self-evident—and she knew the seasons – but most other divisions of time meant little to her. She knew meal times because she was called to attend them – but had no other sense of time or place. Shyama had learned to read and write – but nothing that was written could hold her attention for long. She could speak – but not converse. She left sentences unfinished – hanging in the air. She found herself unable to follow any line of reasoning for more than a few minutes. She was thus increasingly left to her own devices – and came to inhabit the house like a ghost: ignored by all, other than being called for meal times. She ate in silence whilst the family conversed.

When Shyama left the precincts of her home she sometimes failed to find her way back – and searches had to be made for her. The day eventually came when Shyama strayed too far and could not be found. She had wandered down to the river and, after walking some distance along its banks, she crossed over and rested in the shade of some willow trees. Because the day was hot, she wandered in and out of the river to cool her feet, occasionally sitting to gaze at the sparkling patterns on the shallow mountain stream. On standing up to walk home the sun had moved across the sky – and Shyama, confused as to which side of the river she had initially taken, took the wrong direction. She walked for many miles and finally went to sleep under a willow tree on the river bank.

On waking the next morning, she continued to walk. She had not observed the river being joined by a tributary – and when she finally realised that she had been walking away from her home she crossed over to the other bank and set off in yet another false direction. After many days of walking – she came to the conclusion that she would never find her home again.

She would have been hungry but for several kindly dhobi wallahs[5] who gave her portions of their meals. She asked them about her home town – but she could only describe it, she could not name it. Most towns sound similar when described and so no one could help her. Her home town could be one of twenty that lay in all directions – and as she could not designate its size, there was no hope.

As an innocent abroad, she might have been in grave danger – but one evening she met Mahasiddha Ishani[6] – the nondual wandering woman, who said *"You are lost, young lady."*

"No… I know where I am. I am here by the river" replied Shyama. *"I just don't know where my home is any more – and I can't remember the name of my town; so no one can give me guidance."*

"I may not be able to show you the way to go home – but I can give you guidance."

"What kind of guidance can you give me? Is it interesting? Is it like the shimmering water or the wings of a butterfly?" asked Shyama.

"It is like both – and beyond both. It is like lightning in the night sky. It is like a rainbow in dark water. It is like the sound of the breeze in these willow trees."

"Is it like the moon or the sound of a bird?" asked Shyama.

"It is like both – and beyond both. It is also like everything that is ordinary and commonplace."

Shyama pondered for a while. *"Is it like the dust and stones along this track or like the reeds in the shallows?"*

"It is like both – and beyond both. It is like all that is ugly or hideous."

---

[5] Washermen.
[6] Ishani is a name related to the Hindu goddess Durga. The name means 'desire'. Ishani is multi-dimensional: associated with strength, protection, and motherhood, but also war and destruction.

Shyama furrowed her brow seeking images. *"Is it like the howling of wolves and the growling of bears?"*

"It is like both – and beyond both. There is nothing that it is not like. It is like everything there is and like everything that is not."

"That is the first thing I have ever heard that sounded more interesting than the things I see and hear. Is there a way that I can know about that? But… I must tell you… I can never concentrate on anything – my mind always strays."

"What is the longest time you have ever been able to concentrate on one thing?"

"I don't know. Maybe I can only concentrate long enough to dress myself."

"You have already concentrated on our conversation much longer than it takes to dress yourself."

"Yes… You are right… This must be the first time a conversation has interested me."

"I do not believe that you cannot concentrate. Your problem is that samsara does not interest you – and you have no enthusiasm for it."

Shyama asked what Ishani meant by samsara and she replied *"Samsara is the belief in duality, which eventually leads to the belief that the mundane concerns of society are important – and, that we must therefore act as we are supposed to act, according to convention."*

We paused to admire the sketchRæchel had been making of the rocky headland below us – and, before Rinpoche recommenced, I commented *"You could think she sounds like a ditsy space cadet character. But she doesn't have space element neurosis in terms of being depressed or lethargic?"*

"No, she's no lochinkop[7] – she's simply disinterested in success with duality."

"So, if she's not interested in duality, how close is she to actually being in the nondual state?"

---

[7] *Hole in the head* – an idiot. Yiddish (אַ לאָך אין קאָפּ) from the German – *Loch im Kopf*.

"Well, samsara is probably best described as a subset of duality. It's duality as it manifests in the world of contrivances – both as objects and as creatures, human or otherwise. You have the primary duality – and then there's how duality manifests in different civilisations, cultures, societies, and smaller human associations. There are many different societies, each with its social mores." PAUSE "It's not that these societies are samsara in themselves. Samsara is not society's buildings or objects – but they're all reflective of samsara. This is because samsaric beings built them or devised them. Now, should all those beings become realised – those buildings would still be there. The Eiffel Tower[8] would still be there. It's not that the Eiffel Tower will vanish when all beings are realised... simply because a dualised Gustave Eiffel[9] designed it. Simply because dualised artisans constructed it, doesn't mean that the Eiffel Tower is —in itself—samsara. It is simply reflective of samsara."

"Those who work in it, eat in its restaurant, or go to see it" added Khandro Déchen "may all be involved in the reflection of samsara which it temporarily appears to offer. They will feed on that reflection – in terms of how it exists for them in terms of their individual samsaric propensities."

"And of course, Guy de Maupassant[10]—who was known to loathe the Eiffel Tower —ate lunch there every day." Rinpoche laughed. "When asked why—when he loathed the Eiffel Tower—did he eat there every day, Guy de Maupassant answered 'Because it is the only place in Paris where I cannot see the Eiffel Tower.' Some things are so obvious that they come as a surprise. The ugliness of the Eiffel Tower existed in Guy de Maupassant's mind along with his method of avoiding it whilst dining. That is probably one of the least pernicious examples of samsara."

Rinpoche paused. I stared into space momentarily before asking "And... there's less of that samsaric reflection in the natural world – when you're just outside looking at the sea and the sky?"

---

[8] The wrought-iron lattice tower on the *Champ de Mars* in Paris, nicknamed 'La dame de fer' – 'The Iron Lady'. It was constructed from 1887 to 1889 as the centrepiece of the 1889 World Fair. 1,083 feet tall, its square base measures 410 feet per side.
[9] Alexandre-Gustave Eiffel (1832–1923), French civil engineer.
[10] Henri René Albert Guy de Maupassant (1850–1893) – a French author, remembered as a master of the short story.

"Yes, they're not involved in the same way. There's a greater simplicity. The realised state can be experienced through the entire phenomenal world – but it's easier through the natural world. It's more direct. This is an important distinction to make. Sometimes people misunderstand. We have heard a fair few people say 'Oh, it's nice to be at a Buddhist centre away from samsara'. One cannot say that. Buddhist centres —or those who inhabit them or visit them—are also samsara. Everywhere where there are dualised beings is going to look like samsara – if one is dualised. One cannot escape samsara by going to a retreat centre."

"Yes" I replied. "I can see that that doesn't work. So, a retreat centre—if it's run according to Vajrayana principles—could be encouraging you away from dualistic vision more than being in the city centre, for example?"

"Yes… it could" Rinpoche smiled. "Although—if you were a realised being—it wouldn't matter whether you were in Bhutan or Bognor Regis. You could be in the city centre eating something absurdly expensive at a fashionable Japanese Sushi emporium; riding a camel in the Gobi Desert; in a hot-air balloon over the Sargasso Sea; in an igloo in the north of Greenland; or wandering aimlessly in Nether Wallop, Mudford Sock, West Crudwell, Marsh Gibbon, Mamble, Bishop's Itchington, Queen Camel, Compton Pauncefoot in Somerset, or Great Snoring in Fakenham, Norfolk."

"It wouldn't matter where you were" added Khandro Déchen. "For people who are not in the nondual state however – it might be more helpful to be at a retreat centre, by the ocean, or in a forest. As long as you are dualistically conditioned—if you're in a place which evokes that conditioning—the conditioning is going to be stronger than in a place that doesn't evoke conditioning."

"So being surrounded by trees is going to evoke less?" I offered.

"Unless you're a lumberjack, of course" Khandro Déchen responded. "But if you're not a lumberjack… if your only relationship with trees is that you're conscious that they exist—but you have no purpose for them—there's no agenda, and therefore it's easier."

"So, it depends on the individual nature of one's conditioning" continued Rinpoche. "An arboreal conservationist and a lumberjack will have different responses to the same environment." PAUSE "But to get back to the hagiography…" Rinpoche grinned "So… conversation continued. Ishani had explained that 'Samsara is the belief in duality, which eventually leads to the belief that the mundane concerns of society are important – and that we must therefore act as we are supposed to act, according to convention…' "

Shyama then asked "Is that why I have always been scolded for forgetting to finish the task I am allotted, in order to gaze at butterflies, or listen to birdsong?"

"Yes – but you should not believe that butterflies and birdsong are innately more beautiful than domestic phenomena. Your problem is not one of concentration – it is one of not seeing the beauty of all phenomena. When you can witness the beauty of all phenomena – you will find that your concentration is unrivalled."

"Can you teach me how to witness the beauty of all phenomena?"

"Certainly" replied Ishani "but first you must learn to weave the clouds with your mind – by seeing how they are naturally woven."

Shyama requested these teachings and the transmission of the practice – and Ishani instructed her to sit and observe the sky. She had to watch as clouds appeared and disappeared in the sky – how they crossed each other and how they attenuated as they were caught by currents of air. Shyama had to observe the clouds of the different times of day and to notice their relationship to the mountains. "There is nothing to remember in this. All that needs concern you, is the act of watching – and to forget who is watching and what is being watched."

Shyama was confused by this instruction. "But, reverend lady… this sounds just like I am anyway. How can I learn concentration from being as I have always been?"

"The difference is that you are following my instruction. I shall leave you now and come back in a week. In that time I shall make sure you have food – and water is here before you." Ishani indicated the river.

At that moment—in Cornwall—a huge herring gull silently flew so close and so low over our heads that I could feel the movement of warm air from its glide. *"The practice of weaving the clouds with the sky…"* I ventured *"… do all Dzogchen lineages have some kind of teaching or explanation around sky and mind?"*

"That's quite common, yes."

"Why is that analogy always used?"

"Because it's a good one" Rinpoche replied – and we all burst out laughing. *"But more importantly – it was the analogy which Kyabjé Düd'jom Rinpoche and Künzang Dorje Rinpoche employed. Chhi'mèd Rig'dzin Rinpoche also used it!"*

Khandro Déchen then called up the cliff *"That's because the sky is infinite…"* and the laughter started again.

Rinpoche added *"There's the ocean too, of course – but sky is in some ways better."* PAUSE *"I did try courgettes as an analogy once – but that just didn't work nearly as well."* When the mirth had moderated, he returned to the hagiography.

Shyama practised as she had been instructed – and in a week, she had gained clarity. Ishani returned and asked about Shyama's experience.

"I have not wandered away from this place, reverend lady."

"That does not surprise me – but there is more that you can say."

"Yes—there is—I found that I was able to remain staring at the sky whether it had clouds or not. The clouds wove themselves as you said they would – but they wove themselves with the sky."

"Sometimes they became the sky and sometimes the sky became the clouds — but it was the same whichever occurred. Both were the same as my mind — only I was not conscious of myself."

"This is good — and this is what I expected of you. Now you must spend a month looking alternately at the willows and the sparkling of the river in the same way. Collect one hundred and eleven pebbles from the river and make a heap of them where you sit. Gaze first into the sparkling river — then, for every outbreath, move one pebble across to form another heap. When the whole heap of pebbles has moved — shift your gaze to the willows and their movement in the breeze. I shall leave you now and come back in a month. In that time, I shall make sure you have food — and water is here before you." Ishani indicated the river.

Shyama practised as she had been instructed and, in a month, she had gained such clarity that she was able to recall her journey down the river — and to pinpoint the places where she had probably taken mistaken directions. Ishani returned and asked about Shyama's experience.

"I have not wandered away from this place, reverend lady."

"That does not surprise me — but there is more that you can say."

"Yes—there is—I found that I was able to remain staring into the willows or the sparkling river, only moving between them when I had shifted the pile of pebbles. I have now found that I can remain focused on anything I set my attention upon — but more than that: I now have a continuous memory that returns to my birth. Beyond that I know that this memory is empty of a continuous identity. There was someone there in every moment I remember. But none of them exist beyond those moments — and none are here now."

"This is excellent — and this is what I expected of you. Now you must spend a year wandering—looking at everything and hearing everything—remembering everything without a rememberer. I shall leave you now and find you again after the year is over — and at that time you will have attained the nondual state. Simply hold to nothing but empty attention and the empty pleasure of the sense fields.

"You should now beg for alms—because you are a yogini—and water is always before you as long as there are rivers."

Shyama practised as she had been instructed and before the year was over, she had gained her initial experiences of the nondual state. In the moment of her realisation Ishani appeared before her. *"This is the last time we shall meet perhaps – so these are my last instructions. Continue to wander—as I wander—and as you have wandered this last year. Practise tsog'khorlo in the manner in which I shall direct you – and practise it with the yogis and yoginis you meet on your wanderings. Practise the visionary methods in which I shall now instruct you – and integrate your experience of nondual awareness with every aspect of your life. When you are established in the nondual state, you should return to visit your family – but do not stay with them for more than a month. Then you must leave and continue your life of wandering as a yogini."*

Shyama practised as she had been instructed and after three years, she realised the nondual state as the continuum of her experience. She returned to visit her family—who were astonished to see her alive—and spent a month with them. She was so entirely different from the daughter they had known that they asked her for a thorough account of everything that had befallen her. They were still disappointed however – because she had no desire for a societally conventional husband. They tried every means of persuading her to stay with them – but after a month she left and returned to wandering.

Mahasiddha Shyama—the cloud-weaver—helped many people according to their personal dispositions – and enabled many ordinary women to enter the stream of Vajrayana.

As the hagiography concluded Rinpoche looked thoughtful. After a while he added *"Thinking about the idea of samsara as it's used here… it might be more useful to say that Shyama had no enthusiasm for 'the conventional world'. That's what is actually meant. The term 'samsara' can be problematic.*

"That for which she lacks enthusiasm – is the world of indoctrination, programming, and propaganda; the world of predetermined mores, preordained attitudes, predictable opinions, premeditated behaviours, and prefabricated modes of carrying out any activity."

"The world of typical responses?" I asked.

"Yes. Such as 'Hello, how are you?—Not so bad—How are you?—Could be worse—Nice weather for the time of year—Yes, better than last week—How're the children?—As well as can be expected at their age—Did you see the latest episode of 'Depressed People Mumbling at Each Other'[11] *on television last night?"* Rinpoche sighed. *"You become aware of indoctrination when you don't make expected responses. I came across this once and it was really rather peculiar."* Rinpoche smiled. *"We were invited to a dinner party—some twenty years ago—and it wasn't long before I had the distinct feeling that I was 'the invisible man'*[12]. *I was doing my best to be sociable. There was a conversation to which I attempted to contribute – but whatever I said, no matter how hard I tried, no one would take anything I said further. Someone would say something – and someone else would take it up, as one might expect in a conversation and it would go somewhere."* Rinpoche laughed. *"I could never work out what was wrong with what I'd said. I wasn't trying to weird them out. That would have been easy – as I have a surreal sense of humour. I was keen however, to be a pleasant guest. I was attempting to be conventional – but I failed. I couldn't get it right. So in the end, I realised that there was no point in talking."*

"So, what did you do?" I asked.

"Well, I had no wish to make an issue of it by extracting myself from the situation. So, I commented—every once in a while—in order to be friendly. I had to accept however, that I would largely be ignored. That was no great inconvenience. I could accomplish that without effort – but it did seem to be something of a waste of time."

---

[11] For example soap operas, such as *Neighbours* – an Australian television soap opera, which has run since 1985.
[12] *The Invisible Man* – a 2020 science fiction film written and directed by Leigh Whannell, which is a remake of the 1933 film of the same name, based on HG Wells' novel of the same name.

"*So, there's a collective conventionality in terms of communication*" I commented "*in average society?*"

"*Yes*" Rinpoche replied "*and if you don't play according to the rules – you're tactfully excluded.*"

"*So why do people play this game?*"

"*I don't think they know they're playing it. They're only aware if someone's not playing it. They detect this because the person is giving the wrong responses – or responses that sound like non-sequiturs.*"

"*It wouldn't be possible to give an example, would it?*"

"*Well… maybe. It could be like being a merchant banker – and not knowing that all the other people in the room are not merchant bankers. You might say to the person next to you 'What do you make of the current trend in the stock market with respect to the balance of corporate fundamentals against the less accommodative American Federal Reserve?' The person might just stare at you with incomprehension. You'd then realise there was something wrong.*" PAUSE "*Bad example really – because I said nothing technical.*"

"*But still*" added Khandro Déchen "*if you were not aware that there were no other merchant bankers at the table, you'd be perplexed by the fact that no one responded to anything you said.*"

I pondered that for a moment "*Maybe… a lot of people who end up as practitioners have grown up feeling like they didn't quite fit, not knowing quite how to play the game, or not interested in it?*"

"*Possibly – but I've never been keen on the 'stranger in a strange land' idea. I certainly had no sense of being in a strange land apart from my father and the middle / upper middle-class environment. I had good friends and being the vocalist for the Savage Cabbage Blues Band made me fairly mainstream at the time in terms of those who turned 16 to 18 years of age in 1967. As far as I could see – I was no stranger. I think that we're all strangers to certain sectors of the population.*"

"I guess Shyama is just an extreme example of that, of having no enthusiasm for the game at all?"

"Yes…" Rinpoche nodded *"but there's no particular virtue in being a misfit – or being too egocentrically eccentric to speak with other human beings. In my example, I was actually trying quite hard to relate. I was following up on what people were saying. If someone mentioned Brighton, I'd add 'I went to Brighton once and enjoyed roaming around the shops in the Lanes*[13]*.' Then someone would say something entirely disconnected about Barnstable – and everyone would chime in about what a charming resort they'd found Barnstable to be."*

"That was very rude – it sounds as if you were deliberately being excluded."

"No" Rinpoche laughed *"it was probably merely a problem with my semantics. People often find 'difference' of any kind to be frightening or unsettling – even if it's only a question of speaking grammatically when others are busy: 'emigrating to', making 'mute points', 'bigging up', 'decreasing, reducing, sinking, or descending down', 'returning back', 'rebounding again', 'revisiting again', 'revolving round', 'continuing on', 'over-exaggerating', 'going too far over the top' or 'recuperating in health'. Then they speak of 'people that', of larger 'amounts of people' in town – or 'less people' in town."* PAUSE *"It makes me want to extract revenge."* Rinpoche laughed. *"Simply using 'whom' correctly in a sentence, will inform others that you're abnormal."*

Khandro Déchen returned her binoculars to their case and climbed back up the cliff to join us. We sat in a row, watching the white wisps of cirrus high in the blue sky, their patterns mirroring the wave movements on the sea below us. A couple of questions were brewing.

"Can I ask about 'clarity', Rinpoche – with regard to Shyama? The account conveys that when she has been practising for a while – she gains clarity. And then she practices more – and gains further clarity.

---

[13] The Lanes—between the North Laine and the seafront—are a famous part of Brighton and Hove. It is a labyrinthian enclave of narrow alleyways, and hidden squares replete with numerous curious shops and beguiling restaurants.

"And then she practices more and she gains nondual realisation. So, what's the 'clarity' there? It's often used as if it's synonymous with realisation – but obviously not here."

"Well" Rinpoche replied "clarity, is the incidence of 'sparkling through' – in relation to the nondual state. If the nondual state begins to sparkle through – then you begin to develop clarity."

"And you can then develop more 'clarity' as sparkling increases" added Khandro Déchen. "It's not that there's 'more' clarity – it's that the frequency of sparkling increases."

"And is there anything to say" I asked "about empty attention and empty pleasure of the sense fields?"

"Empty attention" replied Khandro Déchen "is simply attention without discursive conceptuality in relation to the attention."

"Without thinking—**my**—attention is on this" added Ngak'chang Rinpoche. "Attention is simply present. It is not elsewhere. It's not—**my**—attention. It's simply attention. One is unselfconscious in respect of attention." PAUSE "And with empty pleasure, it's the same. Non-referential awareness of pleasure."

"It's not 'I hope this pleasure goes on. I didn't have this pleasure before. Hopefully it will be there again later.'" Khandro Déchen laughed. "Pleasure doesn't have to be like that. It can simply **be** there. That is empty pleasure. You're not identifying the one who's experiencing pleasure." PAUSE "Everybody has those moments of empty pleasure – but then they fill them up with referential coordinates which define the pleasure as **my** pleasure."

We sat in silence for another hour or more: endless moments of empty pleasure; gazing at sky and clouds; sunlight sparkling on the water; moments of empty pleasure – and I did my best not to fill them.

Nineteen: Kanhapa – the miraculous exhibitionist

Kanhapa *(nag po pa /* ནག་པོ་པ *)* / Trül-thab Tho-ço Khen *('phrul thabs tho co mKhan /* འཕྲུལ་ཐབས་ཐོ་ཙོ་མཁན *)*
Disciple of: Jalandhara, Tantipa, and Lokamatri
Varna by birth: Brahmin

Drala Jong; late July; an afternoon moving towards evening.

We were sitting on the flagged patio outside the Drala Jong farmhouse enjoying the view. Rinpoche and Khandro Déchen were wearing gö kar chang lo[1] robes—Rinpoche almost all in white—and Khandro Déchen with a red Bhutanese waistcoat and an emerald green robe blouse. She wore this unconventional colour because the blouse had been given to her by Jomo Sam'phel Déchen Rinpoche. Green is worn in the context of Dorje Phurba – but then the other robe garments are black. Ngak'chang Rinpoche's robes were made of rather ancient material dating to the late 1800s. His waistcoat was made of his German great-grandmother's linen tea towels, and his shamtab[2] was made of linen bedsheets. He had inherited these from his mother – or, rather, saved them when she was going to throw them out. They'd had brown marks of age on them and were yellowed from long-term storage. *"My mother"* Rinpoche smiled *"deemed them irredeemable – but I thought it was worth trying to save the fabric. It is marvellously woven – especially the tea towels. Ngakpa Wangdrüp found someone in Switzerland who could remove the stains without bleach. Now they are brilliant white!"* Their wonderfully contrasting woven textures glowed in the evening light.

The farmhouse occupies one side of a large grassed courtyard. Two long Welsh barns form the wings of the courtyard leading away from the farmhouse. The fourth side of the quadrangle is simply the view down the green valley receding into ancient woodland, distant hills, and sky.

---

[1] *gos dKar lCang lo* / གོས་དཀར་ལྕང་ལོ་ — white raiment and uncut hair: the Vajrayana robes.
[2] *sham thabs* / ཤམ་ཐབས་ — lower garment of robes, here the white skirt of the *gos dKar lCang lo*.

One barn houses the shrine hall and the rooms we occupy as custodians. The other barn houses *The Yak and Yogini Bistro*[3] – that is to say, the catering kitchen, dining room, and dGa'tön[4] space. The barns have white, lime-washed stone walls and slate roofs, with wooden doors and shutters over the windows.

Buddleia, wisteria, and rambling roses climb the walls between stone buttresses and rain butts. There is a pond near the centre of the courtyard, its edge graced by a large dignified horse chestnut, and a small orchard of young apple, pear, and walnut trees. Directly before us as we sat was a choir of colour and fragrances of the flowerbed bordering the patio. There were deep pink hydrangeas and glowing orange nasturtiums, purple irises, and golden fennel fronds. The flowerbed was filled with sound. Bees loved the delicate waving beauty of the grape leaf anemones. Rinpoche noticed the bees and recited *"I will arise and go now, and go to Innisfree, And a small cabin build there, of clay and wattles made; Nine bean-rows will I have there, a hive for the honey-bee, And live alone in the bee-loud glade."* PAUSE *"Yeats.*[5]*"* PAUSE *"I've always liked that phrase 'the bee-loud glade' – and the way Yeats isn't afraid of repetition: 'I will arise and go now, and go…' "*

"Can you say what it is that you like about it, Rinpoche?"

"No… *apart from the fact that repetition is unexpected – and it's not as if Yeats wasn't a linguistic master, so he must have had something in mind. It seems to provide… a gentle understated gravitas, perhaps. It's mysterious."*

Our large flock of house sparrows chattered – flitting back and forth amongst the flowers. The sights and sounds of birds—both wild and domesticated—are a prominent feature of life at Drala Jong.

---

[3] The name humorously given to the dining room at *Drala Jong* – inspired by a pre-1950s photograph of a Tibetan lady riding a yak.

[4] *rDo rJe dGa' sTon* / རྡོ་རྗེ་དགའ་སྟོན — Vajrayana Celebration. This is the practice of performance in which both performers and audience participate in authentic individuality, authentic generosity, and authentic appreciation. This is a traditional practice in the Nyingma and Kagyüd lineages. It is not commonly known but continues particularly in the sanghas of gö kar chang lo Lamas.

[5] William Butler Yeats—*The Lake Isle of Innisfree*—1888. A 12-line work comprising three quatrains, first published in the National Observer in 1890.

There are swallows, pigeons, and owls who nest in the barns; sparrows in the farmhouse eaves; and jackdaws, crows, ravens, red kites, and buzzards to be seen in the fields and trees. In the courtyard and surrounding paddock and paths you are likely to encounter the resident fowl: Don Corleone the goose, the duck brothers, half a dozen hens, and our two magnificent cockerels. They all range freely around the land and buildings, putting themselves to roost at night in the large wooden poultry house which stands where we shall—one day—build a labrang to accommodate Ngak'chang Rinpoche and Khandro Déchen – and visiting Lamas.

The two distinctly flamboyant cockerels stride into view, and we comment on their display as they parade. The white cock is the smaller of the two and somewhat gentle and dignified in his bearing. His flecked white feathers and creamy neck plumage contrast brilliantly with his dark green tail and luminous red comb and wattle. The dark red Rhode Island cockerel is the larger of the two and the alpha male. He has deep russet plumage with flashes of oil-on-water colours in his wing feathers. His tail displays the green-black hues of a raven. Whilst the white cockerel is dashing, the red one is glamorous. He is definitely the Gyalpo[6], charismatic and alluring in his demeanour, prone to strutting and crowing as he parades round his domain. That's what he was doing. He had come to the area of lawn right in front of where we were sitting and was sashaying back and forth, *cock-a-doodle-dooing* as he went, looking inordinately pleased with himself.

"I may be anthropomorphising here, but it really looks like he's showing off to us – even though it seems ridiculous to accuse an animal of being an exhibitionist."

"A consummately conspicuous Kanhapa – but, maybe not as condignly contemptible" Rinpoche chuckled. I looked quizzical.

[6] *rGyalpo* / རྒྱལ་པོ་ — king.

Rinpoche noticed and said *"Mahasiddha Kanhapa was known as 'the miraculous exhibitionist'…"* adding with a smile *"and… there's an animal who displays a 'realised human quality' in his hagiography – a camel with a delightful sense of humour."* He raised his eyebrows in query *"Shall we?"*

"Kanhapa with canapés in the courtyard before dinner" I replied *"sounds just perfect."*

"Well, the cockerel in question was no Little Red Rooster" Rinpoche began. *"He was a monk from a wealthy Brahmin family – and thus given to conceit and high cockalorum[7]…"*

Kanhapa studied at the monastic university of Somapuri – under the guidance of Mahasiddha Jalandhara. Kanhapa was a prodigious scholar and highly committed practitioner – but he was enamoured of himself. He had received transmission and teaching from Jalandhara and applied himself single-pointedly to accomplishing the goal according to the instruction he had been given. His perseverance was such, that in twelve months he had experienced visions of the yidam and the yidam's kyil'khor. Kanhapa was proud of his accomplishment and considered himself realised – but he had not long enjoyed the notion before he was verbally assaulted by a hideous naked hag who screamed at him *"Dolt! Who do you think you are to be strutting in this way? Return to your meditation! Realise nonduality! There is no other goal of which it is worth speaking!"*

Kanhapa, utterly horrified, realised that he had been scolded by a dakini – and that however wonderful his experience had been, it was not the nondual state.

Kanhapa practised for another year – and discovered to his delight that when he walked on rocks, he could leave imprints of his feet in them. Again, he was proud of his accomplishment and preened himself in a way that would have been too disgusting had there been any witnesses.

---

[7] Cockalorum is an 18th century term for braggadocio, extreme vanity, having a vastly inflated opinion of oneself.

No sooner had he congratulated himself on his realisation, than he was verbally assaulted a second time by the hideous naked hag who screamed at him *"Fool! Vanity of vanities! Why do you waste your time with this cretinous conceit? Return to your meditation! Realise nonduality! There is no other goal of which it is worth speaking!"*

Kanhapa, entirely confounded, realised that he had been reproached by the same dakini and that, however wonderful his sign of progress was, he had not realised the nondual state.

Kanhapa practised for another year – and at the end of his final session he found himself having risen in the air, such was his one-pointed absorption. This time he was immensely self-satisfied. His realisation, he reasoned, could now not be doubted. But as soon as this idea emerged, he was verbally assaulted a third time by the hideous naked hag who screamed at him *"Buffoon! What sort of bombastic balderdash is this? Return to your meditation and realise nonduality! There is no other goal of which it is worth speaking!"*

Kanhapa, completely aghast, realised that he had been reprimanded yet again by the dakini, and that however amazing it was to levitate – it was not a mark of the nondual state.

Kanhapa practised for another six months – and at the end, five damarus sounded in the sky above his head. This time he was sure that his realisation had been heralded. Again, as soon as this notion formed itself, he was verbally assaulted a fourth time by the hideous naked hag who screamed at him *"Idiot of idiots! Is there no end to your bumptious brashness? Return to your meditation. Realise nonduality! There is no other goal of which it is worth speaking!"*

Kanhapa, completely aghast, realised that he had been reprimanded yet again by the dakini, and that however amazing it was for damarus to sound in the sky – it was not a characteristic of the nondual state.

Kanhapa practised for another three months – and at the end, a cloud like a Dharma canopy appeared as well as five damarus sounding in the sky. This time he was sure that his realisation had been heralded. Again, as soon as this notion formed itself, he was verbally assaulted a fifth time by the hideous naked hag who screamed at him *"Imbecile of all imbeciles! Is there no limit to your narcissistic grandiloquent pretensions? Return to your meditation! Realise nonduality! There is no other goal of which it is worth speaking!"*

At that moment, the white cockerel strutted purposefully towards us, looking particularly pleased with himself and we all burst out laughing. *"These displays of relative siddhis are interesting"* I interjected. *"When he has the vision of the yidam and the yidam's kyil'khor at the beginning, that seems slightly different to the other accomplishments to me, but it's still just a relative siddhi?"*

"That depends on how tangibly it is experienced. If it's purely in the mind, that's one thing – but if it becomes external and you're part of it... that's entirely different."

"How do you know if it's in the mind or it's external?"

"Well, if it's mind, you're seeing it – and you know you're seeing it in mind. But if you're experiencing it in the physical dimension, that will be obvious – unless you're psychotic." Rinpoche gestured to the vista before us.

"It's when Drala Jong vanishes and becomes the copper-coloured mountain[8] *and there is no Drala Jong"* Khandro Déchen continued. *"When there's simply the copper-coloured mountain and you are actually there, that's utterly different from having your eyes closed and seeing it."*

---

[8] Nga-yab Zang-dog Palri *(rNga g.Yab zangs mDog dPal ri* / རྔ་ཡབ་ཟངས་མདོག་དཔལ་རི) – the Glorious Mountain in Chamara; the dimension of Guru Rinpoche. Chamara is the central one of a configuration of nine islands inhabited by savage rakshasas. In the middle of Chamara the majestic copper-coloured mountain rises into the sky. On its summit is the magical palace Lotus Light, manifested from the natural expression of primordial wakefulness. Here resides Guru Rinpoche in an indestructible bodily form transcending birth and death for as long as samsara continues and through which he incessantly brings benefit to beings through magical emanations of his body, speech, and mind.

"So—if he was psychotic—if he was experiencing some sort of hallucination" I asked "he might experience the vision as reality. Would he then think he was actually there?"

"Perhaps" replied Rinpoche. "At this point in time, we can't know what he was experiencing."

"All we can know" added Khandro Déchen "is that the dakini told him it was nonsense. That's the main point."

"We know that" laughed Rinpoche "because the dakini tells him it was a nyam[9]."

"Is there a difference between some of these miraculous relative siddhis and nyams?"

"Nyams—mainly—are not relative siddhis. Nyams can be fairly humdrum. They can be bizarre or even wondrous. They can be blissful or horrific. The relative siddhis are beyond nyams."

"Relative siddhis are not common for average human beings or even average practitioners" added Khandro Déchen. "You could move outside the conventional realm and gain experiences – but you could still describe those as nyams."

"You see… relative siddhis are nyams" added Rinpoche "but not all nyams are relative siddhis." PAUSE "So… Kanhapa felt chagrined in having been castigated yet again…"

He'd been called successively: a dolt, a fool, a buffoon, an idiot, and an imbecile. He reflected on these names peevishly and—when he had worked himself into a sufficiently petulant frenzy—he decided that marvels associated with Buddhas may not be exactly the same as the nondual state – but they were as near as made no difference.

He decided that having his progress criticised at every turn was becoming an obstacle and took himself off to another place where he might not be disturbed by naked hags – be they dakini emanations of wisdom or not.

---

[9] *nyams* / ཉམས — temporary meditative experience, transient meditational moods, experiential sign of the development of practice.

Kanhapa took great pains to seclude himself – and to this end he set up an elaborate series of protective magical rings, by means of which no one could disturb him. Kanhapa was possessed of mundane siddhis and so this was a feat of sorcery that was well within his capacity. Safe within his cocoon of self-adulatory smugness he began to practise again – and this time nine Dharma canopies opened above his head and nine damarus sounded in the sky. This time however, the vituperate naked hag did not appear – and Kanhapa was able to bathe in his own glory. *"At last! I have gained the ultimate siddhi!"* he sang out in great joy. *"I shall arise now and go— and go to the Isle of Langkhapuri—with my entourage. I shall convert the Tirthikas there!"* Then with infantile self-adulation he proclaimed *"Once I have accomplished this, I shall be the equal of my vajra master, Jalandhara."*

"I guess it's possible to set up a cocoon of self-adulatory smugness without using siddhis to create magic circles?" I asked. *"I was thinking of 'god realm celebrities' surrounding themselves with sycophants?"*

"Yes…" Khandro Déchen answered *"but you don't have to be rich or famous to do that. That is possible whenever we create a little world for ourselves – one in which we can feel superior. That is a trap into which we could fall – if we decided to ignore the ignominy of it. We have a world in which we are understood in a certain way – and we could take that as meaning more than it does."*

"So, unaware of the deluded depravity of the situation" Rinpoche continued the hagiography *"Kanhapa set out for Langkhapuri with a large entourage, who were all impressed by his powers…"*

When he arrived at the shore, he decided that he would commence with a miracle display. He would walk on the water: what need had he of a boat? That was for the lower orders. As he trod the rippling surface of the water, he felt such pleasure that he began to skip – all the better to impress his entourage with his spiritual prowess. The thought arose in his mind *'Ha! Even my vajra master, Jalandhara, is not capable of feats such as this!'*

The moment this ignominious thought made its fæculent passage through his mind, he sank like a stone and the waves tumbled him onto the beach covered with sand and seaweed. When Kanhapa looked up, he saw Mahasiddha Jalandhara seated upon a camel. Both Jalandhara and the camel gazed down at him with sad expressions. *"I am sorry to see you in this sad state, Kanhapa"* sighed Jalandhara as his camel belched languidly in Kanhapa's face. *"What would you mean by breaking the root vows in this sordid manner? No wonder my camel broke wind in your face…"*

Kanhapa could not answer and stared at Jalandhara, as dumb as an ox.

"What purpose was there in teaching you if you behave like this?"

Again, Kanhapa had no answer.

"I even requested a powerful dakini to visit you with guidance – but although you took advice four times, in the end your peevish pride got the better of you, didn't it?"

"Yes…" Kanhapa finally replied.

"What is the sense in practising Vajrayana if your main interest is self-glorification?"

Kanhapa was silent and so Jalandhara asked *"Well…? Answer me…"*

Kanhapa apologised profusely and promised he would not make the same mistake again.

"No…" replied Jalandhara *"…you will not, Kanhapa – because I can no longer teach you."*

Kanhapa begged for forgiveness. He begged to be allowed to resume his place as Jalandhara's disciple – but the Mahasiddha smiled sadly.
"Naturally I forgive you – but nonetheless, I cannot teach you. You must seek out my disciple Tantipa—the wondrous wisdom-weaver—in Pataliputra and beg him for transmission. If you promise faithfully to follow his guidance—without self-infatuated guile—you may yet realise the nondual state. But you—must—give up this vile fascination with mundane siddhis.

"As the Ḍākinī told you 'Return to your meditation and realise nonduality! There is no other goal of which it is worth speaking!' Now forget your obsession with glory and seek Mahāsiddha Tantipa."

With that Jalandhara and his camel vanished. Kanhapa—suitably humbled—decided to follow Jalandhara's instruction. As soon as he committed to following Jalandhara's instruction the damarus tintinnabulated in the sky for all to hear and Dharma canopies appeared above him. It came as a severe blow to him that Jalandhara could no longer teach him – but he could still take him as his vajra master in following his instruction.

Fortunately Kanhapa's entourage had seen Jalandhara. Unfortunately, they had not heard his words. Unfortunately, they had heard the damarus and seen the Dharma canopies above Kanhapa's head – and were therefore happy to follow Kanhapa on his quest. They decided that Kanhapa's aqueous contretemps was simply a sign that it was not worth going to convert the Tirthikas of Langkhapuri – and Kanhapa did nothing to dissuade them of that idea.

By the time the party arrived in Pataliputra, Kanhapa again felt himself to be on a noble mission which would avail him of the nondual state. His siddhis had returned after his unfortunate dunking in the sea – and he decided that the best way to find Tantipa, the wisdom-weaver would be to snap the threads of every weaver's loom with his gaze until he came to a weaver whose threads he could not snap. The plan worked. He found Tantipa and left a dozen distraught weavers all diligently setting up their looms again.

"Why did you not simply ask my whereabouts?" asked Tantipa. *"My name is not unknown here? Wait here while I go and pay for the inconvenience you have caused. These men have families to support – their time and thread bring their income."*

Kanhapa apologised for his foolishness – and said that he would go himself to pay the weavers handsomely for their inconvenience.

Nineteen: Kanhapa – the miraculous exhibitionist

When he returned Tantipa sighed *"I know who you are. You are Mahasiddha Jalandhara's failed disciple. I know why you are here. It is because your erstwhile vajra master has entrusted you to my guidance. I know what is needed – but can you promise that you will do whatever I ask?"*

Kanhapa said that he would follow Tantipa's commands faithfully – whatever they were. *"Then come to me tomorrow and I shall take you to the charnel ground. Ask your entourage to remain here and await your return."*

Kanhapa arrived the following morning before dawn—as Tantipa had instructed—and they walked to the charnel ground. Kanhapa had thoughts of stating a preference for flying there – but decided against making the suggestion when he saw Tantipa's face at the moment he had that thought. Tantipa sneered at him and shook his head in despair. They arrived at the charnel ground and walked some way within it. They arrived at a clearing – and there they found five dead creatures: a human being, a cow, a dog, an elephant, and a horse.

Tantipa motioned for Kanhapa to be seated. *"Now Kanhapa – before you receive transmission, we must practise tsog'khorlo together. These are the five meats*[10]. *You must eat a portion of each one from a skull bowl*[11].*"*

"So these meats and nectars, Rinpoche…" I pondered *"could you perhaps elaborate a little?"*

---

[10] The five meats – shar nga *(shar lNga /* འར་ལྔ *)*. These are: human flesh – *shar chen /* འར་ཆེན; cow flesh – *nor shar /* ནོར་འར; dog flesh – *khyi shar /* ཁྱི་འར; elephant flesh – *gLang shar /* གླང་འར; horse flesh – *rTa shar /* རྟ་འར.

[11] Skull bowls of human bone are utilised in tsog'khorlo *(tshogs 'khorlo /* ཚོགས་འཁོར་ལོ */ ganachakrapuja)*, the Feast Profferment which celebrates the vajra master and mends breaches in damtsig. Two skull bowls are used which contain the sha nga düd-tsi nga *(shar lNga bDud rTsi lNga /* འར་ལྔ་བདུད་རྩི་ལྔ *)* – the five 'meats' and the five 'nectars'. The 'meats' are usually represented by any kind of meat and the nectars by alcohol. The five 'meats' and the five 'nectars' represent things that are usually considered foul and disgusting. This profferment symbolises transcending the concept of samsara and nirvana as a mutually-exclusive polarity. It symbolises transcendence of the 'pure-impure dichotomy'. These profferments are important in the three Inner Tantras. Smaller skull bowls are made of metal, and these are preferable for a chogtsé (throne table).

"The five meats and five nectars[12] *represent the overthrow of mundane religion."*

"Mundane religion…?" I asked. *"How would you define that?"*

"The spiritualised path of societal control, collective mandate, consensus reality, and pedestrian mediocrity." PAUSE *"You see… where religion becomes a set of laws which have to be obeyed—rather than a body of knowledge which needs to be discovered—reality requires revelation. Political correctness and spiritual correctness must be overturned. Having said that however, I should place the five meats and five nectars in context."* PAUSE *"These substances represent what was reviled by those who adhered to Brahmanic tendencies which remained in Buddhism. Even though Buddhism was no longer part of the Hindu culture from which it sprang – some elements of Brahmanic law remained as cultural accretions."* PAUSE *"It's not so different in one way from Christian society in which there are pre-Christian forms such as Easter eggs and Easter rabbits. There are Christmas trees, holly, and mistletoe. Of course these do not undermine Christianity – but Brahmanism and the four denials undermine Buddhism."*

"Yes." PAUSE *"So, for us—apart from human flesh—we can eat what we please."*

"Yes – so the five meats and five nectars no longer perform quite the same function. We could now say that the five meats and five nectars represent the fascistic aspect of political correctness and spiritual correctness."

"Spiritual correctness?"

"Yes" responded Khandro Déchen. *"It's the spiritual correlate of political correctness. It's not a known term as yet – but it's one of Rinpoche's neologisms. It relates to a 'safety first' approach to religion in which nothing surprising is allowed to happen."*

"It's the state of mind" Rinpoche added *"which takes objection to Vajrayana as being different from Sutrayana – and, in which being vegetarian or vegan, abstemious, and gender-fluid are seen as mandatory.*

---

[12] düdtsi na-nga *(bDud rTsi sNa lNga* / བདུད་རྩི་སྣ་ལྔ་). These are: urine – *gCin* / གཅིན་; excrement – *sKyag* / སྐྱག་; blood – *khrag* / ཁྲག་; semen – *khu* / ཁུ་; and, pus – *chu ser* / ཆུ་སེར་.

"Not that there is anything wrong with those options per se – it's when they became mandatory. It's when they are seen as being ultimate *rather than* relative *stances.*" PAUSE *"As to the five nectars, we're free to experiment – but we have no obligation to avoid these nectars in terms of legality. The five meats and five nectars were almost universally—not—taken literally in Tibet. They simply represented the requirement to go beyond codified limits."*

"In the West, Buddhism is not encumbered by Brahmanism" continued Khandro Déchen. *"It's encumbered by neo-puritanism and neo-Protestantism."*

"In the current milieu" added Rinpoche *"we suffer from the politicisation of ethical values – and, cosseting demands for safety."* PAUSE *"This leads to originality and natural kindness being crippled. Simply partaking of meat and alcohol—for many Western Buddhists—therefore, serves the original purpose of the five meats and five nectars."*

"So" I asked *"do you think that's why Chhi'mèd Rig'dzin Rinpoche told you to give up being vegetarian and abstemious?"*

Rinpoche was silent for a few moments *"It could well be."* PAUSE *"He couched it in terms of my being a Buddhist rather than a Hindu – as he was well aware of the Western fashion for mixing Hinduism and Buddhism as if they were more-or-less the same. Without naming names, a fair few of the first Western students of Himalayan Lamas originally studied with Hindu teachers. This experience was a problem compounded by there being Newari Buddhists in Nepal – and Newari Buddhism is an admixture of Hinduism and Vajrayana. This being the case – there would have been those who came to see Buddhism and Hinduism as a little too similar."* PAUSE *"So, Chhi'mèd Rig'dzin Rinpoche always defined* exactly *what the differences were – particularly in terms of karma and the fact that nonduality in Buddhism is not monistic. Many people labour under the illusion that advaya*[13] *and advaita*[14] *are the same.*

---

[13] Nyi'mèd *(gNyis 'med* / གཉིས་མེད) – nonduality.
[14] 'One' with nothing secondary.

"*Advaya is nondual in terms of 'emptiness' and 'form' being nondual. Advaita—as in Advaita Vedanta*[15]—*is the 'nonduality' of undividedness of God and God's creation. From the Buddhist perspective Advaita Vedanta is monist – in positing that everything is one. Buddhism posits a 'pluralist nonduality' rather than a 'monist singularity'. In Buddhism, 'identity' is impermanent – but its proliferation of transient appearances is endless. There is no dissolution into emptiness without arising from emptiness.*"

"*In ancient India*" Khandro Déchen added "*this tsog'khorlo—or ganachakra—profferment overturned the 'purity-obsession' of Brahmanism – but it now has equal importance in overturning 'tyrannical puritanical tendencies' which have no function in Vajrayana. The humanitarian value of certain aspects of political correctness are not in question – simply the idea that they can override Vajrayana.*"

"*The important point to remember*" Ngak'chang Rinpoche continued "*is that Vajrayana cannot be judged according to criteria which are not based on nondual realisation.*" PAUSE "*And on that note – back to Kanhapa…*"

Kanhapa was revolted by the idea because he had only ever eaten the five meats symbolically. As this was Tantipa's first command however – he felt he could not disobey him. He pulled out a knife in order to cut the smallest possible token of each creature – but no sooner had he done so than Tantipa shouted "*Out of my way, you blithering buffoon! That's not the way to do it!* **This** *is the way the five meats are eaten!*" Thereupon Tantipa ravaged the corpses like a wolf. He tore at their flesh with his bare teeth—taking a healthy bite of each—and then shouting "*Now you!*"

Kanhapa obeyed but performed the task with great revulsion. Tantipa then pointed out a group of five skull bowls that lay at the base of a tree – each filled individually with urine, excrement, blood, semen, and pus.

---

[15] Advaita Vedanta (अद्वैत वेदान्त) School of Hinduism is the oldest scholarly tradition of orthodox Hinduism – and also a popular, syncretic tradition. Advaita means 'non-secondness' rather than 'nondual' – and equates with monism. It posits the idea that Brahman alone is ultimately real, whilst the transient phenomenal world is an illusory appearance of Brahman (God).

The tree that overhung the skull bowls was festooned with snakes, and a leopard and tiger sat at the base of the tree snarling. *"Now Kanhapa – we must practise the second part of the tsog'khorlo. These are the five nectars. You must drink a portion of each one."*

Kanhapa—already nauseated by the five meats—was utterly disgusted. He had before, drunk the five nectars symbolically – and although this was only Tantipa's second command, he said that he could not obey him. Tantipa drank from each of the skull bowls with a smile. Tantipa said nothing of Kanhapa's having broken his promise. He simply blew loudly on a conch – and a group of yogis and yoginis emerged from the trees. They gathered up the five skull bowls and stripped the flesh off the five creatures. They laid the offerings on a butcher's cart—harnessed to four lions—and left the charnel ground.

"We shall now invite your entourage to the tsog'khorlo – but it shall be held in the parkland."

Tantipa and Kanhapa walked back to town following the butcher's cart and met Kanhapa's entourage. Tantipa invited them all to the tsog'khorlo and they were overjoyed to be included by a Mahasiddha such as Tantipa. Kanhapa however, became highly agitated concerning the prospect of how his entourage would react to the five meats and five nectars – and hid his face whilst they ate and drank. After a while Kanhapa looked around him and discovered that the offerings appeared to be delicious – and joined in with the feast.

"These were the substances you found so revolting in the charnel ground" said Tantipa. *"How is it now, that you have such an appetite for what you previously found so disgusting that you broke your vow with the second command I gave you?"*

"But these are not the same offerings – you have transformed them into a glorious feast."

Tantipa smiled *"And would I not have done the same for you – had you been wholehearted in following my vajra command?"*

Kanhapa felt deeply ashamed when he heard these words. He begged forgiveness – but Tantipa said *"Naturally I forgive you—just as the great Jalandhara forgave you—but I cannot teach you. You must leave this place and hope for one last opportunity before you die."*

As Rinpoche paused, Ja'gyür asked *"When you break the root vows like that, in terms of the relationship with the vajra master, is there a point at which it's irreparable?"*

"According to Künzang Dorje Rinpoche these vows are never irreparable" Rinpoche replied. *"There are different views on it however."*

"We would accord with Künzang Dorje Rinpoche's view, of course" Khandro Déchen smiled. *"But usually if you don't repair vows within three years, they're considered irreparable. That however, is somewhat arbitrary – because you could ask 'What about three years and a week? How would that be?' and receive the answer 'Yes, that's alright.' Then you could ask 'Well, what about three years and a month?' and be told 'No, that's too long.' Wherever the line is drawn, it becomes nonsense – but what actually counts is the position taken by one's own Lama. So, Jalandhara and Tantipa were correct – and so was Kyabjé Künzang Dorje Rinpoche."*

"So…" Ja'gyür began – but said nothing further.

"I never discussed vow breakage with Kyabjé Düd'jom Rinpoche – so I do not know what his view was. However, there's nothing hardwired which occurs at the end of three years." Rinpoche replied. *"The lights don't fuse. The longer you leave it however – the more difficult it becomes."*

"So, duration makes it increasingly difficult" added Khandro Déchen *"but it's never impossible as long as one wishes to repair the vows. The obstacle is only* not wishing to repair the vows.*"*

Rinpoche returned to the hagiography *"Kanhapa left with his entourage – who all thought that his meeting with Tantipa had been a profound success…"*

They travelled for nine years meditating in different places – but wherever they went Kanhapa found his meditation dull. The greater of his mundane siddhis slipped from him, and he felt as if he had returned to the state of being before his first sign of attainment had appeared. In a state of deepening depression, he, and his entourage, reached the outskirts of Bhadakhora, where they sat and rested in a grove of trees.

In the middle of the grove there were several large trees laden with ripe mangoes – and the Kanhapa party were all both hungry and thirsty. Kanhapa had no power to manifest food or drink so he led his party toward the trees. On reaching the mango trees he perceived that the fruits were all in the higher branches – and so he caused the branches to droop in order that the mangoes could be easily picked. As soon as the mangoes came within reach, a force greater than Kanhapa could resist, made the branches assume their previous position. He tried again and the same thing happened. Kanhapa standing there—perplexed and thirsty—noticed a young low-varna girl sitting by the largest tree eating a mango.

"Who are you, young girl – and how did you manage to obtain a mango when they are so high in the trees?"

"Why, I am Lokamatri[16] *– the guardian of these trees. My permission is required if anyone wishes to eat these mangoes."*

Kanhapa shook his head in disbelief and asked *"By whose magic do the branches of these trees resist my command?"*

"There is no magic, Kanhapa – merely awareness and unbroken vows."

"You cannot tell me that it is you—a low-varna girl—who prevents me lowering these branches" laughed Kanhapa. *"If it is you – show some sign of your power."*

---

[16] Kama la-cha *(ka ma la ca /* ཀ་མ་ལ་ཅ *)* The name means 'mother to the world'. It is another name for the Goddess Lakshmi.

"*No...*" smiled Lokamatri.

"*Then I will show you a sign of my power!*" scoffed Kanhapa.

"*If you like*" smiled Lokamatri – at which Kanhapa raised his hand and performed a gesture to cause Lokamatri pain. No sooner had he performed his gesture than Kanhapa crumpled to the ground in agony. He struggled to his feet and attempted another occult assault on Lokamatri – but his bowels immediately opened and he fouled himself with his own urine and fæces. Humiliated and enraged he tried again but his whole body writhed as if constricted by snakes and stung by scorpions. Kanhapa fell to the ground screaming – but Lokamatri smiled and addressed him softly.

"*All you had to do, Kanhapa – was to have asked me whether you and your entourage might eat mangoes from these trees.*"

Immediately, Kanhapa's entourage—all terribly thirsty—called "*Please, Lokamatri, may we be allowed to have mangoes from your trees?*"

"*Certainly*" Lokamatri sang out. "*You may—all—have mangoes! All apart from this vainglorious monk Kanhapa. He has yet to make his request – but as soon as he does, he may also have mangoes.*"

At these words Kanhapa wept – and pleaded for a mango. Lokamatri rose from her seat and plucked a mango for Kanhapa. She offered it to him, saying "*The suffering you brought on yourself was entirely unnecessary – as is all the suffering of samsara. Knowing this should give rise to great compassion for those who hurt themselves through their own delusion. The siddhis which arise from accomplishment are as nothing in comparison with authentic devotion to the vajra master. You have broken vows with both Jalandhara and with his disciple Tantipa – but they have not broken their commitment to you. That is why I am here – and why you have a final opportunity to renounce your self-adulatory obsession with power.*

"An intoxicated pachyderm has power such as yours – and your behaviour is little different from an inebriated elephant. Tell me now, do you truly wish to change your life and become an authentic disciple?"

Humiliated in front of his entourage—and psychically devastated by Lokamatri—Kanhapa came to his senses. *"I would do anything if I could see my vajra master Jalandhara again and confess my contemptible stupidity. I now have no wish for anything but to be his disciple again."*

"You have spoken well, Kanhapa. From this point on you should no longer be a monk – there is too much vanity in that for one such as you once were. You must now be a yogi with uncut hair and white clothes."

"I will follow your instruction – and I shall renounce realisation until all beings attain it. I shall renounce all siddhis until they may be of use to others."

At that moment Jalandhara rode into the mango grove on his camel. He sat gazing at Kanhapa. On seeing his former vajra master, Kanhapa threw himself to the ground – and at that moment he experienced a flash of the nondual state. Jalandhara recognised his disciple's experience and smiled down at him lovingly – but the camel belched in Kanhapa's face.

"Forgive my camel…" smiled Jalandhara *"but his memory of offence is far longer than mine. He will require my assurance before he will befriend you. However, it seems that you may become my disciple again if it is your wish."*

It was most definitely Kanhapa's wish and he was immediately accepted. In recognition of his acceptance Jalandhara's camel playfully knocked him to the ground with an affectionate nuzzle. This caused Kanhapa to laugh and it was clear from this, that Kanhapa was no longer stifled by his own pride.

Kanhapa practised for a further three years and his realisation of nonduality became integrated with the stream of his experience. He never manifested siddhis again, or even admitted to having them.

He became the *siddha-without-siddhis* and encouraged his disciples to abjure all interest in miraculous phenomena. None therefore are recorded as Mahasiddhas. *"There was once…"* he told them *"… no end to my narcissism and fascination with siddhis – but although I gained powers, they led only to humiliation and degradation. It was my greatest fortune to have been allowed a final chance to abandon my error and return to the devotion I should have naturally owed my vajra master, the Mahasiddha Jalandhara. It was only through him that I realised nonduality."*

"Didn't you write poetry called 'siddha-without-siddhis', Rinpoche?"

"Yes – a long time ago. It had a line in the first stanza which ran something like this: 'I'm sorry if my presence orchestrated disappointment and caused you irritation; It was nothing but a shimmering between bewilderment and wonderment – so, relax and allow the siddha-without-siddhi to manifest as he will…' It looked at the different ways in which a certain Tibetologist found me wanting… I sent it to him some days after I'd given a talk at the Institute of Integral Studies [17]. *"*

"Did he respond?" asked Jagyür.

"No – but I didn't expect a reply. He'd invited me to speak on my life of training as a Lama – but had informed the class beforehand that he was going to expose a fraud. The students told me this later. It was vaguely amusing because his obnoxious manner caused the students to take my side and apologise for his rudeness and hostility. [18] *They came to a talk I gave elsewhere in order to meet me under less divisive circumstances."* PAUSE *"I called the piece 'Siddha-without-siddhi' because the Tibetologist asked me what siddhis I had."*

"What did you reply?"

---

[17] The Institute of Integral Studies is a private university in San Francisco, California, founded in 1968. The institute has no official spiritual association – but it grew from followers of Sri Aurobindo.

[18] See: Ngakpa Chögyam—*Goodbye Forever – the Miscellaneous Memoirs of an English Lama*—Volume VI—Aro Books WORLDWIDE—to be published in 2025.

"I asked 'What made you imagine I had siddhis?' At that he seemed vaguely thrown —and didn't know how to follow on—so I said 'Willingness to deal with whatever arises is my only accomplishment – but I can't say that it's been rigorously tested.' Then the evening ended and he left without saying goodbye."

We watched the swallows in their evening dance, swooping and diving through the courtyard at such speed that it was difficult to track their flight. We listened to the 'heading-to-bed' clucking of the chickens as they were herded down the lawn by the strutting cockerel, Gyalpo. I asked *"Is it possible to achieve the nondual state and still be a little bit self-enamoured, still be interested in self-glorification?"* Rinpoche laughed and shook his head *"No."*

"Can you explain why that is?"

"Being self-enamoured is an aspect of duality. Who is this 'self' of whom 'you' are enamoured? There cannot be two people involved" Ngak'chang Rinpoche commented.

"And beyond that – if you're beyond duality, you're not going to be self-enamoured" Khandro Déchen laughed. *"It would be pointless – like saying 'I'm breathing' or 'I'm not dead'. Why make such a statement?"*

"You can't be wet and dry at the same time" added Rinpoche. *"You can't be hot and cold at the same time. Once you become an adult – you have bowel control. So, if you have bowel control – you don't suddenly lose it for no evident reason. You can't say 'I'm a mature, healthy, independent, self-reliant adult – but occasionally I foul my britches in the most unlikely places.' That does not happen. It would be like saying 'I'm in the sea, swimming, and I'm wet – but there are people in the sea who are not swimming properly because, occasionally, they find themselves dry.' It would make as much sense as that. You're either in the sea swimming and you're wet, or you're not. To be dry you have to get out of the sea again and either use a towel or dry in the sun."*

I was laughing as Rinpoche continued *"What does happen – is that there's a phase of practice where one has brief experiences of the nondual state. One doesn't remain stable in them. You find them in practice – but then you lose these brief experiences of the nondual state. It depends how often they occur. If they happen often enough – like a strobe light in a dark room, when the strobe flashes fast enough, you can see the room. If the strobe is too slow, then maybe you can't walk across the room because it's dark too long to get sufficient sense of the room. Once it hits a certain frequency however, you begin to be able to see the room. It's an appalling analogy – but it could be somewhat like that. Then the experience affects people, even when they're not stable in the experience of nonduality."*

"So, it's possible for somebody to have had some nondual experiences" I asked *"but when they're not remaining with that, then they can still be ridden by their neuroses?"*

"Yes… to a certain extent…" replied Khandro Déchen *"although at that point, even if you've had just one such experience—or you're having one a week—you're not going to get into horribly high-level neurosis. Even with regular practitioners a degree of self-control becomes available. That's how we know if people are practising or not. It shows in their behaviour."*

"As long as people have patellar reflex responses to anything" Rinpoche added *"it means they haven't stabilised shi-nè, let alone lhatong, nyi'mèd or lhundrüp* [19]. *For those who have good experience of shi-nè however – they will no longer be subject to automatic or autonomic emotional responses."*

Two crows landed on the roof of *The Yak and Yogini Bistro* and cawed conversationally with us. *"I remember when I was about nineteen"* Rinpoche continued. *"I'd just come back from India the first time. I'd been invited to a party. It was someone at Art School, whose parents were rather wealthy. They lived in a mansion with a floodlit trout lake. I turned down the drive from the main road on my motorbike – and it must have been about five minutes before I arrived at the house.*

---

[19] rNal 'byor bZhi / རྣལ་འབྱོར་བཞི་ – the four naljors, preliminary silent sitting practices of Dzogchen sem-dé: zhi gNas / ཞི་གནས་, lhag mThong / ལྷག་མཐོང་, gNyis med / གཉིས་མེད་, lhun grub / ལྷུན་གྲུབ་

"There was a massive, semi-circular flight of twenty or thirty stone steps up to the front door – and a strobe playing down the steps. People couldn't walk up the steps without falling over. They had to crawl up on their hands and knees because the strobe was making it impossible to traverse the steps. When I approached them, I started blinking in time with the strobe in such a way as not to see the light – just the dark phase, which wasn't completely dark. Due to this simple device, I walked up the stairs without falling over. Everyone thought it was miraculous – because they couldn't manage it. They couldn't manage it—of course—because they were not blinking. That's probably a useless analogy, but it's some sort of example of something intermittent – and how you can work with it."

I was quiet for a while, listening to the intermittent rustle of the early evening breeze in the horse chestnut by the pond, and the feathery whisper of the wisteria fronds moving against the wall of the barn. There was the sound of sparrows twittering from the eaves above our heads and distant lowing from the field of Friesians. *"Despite all the opportunities he's given"* I began *"it seems as if the main problem is that he's never honest with his entourage. He keeps them there by being dishonest. He doesn't say 'Actually, I messed up'. Instead, he pretends that he didn't mess up every time – until he's finally humiliated directly in front of them, in the mango grove. It made me wonder… if he had managed to keep his humiliation secret from his entourage – would he merely have just carried on in his delusion?"*

"That's probable" Rinpoche sighed. *"Although when you say 'he was humiliated' – he humiliated himself. He kept trying to attack the young woman – but everything he threw at her, bounced back at him. She simply sat quietly allowing him to humiliate himself. Which—of course—is why she said 'You—could—simply have requested a mango. If you had asked for a mango, I would have given you a mango.' It could have been that simple."*

"Of course" Khandro Déchen grinned *"his entourage did simply request mangoes – and their requests were granted. They each received as many mangoes as they desired."*

"*The hagiography relates that Kanhapa has vanity in being a monk*" I wondered out loud. "*Why would there have been more vanity in being a monk than in being a Mahasiddha?*"

"*Not—more—than being a Mahasiddha*" Rinpoche chuckled. "*The vanity in 'being a monk' is connected with the Brahmin varna and their obsession with purity. So, Kanhapa was proud of being a monk, proud of his celibacy, proud of his purity – and proud of everything concerned with monasticism. To be a tantrika however, means going beyond the pure-impure dichotomy – and that would not have held any attraction for a Brahmin.*"

"*It's not attractive to many Western spiritual practitioners either*" added Khandro Déchen "*in terms of who they choose as their Lamas. Many Western people would rather have a monastic Lama – even though they're not monastics themselves. It's the huge myth of 'renunciation being the answer'. We need to grow out of that – or Vajrayana is out of the question.*"

I obviously had a question writ large on my face – which prompted Rinpoche "*The huge myth is that if* **you** *can abstain from sexuality—when* **I** *would not want to abstain—then* **you** *must be realised.*" PAUSE "*That makes as much sense as saying that if I can abstain from travelling to Lapland to witness the aurora borealis – I must have greater realisation than someone who deliberately goes there to see the phenomenon.*" PAUSE "*Or, if I'm an emaciated hair-shirted flagellant – I must have profound wisdom. If I'm a humourless, tight-lipped, emaciated absentee from sensory reality – I'm as good as 'enlightened'. This kind of anxious timidity is tragic.*" PAUSE "*It's the same with abstention. Ex-alcoholics may be abstemious – but it doesn't mean they're in line to be canonised.*"

"*Wasn't there a Saint Timothy the Teetotal?*" smiled Khandro Déchen.

"*In all probability*" Rinpoche grinned. "*On which note… I believe it might be time for the Drinking Song of Kyabjé Düd'jom Rinpoche Jig'drèl Yeshé Dorje.*"

Twenty: Sarvagjna – the eccentric monocular seamstress

Sarvagjna *(sar bag jna /* སར་བག་ཇན་ *) /* Tshar-zhar Tsembuma *(mTshar zhar tshem bu ma /* མཚར་ཞར་ཚེམ་བུ་མ་ *)*
Disciple of: Shyama
Varna by birth: Harijan

Cornwall – a prismatic August dusk on the Lizard peninsula.

We had come to Lizard Point for either piscatorial pommes frites or traditional fish pie. We would then take a postprandial evening stroll amongst the huge boulders and rock pools of Kynance Cove. Lizard Point is the most southerly tip of mainland Britain – with dramatic cliffs and majestic seas. The coastline has been shaped by the power of the Atlantic Ocean and the waters off the point can be hazardous. We swim there nonetheless. There have been beacons lit on this coast to guide seafarers to safety since the 1500s. The twin-towered lighthouse which currently stands on the site was opened in August 1752. At that time each tower was topped by a coal-fired brazier, kept alight by two burly bucolic burghers with bellows. If they relaxed their efforts—and the fires dimmed—they would be reminded of their task by the lighthouse overseer giving a loud blast on his cow horn. Today the lighthouse is unmanned and fully automated – but it still booms loud haunting warnings across the point when there is fog or visibility is poor.

We had parked at the lighthouse and walked down the coastal path to *Polpero Café*. As England's *Most Southerly Café*, it sits in an astonishing position poised on the edge of the clifftop with sumptuous views in every direction. From the terrace of the café, choughs may be seen – and seals can often be espied in the roiling sea below; sometimes dolphins – and even occasionally basking shark or whale. The café is invariably lively. Visitors come from all over the world for the vistas, wildlife, and the café's viands – especially the famous fish pie.

Despite the bustle we had struck lucky. We had seats at our favourite table—right on the edge of the terrace—with nothing but glittering sea before us. We ordered fish pies and, after we had eaten, we sat gazing out to sea with the rubicund sun steadily sliding towards the horizon amongst the cinnabar and crimson of a glorious sunset. There was a breeze off the sea and I noticed Rinpoche adjusting the scarf wrapped elegantly around his neck. It was a particularly pleasing colour – deep-emerald green with white polka dots. *"That's a lovely scarf, Rinpoche"* I commented. *"Where did you buy it?"*

"Thank you—but I didn't buy it—not as a scarf, at least."

"There's a story behind it?"

"Almost always…" Rinpoche chuckled. *"About a decade ago, I bought an 'aviators' scarf' from the J. Peterman catalogue. It was Prussian blue with cream polka dots. It looked splendid – but, basically, it was simply a frayed length of cloth sewn into a tube. Unfortunately, I left it briefly unattended on an æroplane. It vanished. Someone obviously thought they required it more than I did"* he smiled. *"I decided I would buy a replacement – but J. Peterman had run out of them and hadn't yet put them back into production. At that point, it occurred to me that—for what it was—the scarf was not cheap. It then occurred to me that all I needed to do was buy a length of polka dot fabric and sew it into a tube. That provided me with the same scarf for less than a tenth of the price. So now, I have a dozen of them – each in a different colour to match different coats and jackets. They're better than the purloined original because I made them four times wider and thrice as long. When folded four times, air pockets are created. This makes them as warm as woollen scarves – but without the itchiness."*

"Now, there's no particular reason why anyone couldn't invent a scarf – but people don't do that" I commented.

"Quite so" Rinpoche chuckled *"but it doesn't take any massive intellect. The idea simply has to occur. People seem largely unaware however, that they are free to invent."*

Twenty: Sarvagjna – the eccentric monocular seamstress

"It doesn't often occur to you though – that you can do that" added Khandro Déchen. *"Everyone's free to do so – as Sarvagjna was free to do with her many curious assemblages of clothing."*

I must have adopted a questioning expression as Khandro Déchen grinned *"Mahasiddha Sarvagjna – the eccentric monocular seamstress."*

"Hers is not a lengthy hagiography" Rinpoche continued *"so I could probably recount it whilst we finish this jeroboam of Chablis and wait for the accounting."*

As we all nodded eagerly, Rinpoche began. *"Sarvagjna didn't have an easy start in life. She was born with a deformity: she had but one eye, on the left side of her face. Where her other eye should have been – there was no trace even of an eye-socket…"*

Born into a Shudra family, she was orphaned at the age of five and had to make her own way in life as a beggar. Sarvagjna lived as a beggar until she was an adolescent. Up to that age she learned to enjoy life in whatever way she could. Sarvagjna had no friends. She was shunned by other beggars – and therefore became accustomed to solitude. She found shelter wherever she could – and found solace in the daily wonders of nature. There were always animals, birds, flowers, and trees at which to marvel – so, at the age of nine she began to roam. At first, she did not travel far from her place of birth in Andhra Pradesh – but by the age of eleven she was wandering throughout India, simply to see whatever she could see.

She had no specific intention in her wanderings other than to survive and enjoy her survival as best she could. She saw many different creatures – all of which gave her joy to witness, even when they were dangerous. In Andhra Pradesh her heart was gladdened by the Nelumbo water lilies and the lively blackbuck antelopes. She sat and watched them for days whilst gathering whatever she could find to eat from begging in local villages.

In Arunachal Pradesh she gazed upon sedate Gayal cows and the marvellous great hornbills. Assam entranced her with its single-horned rhinoceri, the white-winged wood ducks and abundant orchids. In Bihar there were majestic Gaur bison and delicate house sparrows twittering in the white orchid trees. In the more remote areas Sarvagjna learned to forage for food – and became quite adept at sustaining herself on what she could find in the way of wild fruits and vegetables. She preferred this to begging, as it left her free to explore the natural world. She far preferred the wilderness to the towns and villages, as there was no one to gawk at her – and remind her that she was a freak. On her own she was simply a girl – simply an adventurer.

In Jharkhand, Karnataka and Kerala, she found lotus flowers – and was thrilled to see elephants. She enjoyed the trumpeting sounds they made. Free from the vagaries and humiliation of begging, Sarvagjna became highly resourceful and enjoyed the freedom her independence gave her. Chhattisgarh was replete with wild water buffalos – as was Goa where there were also plentiful Gaur buffaloes and black-crested bulbul birds.

The wonderful variety of the natural world appeared to Sarvagjna as a magnificent treasury – and she occasionally wondered why no one else seemed to venture far from the beaten track. In Gujarat she saw the greater flamingos amongst the Golgotha marigolds – and lions, at a distance. She remained hidden in order to watch them, which involved remaining motionless. It also involved ingenuities such as rubbing her body with the sap of shrubs in order to hide her human scent. There was always a *way* to survive in the wilds. She found that she was able to learn it all from first principles – and by observing how the animals themselves survived.

In Himachal Pradesh she witnessed tragopan birds and snow leopards. She found the snow leopards utterly beautiful when she espied them through the high-altitude rhododendron trees and deodars. In Meghalaya there were clouded leopards.

In Jammu and Kashmir she saw black-necked cranes and stags. She loved to watch the stags as they ran through the hills or flitted amongst the Himalayan horse-chestnut trees.

In Maharashtra there were Puducherry squirrels, giant squirrels, and yellow-footed green pigeons. There were mangoes to eat and all manner of other delicious fruits. In Mizoram there were Hoolock gibbons and in Tripura there were langur monkeys. In Sikkim, red pandas and blood pheasants made their homes amongst the rhododendrons and in Rajasthan she delighted in the great Indian bustards. Tamil Nadu had its emerald doves and Uttar Pradesh its Sarus cranes and white-breasted kingfishers.

"This is quite a catalogue of wildlife!" I hooted. Listening to the hagiography I'd been transported to those eastern lands with visions before me of the incredible animal beings Sarvagjna encountered. I was brought back however—to the Lizard—by Peter, the café proprietor asking *"Would you mind terribly, making room for new diners arriving? I hate to move you on… but…"* It was clearly time to leave. *"Certainly"* replied Rinpoche. *"I'm so sorry, we were forgetting the time – in story-telling."* Peter smiled – and looked relieved that we hadn't taken his request amiss.

"Let's continue the hagiography down in the cove" Khandro Dechen suggested. We paid the bill and traversed the coastal path back to the car. After a short drive to the Kynance National Trust parking place, we wended our way through the rounded boulders and grassy hillocks of the path down to the shore. Kynance Cove is famous for its white sand and turquoise sea – but, in particular, for its remarkable rock stacks, islands, and caves. These were formed when the red and green serpentine of the Lizard was broken into blocks and invaded by granite and basalt. The softer rocks were eroded by the sea leaving the stacks which are the cove's dramatic defining feature. The four largest stacks have interesting names: *The Bishop, Gull Rock, Asparagus Island,* and *Steeple Rock.* If you're there around half tide as we were, a strange snorting can be heard.

It comes from *The Devil's Bellows*, a blowhole on *Asparagus Island* which was caused by the sea tunnelling along a fault. There's a second blowhole too which is amusingly called *The Post Office* – because there is apparently sufficient suction to draw a letter into it. We've never tried.

Kynance is undoubtedly one of the most beautiful coves in Cornwall – and, as a result, it is one of the most painted and photographed. It is also one of the most frequently visited – particularly after its magnificence was featured in an episode of the historic drama series 'Poldark'. On summer days it is unpleasantly busy, which is why we much prefer visiting in the late evening – after the holidaymaking hordes have headed home for the night. This evening we had the cove to ourselves. We were able to silently appreciate the shapes of the extraordinary rock formations – otherworldly in the twilight. It was a magical place – an enchanted time at the margins of sea and shore, at the margins of day and night. As we settled to sit at the tide's edge, perched on rocks, damp with sea spray, the smell of kelp and the evening cries of gulls filled the senses. *"So..."* Rinpoche announced *"to return to the story..."*

Sarvagjna's life continued in this wandering style, crisscrossing the wilds of India, until she was sixteen years old. On leaving the eaves of a wood she saw a sight she had never previously witnessed. She saw Mahasiddha Shyama—the cloud-weaver—sitting on a hillside in Jammu. Usually, Sarvagjna would have avoided human beings – but she found herself curious. Shyama was not like other human beings, inasmuch as she simply sat staring into the sky. Shyama was motionless. Sarvagjna sat and observed her from a distance – also motionless. Many hours passed and neither person moved. Finally, Sarvagjna was unable to contain her curiosity and began to move closer to Shyama. Once she came close enough, she asked *"Who are you?"*

Shyama gazed at her in a kindly manner *"I am Shyama—the cloud-weaver—and I have been waiting for you. I have been waiting for some years."*

"How do you know who I am?"

"That is not a mystery" replied Shyama. *"You are a young lady who wanders through the lands. You are not lost, as I was once lost – because you are not trying to find your home, as I was once trying to find my home. You are like me however – and like me, when I was young. You need a teacher – as I needed a teacher when I was young."*

"It's true… what you say is true." Sarvagjna paused. *"I do roam through many lands. I am not lost – and I am not trying to find my way home. I have no home. I wish to have no home. As to needing a teacher however, I already know all I need to know to survive in the wilds – what else is there to know?"*

"I had no idea that I needed a teacher…" Shyama smiled *"…many years ago when my teacher found me. I was lost in the wilds – but one evening Mahasiddha Ishani— the nondual wandering woman—appeared and said 'You are lost, young lady.' I replied 'No, I know where I am. I am here by the river. I just don't know where my home is any more.' Mahasiddha Ishani then said 'I may not be able to show you the way to go home – but I can give you guidance.' I found that interesting and asked 'What kind of guidance can you give me? Is it like the shimmering water or the wings of a butterfly?' to which Mahasiddha Ishani replied 'It is like both – and beyond both. It is like lightning in the night sky and rainbows in dark water.' You look like a young lady who might find that interesting."*

Sarvagjna felt a little uneasy – because no one had spoken to her for years and it was not immediately easy to fall into conversation. *"Yes…"* she replied *"… it is interesting… everything in the wilds of nature interests me – but… what is there to teach on such things. Are they not simply there and simply to be seen and heard?"*

"Yes" smiled Shyama. *"I cannot teach you anything more than you have seen and heard – because you have seen and heard far more than I have ever seen and heard. I have not seen the many different lands that you have seen. I have not seen the many animals, birds, flowers, and trees that you have seen – but I know their nature and I know the nature of Mind, which is the mirror in which they manifest.*

"I also know the same of taste, fragrance, touch, and ideation. I know the nature of everything that manifests in the mirror of the sense fields – because Mahasiddha Ishani—the nondual wandering woman—gave me teachings on the means whereby a person could discover such knowledge."

Rinpoche paused as a seagull alighted on the rocks in front of us, stridently announcing its arrival, and I asked *"Can you say more about what 'mirror of the sense fields' means, Rinpoche?"*

"Not much more than what exists within those words" Rinpoche replied. *"Dzogchen men-ngag-dé has that quality. As Künzang Dorje Rinpoche explained"* Rinpoche then rendered the explanation in Tibetan syntax *"… Men-ngag 'no word' meaning – so only words which practice describing. No more words coming – or cannot be Dzogchen men-ngag-dé calling.' The language is experiential – so, unpacking it is not possible in conventional prose."*

Khandro Déchen leaned forward towards me pulling her coat over her legs. *"The mirrors of the sense fields are the way in which what you sense reflects the nondual nature of Mind."* PAUSE *"Giving that as an explanation however, wouldn't explain anything to someone who didn't have that experience"* she smiled.

"It would be semantic semolina." Rinpoche laughed. *"So, Sarvagjna—by now—had lost her sense of unease. Her curiosity had become stirred, as it was stirred on seeing snow leopards or other rare creatures…"*

Sarvagjna wanted to ask *'What is this knowledge?'* but felt wary of asking anything that might lead in a direction she might not wish to take. She had learned how to survive and an important aspect of survival was avoiding people. She had learned to distrust people.

"You have curiosity" smiled Shyama.

"Yes – but… how do you know that?"

"That is simple to tell. You sat and watched me for hours. Then you approached me and asked who I might be. Now you are curious as to what this knowledge is of which I speak. Is that not true?"

Sarvagjna smiled for the first time in their exchange and agreed that what Shyama had said was true.

"But I am also curious… I am curious as to why you wear an upper garment as a lower garment – and a lower garment as an upper garment?"

"That is simple to answer" laughed Sarvagjna. *"The upper garment I found in a midden is of stouter material than the lower garment I found – and therefore protects me better."*

"And…" pondered Shyama *"how did these vestments come to be as they are… they seem to be sewn together in a manner I have never seen before?"*

"That is also simple to answer. Needles I found—and thread I made from rags—and from these I keep myself clothed. Whenever my clothes wear thin or tear, I add pieces of whatever I find. That is why—in this cold climate—I have an array of sleeves that form a cloak to keep me warm. The sleeves have air within them – and no cold can penetrate them."

"A ha! Just like your scarf, Rinpoche!" I interrupted.

Rinpoche smiled and nodded *"Chhi'mèd Rig'dzin Rinpoche is a far more impressive exponent of that Art – particularly in the arena of mix-and-match. He manages to conjure the segue between Mahatma Gandhi and Jimi Hendrix—Beau Brummel and Attila the Hun—Arnold Schwarzenegger and Quentin Crisp. The empty mirror of Chhi'mèd Rig'dzin Rinpoche who displayed them – being Guru Rinpoche."*

"We'll show you some photographs when we're next at Drala Jong" Khandro Déchen added and Rinpoche continued with the hagiography.

Shyama looked at Sarvagjna *"You are a resourceful young lady. That is a valuable prerequisite for one who follows a religious calling. What is your name?"*

"I was named Sarvagjna¹ – but no one has used that name for many years and I have no real need of a name… or to follow a religious calling. It is not possible to become a nun if you have a deformity such as mine."

"What is this deformity of which you speak?"

Sarvagjna was perplexed by this question *"Can you not see that I am monocular?"*

"Yes – but I do not see that as a deformity. The only real deformity is the deformity of duality."

"That may be" Sarvagjna replied *"but in the world of people—which I have rejected—my deformity is not regarded in such a light. That is why I have lived in the wilds since I was a young girl. I have learned to live as animals live in order to survive. I have learned to avoid the ridicule of ordinary people who see me as a freak."*

"Being a Buddhist yogini, I also live in the wilds—most of the time—and I avoid most ordinary people, who I see as freaks of dualistic derangement. The same could be true for you."

"Maybe – but you have two eyes and I have one, so it is easy for you to speak as you do."

"You are not easy to persuade – and… that is a good quality in a yogini. However, you must be curious as to what else exists other than the wilds of nature and the many creatures it contains?"

Sarvagjna thought about this for some moments and replied *"Yes… I am curious about that – and, I am curious about what it is that is like the shimmering water, the wings of a butterfly, lightning in the night sky, and rainbows in dark water – but beyond them all. Is this the knowledge that yoginis have?"*

---

[1] The name Sarvagjna is actually a male name, meaning 'One who knows everything'. In Hindu numerology, those with the name Sarvagjna have the Namank *(destiny number)* 'four', which pertains to altering life in a positive manner.

"It is knowledge that you could have—if you would accept the teachings I have to offer—but that is up to you. All I have to say is that this is the moment to decide. If you do not take this opportunity now – you may never find me again and the chance will be lost. There must have been many times when you took an opportunity to see some rare creatures – knowing that such opportunities seldom present themselves. This is one such opportunity."

"Then I will take it" Sarvagjna replied and sat down next to Shyama.

Sarvagjna spent a month with Shyama learning the nature of practice and receiving teachings on the nature of Mind.

"You must learn" advised Shyama *"to be as comfortable in the villages and towns as you are in the wilds – because there is no fundamental difference. Both the wilds—and the places human beings have domesticated—are part of the realm of phenomena. You must learn also, that the vestments of society and the vestments of your ingeniousness – are of the same fundamental character. When you realise the nature of Mind – you will be accepted as a woman who knows the nature of Mind: a yogini. When you are accepted as such you will be able to make whatever clothes suit the individual – and, to teach through the creation of clothing which allows the wearer to experience the world as a unique juncture. Your experience of the wilds—and your new association with the habitations of human beings—will benefit all who are open to learning what an eccentric seamstress has to teach, concerning how the human condition is the camouflage of the nondual state."*

Sarvagjna absorbed this teaching and practised as she had been instructed. She met Shyama a year later in the same place she had first met her. Sarvagjna had gained a high level of realisation and thus was ready to receive her final instructions from Shyama.

"This will be the last time we meet in this life Sarvagjna, so listen carefully to my final instruction:"

Take all situations as the wilderness.
Take all clothing as the natural appearance of the creatures who inhabit the wilderness.
See the civilisation of the villages and towns to be no different from the undomesticated realms of nature.
Manifest as the unconstrained animal who is at home wherever she finds herself, and in whatever company she finds herself.
When you have realised the nondual state – be of benefit to all who are open to learning what an eccentric seamstress knows of the human condition as the camouflage of the nondual state.

Within a year Sarvagjna realised the nondual state and became known as Mahasiddha Sarvagjna – the eccentric monocular seamstress. She travelled widely before arriving in Sindh where she established an 'occasional home' in Aror—near Rho-hri—on the outskirts of the village. She was honoured in Aror as a holy woman and whenever she returned there from her travels local people came to receive her blessings. Certain siddhas sought her out, requesting raiment made to her design – and, when she agreed to a request, she made clothes for them which fitted their being, as creatures of the natural state.

As Rinpoche concluded the hagiography in the dwindling purple light, I mused *"Sarvagjna clearly has many of the same qualities that we've discussed before with Minapa and Goraksha – in terms of spending a lot of time in solitude. So, presumably—as she's also so skilled and at home in the natural world—she's like them in being poised for practice. With Sarvagjna however, there's also this sense of her venturing off the beaten track, of inhabiting the margins. It's making me wonder if the margins are a particularly fecund place for practice?"*

"Yes, indeed" replied Khandro Déchen. *"The margins are usually where the rulebook runs out – in terms of how to be and what to do. The margins are dawn and dusk. They're the margins of the seashore which are alternately seabed and shoreland. Both exist in alternation."*

"Then of course" added Rinpoche *"there are the margins of society in which the mores are unclear – where one might ask 'What is this situation? Is it a situation where people are critical of each other – or is it not? How do I know what is the right thing to say here?' There's a sense of the clandestine."* PAUSE *"On the other hand, I remember being in Harlem, New York, with two New Yorker students. We were going to a concert called 'Juke Joint and Gospel' which was to showcase the crossover between Blues and Gospel music. Well… the two students were a little lost and couldn't find the place. I kept suggesting we ask someone – but they were highly reticent about that. I suggested periodically as it became increasingly evident that we might never find the place – but each time they declined to ask a local. In the end I approached a local Black American gentleman and enquired. He smiled and replied 'Sure Homes – you just take left down on the next block. Enjoy the show.' I thanked him and returned to our students. I gave them the directions I'd been given and asked 'What d'you think he meant when he called me 'Homes'? Was it Holmes – as in Sherlock Holmes?' They burst out laughing and told me he was making a joke, because 'Homes' was short for 'home boy' – which was to say 'one of us'. Joke or not – I took that very kindly. They were nervous about approaching Harlem locals in case it caused 'some sort of problem'. They were very far from racist – just highly nervous about causing offense… whereas I had no sense at all that a genuine enquiry might cause offense. It was probably in my favour that I was an Englishman who appeared to have stepped out of the 1950s."*

"To return to being marginalised and living in the margins – if you don't give the statutory answers in a particular group" continued Khandro Déchen *"you're aware that you've become marginalised. It's an uneasy place, where it's not clear which way it might go. As a practitioner it's a matter of being at home there, at home in the uncertainty – of being comfortable with being uncomfortable. Of being comfortable with not knowing. Of being comfortable in being able to move from one domain to another – and adapt accordingly, recognising there are different rules in operation. It's being able to work with whatever the prevalent rules or mores happen to be – because they're all empty. The rules and mores are all temporary. They're all impermanent, provisional, fleeting, or momentary… even though the moment may be a month or a millennium."*

"So, in terms of what Sarvagjna does" I asked "she's simply learning how animals are – and what the rules are in their domains?"

"Yes – she learns how to be unobtrusive, how to avoid being eaten" replied Khandro Déchen. "She's aware that you don't absolutely have to be eaten – as long as you function in understandable ways within whichever particular realm it happens to be."

"She's so resourceful too" commented Ja'gyür. "Shyama says that's a valuable criterion for a religious calling. I can see that patience or a willingness to be in solitude is useful – but what is it about resourcefulness that makes you primed for practice?"

"… I'd—almost—rather say the reverse" replied Rinpoche with uncharacteristic caution. "It's practice which makes you resourceful. Sarvagjna has already entered the sphere of practice without knowing it – simply through learning to be still and silent. Being authentically resourceful is being free to be able to influence what is there in terms of survival, with pragmatism. For example: if you're freezing to death – and all you have is a carpet, it could occur to you that there are better ways to deal with the cold than merely rolling yourself up in the carpet. If you're resourceful – you're going to make clothing out of the carpet. You're going to tease some thread from the ends of the carpet in order to stitch it together so you can wear it."

"If you're not resourceful however" added Khandro Déchen "you'll just see it as something on the floor that's not going to keep you warm. So, resourcefulness is being able to see that things aren't necessarily limited to the function they're deemed to have according to common conceptions."

"So, you can be free to invent – as you said back at the café" I commented. "You're saying that being inventive is another quality of a practitioner?"

"Yes. Invention is crucial. Being able to invent comes out of being resourceful. Naljorpa Rangdröl was brilliant in that way. If you look at the gÇod damaru case he made for me – it's a brilliant combination of unlikely elements. It's partially sewing – but there are brass hinges which are bolted in place.

Twenty: Sarvagjna – the eccentric monocular seamstress

"He combined elements you wouldn't normally ever see together – because a tailor wouldn't ever think of employing such unlikely materials. He couldn't find anything that worked for the strap, so he plaited it from lengths of cord-binding. He could do that because he approached it all from first principles. He wasn't a tailor, milliner, cordwainer, or a bagmaker, so he had to work it out. When you're presented with having to originate something—where you don't have expertise—then you have to be creative." Rinpoche laughed *"It doesn't always work out well of course. I made a throne once…"* he laughed *"… but because I'm not a carpenter—let alone a joiner or cabinet maker—I built it like a battleship. It was made of* two-by-four[2] *and clad with plywood. You'd have had to take a sledgehammer to it to break it. I didn't know how to create carpentry joints, so I fixed it together with steel angle brackets. It was unbelievably strong – but it was a monster to move around. It worked – but it wasn't portable"* he grinned. *"It's probably still sitting at Spirit Horse Camp*[3] *– unless it's rotted."*

"In terms of being a useful quality for a practitioner" I queried *"could you say that an inventive mind is, by definition, less restricted by conditioning? It's able to move outside of boxes more easily?"*

"Possibly…" Rinpoche answered *"but I'd say there are two kinds of inventive minds. There's the inventive mind which turns towards fiscal profit… and the inventive mind which is simply inventive because of the natural joy of invention. They both require openness. Where you have pure inventiveness however—where you simply have random ideas arising in response to reality—that is more perfectly open-ended. "Where someone is looking to make a million from what people are going to buy – that is far more limited. Then there's looking at how to kill the largest number of people in the shortest period of time."*

"That's definitely limited" laughed Khandro Déchen.

---

[2] This refers to wood of the dimensions 2 inches by 4 inches – a standard in the building trade.
[3] Spirit Horse Camp—established by Shivam O'Brien and Erika Indra—is described as *'a summer off-grid retreat centre, consisting of a village of Celtic roundhouses and yurts, waterfalls, sacred fires and temples, cradled in 200 acres of Welsh forest.'* Ngak'chang Rinpoche and Khandro Déchen gave 10-day retreats there during the 1990s.

"It's all inventive – but, highly trammelled invention." Rinpoche looked out to sea.

"Whereas... you could look at Leonardo da Vinci" Khandro Déchen suggested "and see what he invented. He was prolific. He turned his mind to everything, even helicopters. He simply kept on having ideas and making drawings. Imagine how it might be if you allowed such open-ended inventiveness to manifest." PAUSE "When we were still going to Montana, Rinpoche invented several pieces of horse tack. He made a conversion strap to turn a side-pull bosal[4] into a halter-bridle, because—although halter-bridles were available—there was no bit-less version. He added Mexican-style leaf-flaps to the end of his reins, and designed a saddle-mounted scabbard for his 15-inch Bowie knife."

"That was quite a time for invention" Rinpoche continued. "It was probably a reaction to living for extended periods around horses – and riding every day."

It was becoming quite dark by this point. It was not so easy to see our way as we started the climb from the cove back to the car. I was picking my way carefully across the rocks, aware of the limitations of my night vision and thinking about 'the human condition as the camouflage of the natural state'. I put this to Rinpoche and added "It's obviously not that the nondual state is trying to camouflage itself – is it?" and Rinpoche answered from ahead.

"No" Rinpoche chuckled "it's Shyama's poetic style. She's simply using words that are in her own experience. It comes from the way in which Sarvagjna succeeds in watching dangerous animals by using camouflage. So, the nondual state is camouflaged by the dualistic state."

"This is linked to the teaching that 'Buddhas see sentient beings as Buddhas whilst sentient beings see Buddhas as sentient beings'. That is important" Khandro Déchen added. "So, what people see is the camouflage."

---

[4] A bitless bridle or hackamore which employs pressure on the horse's nose via a rawhide strap.

"It's not that nondual beings wear *camouflage"* Rinpoche explained. *"It's that dualised beings project the illusion of camouflage onto them. It's similar to the way in which we project onto Rock stars or film stars. Most people can only understand the world through their own preconceptions."*

"So—for example—whatever you say" Rinpoche continued *"someone without understanding is going to respond 'Oh – 'that' is like 'one of those', isn't it?' The rôle of the teacher then, is to say 'No, it's not like 'that'. It's not like 'this' either. Nor is it like 'anything else' in any 'other category'. It's not like anything you can imagine – as long as your imagination is based on pre-existing formulations."* PAUSE *"Basically, one needs to cease in terms of generating similes – because they're all going to be erroneous to some degree."*

"So we have to give that up, let go of it completely" I replied *"because that's how we are with everything: 'Oh, it's one of those.' Sometimes if we're more open we'll say 'Oh, it's one of those but it's a bit different.' But no, it's not even one of those but a bit different. It's just not 'one of anything'. It's something else."*

As we reached the car, I watched Rinpoche take off his ankle-length Levi coat, emerald green polka dot scarf, and Montana Crease hat. He stowed them carefully in the boot. I thought of Sarvagjna making clothes for people which 'fitted their being, as creatures of the natural state' and asked *"Can you say more about what kind of clothes they are – that 'fit' being, in terms of a person?"*

"That concerns what naturally arises from the authentic appreciation of a genuine individual. Clothes would fit one's being because they are not being manipulated to make a statement. By that, I mean a statement which communicates something to others in terms of status, prestige, distinction, celebrity, or whatever. One's not wearing something because it's fashionable. One's not wearing something to impress an audience of onlookers. If you manipulate in that way – then the clothes don't fit your being."

"It might fit somebody else better" grinned Khandro Déchen. "The most charming example of this was when Mike in the Windsor Fruit and Vegetable shop in Penarth said to Rinpoche 'Oh, Doc[5], I've found one of your buttons. I knew it was yours, because it had 'Christian Dior' on it.' Rinpoche was amused and replied 'It's not Christian Dior – the **CD** stands for Civil Defence. It was a dark blue British paramilitary coat" added Rinpoche "which my father used to wear when he belonged to the Civil Defence after WWII. Mike had a hearty laugh about that."

"So" Khandro Déchen concluded "clothes which don't fit your being, are clothes you wear which are not derived from authentic appreciation. They might not even fit the fashion designer's being. As long as you're wearing whatever-it-is because it's someone else's concept—which you've accepted under the false pretence that it suits everyone who is 'in fashion'— rather than something you authentically like yourself… it's never going to be natural."

With that Rinpoche closed the boot. Time to head back to Pink Cottage for practice and a good night's sleep.

---

[5] Ngak'chang Rinpoche is known as 'Doc' by those who are not Buddhist. The name is based on the fact that he has a doctorate. Ngak'chang Rinpoche's monothematic memoirs of his life in the field of the Arts—called 'an odd boy'—were written under the name 'Doc Togden'. The name on his passport is Dr Chögyam Togden.

Twenty-one: Manibhadra – the perfect housewife

Manibhadra *(ma ni bha dra /* མ་ནི་བྷ་ད་ *) /* Khyim'dzin Kündzogma *(khyim 'dzin kun rDzogs ma /* ཁྱིམ་འཛིན་ཀུན་རྫོགས་མ་ *)*
Disciple of: Kukkuraja and Niguma
Teacher of: Naropa
Varna by birth: Kshatriya

Frogs' Leap, Penarth, South Wales.

Ja'gyür and I had been invited to dinner with Ngak'chang Rinpoche and Khandro Déchen at their home in Penarth. We had partaken of *Land Chestnut Flanquette*[1] and prior to retiring to the drawing room to continue the conviviality there were some household duties to perform. The kitchen beckoned as the domestic accoutrements—pots, pans, baking trays, crockery, and cutlery—needed washing, drying, and stowing. The kitchen has a Victorian tiled floor, reclaimed pitch-pine cupboards, and a beautiful black granite counter quarried in Kafiristan[2] which flickers with flecks of red and green. There's a deep ceramic Belfast sink – but it is never seen filled with unwashed dishes. Rinpoche and Khandro Déchen always clear up immediately after dining. Plates and cutlery are washed; pans are scoured; ingredients and implements tidied away; and all surfaces wiped down. Rinpoche donned his ankle-length Levi 501 Serge de Nîmes apron and took his usual place at the sink. The Serge de Nîmes apron is his own design and made from the remaining good pieces of five pairs of his worn-out Levi's.

When I commented on the length of the apron, Rinpoche replied *"The problem with almost all aprons is that they seem to have been designed prior to the 1960s – in terms of the length of the average lady's skirt or dress. This is peculiar because it would assume that ladies were not discommoded by food or water spillage on their stockings."*

---

[1] A comical name once used for this dish – which has endured for reasons entirely obscure. *Flanquette* is a sexual position.
[2] Kafiristan is an historical region that covered present-day Nuristan province in Afghanistan. It is bounded by the Hindukush on the north, the Chitral of Pakistan to the east, the Kunar Valley in the south, and the Alishang river in the west. Kafiristan took its name from the enduring kafir (non-Muslim) Nuristani inhabitants who were once Buddhist.

"It's certainly a handsome addition to your sartorial look-of-the-day" I smiled. Rinpoche was wearing top-to-toe Levi's with an expansive rüchèd Levi tie made from a worn-out Levi shirt.

"Well" Rinpoche replied with glee "it's Art – and I see the Culinary Art as covering the entire process from perusing recipes and purchasing ingredients, to food preparation, thence dining and dealing with the aftermath. It is all Art – and when several people are in a kitchen it becomes ballet, if you want to avoid breakages."

Rinpoche worked at weekends—between the ages of 16 and 18—in the Army kitchens in Aldershot. He still employs washing up methods upon which the Army insisted: cleaning under violently-hot running water. Sink plugs were prohibited.

"Working for the Army was valuable in various ways. The Army was a good and fair employer and I was able to converse with soldiers as human beings. This meant that I was spared the standard hippie prejudice against soldiers. I realised they were simply people who wanted a better life than was offered by factory work. They were decent fellows – and took my part against the rather uncivil civilian foreman."

"The civilian foreman didn't like you?"

"No" Rinpoche laughed. "He thought I was a criminal pervert – a drug-ingesting, libidinous, degenerate debauchee."

"Why?" I laughed.

"Because I had long hair. Anyone with long hair at that time was considered a depraved, dissolute, miscreant reprobate – by some people at least. He threatened to have me searched for drugs on an almost weekly basis. I'd tell him he was more than welcome to search me hourly if he liked – and that rankled with him. The soldiers told him 'Leave him alone, you fat bald-headed, loofah-nosed old bugger – John's a good lad.' They called me 'John' after John Lennon because I wore those round National Health spectacles, as John Lennon used to wear."

"Like the glasses you wear now?"

"No – they had rims. When I left school, and went to Art School, I discovered the older rimless type in antique shops. They were so cheap that I bought a few dozen of them and have been wearing them ever since. I like them because they make no fashion statement – they're merely lenses which connect at the nose and wrap round the ears. They're neither in fashion nor out of it."

"Can I just go back to 'loofah-nosed' – what d'you think they meant by that?"

"Maybe it's Aldershot, or Home Counties slang for rhinophyma[3]. That comes from Greek: 'rhis' meaning nose – and 'phyma': for skin tumour. And, I must say, his nose did resemble a loofah[4]."

Rinpoche put on his Marigold gloves to begin the process of washing up – and this completed his professional appearance as the *master of abstergement*[5]. Not for the first time—whilst watching Rinpoche in aproned action in the kitchen—I thought of Mahasiddha Manibhadra, the perfect housewife. It occurred to me that although I had known for some years that Rinpoche was the incarnation of Manibhadra, I didn't actually know much more about her. *"Do you have any memories of being Manibhadra"* I asked Rinpoche *"or how you discovered that you were?"*

He shook his head as he rinsed the silver knives and forks under the hot tap. *"Kyabjé Düd'jom Rinpoche Jig'drèl Yeshé Dorje told me – but I have no memory of it. Sadly, nothing remains accessible."* Rinpoche paused. *"The memory loss is due to Aro Yeshé having died in an avalanche. Several thousand tons of ice and snow tend to create discontinuity. If, when you die, there is no opportunity to be aware of the elemental dissolutions and the bardos – you become scrambled."* He smiled *"…like eggs, perhaps."*

---

[3] A disfiguring nasal deformity due to the proliferation of sebaceous glands and underlying connective tissue.
[4] A loofah is the fruit of the species Luffa ægyptiaca and Luffa acutangulais, of the tropical / subtropical gourd family *Cucurbitaceae*. When the fruit is fully ripened, it is highly fibrous and serves as a scrubbing sponge in bathrooms.
[5] Rinpoche employed the words: absterging, washing up, scrubbing, cleaning, wiping, cleansing, rinsing, mopping, or sluicing down.

Khandro Déchen paused in her putting away of a huge copper pan. *"You remember the avalanche though, don't you?"*

Rinpoche nodded *"In a manner of speaking."*

"What do you remember of it?" I asked.

"Being cold" he laughed. *"The memory came to me when I was watching footage of an avalanche on television with the family when I was a child. I became rather upset – but had no idea why. I didn't display my distress to my parents – but I felt frightened and sat there 'frozen', as it were."* Rinpoche was quiet for some moments. He then looked up from the washing up and grinned *"Although I can't remember anything of being Manibhadra, we do have her hagiography in the collection from Jomo Pema 'ö-Zér's gTérma of the Eighty-four Mahasiddhas. I could recount it if you like."*

We said that we'd like that very much. So, washing up completed, Rinpoche removed his apron and gloves and we settled in the drawing room – ready to listen and become rapt.

"Manibhadra was born in Kamarupa[6]" Rinpoche began. *"She was the daughter of a wealthy merchant and a marriage had been arranged with the son of an equally wealthy family…"*

Being prosperous, the family supported all religious mendicants who called at their home – and on one occasion they were visited by Mahasiddha Kukkuraja, the caninophile. Manibhadra welcomed Kukkuraja into the house and arranged for their servants to present him with a fine meal. Manibhadra had grown to an age where she had developed a keen sense of curiosity and so she sat with Kukkuraja as he ate.

---

[6] Kamarupa was the first historical kingdom in Assam, existing from 350 to 1140CE. It was ruled by three dynasties from their capitals in present-day Guwahati and Tezpur. It covered the entire Brahmaputra river valley, North Bengal, and parts of Bangladesh. Although the historical kingdom had disappeared by the 12th century to be replaced by smaller political entities, Kamarupa persists as a gestalt, as both ancient and mediæval chroniclers continued to call this region Kamarupa. The name survives in 'Kamrup', a present-day district in Assam.

When he had finished eating, Manibhadra asked *"You are obviously young, handsome, and intelligent – so you could easily become as rich as my father, so why do you live by begging?"*

"You ask me this question…" Kukkuraja laughed *"because you know nothing of the nature of wealth."*

"That is interesting" commented Manibhadra. *"What is the nature of this wealth, of which you say I know nothing?"*

"Its nature is that anyone may have it."

"If anyone could have it…" laughed Manibhadra *"why is it that they do not avail themselves of it?"*

"Because they see wealth such as yours, as the real wealth – and care nothing for the wealth which is primordially theirs."

"Ah… I see…" smiled Manibhadra *"you speak of religion. I have no great interest in religion."*

"That does not surprise me" laughed Kukkuraja.

"Do you think I am so foolish, then – that I would not understand?" asked Manibhadra – but not with disrespectful snappishness.

"Not at all. A fool would not ask me such questions. No… I said that it did not surprise me, for other reasons entirely. Institutional religion, you see, is not so very interesting. Mainly it is a way of passing time – or of trying to secure a better rebirth. Many are foolish enough to hedge their bets – claiming that they earnestly wish to practise but that they are ill-prepared for it in this life. So what they do, is to accumulate merit so that they can be practitioners in their following lives."

"Is this of no value then?"

"It is of some value, yes – but not of great value."

"But is it not better than unkindness or cruelty to others?"

"Yah, it is better than that – but there is nothing more to be said in its favour. Those who adhere to poverty are little better."

"But is not poverty something that was enjoined upon monks by Shakyamuni Buddha?"

"Certainly – and if one practises as Shakyamuni Buddha taught, I have no fault to find. Most of these ascetics however, are merely addicted to asceticism – and as vain as peacocks on that basis."

"But are you not an ascetic?"

"No… but neither am I a hedonist. I am not addicted to either extreme. If it were of benefit to beings for me to be conventionally wealthy, I would gather wealth. If it were of benefit to beings for me to be conventionally austere, I would practise austerities. As it is, I simply live as I live – without concern either for possessions or possessionlessness. If great wealth comes my way, I accept it. If it is required elsewhere, I give it away."

On hearing this Manibhadra gained a sense of curiosity that she had not experienced before. "Please, venerable sir – will you tell me then about the nature of real wealth."

"That, young lady, will have to wait 'til tomorrow – as I have visits to make in this town. If you would like to hear of the nature of real wealth, I shall be happy to tell you all you need to know – but before I return, I would like you to notice what can be seen with your eyes and heard with your ears. I would like you to pay attention to all your senses and see what can be found interesting – especially those things to which you would usually not pay too much attention."

Manibhadra assured Kukkuraja that she would follow his suggestions – and bade him farewell, looking forward to their further discussions. After he left, Manibhadra noticed that her vision and hearing were not what they were before. It was not that she saw anything or heard anything utterly marvellous – but she became astonishingly conscious of the fact that she continually saw and heard the world.

Then she discovered that she continually touched the world, that there were always fragrances in the air, and that food and drink were somehow experiences that contained more than she expected.

As Rinpoche paused, I mused *"Manibhadra seems to experience an immediate effect from Kukkaraja's instruction. Is that because he has actually transmitted something to her? Or is it simply that she's doing what he told her to do, which was to open her sense fields and pay attention?"*

"Both."

"There's transmission" Khandro Déchen added *"but then, anyone could do what she does – without the necessity of transmission."*

"Quite so" Rinpoche continued. *"Anyone could decide to say 'I'll see what happens if I just look at colour.' If one did that, one would notice an immediate difference if one decided to devote the next couple of minutes to doing it."* PAUSE *"Just looking at this wall ..."* Rinpoche indicated the wall by his chair, a plain white plastered wall *"... do you see how interesting the wall is? The odd shapes of irregular plaster... it's fascinating. You might not have noticed before – but there are minute crevices and angled planes. Maybe something was there before, maybe a light switch which has been removed."* Rinpoche smiled as we all stared at the small patch of empty wall for some minutes.

"By the time that Kukkuraja returned" Rinpoche continued *"Manibhadra felt strangely disconcerted yet somehow ebullient: she had lost who she had been before she had met Kukkuraja..."*

He greeted her cordially and ate lunch. Once having eaten, he commenced *"For one who remains in the nondual state – possessions and possessionlessness have the same taste. One possesses whatever enters the sense fields – for as long as they remain. One thus owns everything and carries nothing. One is not hampered by the need for objects."*

"I understand that... but I do not feel hampered."

"I imagine that you do not – but… let me ask you a question. Have you ever left home? Are you free to travel wherever you please?"

"No… I have never left home and should I desire to do so… you are right, I am not free to travel wherever I please – but my home is pleasant and I have never wished to go anywhere else."

"Yes, young lady… your home is pleasant – but you will not live here forever. You will have to marry and when you marry it will not be your choice."

"Yes… my marriage is already arranged. I had not thought so far – but the time is sooner than I would wish it to be."

"And if you renounced marriage – you would have no wealth, would you?"

"No… I would not. I would probably be cast out and have to beg for my living. My parents are kind – but they would not brook my disobedience."

"So… tell me – of what worth is your wealth, when it is contingent upon the dictates of others? Your husband may well be a good and kind man – but the choice is not yours. Your life is not your own. I do not say this to unsettle you or to cause you to disobey your parents – I merely answer your question as to why I have no interest in conventional wealth. If I was a conservative man—and conventionally wealthy—and had a daughter such as you, I would be forced by conformist society to make the same demands of her as your parents have made of you – and I would not wish to act in such a way."

"But my parents only wish the best for me."

"I have no doubt of it. It is the way they see the world. I do not judge your parents for being as they are – I only say that I would not wish to be in their position. To be wealthy as they are, is not to be free or to allow others to be free. When you gain the conventional wealth of society through following the rules of society – you become the prisoner of that wealth and of that society."

Kukkuraja paused—observing Manibhadra closely as she absorbed the portent of his words—and finally said *"Again… I have visits to make in this town. If you would like to hear more of the nature of real wealth, I shall be happy to tell you – but before I return, I would like you to continue in noticing that which is seen with your eyes and heard with your ears. Pay attention to all the senses – but avoid commenting internally with thought, in terms of your sense perceptions."*

Manibhadra promised Kukkuraja that she would follow his instructions and bade him goodbye till the next day. She told him that she was eager for their further discussions and Kukkuraja nodded with a smile which seemed to betoken something. After he left, Manibhadra perceived that her vision and hearing were entirely other than they were before. She saw what had previously been ordinary – and found it to be extraordinary. The mundane appeared mysterious and the commonplace became astonishing – but everything remained exactly as it was. Nothing was actually different – but everything was somehow fresh and vital as if she had only ever perceived the world through a fine layer of dust before. If this was what could occur after two meetings with Kukkuraja—and through following fairly simple advice—what more could be possible?

By the time Kukkuraja returned, Manibhadra was impatient to speak with him. She felt enigmatically perturbed yet somehow passionately alive. She had misplaced who she had been even the day before, when her whole sense of sensory perception had changed. Kukkuraja arrived, acknowledged her affectionately and ate lunch. Once having eaten, he embarked from a new perspective on what they had discussed before.
"Do you find the sky beautiful at the end of the day when the clouds are raddled with many different shades and hues of red?"

"I do!" she replied. *"How did you know?"*

"Oh, that is nothing to know – I find it beautiful too. The sky was beautiful last night. I find many things beautiful – but… tell me, who owns all this beauty? Who owns the sky?"

"No one owns the sky – it is simply there."

"That is true, young lady. It is also true that anyone can own the sky…" Kukkuraja nodded. *"Who would you guess, to be a sky-owner?"*

"You?"

"Well yes…" Kukkuraja laughed *"… but other than me or anyone like me?"*

Manibhadra pondered for a while and finally ventured *"Those who truly own the sky… must be those who love it the most – those who appreciate it the most."*

"Yes. You are correct – but what of those who are disinterested?"

At this question Manibhadra's eyes lit up *"They!"* she exclaimed *"… they surely are those who cannot own even a moment of it! To them it cannot be wealth – but to those who love it, it is wealth."*

"Now you understand the meaning of authentic wealth and why it is available to everyone."

"But still…" pondered Manibhadra *"one cannot buy anything with that wealth."*

"No—I would not deceive you—you can buy nothing but pleasure with that wealth. Conventional wealth will buy you anything that can be bought – but it will not buy you the pleasure of seeing the sky if you do not already have it."

Manibhadra was amazed to hear this and realised that the nature of reality was nowhere close to what she had imagined before she met Kukkuraja. She asked him if he would be her teacher – and Kukkuraja agreed. *"Come to my island then. You will find me in the middle of the lake at the centre of the charnel ground."*

"Is that not a terrifying place?" she quailed.

"According to some… yes… You will find that any place is what it is—and appears as it appears—to whomever sees it. However… don't be frightened. You will be helped. Everyone knows where I live."

"There is no one who will not assist you once you arrive at the charnel ground – but you must not come dressed in your wealthy finery, for if you do, you will never find me."

Manibhadra agreed to the proposal, deciding that she could borrow a servant's clothes. She prepared to leave home when her parents had gone to sleep – but it proved impossible to take the clothes of any of their servants without drawing attention to herself. In desperation she decided to look for cast-off rags along the way, but she found none. The scavengers had removed everything from the streets.

Boraccio—the Norwegian Forest cat—jumped up onto Rinpoche's lap and I took advantage of the pause to ask *"Do all practitioners have to be willing to move beyond their 'comfort zone' to some extent?"*

"Comfort zone…" Rinpoche wrinkled his nose. *"Is that like a 'rest room' – the American word for defæcatorium? Some people even find 'rest room' a little risqué and are calling them 'comfort stations'. You know… even the words 'toilet' and 'lavatory' are just French and Latin words which pertain to washing. Personally, for historical reasons, I prefer 'loo' if one must use a euphemism. 'Loo' derives from the old pronunciation of l'eau – as in 'gardez l'eau'. That's the approximate Middle-French for 'watch out for the water' – a cry which warned passers-by below, that the contents of a chamber pot were being ejected from an upper floor window."* PAUSE *"But let us return to your question about being willing to 'move beyond the comfort zone'."*

"Yes" I laughed *"being willing to go to some version of a terrifying place?"*

"Well yes" Rinpoche replied *"there are terrifying places and versions of terrifying places which are only terrifying to the imagination."* PAUSE *"There are always choices to be made in life. You can choose comfort, or you can choose challenge. It's a question of whether the challenge is worthwhile or not. That's not necessarily simple to quantify. Sometimes people back out of things merely because they have some slight trepidation – or because they're nervous. Some people want too much assurance that success will be forthcoming."*

"*Such people never do anything*" added Khandro Déchen "*because the assurance is not there. When Rinpoche headed out to India at the age of nineteen—for example —if he'd required assurances that every single thing was going to be alright... If he'd required assurances that he'd get home again safely – he might not have set out.*"

"*There was some assurance in terms of it being a 'known hippie trail'...*" Rinpoche grinned "*and other people had done it before. It wasn't a journey to a war-torn country.*"

"*But there was still no guarantee with respect to what would happen*" I commented.

"*No indeed, there's never any guarantee of what will happen under any circumstances – unless you jump from a great height. That usually guarantees death. Other than that, it's simply a matter of making choices. With any choice – there's the likelihood it might alter your life. There's always the possibility one might come to regret the choice. Moving house, changing your job, commencing a new relationship, marrying, divorcing – whatever choice you make, you may come to regret it.*"

"*There's always that possibility with any choice*" added Khandro Déchen "*but then you cannot avoid making choices. If you merely shillyshally, then you never do anything – and become miserable anyway.*"

"*Exactly. 'Procrastination is the thief of time', as the saying has it. Vacillation, dithering, indecisiveness, equivocation, hesitancy, indecision, and irresolution are the modus operandi of failure. As Stan Hollaway—an old school comrade—used to say: 'He who hesitates is a toss-bag.' So Manibhadra makes her choice. She sees something as possible – and she goes for it.*"

"*On arriving at the charnel ground*" Rinpoche continued the hagiography "*Manibhadra found herself with a considerable dilemma as to her apparel – and, to the agreement she had made with Kukkuraja...*"

She could not enter the charnel ground—or see Kukkuraja—in her finery – so she sat for some time trying to find a solution to her problem. After an hour she realised that there was no answer – and so, in desperation, she decided that she would have to go naked.

She removed her clothes and placed them under a rock by a conspicuous tree where she would be able to find them again. As soon as she had hidden her clothes a yogini approached her *"So, Manibhadra, welcome – you have come as expected and your appearance is suitable to present you to Mahasiddha Kukkuraja. I will now guide you to the lake where a boatman will take you across to the island where Mahasiddha Kukkuraja lives."*

The boatman passed no comment on her nakedness – neither did he appear in any way surprised. The boatman simply helped Manibhadra aboard his small boat and began to row toward Kukkuraja's island. As the boat drew closer to the island, Manibhadra began to hear the howling, growling, and baying of what seemed to be many dogs. She felt anxious and asked the boatman *"Is this not a dangerous island with so many fierce dogs?"*

"Yes, Manibhadra, it is dangerous – but not for you. It is only dangerous if you attempt to come here uninvited or with self-serving intentions."

"So, what will these dogs do when they see me?"

"That I do not know – but it is not wise to worry. Mahasiddha Kukkuraja has invited you to attend him – and so there will be no difficulty or danger for you."

The boat finally came to rest on the shore of the island and Manibhadra stepped out of the boat and into the baleful gaze of a score of dogs. Their howling, growling, and baying subsided as they discerned her presence and Manibhadra stood gazing at them for some time before walking toward them. She had no choice but to walk up the shingled spit of the beach where they were crowded. The nature of the rock-strewn island had created a narrow defile beyond the landing place – and so Manibhadra had to approach the dogs or turn back. Having ventured this far—even to the extent of divesting herself of clothing—she decided she may as well brave the ordeal. No sooner was her decision made however, than the dogs quietened—moved aside to let her pass—and stood wagging their tails in a friendly manner. The dogs then followed her until she reached the place where Kukkuraja resided.

"It is good that you have come without your finery, Manibhadra…" Kukkuraja commented when he saw her approach *"but… is it not disreputable, according to society, to be naked?"*

Manibhadra was embarrassed – but replied *"Yes, it is disreputable – and if I was discovered I would lose my varna and become an untouchable. It was difficult for me to risk my reputation and to overcome my embarrassment – but I have understood that caring about appearances will not enable me to receive your teaching and transmission. Receiving your transmission and teaching was more important to me than my modesty or embarrassment."*

"You have spoken well, Manibhadra – so now I shall give you transmission and teaching on the nature of Mind and the infinite purity of the phenomenal world."

Manibhadra expected to be back at home before dawn – but Kukkuraja had prepared to spend nine days giving her teachings and transmissions. It was vital that she could conspire to wake in her own bed as if nothing had happened and her parents would be none the wiser – but it was yet more vital that she remained with Kukkuraja. She realised that this was an opportunity which was not easily available – and, if she made some lame excuse about having to go home in case her parents worried about her, the chances of ever seeing Kukkuraja again would be slim. Kukkuraja—having some awareness of her internal writhing—told her *"Do not be concerned, Manibhadra, a messenger has already been sent to your home to inform your parents that you will be away from home for nine days – and that no harm will come to you."*

This was both reassuring and terrifying to Manibhadra. It was reassuring because her parents would not be tortured by uncertain wonders. It was terrifying because her parents *would* be tortured by uncertain wonders. Kukkuraja knew quite clearly what was in her mind – and commented *"I shall leave it to you, what you say to your mother and father when you return. I cannot promise that they will be happy—they will not—but it will pass. They may feel that they cannot forgive you – but they will.*

"Like most people they will need to have explosive emotions before they learn to allow them to subside. I am confident that you will behave in the best way and address them in a manner that will enable them to accept you in your new life."

And so, the teachings and transmissions were given day-by-day – and by the time her period of instruction was concluded, Manibhadra was equipped to practise for the years ahead without further need of tuition. On Manibhadra's parting, Kukkuraja said:

Phenomena are empty of conventional value – yet their authentic value is without limit.
The sense fields are the greedy hands by which we manacle ourselves to dualism
Yet they are also the repository of infinite empty-wealth.
Desire to possess the form of phenomena, as if the form were not empty,
This is the cause of unsatisfactoriness.
Appreciation of the empty-lustre of phenomena,
Knowing that their emptiness is form,
This is the portal of the nondual state.

Manibhadra—her training concluded—set off for her home. She found the place where she had left her clothes – but they were gone. In their place she found only white raiment, ragged – yet clean. She had no choice but to return to her home dressed as a religious mendicant.

On seeing Manibhadra, her parents were outraged. They were horrified by her wild appearance. They were furious at her having left home without a word – and thus causing a scandal in the family. Such was their parental disapproval for absconding and bringing their family into disrepute, that Manibhadra received a thrashing.

Manibhadra accepted her thrashing without complaint. Once it was over however, she explained with astounding serenity *"According to conventional mores, I have deserved the thrashing you have given me. I make no complaint.*

"You were right to do what you have done according to societal convention – but societal convention knows nothing of authentic reputation. Reputation such as yours would now merely be a burden to me – because I have received transmissions and teachings from the Mahasiddha Kukkuraja. My reputation—according to the convention of Vajrayana—is unstained, and my wealth is therefore without measure. You would be just in denying me my inheritance for the conventional shame I have brought upon my family – and I would have no grievance against you. The loss of wealth would make no difference to me – as I shall be happy whatever happens."

On hearing their daughter speak in this calm yet dignified way, her parents were shocked yet pacified – in a disquieted and unsettled way. It was hard for them to comprehend their daughter in terms of who they considered themselves to be. They sat in silence for some time hypnotically bemused by the spectacle of their daughter sitting before them in a manner almost like a Maharaja. After a while they asked *"You… would not then, wish to marry…"* but it was more like a plea than a question.

She replied *"I would be happy to keep the commitment you have made on my behalf – as now all activity will eventually be inseparable from the nondual state, now I know how to practise."*

"So… you will then marry?" they asked again, almost able to understand her answer.

"I will marry" she replied – and both her parents wept with relief. Once her parents had recovered themselves, Manibhadra asked *"I have only one request to make of you – and that is that I wish to be allowed, before I marry, to spend my time as I wish – engaged in meditation. I will, of course, see my husband-to-be on all proper occasions on which I shall comport myself appropriately and pleasantly as a prospective wife should."*

Her parents nodded in what could have passed for approval. They then left Manibhadra to her own devices – realising that they had both regained their daughter and lost her at the same time. They were deeply ashamed of the thrashing they had given her.

They apologised repeatedly – but Manibhadra told them each time that she had no sorrow, no anger, and no grievance toward them at all. *"My dear mother and father – you simply live within the bounds of the conventions of society. You have thus acted as any parent would act who was similarly placed. It is only due to what I now know—from what I have experienced—that makes it possible for me to understand your perception as I do. You may no longer understand me – but I understand and sympathise with you. Be cheerful now, my good parents, and be happy for the future – because it will be exactly as you desire."*

In the remaining few years before the marriage took place, Manibhadra devoted herself to the accomplishment of the teachings she had been given by Kukkuraja – and by the time of her marriage she found herself able to experience the nondual state. At that point in time, she again met Kukkuraja who was happy with her progress. He told her that before she married, she should make one journey to the charnel ground of HaHa Gödpa[7]. There she would meet Niguma[8] and receive the final teachings which would enable her to rest continuously in the nondual state. Her parents allowed her to make the journey. They had serious misgivings, but —because they could not otherwise fault the behaviour or demeanour of their daughter—they felt they had no choice but to concede. They recognised—as far as they were able—that their daughter had become a 'holy woman' and was therefore outside their understanding. They were assured that she would return – and gave the appearance of being satisfied by her promise. *"Everything will remain exactly according to my commitment – I shall marry as promised and shall be the model wife to my husband that you would wish me to be."*

---

[7] *ha ha rGod pa* / ཧ་ཧ་རྒོད་པ་ — the Charnel Ground of Wild Screaming 'Ha Ha' Laughter, in the north-east.
[8] *ni gu ma* / ནི་གུ་མ་ / 10th century – the sister of Naropa *(na' ro pa* / ནཱ་རོ་པ་ / 956–1040). Niguma transmitted the Six Yogas of Niguma to Khyungpo Naljor *(khyung po rNal 'byor* / ཁྱུང་པོ་རྣལ་འབྱོར་ / 990–1140), the founder of Shangpa Kagyüd. She achieved rainbow body.

Manibhadra met Niguma in the Charnel Ground of HaHa Gödpa just as Kukkuraja had predicted. It was a far greater ordeal in terms of fear than Kukkuraja's dogs had been – but Manibhadra was not the same person she had been. The harrowing screams that appeared to emanate from the ground itself, were therefore only marginally disquieting. Niguma gave her all the teachings and transmissions required to attain nondual realisation and concluded saying:

> *"Because demonstrable reality is not as we imagine it to be*
> *It cannot be revealed in conventional language.*
> *The essence of reality is free of dependency on conventional rationality*
> *Therefore, it cannot be investigated or examined.*
> *It is free of demonstrable examples even though examples exist as allusions.*
> *It is beyond the realm of the conceptual mind.*
> *It is neither eternal nor transient – neither samsara nor nirvana.*
> *It is apparent – and yet empty. It is neither real nor unreal – neither arising nor non-arising.*
> *All negative disharmonious conditions are the source of siddhis – because negative conditions intensify experience.*
> *Since you understand the true nature of negative conditions, you do not need to avoid them – but integrate your awareness with them.*
> *Practise the natural state free from attachment and nonattachment;*
> *Renouncing nothing, accomplishing nothing, attaching to nothing, detaching from nothing, purifying nothing, and rejecting nothing – you will be possessed of perfect behaviour in whatever your body requires.*

Manibhadra received the teaching and transmission and attained the nondual state before she left the charnel ground. She then returned home and informed her parents that she was now free to marry. Once married, she astounded her parents in being *the perfect housewife*. She was everything her husband could have wished her to be. Her mother and father-in-law were delighted and all thought of her mysterious nine-day disappearance was forgotten.

She spent many years as the societally perfect wife and mother – but when her children reached adulthood and married, she manifested her realisation externally. She rose into the sky naked and radiating rainbow light. She was seen by the entire township, who came to receive her teachings and the transmission of her presence. Her husband then became her disciple and gained accomplishments.

As Rinpoche concluded the hagiography, I was intrigued by Niguma's transmission: 'all negative disharmonious conditions are the source of siddhis'. *"Does this mean that there's the possibility of any difficulty becoming a source of siddhis?"*

"Certainly" Rinpoche nodded. *"If you have a difficulty – you can strive to overcome that difficulty."* PAUSE *"That's what it actually means. It doesn't mean that if you lose weight, you'll be able to walk through walls."* PAUSE *"If there's no difficulty, there's nothing to overcome. If there's nothing to overcome – there's nothing to be enacted in terms of development as a human being. If there's nothing to be enacted – there's merely an inert phlegmatic lethargic sterile stasis. As soon as there's challenge – the more 'difficult' it is, the more power has to be exerted with regard to surmounting it."*

"Then…" added Khandro Déchen *"you discover a resilience of which you were previously unaware."*

"And when Niguma says negative conditions intensify experience" asked Ja'gyür *"is that simply because conflictive emotions are more intense?"*

"Yes. It's that simple" Khandro Déchen answered. *"It's all at the level of sensation. Negative experiences increase sensation – and if you know how to find the presence of awareness in sensation, then that is it. So, it generally depends on how you see life. It's perhaps like being a racing driver, for example. It's whether an experience registers as exhilaration or terror. It's a matter of choice."*

"Falling in love and having a panic attack" Rinpoche grinned *"are physiologically identical. It is simply a question of how that sensation is translated by conceptual consciousness."*

As Ja'gyür refreshed our wine glasses, I continued with questions. *"Where Kukkuraja says 'ownership doesn't require physical possession – we own whatever enters the sense fields where we're not hampered by the need for objects…' I assume he's not saying that 'owning objects' is in itself problematic?"*

"You assume correctly" Rinpoche smiled.

"But needing to own" I continued *"or 'owning without appreciation' – is that what's problematic?"*

"Yes" Rinpoche nodded. *"It doesn't mean you can't own* anything*. It means that 'having nothing' should* not *be problematic. You can* appreciate *without having to* own*. Richard, a friend at university in Exeter, was living in an apartment – in a rather nice Georgian mansion owned by the University. One day, a wealthy student—who was a friend of his—threw him the keys to his banana-yellow Lamborghini Miura*[9] *and said 'Go take a ride.' And so, my friend and I got into the car and spent the day exploring the countryside. We had a splendid time – but at the end of the day, my friend seemed dejected. I enquired as to his mood and he replied 'It's not likely that I could ever own a car like that. I find that depressing.' I replied 'Neither is it likely that I'll ever own such a car – but I've had a whole shoal of fun as a passenger in it. I don't have to ruin my day by thinking about the fact that I'll never own a Lamborghini Miura. I'd rather have a reconditioned 1966 Rolls Royce Silver Cloud in any case."*

"Did that help Richard?"

"Not much" Rinpoche laughed. *"Richard wasn't Manibhadra."* PAUSE *"Maybe he'll remember it one day – and it might be of use. I hope so."*

---

[9] *Lamborghini Miura* – 350GT, 4-litre, 4-cam, V-12 engine delivering 375 HP and 266 Ft/lbs torque, with a top speed of 180 mph.

"Wealth is how **much** *you appreciate"* Khandro Déchen added *"and poverty is failure to appreciate."* PAUSE *"That's not to say that those who are actually poverty-stricken—in real terms—should be ecstatic about it. I guess if you were* realised *you could be happy – but poverty without nondual realisation is not big fun."*

"No" I pondered. *"It also made me think about the idea of being willing to give up conventional wealth, of owning nothing, and surviving by begging for alms. Would there actually be any practice-value in giving everything away?"*

"Well giving everything away" replied Khandro Déchen *"is only functional in a country where mendicancy is operative. Where it's not, you need to look after yourself in order that you can practise. If leaving yourself destitute, leaves you no time to practise because you're always in the social security office – that is not that useful."* PAUSE *"Giving everything to the local Buddhist centre in return for a room and board… where they'll look after you – and cover your dental work… that could work. Mendicancy in the West however… living on the streets and begging, would merely shorten your life. It would shorten your practice time, which is not wise. Dung-sré Namgay Dawa Rinpoche*[10] *is well aware of this, and makes sure that none of his students—who offer work to the centre—are deprived of a working life which allows them to pay into social security."*

"Whereas having a great deal of money and being benevolent with it" Rinpoche added *"where it's your own choice where you make donations – that, might actually be the best use of the money. As Kyabjé Künzang Dorje Rinpoche said 'You might be the best judge of where money would be most useful. You might be able to do more authentic good with your millions than whatever a gompa might choose to do with it.' He was quite direct about the matter."*

"It's the desire for wealth for its own sake that's the problem" Khandro Déchen continued *"rather than 'having wealth' – or 'the wealth itself'. If you have great wealth and you never make use of it to benefit anybody else, then that is a* **definite** *problem.*

---

[10] *gDung sras rNam rGyas zla ba rin po che* / གདུང་སྲས་རྣམ་རྒྱས་ཟླ་བ་རིན་པོ་ཆེ — a Nyingma Lama in New York, who is a grandson of Kyabjé Düd'jom Rinpoche Jig'drèl Yeshé Dorje.

"This is because wherever you go, you can see people who could be helped. Even when you don't have so much money – you can still be helpful. However, it doesn't matter how much money you have – you still can't help everybody. You therefore have to make choices. It's a practical matter. You help those whom you are best at helping – this is also what Künzang Dorje Rinpoche was expressing."

"But I could probably always help more than I do" I sighed. "I could always do a bit more."

"Doing a bit more is probably always a good idea" replied Khandro Déchen "in the same way in which you can always push yourself to exercise more, or practise more. But then – don't push beyond the point where you damage yourself."

"If you give so much away that you damage your situation" continued Ngak'chang Rinpoche "that would be problematic in terms of practice. That would be contraindicated from Künzang Dorje Rinpoche's perspective. He was always eminently practical." PAUSE "Below a certain level of income – time is eaten up with the bureaucracy and mechanics of survival. Time which could be used for practice and helping people in other ways is squandered on making ends meet. Time can be wasted when you lack money. So, practitioners shouldn't give away so much that they would cause themselves problems in respect of time." Rinpoche paused, then smiled "Actually we have a slight 'time problem' now – inasmuch as it's later than it was earlier. Maybe it's time to retire."

We all headed to the kitchen. Rinpoche rinsed the wine glasses and prepared nocturnal beverages: cloudy apple juice for Rinpoche and red grapefruit juice for Khandro Déchen – each diluted with sparkling water. Khandro Déchen prepared violently strong Lapsang Souchong tea for the protector offering.

"Kukkuraja talks about the problem with 'organised religion'…" I commented.

"Organised religion?" Rinpoche mused. "I would say that he referred to 'institutional religion'. People do use the term 'organised religion' – but I find myself wondering what it means. What would 'disorganised religion' be?

"If it was disorganised then it wouldn't even be possible for two people to meet – let alone do what we're doing now."

"Yes" replied Khandro Déchen. "I think people actually mean 'institutional' – there is nothing fundamentally wrong with organising situations which involve people who are cooperating in a venture. The approach in which the same rules apply to everyone regardless of their personality, aptitude, experience, or intelligence—that—is a problem. A situation where activities are carried out by rote. I think people are referring to the sense in which 'edicts are issued from on high' – dictates of dominance and control. That is 'institutionalism' in its worst sense."

"Ah yes" nodded Rinpoche. "I think what some people mean by 'not wanting to be part of an organised religion' – is their need to be the sole arbiters of everything. I think that often means not wishing to learn anything from anyone anywhere – especially if it means being less selfish."

"Yes" Khandro Déchen laughed "that seems to be the meaning behind it. Anything which constrains the 'me obsession' is seen as organised religion."

"Right, so, Kukkuraja says that 'institutional religion' can just be a way of passing time or trying to secure a better rebirth. I guess if you did give all your money to a local Buddhist centre, it would buy you lots of merit" I joked. "Actually, I find the whole idea of 'accumulating merit' weird."

"Yes" Rinpoche yawned. "Dzongsar Khyentsé Rinpoche wrote about this." PAUSE "He said that 'merit' was not a good translation of sônam [11] – with which we would agree entirely. For me, 'merit' has Boy Scout connotations. Dzongsar Khyentsé Rinpoche said sônam should be translated as something more like 'capacity' or 'method' – the 'capacity of greater power to perform an act'. The problem with the idea of 'accumulating merit', is – where are we accumulating it? It can only be accumulated 'of yourself, as yourself' – otherwise where would it be?" PAUSE "It's always only in yourself—in your continuum—that sônam exists. If it's power or capacity—which you develop as sônam—then it's at your disposal."

---

[11] bSod nams / བསོད་ནམས་ / punya.

"So, if you exercise—if you lift weights—then the sônam is there in your arms. Then, when someone's having problems with a heavy suitcase, you help – because you've got that sônam at your disposal." PAUSE "So it's simpler to understand 'merit' in terms of weightlifting and the results of weightlifting, than in terms of some kind of 'cosmic bank account' – where you have 320,172.54 units of merit. If you develop strength however, then you have the capacity to do something to help others."

"You have **strength** *to accomplish*" added Khandro Déchen. "If there's a retreat and there's work to be done, there'll **always** be people who suddenly need to go to the toilet for half an hour – or suddenly have to go somewhere else, or hide in another room. But if you **always** *volunteer to help*: then you're a person who helps. Then people appreciate you. Then you enjoy helping – and then, that's a capacity which develops, rather than the 'capacity' for slinking and skulking."

"*The capacity for slinking and skulking*" Rinpoche laughed "*skiving—ducking and diving—shirking, sidestepping, malingering, or playing truant… is not to be desired.*"

"Sometimes you hear 'merit' being talked about as a kind of *luck*" I mused.

"*Luck!*" Ngak'chang Rinpoche laughed. "*Thomas Jefferson talked about luck. He said 'I found in my life, that the harder I worked – the more luck I had.' That's more-or-less what I've found.*"

"*I think Rinpoche has a story about luck…*" Khandro Déchen suggested.

"The car transporter?"

"Yes – that's the one."

"When I was younger, so much younger than today[12], my motorcycle broke down about ten miles outside of Guildford. I had no money to call somebody to come and pick up my motorcycle and take it into Guildford to be fixed. So, I thought 'I guess I'm going to have to push my motorcycle to Guildford.' I had no other choice.

---

[12] Ngak'chang Rinpoche is quoting: Lennon/McCartney—Beatles—*Help*—Help—1965

Twenty-one: Manibhadra – the perfect housewife

"So, I started pushing – and it suddenly occurred to me that I could try flagging a ride from large vehicles. I stuck out my thumb – and, within minutes, the first vehicle to pass was a car transporter. It stopped. The man chained my bike on the back, drove me to Guildford and dropped me – outside the repair shop. I took the motorcycle in for repair – and then when I walked out the door I bumped into my father. He rarely visited Guidlford, by the way. He took me home for lunch – and that's the end of the story." We all laughed and Rinpoche continued "If it hadn't occurred to me that somebody might help me—and if I hadn't stuck my thumb out—then I probably wouldn't have got to the shop before it closed, and would have had to sit outside with my bike all night waiting for the repair shop to open."

"So, you could call that luck" added Khandro Déchen. "You could say Rinpoche had sônam—the merit—to think of hitching a lift on a car transporter. Or you could understand it in terms of having the capacity to think of hitching. Capacity can be intelligence, capability. You assess the potential of the situation in which you find yourself – and take the appropriate action."

Rinpoche stood there in his denim apron – a tea towel in one hand and a dishcloth in the other. "Y'know…" he said "one of the things that's good about there being a Mahasiddha called 'the perfect housewife' is that it's more offensive now than it was at the time."

"The perfect housewife would not have offended society at that time" added Khandro Déchen "but it would offend a certain section of society now, mainly women – but some men too, which is all to the good."

"I was a 'house husband' for a while with a lady friend back in the late 1970s. She had a career—not too well remunerated—so I stayed at home, preparing meals – and saving money. Looking after her—making her life as pleasurable as possible—was rewarding. I thoroughly enjoyed it. It can be a good idea for many couples. The one who can earn the most goes out to work. It doesn't matter which one of the couple it is. The other stays at home and saves them both money by home cooking, wine making, bottling preserves, making jams and chutneys, growing vegetables – etcetera.

"What I noticed was that whenever we were out at some function, I would be asked what I 'did'. I would reply 'I'm just a house husband' – and everyone would say 'Oh how very interesting!' My feminist partner would then be outraged – and say later 'They wouldn't say it was 'very interesting' if you were a woman! Just because you're a man it's suddenly 'very interesting!' I despair.' This is also interesting from the point of view of societal conditioning."

"Anything unusual is interesting from the conventional point of view" Khandro Dechen added. *"That was about fifty years ago – hopefully it wouldn't be so unusual at this point in time. Housekeeping is an important rôle, if it's—seen—as an important rôle."*

"I concur entirely" I smiled. *"A couple can make their lives far more pleasant in that way than both having to go out to work. If one of them can only get a low income, it's better to stay home and make the income stretch further. It just needs the rôle to be properly appreciated, rather than getting rid of the rôle. There's nothing wrong with the rôle at all."*

"What's delightful" Rinpoche smiled *"is that what was not offensive a few thousand years ago—Mahasiddha Manibhadra – the perfect housewife—is now offensive, to those who decide to be offended. So—as you can see—the Mahasiddhas are still performing their function in challenging conditioning. They are simply challenging conditioning in different and unexpected ways."*

With that, Rinpoche wafted his tea towel and dishcloth in elaborate flourishes. Just for a moment, I saw the tea towel and dishcloth as the silks in the hands of Manibhadra – especially as Rinpoche seemed to me to be wielding the cloths with the same mudras as appear in the thangka of Mahasiddha Manibhadra – the perfect housewife.

www.ingramcontent.com/pod-product-compliance
Lightning Source LLC
Chambersburg PA
CBHW060910300426
44112CB00011B/1412